ASIA
6185

Other tribes, other scribes

D0963141

Entrevue de Biron avec les Patagons

This illustration is taken from the frontispiece of J. P. Bérenger,
*Collection de tous les voyages faits autour du monde par les différents
nations de l'Europe*, Vol. 5. Geneva, 1778–9. See Chapter 2.

GN
345
.B66
1982

Other tribes, other scribes

Symbolic anthropology in the comparative study of cultures, histories, religions, and texts

JAMES A. BOON

Professor of Anthropology and Asian Studies
Cornell University

CAMBRIDGE UNIVERSITY PRESS

Cambridge
London   New York   New Rochelle
Melbourne   Sydney

Published by the Press Syndicate of the University of Cambridge
The Pitt Building, Trumpington Street, Cambridge CB2 1RP
32 East 57th Street, New York, NY 10022, USA
296 Beaconsfield Parade, Middle Park, Melbourne 3206, Australia

© Cambridge University Press 1982

First published 1982

Printed in the United States of America

Library of Congress Cataloging in Publication Data
Boon, James A.
Other tribes, other scribes.
Includes bibliographical references and
index.
1. Ethnology – Philosophy. 2. Ethnology –
Methodology. 3. Symbolism. I. Title.
GN345.B66 1983 306 82-9516
ISBN 0 521 25081 1 hard covers AACR2
ISBN 0 521 27197 5 paperback

To my teachers

"Spectatorship" is in England a filial characteristic, linked with dependency and submission, while in America spectatorship is a parental characteristic linked with dominance and succoring... An Englishman when he is applauding another is indicating or signaling potential submission and/or dependency; when he shows off or demands spectatorship, he is signaling dominance or superiority; and so on. Every Englishman who writes a book must be guilty of this. For the American, the converse must hold. [*Other tribes, other scribes.*] His boasting [booking] is but a bid for quasiparental approval. [Confessed.]

Gregory Bateson, Steps to an Ecology of Mind

The only counterpart of the dialectical method is pure empiricism. If we can find no universal law by virtue of which one cultural form necessarily issues from another, until at last the whole cycle of forms has been comprehended – then, it would seem, the totality of these forms can no longer be looked upon as a self-contained cosmos. Then the particular forms simply stand side by side: their scope and specific character can be described, but they no longer express a common ideal content. The philosophy of these forms would then necessarily amount to their history, which, according to its object, would define itself as history of language, history of religion and myth, history of art, etc. At this point a strange dilemma arises. If we hold fast to the postulate of logical unity, the universality of the logical form threatens ultimately to efface the individuality of each special province and the specificity of its principle – but if we immerse ourselves in this individuality and persevere in our examination of it, we run the risk of losing ourselves and of finding no way back to the universal.

Ernst Cassirer, *The Philosophy of Symbolic Forms*

Contents

vii

Preface

They have a way in their language of calling men the halves of one another.

Montaigne, Of Cannibals

How can I inscribe the power of symbol systems to establish cultures that appear intellectually consistent, emotionally compelling, and convincing even as they change? Yet any culture viewed from outside – one's own in particular – appears as thoroughly arbitrary, indeed outlandish, as all the others. How can I demonstrate that the difference between any two human languages, and cultures, is as intriguing as the possibility that chimpanzees, for example, might have language? Indeed, chimps as a species would require many thousands of mutually unintelligible languages, each capable of concerted misinformation, to rival human communication. How can I use somber-sounding analytic distinctions like arbitrary/motivated, conventional/constitutive, models of/for, without reducing cultures to numbing jargon? Indeed, without comparative analytic frameworks, every culture, whatever its "genius," remains impenetrable. Such are, rhetorically, the dilemmas of the anthropologist of symbolic forms.

Anthropology is as abstract as information theory yet as palpable as the eerie confrontation between the New World and the Old, represented in the frontispiece. That encounter (and others like it) never precisely happened. Yet this inevitable "misrepresentation" – there were neither giant Pantagonians nor generally enlightened European emissaries – cannot be explained by simple empirical error. Rather, the explanation lies in the fact that cultures meet indirectly, according to conventional expectations of the cultures themselves. The comparison of cultures requires not that we reduce them to platitudinous similarity but that we situate them apart as equally significant, integrated systems of differences. A "culture" can materialize only in counterdistinction to another culture. This statement is no hocus-pocus but merely acknowledges that before any culture can be experienced *as a culture* displacement from it must be possible; and contrary to notions of the Enlightenment, there is no place outside it to be except in other cultures or in their fragments and potentialities.

ix

The same paradox applies to language(s), or really (language)s. Any given language and culture seem perfectly adequate for the discernible needs of communication; yet within a given language and culture, other languages and cultures can be rumored; we even find ourselves believing in them, although we never experience them directly. Cultures interpenetrate symbolically, as they are constituted. Anthropologists from any culture (and they exist in every culture) engage in translating and interpreting the rumors of other cultures. Professional anthropologists (and their analogs exist in every culture and in every time) specialize in the diverse signs and symbols by which humans communicate according to variant social forms that are differentiated and perpetuated, even as they change.

This book develops related issues. Several chapters (1, 4, 7) introduce notions of signs and symbols from linguistics and culture theory. By renouncing the belief that a purposive direction underlies the history of language, linguists have managed to render change intelligible. Similarly, semiotic approaches often reject causal determinism in favor of systematic diversity, enriched translations, and comparative interpretations.

Other chapters (3, 6) compare ideas of social and institutional differentiation in the writings of Durkheim, Mauss, Weber, Marx, Hocart, and others. Durkheim never quite outgrew evolutionism, and Weber just barely saw beyond the historical specter of routinized bureaucracy. Yet their works helped dissipate confidence that civilizations develop with an irreversible thrust. After Durkheim and Weber, no progressive teleology could be either casually inferred from some primitive past or prophesied into an uncertain future. Both writers were too attentive to the specifics of ethnography and history, especially in the ideals and values we call religion.

Another issue (Chapters 1, 3, 5) concerns the telltale conviction of professional anthropology that diversity of human meaning is properly investigated "in the field" during fulsome experiences preferably documented in monograph form. Fieldwork is often misconstrued as an experimental laboratory and has become a central disciplinary doctrine. My attitude toward fieldwork is playful, because I find the concept an ideal and action that should be simultaneously debunked and preserved. Accordingly, Part I begins with reflections on fieldwork and the kinds of writings it is expected to produce. I trace ideals of descriptive reportage to certain Enlightenment assumptions, which I then critique from historical perspectives. Part II turns to several prominent bodies of comparative social theory, which I reread with an eye toward tribal and traditional civilizations in an effort to interconnect them. My critique of Enlightenment assumptions continues apace as I turn to a review of issues and elements of the semiotics of cultures. These chapters lay the foundation for Part III, where comparative social theory and mythology, structural analysis, and interpretive theories of texts and contexts, both ethnographic and historical, are combined in a discourse of cultures.

Throughout these sections I adjust concepts relating to kinship and marriage, religion, social hierarchy, mythic codes, ritual performances, intellectual history, and literary criticism to treat aspects of cultural comparison, with examples from Bali (my own fieldwork area) and variant Indo-European traditions. Introductory and concluding sections explore topics ranging from anthropology's understandable obsession with sensational customs to inklings of philosophic negativity – even *frissons* of nothingness – disturbing recent studies. The Appendixes contain several concerted reviews of developments and debates in structuralism and symbolic interpretation. The book's fluid discussion of fieldwork values, historical hermeneutics, comparative typologies, contemporary semiotics, and exotic societies and texts remains suggestive at best. My aim is to provide convincing examples of the interrelationship of these concerns.

My subject matter and its organization draw inspiration from a challenge expressed by Clifford Geertz:

To take the giant step away from the uniformitarian view of human nature is, so far as the study of man is concerned, to leave the Garden. To entertain the idea that the diversity of custom across time and over space is not a mere matter of garb and appearance . . . is to entertain also the idea that humanity is as various in its essence as it is in its expression. And with that reflection some well-fastened philosophical moorings are loosed and an uneasy drifting into perilous waters begins. [Geertz 1973:36]

I proceed in a manner less sequential than episodic; my method is dialectical, drifting. Sources proliferate as the book advances; critique strengthens motives; and if a critique requires adversaries, I choose materialism and psychologism and their contraries, idealism and behaviorism – the misleading alternatives of a lingering positivist, even utilitarian, ideology (rife in the Enlightenment and partly restored in the anthropological school of functionalism). At the core of the study lies the fact that not only are cultures plural, but so are the methods for investigating them. Cultures, histories, and methods communicate discursively across a semiotic paradox, because methods themselves are produced from cultures proceeding through time.

I proceed by interrelating opposed yet complementary comparative approaches: Frazer/Malinowski (Chapter 1) interpretation/analysis (Chapter 2), Marx/Mauss (Chapter 3), Saussure/Peirce (Chapter 4), intercourse/discourse (Chapters 6 and 7), and so on. An organic solidarity between two approaches – one associated with *L'année sociologique* (particularly Durkheim, Mauss and, subsequently, Lévi-Strauss), the other associated with Weberian and Parsonian frameworks shifted to anthropology (particularly in the works of C. Geertz and D. M. Schneider) – remains a covert structure, the cryptotype, in Whorf's sense, of the entire study. If forced to synthesize these oppositions, I would find least objectionable a radically cross-cultural version of Kenneth Burke's

Augustinean–Coleridgean–transcendentalist–pluralist "dramatism" of polar meanings and motives (with a tilt toward negative dialectics). But then, I'm American; and any synthesis, even this one, will be finally rejected.

Also American, among other things, is one of the book's recurrent devices, which an illustrious predecessor has categorically excused:

> No apology is needed for following the learned custom of placing attractive scraps
> of literature at the heads of our chapters. It has been truly observed by Wagner that
> such headings, with their vague suggestions of the matter which is to follow
> them, pleasantly inflame the reader's interest without wholly satisfying his curiosity,
> and we will hope that it may be found to be so in the present case. [Twain
> and Warner 1873/1969:xxii]

Unlike Mark Twain, however, the present work lets only a bit of French and German and an occasional Indonesian term or Latinism obscure its policy of relentless translation. On the other hand, in 1873 young Twain presumed to set his mottoes "in a vast number of tongues," for the reason, he explained, "that very few foreign nations among whom the book will circulate can read in any language but their own; whereas we do not write for a particular class or sect or nation, but to take in the whole world." Then in 1899, still twinkling, the ever-thoughtful Twain finally did his readers the courtesy of appending a translation of his quotations – including Chinese, Chippeway, Ethiopic, Old French, Sindhi, Italian, Choctaw, Japanese, Egyptian, German, Latin, Old Irish, Hawaiian, Javanese, Sioux-Dakota, Arabic, Arrawak, Hebrew, Yoruba, to name a few – but only so as to renew *The Gilded Age*'s copyright (Felheim 1969:viii)! Mottoes and epigraphs are also forms of acknowledgment. This book is in part an elaborated set of mottoes, acknowledging the authors and cultures that are its sources yet paradoxically interlacing them in one language – to which Twain did not resort until twenty-six years later!

Finally, I adopt a policy elsewhere promoted by Edmund Wilson: I give considerable space to quotations of authors, times, and cultures. I purposely cite at greater length than is customary. The company is diverse – Frazer, Weber, Malinowski, Durkheim, Lévi-Strauss, Samuel Purchas, Robert Lowie, Hocart, Clifford Geertz, pre-Enlightenment arguments, Balinese culture, Talcott Parsons, Ruth Benedict, cross-cousins, the *Ramayana*, Saussure and Peirce, and Edmund Wilson himself, as well as others–making it vital to let the texts unfurl in order to catch their multiple drifts. Besides Twain and these other authors, times, and cultures, I should add more conventional acknowledgments to this initial *avertissement*. Portions of this work have appeared in several publications with patient editors. Stephen Graubard included part of Chapter 2 in a 1980 *Daedalus* issue, "Intellect and Imagination," where it was called "Comparative De-enlightenment: Paradox and Limits in the History of Ethnology." Irene Porter-Wennis and Jean Umiker-Sebeok edited a special issue of *Semiotica*, "Cultural Semiotics" (1979), in which part of Chapter 4

appeared as "Saussure/Peirce *à propos* of Language, Society, and Culture."
Charles Keyes and E. Val Daniel include much of Chapter 6 in a collection
called *Karma: An Anthropological Inquiry* (Berkeley: University of California Press, 1983). Finally, David Wagenknecht included portions of Chapter 7
as "An Endogamy of Poets and Vice Versa: Exotic Ideals in Romanticism/
Structuralism" in an issue of *Studies in Romanticism* entitled "Structuralism
and Romanticism" (1979).

During the course of writing, I benefited from the responses of discerning
audiences. Materials in Chapter 1 were presented at a Brown Symposium at
Southwestern University organized by T. Walter Herbert in 1980 and at a
conference at Emory University entitled "Intellect and Imagination," organized by an industrious committee including Robert Paul. Johannes Fabian
enabled me to try out parts of Chapter 2 at Wesleyan University in 1978.
Chapter 3 has developed in part from graduate seminars taught at Duke and
Cornell universities. Different parts of Chapter 4 have been discussed at talks
organized by Hildred Geertz and James Fernandez at Princeton University and
at a panel ("Reading and Writing Ethnography") at the American Anthropo-
logical Association meetings (1975) organized by Roger Abrahams and John
Szwed. Chapter 5 originated in a talk at the Institute for Advanced Studies,
Princeton, organized by Clifford Geertz. I discussed related materials at the
University of North Carolina, thanks to James Peacock, Ruel Tyson, William
Peck, and others; in a special seminar and a talk at Cornell's Society for
the Humanities that were organized by Michael Kammen; and at a talk at
Brown University that was arranged by William Vanech. Parts of Chapter 6
were discussed at two Social Science Research Council conferences on
Southeast Asian aesthetics organized by A. L. Becker and Benedict Anderson, and David Szanton, first at the University of Michigan, then at Cornell;
talks based on Chapter 6 were presented at McGill University, thanks to
Lee Drummond, and at a panel on "The Anthropology of Experience" in 1980
organized by Edward Bruner and Victor Turner. Finally, Chapter 7 benefited from long discussions with Bob Montiegel and many others associated
with National Public Radio who were involved in the series "A Question of
Place."

This book was begun at Duke University and was written largely at Cornell
University, where I have enjoyed the resources of the Department of Anthropology, the Southeast Asia Program, and the Society for the Humanities.
Three trips to Indonesia (with results that figure in Chapter 6) were made
possible by the Ford Foundation (1971), research fellowship from the National Institute for Mental Health, (1972), and the American Philosophical
Society (1981). My research in Bali in 1972 was sponsored by the Lembaga
Ilmu Pengetahuan Indonesia. Topics in Chapter 5 were pursued during two
years at the Institute for Advanced Studies, Princeton (1973–75), and during a
year as a fellow at Cornell's Society for the Humanities (1978–9). I am

particularly grateful to historians O. Ranum, R. Trexler, and C. Holmes, who tolerated my trespasses during these stints.

The length of even a partial list of individuals whom I feel encouraged this study is perfectly embarrassing. I thank most of all my teachers, colleagues, and students who were willing to engage in free-wheeling, unhurried conversations about social, textual, and interpretive issues that are as irresolvable as they are inescapable: C. Geertz, J. Peacock (who first taught me cultures), J. T. Johnson (who first taught me texts), D. M. Schneider, A. T. Kirsch, M. Singer, R. J. Smith, J. Eidson, D. Greenwood, R. Blair, L. Rosen, D. Holmberg, L. Hochberg, and others.

For additional encouragement, I also thank C. Lévi-Strauss, W. Lippincott (whose suggestion in 1976 led to this book), O. Wolters, D. Brent (who solicited responses to Chapter 5), S. Gilman, P. Hohendahl. J. Culler, C. Chase, M. O'Barr, A. Yengoyan, H. Varenne, K. March, R. Rosaldo, the late M. Rosaldo, C. Greenhouse, B-J. Isbell, J. Pemberton, I. Jacknis, S. Mintz, J. Hunnicutt, D. Segal, S. Greenblatt, S. O'Connor, S. Errington, E. Friedl, G. Stocking, B. Babcock, J. Elliott, G. Neville, B. Lambert, R. Asher, M. DiGiglio, A. Seeger, D. LaCapra, J. Shklar, P. Friedrich, W. O'Flaherty, W. Sturtevant, S. Kaplan, and M. Fisher. Many have been omitted from this list but none forgotten. Special thanks to Joan Oltz and Marge Ciaschi. Finally, enduring gratitude to Olivian, Catherine Olivia (Tili), and Jessica Alexis Boon.

James A. Boon
Ithaca, New York

Part I
Initiations

So the suffering which [ascetic practices] impose is not arbitrary and sterile cruelty;
it is a necessary school, where men form and temper themselves, and acquire the
qualities of disinterestedness and endurance without which there would be no religion.
If this result is to be obtained, it is even a good thing that the ascetic ideal be
incarnated eminently in certain persons, whose specialty, so to speak, it is to represent,
almost with excess, this aspect of the ritual life; for they are like so many living
models, inciting to effort. . . But these exaggerations are necessary to sustain among
the believers a sufficient disgust for an easy life and common pleasures. It is necessary
that an elite put the end too high, if the crowd is not to put it too low. *It is necessary
that some exaggerate,* if the average is to remain at a fitting level.
   . . . So there is an asceticism which, being inherent in all social life, is destined
to survive all the mythologies and all the dogmas; it is an integral part of all human
culture.

Durkheim, *The Elementary Forms of the
Religious Life* (emphasis added)

1. Introduction: The exaggeration of cultures

We are so made that we can derive intense enjoyment only from a contrast and very little from a state of things. (Goethe, indeed, warns us that "nothing is harder to bear than a succession of fair days." [*Alles in der Welt lässt sich ertragen, / Nur nicht eine Reihe von schönen Tagen.*]) But this may be an exaggeration.

Freud, *Civilization and Its Discontents*

Anthropology heightens our sense of human diversity, often routinely, sometimes painfully, sometimes making us giddy. Consider Max Weber – sociologist, political economist, philosopher, typologist, historian, translator – but nevertheless, I insist, an anthropologist. Even when discussing the ideal-type of otherworldly religious interests, Weber intersperses his values of the beyond with contrapuntal attitudes toward the here and now. Arguing that rationalized religions have sublimated the orgy into the sacrament, he contrasts a puritan sense of divine election with other concrete ideas:

The Buddhist monk, certain to enter Nirvana, seeks the sentiment of a cosmic love; the devout Hindu seeks either Bhakti (fervent love in the possession of God) or apathetic ecstasy. The Chlyst with his radjeny, as well as the dancing Dervish, strives for orgiastic ecstasy. Others seek to be possessed by God and to possess God, to be a bridegroom of the Virgin Mary, or to be the bride of the Savior. The Jesuit's cult of the heart of Jesus, quietistic edification, the pietists' tender love for the child Jesus and its "running sore," the sexual and semi-sexual orgies at the wooing of Krishna, the sophisticated cultic dinners of the Vallabhacharis, the gnostic onanist cult activities, the various forms of the *unio mystica*, and the contemplative submersion in the All-one – these states undoubtedly have been sought, first of all, for the sake of such emotional values as they directly offered the devout. In this respect, they have in fact been absolutely equal to Dionysian or the soma cult; to totemic meat-orgies, the cannibalistic feasts, the ancient and religiously consecrated use of hashish, opium, and nicotine; and in general, to all sorts of magical intoxication. [Weber 1958a: 278]

The discipline of anthropology collectively performs in its fieldwork the kind of whirlwind cultural tours of which Weber so compellingly wrote. Yet Weber's work illustrates that nonfieldworkers can gain vivid knowledge of remote traditions, if only from books and if only by contrast. By the same token today's fieldworkers can learn from Weber not to mistake "their islands" as sole exemplars of humankind. The accumulation of anthropological

3

field experience in fact confirms a profound implication of Weber's comparative sociology of religions: Every culture is equally an extreme, including
one's own, even in its rationality and common sense.

But if no exotic population is a universal paragon, why visit? Why, for
example, like Victor Turner, map multivocality of symbols among the Ndembu
of Africa to help refute positivistic views that words are simply referents to a
preexistent inventory of meanings? Or why, like Clifford Geertz, disclose
phenomenological depths of social experience in politicized Java, performative
Bali, and manipulative Morocco? Or if, like Weber, one stays home, why
turn to documents of India and China; why not investigate degrees of economic,
political, and spiritual bureaucratization in Germany without going so far
afield? At first glance, there appear to be decidedly easier ways of investigating
matters. We might simply leave aside all those Bhakti cults, Dervish orgies,
and cannibalistic feasts; human meaning can be quite well studied by just
about anyone just about anywhere. Many phenomenologists study meaning
by reflecting on themselves or on their sense of bounded selfhood versus
diffuse otherhood. Hermeneuticists circle through texts, sacred and otherwise,
with spiraling enthusiasm and insight. Academic philosophers ponder their
own discussions in tight-knit groups. Many varieties of literary critic, philologist, and religious historian delve into documents of sensibility and belief.
Anthropologists of symbolic forms borrow elements from all these endeavors
(at the same time borrowing the accompanying drawbacks) and complicate
matters by accentuating cultural extremes. Once back from the field, however, one confronts all the pitfalls of subjectivity, inexplicability, and
nonconceivable falsifiability that characterize other interpretive pursuits (but
they have fewer excuses than anthropology!). The disciplinary madness stems
from a perpetual suspicion having the force of conviction: Without contrastive
sweep, fundamental (not to mention superficial!) aspects of human meaning
would remain unknown to us. Indeed, optimum contrast is needed to disclose
the very terms of cultural discourse. Like comparative linguistics and folklore, the anthropology of meaning takes the greatest scope and humblest
materials as a means to guard against artificial standardization – and elitism as
well. Our own streetcorners are perhaps microsocieties, and our own quad-
rangles enclose semantic universes; but studying them alone cannot reveal the
ultimate cultures that they contrastively represent. Hence anthropology's apparent inefficiency, its worldwide circumlocution, and its most distinctive
fetish.

Fetishism of the field

In fact, the field research with which every ethnographic career begins is mother and
nurse of doubt, the philosophic attitude *par excellence*.

Lévi-Strauss, "The Scope of Anthropology"

To meet the age-old challenge of discovering the significance of human diversity, the thoroughly modern anthropologist packs her or his belongings, obtains visas if necessary, and boards a ship or plane (or bus or subway) to real or imagined exile, ready to suffer all the petty delays, cross-cultural misunderstandings, and confusing self-doubts that ordinary travelers, thanks to the successors of Cook's tours or Baedeker's guidebooks, avoid. Anthropologists snoop where nobody else foreign or native would either dare or care, in order to interpret diverse cultures in heightened contrast.

Fieldwork is a peculiar idea: a prolonged episode, ideally (since Malinowski), during which a lone researcher visits a remote population. The experience, not quite authentic when an entire expedition pursues it, must be hauntingly personal and richly particular; yet it becomes the basis for intercontinental comparisons. The prescribed method of fieldwork requires being there, participating and observing, and speaking the language. The ideal-type anthropologist (each individual anthropologist, of course, need not conform) clarifies – literally as a pedestrian – the highest-flying issues in human meaning: Icarus with dirty feet.

Fieldwork results often help support social and cultural generalizations that accentuate the exotic. Much of the history of professional anthropology has been marked by theories that make obscure rituals, myths, or praxis into touchstones of religion and society in general. Take, for example, suggestions that positive rules of exogamy – as bizarre to Americans as a requirement that Republicans marry Democrats – reveal basic properties of human communication. Do such "total anthropological facts" actually escape chauvinism? What explains the passion of Emile Durkheim's circle in France, of Franz Boas and his followers in America, and of J. P. B. de Josselin de Jong's school in Holland for dualism and exogamous clans?[1]

These questions have given rise to endless quandaries. Does apparent nonchauvinism subtly mask solipsism? Indeed, ethnographers themselves occasionally seem to resemble the exotic cultures they unveil, as in Lévi-Strauss's "neolithic mentality," his self-confessed sense of identification with preliterate modes of information (1977). Such confessions aggravate suspicions that comparative anthropologists merely project a self-image when they claim to communicate cross-cultural understanding (cultural interpretation) or to understand cross-cultural communication (structuralism). Yet when Professor X looks suspiciously like culture X, we are obliged to remember that investigators themselves emerge from a society and history conforming to cultural patterns (cf. M. Douglas 1975:74ff.): The investigator is *native* to some culture or other. Many provocative episodes in anthropology (broadly construed) involve particular observers and cultures "finding each other" – Cushing and Zuni, Hocart and Fiji, Tocqueville and America. This discovery is a matter of more than simple subjectivity, if only because the exotic culture with which the investigator identifies represents what the investigator's native culture, insofar as he understands it, is *not*. Cross-cultural discourse emerges from anthropologists' sense of antithesis. Perhaps, dialectically, that's the best we can do.

More quandaries arise from the fact that any interpretation is culturally embedded. Perhaps anthropology is simply a roundabout ethnocentrism. Perhaps concern with exotica merely keeps scholars off certain political streets. This possibility looms more darkly if we recall the British in India, the Dutch in Indonesia, the Bureau of Indian Affairs on the reservations, the sociologists in Levittown, or all academic observers in the Third World. Can infrastructures (politics, economics) and/or superstructures (religion, ideology) account for the existence of comparative anthropology or for the cultural diversity it highlights? Are different anthropologies handmaidens of political, national, or philosophical interest groups without realizing it? Perhaps, we may say pessimistically. But more optimistically: What a way to serve interest groups! Why not simply dismiss clan-exogamy, totemism, or other exotic usages; why strive to identify them in the first place? One need not expect anthropology absolutely to transcend all ideologies; yet, following Weber, one may hope that comparative social science can avoid playing directly into the hands of a particular power sector. Perhaps, ironically, that's the best we can do.

Counterparts of anthropologists in less specialized culture include shamans, tricksters, clowns, and kind-fools. These figures, like professional anthropologists, doubt the absoluteness of their own culture; they displace the immediacy of their audience's social lives. It is therefore appropriate to greet the work of anthropologists (and our equivalents) with a dash of skepticism. More quandaries result. Perhaps ethnography is ultimately unverifiable. Because every "other" can only be known through translation, must anthropology dissolve its subject in the act of reaching it? Perhaps anthropology in any society necessarily produces only what that society's internal conditions require it to conceptualize as *other than* itself. (But our view of others may well be no more ideologically fantastic, or even figmentary, than their view of us; in any case figments, too, are culturally produced.) I am personally less skeptical about these issues, although I recognize that there are sources other than anthropology that provide contrastive perspectives on ourselves. Science fiction makes our norms problematic; religion and literature imagine heavens and hells, Utopias and Gomorrahs. I suspect, however, that anthropology's busy documentation of the customs and conventions of all human extremes does make a distinctive contribution to our sense of contrast. No science fiction, after all, quite matches the actual variation in human death rites. No Utopian dream has outstripped tribal ideals of the intermarriage of clans, perfect reciprocity-plus-difference.

Professional anthropologists of late have been willing to confront such quandaries and to stress the ways in which the crossing of cultures twists basic issues in knowledge and method. Lévi-Strauss, for example, in the finale of

Mythologiques, returns to the polemics of *Tristes tropiques* and *The Savage Mind*. He decries the "rut of existentialism,"

this auto-admiring enterprise, not without *jobardise*, in which contemporary man is enclosed in a tête-à-tête with himself and falls in ecstasy before himself – cutting himself off from a scientific knowledge he scorns and from a real humanity whose historical depth and ethnographic dimensions he ignores, to set up a tiny world, closed and reserved: ideological Café du Commerce where, transpiring within the four walls of a human condition cut down to the size of a particular society, its frequenters sift anew the whole day through problems of local interest, beyond which the smoky atmosphere of their dialectical tobacco-talk prevents them from expanding their vista. [1971:572; my translation]

Many, needless to say and to put it mildly, would dispute this view of existentialism. Others would hurl Lévi-Strauss's accusation at different philosophies or anthropologies; some would aim the same charge at the accuser. All might nevertheless doubt that rhetorical tobacco-talk or at-home heuristics permit adequate investigation of the so-variable human tribe. Still, although we may board the plane, the assertion that we ever *really* get away, even in encountering the exotic, remains profoundly problematic.

The field (of symbols) affords a presumably privileged avenue of escape from the ideological café. Yet doing fieldwork has seldom brought forth a truly self-conscious ethnography and ethnology, this veritable "prose of the world." Traditionally, few field accounts – Gregory Bateson's *Naven* (1936/1958) is one vibrant exception – explored their own symbolic foundations as descriptions. Fewer still – here the classic exception is *Tristes tropiques* – explored their own nature as discourse. Recently the symbolic basis of the fieldwork experience, in particular the intensive writing that presumes to represent its findings, has itself become a subject of scrutiny.[2] In the past more conventional champions of the fieldwork ordeal routinely implied that cultures can be penetrated simply by entering *their* jungles, real or asphalt, and by participant-observing their daily affairs, particularly regular family life. Visit the island and enter the kinship system – then just write it up, sooner or later.

Margaret Mead in her early work promoted an oversimplified view of fieldwork. In 1937, when her study of Samoan adolescence was a popular success, Mead was ready to wrap up New Guinea. She wrote Ruth Benedict:

I am more and more convinced that there is no room in anthropology for philosophical concepts and deductive thinking. Of course Papa Franz [Boas] has always stood for empirical thinking, but he has never really determined what the data are in social anthropology on which the thinking is to be based...[Radcliffe-] Brown has no tact and no political sense and needs a nurse. [1959:334][3]

So Baconian a view of fieldwork sustains equally simplified confidence in its results. Three days later the Tchambuli had fallen into the ethnographer's pocketbook:

I've had a tremendous spurt of energy and I've gotten the key to this culture from my angle – got it yesterday during hours of sitting on the floor in a house of mourning. Now it's straight sailing ahead, just a matter of working out all the ramifications of my hunch. In fact I think we've both [Mead and Reo Fortune] had our big moments in this culture and the rest of the time will be just steady working ahead, verifying, recording, amplifying, and learning the dashed language which is really awful. [1959:334]

Even as the ink dried, Mead was off to yet another island, this time Bali, aiming again to determine "what the data are." Her subsequent work in psychological anthropology belied her initial faith in fieldwork untainted by philosophical deduction. Yet Mead's earlier position reflected a naivete that persists in American anthropology.[4]

British anthropologists, too, disdain deduction. Their views usually take the guise of caustic rebuttals of armchair theorizing. Even Evans-Pritchard, hardly inductivist in his own work, when it came to legislating the norms of the profession could not resist swipes at *penseurs* who had never really roughed it. Durkheim himself, elsewhere credited by Evans-Pritchard with making social theory answerable to tribal systems, here falls victim: "One sometimes sighs – if only Tylor, Marett, Durkheim and all the rest of them could have spent a few weeks among the peoples about whom they so freely wrote" (1912/1965:67). This rhetoric with a small *r* is standard in empiricist simplification. Are we to believe that contact of a few weeks, a few years, or a few lifetimes between Durkheim and Australians (or Pueblos or archaic Chinese!) would have altered the views underlying *The Elementary Forms of the Religious Life* or *Primitive Classification*? On the other hand, should we be surprised that Spencer and Gillen or other long-term Australian ethnographers failed to produce general social theories? Such tossed-off remarks – "if only all the rest of them had performed fieldwork" – reinforce the mistaken view that cross-cultural interpretations happen empirically. Worse, these statements ignore the potential for a disciplinary division of labor. Worst of all, they prolong the fallacy that fieldwork is fundamentally "descriptive" and comparison more vaguely "theoretical." Empiricists often advance methods of description and theories of comparison without stipulating that we require methods of comparison and theories of description in equal measure.[5]

The contemporary identity of the anthropological profession centers, rightly I think, on fieldwork – in act and ideal. This statement means neither that the history of the discipline commenced only with fieldwork nor that every anthropologist must practice it but only that fieldwork epitomizes what anthropologists do when they write. Yet cultures cannot be penetrated simply with passports, survey sheets, statistics, genealogies, and dictionaries (or by intuition, benign tolerance, indomitable self-confidence, or studious self-effacement) – although each of these may on occasion be helpful. Rather, cross-cultural interpretation must be *made* to happen, using symbolic conventions derived from sources outside the conditions of fieldwork proper, as it is narrowly construed in the functionalist school (cf. Wagner 1975). Part of the business of anthropology is to make explicitly exotic populations appear implicitly familiar and explicitly familiar populations appear implicitly exotic. Although both sorts of population are *experienced* anthropologically "in the field," they are *interpreted* anthropologically in books.

Functionalist books versus Frazer

What does the ethnographer do? – he writes.
C. Geertz, *The Interpretation of Cultures*

Whereas "isms" *look* positive, they are all negatively infused, taking their form antithetically to other "isms" (some elements of which, paradoxically, they often end by incorporating).
K. Burke, *The Rhetoric of Religion*

Anthropological functionalism commenced broadly, in fact sweepingly, and only narrowed as it prospered. Bronislaw Malinowski, "godfather and standard-bearer" of functionalism in Britain, first championed the idea of fieldwork as making possible total immersion in a particular society (1963:xxviii). Yet he concluded his initial book-length account of "native enterprise and adventure" in the Trobriand Islands not with final field data about *kula*-type inter-island exchange networks but with a florid salute to comparative studies extending well beyond Melanesia:

> Thus the details and technicalities of the Kula acquire their meaning in so far only as they express some central attitude of mind of the natives, and thus broaden our knowledge, widen our outlook and deepen our grasp of human nature.
> What interests me really in the study of the native is his outlook on things, his *Weltanschauung*, the breath of life and reality which he breathes and by which he lives. Every human culture gives its members a definite vision of the world, a definite zest of life...
> Though it may be given to us for a moment to enter into the soul of a savage and through his eyes to look at the outer world and feel ourselves what it must feel to *him* to be himself – yet our final goal is to enrich and deepen our own world's vision...
> The study of Ethnology – so often mistaken by its very votaries for an idle hunting after curios, for a ramble among the savage and fantastic shapes of "barbarous customs and crude superstitions" – might become one of the most deeply philosophic, enlightening and elevating disciplines of scientific research. [1922/1961:517]

Argonauts of the Western Pacific (1922) on Trobriand trade and economic life became an instant classic. This happy fate was foreseen by James G. Frazer, the eminent Scottish comparativist whose celebrated *Golden Bough* (1890, 1911–15) had inspired Malinowski to pursue anthropology. Frazer's preface to *Argonauts* expresses boundless praise:

It is characteristic of Dr. Malinowski's method that he takes full account of the complexity of human nature. He sees man, so to say, in the round and not in the flat. He remembers that man is a creature of emotion at least as much as of reason, and he is constantly at pains to discover the emotional as well as the rational basis of human action. The man of science, like the man of letters, is too apt to view mankind only in the abstract, selecting for his consideration a single side of our complex and many-sided being. Of this one-sided treatment Molière is a conspicuous example among great writers. . . Very different is the presentation of human nature in the greater artists, such as Cervantes and Shakespeare: their characters are solid, being drawn not from one side only but from many. [1922/1961:ix]

The implicit compliment – Malinowski stands to ethnography as Shakespeare to literature – was gradually forgotten by its beneficiary. As Malinowski developed functionalist method and theory, his followers professed diminishing esteem for Frazer, the "father of institutionalized academic social anthropology" (Jarvie 1969:1).

Frazer's *Golden Bough* became the antithesis (along with evolutionism and diffusionism) of developing functionalism. I. C. Jarvie reviews the matter as purely political strategy:

Bronislaw Malinowski plotted and directed the revolution in social anthropology. It was a genuine revolution, aiming to overthrow the establishment of Frazer and Tylor and their ideas; but mainly it was against Frazer. . .

One should not be misled by the curiously affectionate personal relations between Malinowski and Frazer. Admittedly Frazer wrote a nice foreword to *Argonauts* and Malinowski wrote a magnanimous tribute to Frazer after the latter's death; but this should not disguise the fact that Malinowski started a war for control and won it.

Malinowski's new ways were fieldwork ("come down off the verandah") and functionalism ("study the ritual, not the belief"). . . The difference between Frazer's work and Malinowski's is not merely in methodology, as it should have been. In Malinowski's hands the science of man was twisted into an inductivist and relativist science, with no clear connections with the basic metaphysical problem of the unity of mankind at all. In all this I think the role of Radcliffe-Brown was that of a consolidator. His contribution was to strengthen the doctrine of functionalism by bringing in the element of structure; in almost all else connected with the revolution he went along with Malinowski. [1969:173–5]

With hindsight the reason for the apparent revolution appears clear enough. Frazer deemed primitive life and ritual – echoed in our own folklore, superstitions, and ceremony – an allegory of a sensational tragic theme that underlies basic religious and political institutions: The officeholder is slain to perpetuate the office. As we shall see, the only thing that is whole in *The Golden Bough*, eventually thirteen volumes long, is the allegory itself. In contrast, functionalists came to construe primitive groups as routine individuals interrelated through the stable mechanisms of their whole-societies, whose workings could be thoroughly documented by the lone participant-observer. Theirs was an open-air anthropology freed from the complacencies of the armchair. The standardized history of modern British social anthropology is often presented as a self-congratulatory chronicle of the scientific fieldwork method emerging triumphant from Victorian blather.

The contrast between Frazer and Malinowski was exaggerated by functionalists in retrospect (and was reexaggerated later in Jarvie's tabloidlike account). Their compatibility ran deeper than a token tribute paid by the elder in the novice's professional birth announcement and later reciprocated in the elder's official death notice. The functionalist emphasis on ritual rather than belief (or, more fancily, on action rather than idea or perhaps, nowadays, on praxis rather than exegesis) in fact recalls Frazer's methodological advance over Tylor's less paradoxical *Primitive Culture* (1871/1958). Tylor had reduced nonliterate religions to beliefs in the pervasive agency-spirit of matter, the primitive doctrine of animism. Frazer bypassed the pale foreshadowing of doctrine to emphasize the rich array of primitive rite. *The Golden Bough* internalizes the contrast between itself and its subject matter; its prose paradoxically describes unbelievable rites believably. Tylor's *Primitive Culture* attempted merely to collate and to compare native creeds implicit in field reports. *Primitive Culture* offered not a prose of rites but a creed ("animism") of presumed native creeds. (Any discrepancy between source material and ethnological account remains back in the piecemeal field reports by missionaries, civil servants, or travelers). Frazer, on the other hand, introduces a basic discrepancy (we might call it rite/write) into ethnological tomes themselves, as a motive force generating *The Golden Bough*'s expanding volumes of prose. This contrast between Tylor and Frazer suggests a development from one-dimensional reportage to multidimensional representation. Why else would Eliot, Joyce, Lawrence, and "all the rest of them" have thrived on Frazer?

Thus Malinowski's emphasis on rites itself derives from Frazer. Unlike Frazer's work, however, Malinowski's prose accounts adopt mechanistic models and conventions of space–time isolates that are associated with realist and naturalist novels (and literary theories). Nevertheless, and this point is crucial, both Frazer and Malinowski could be – in the Auerbachian sense implying representational illusionism – *read*. Moreover, judging from the early reactions to Malinowski's books of even professional anthropological readers, Frazer became passé less because Malinowski converted Frazer's rambling evolutionism into systematic science than because Frazer's expanding literary allegory was updated by Malinowski until it resembled narrative realism. As A. I. Richards has recalled: "In comparison with works such as those of Frazer, Crawley, Westermarck, or Durkheim which we read at the time . . . , [Malinowski's] work seemed lively and stimulating, and we began actually to visualize ourselves 'in the field.' The couvade was no longer a laughable eccentricity but a social mechanism for the public assumption of the father's duties towards the child" (1957:19). "Actually to visualize ourselves 'in the field' ": Richards read Malinowski as Emma Bovary read novels.

The most conspicuous continuity between Frazer's and Malinowski's writing was their means of legitimating interest in matters savage. Like Frazer, Malinowski drew an analogy with the mythical Mediterranean to lend an instant aura of grandeur to Trobriand usages. Malinowski wrote *Argonauts of the Western Pacific* before risking *The Sexual Life of Savages*. The word "Argonauts" alone suggests the sort of synthesis he advances in the Frazerian conclusion to his 1922 opus. The parallel between practicing Melanesians and heroes from classical legend enabled Malinowski to convert humble Trobrianders into a book – a monograph – about exploits less exotic than remote. Malinowski gave his readers fair warning:

> Thus the first and basic ideal of ethnographic field work is to give a clear and firm outline of the social constitution, and disentangle the laws and regularities of all cultural phenomena from the irrelevancies. The firm skeleton of the tribal life has to be first ascertained. This ideal imposes in the first place the fundamental obligation of giving a complete survey of the phenomena, and not of picking out the sensational, the singular, still less the funny and quaint. The time when we could tolerate accounts presenting us the natives as a distorted, childish caricature of a human being is gone. This picture is false, and like many other falsehoods, it has been killed by Science. The field Ethnographer has seriously and soberly to cover the full extent of the phenomena in each aspect of tribal culture studied, making no difference between what is commonplace, or drab, or ordinary, and what strikes him as astonishing and out-of-the-way. [1922/1961:10–11]

Today this passage, too, sounds like an oblique attack on Frazer, but judging from his introduction, Frazer himself did not think so. Moreover, the material in *Argonauts* was no more objectively drab and commonplace than the title. Nor was the kula the sum, average, and common denominator of all Trobriand activities; rather, it was a particularly intense and well-formed set of institutions, certainly as select as, for example, the Zuni ceremonies, Dobu magic, and Kwakiutl potlatches that later informed Ruth Benedict's justly celebrated *Patterns of Culture*. Why else would the kula account have so influenced Benedict herself, or that arch-deductivist, Marcel Mauss (1925/1967)?

Finally, like Frazer, Malinowski lingered over the sensational. Even in books less Frazerian than *Argonauts*, he dressed drab practices in literary analogy, sometimes in a way that was convoluted and negative:

> The whole mortuary ritual is, in fact, perhaps the most difficult and bewildering aspect of Trobriand culture for the investigating sociologist. In the overgrowth of ceremonial, in the inextricable maze of obligations and counter-obligation, stretching out into a long series of ritual acts, there is to be found a whole world of conceptions – social, moral, and mythological – the majority of which struck me as quite unexpected and difficult to reconcile with the generally accepted views of the human attitude towards death and mourning. Throughout this ritual, the unfortunate remains of the man are constantly worried. His body is twice exhumed; it is cut up; some of its bones are peeled out of the carcass, are handled, are given to one party and then to another, until at last they come to a final rest. And what makes the whole performance most disconcerting is the absence of the real protagonist – *Hamlet without the Prince of Denmark*. For the spirit of the dead man knows nothing about all that happens to his body and bones, and cares less, since he is already leading a happy existence in

Tuma, the netherworld, having breathed of the magic of oblivion and formed new ties... The ritual performances at his twice-opened grave and over his buried remains, and all that is done with his relics, are merely a social game, where the various groupings into which the community has re-crystallized at his death play against each other. This, I must add with great emphasis, represents the actual contemporary view of the natives, and contains no hypothetical reference to the origins or past history of this institution. Whether the dead man always had his spiritual back turned on the Trobriand mortuary ritual, or whether his spirit has gradually evaporated from it – it is not for the field-worker to decide. [1929:148–9; emphasis added]

The passing, sober resolution of *The Sexual Life of Savages* (1929) hardly registers after the evocative account of exhumation and, above all, the theatrical allusion to the drama of the Dane. Malinowski's structural-functionalist successors tried to purge such colorful "digressions" from the monograph genre. Evans-Pritchard, for example, branded them with the least flattering comparison he could think of, linking them with Mead's *Coming of Age in Samoa*, this "discursive, or perhaps I should say chatty and feminine, book with a leaning towards the picturesque, what I call the rustling-of-the-wind-in-the-palm-trees kind of anthropological writing, for which Malinowski set the fashion" (Evans-Pritchard 1962:96). But the eventual deprecation of some of Mead's and Malinowski's liveliest discourse should not prompt us to forget that the Malinowskian monograph was launched as the flagship *Argonauts* on Frazer's literary vogue. Although the genre rode that vogue's crest into other, less literary lagoons, they were never, while Malinowski himself stood at the helm, commonplace, drab, or ordinary. (My extended metaphor should help prepare us for Frazer's style.)

What do *functionalists* do? They write, too. The monograph, together with the fieldwork method, formed the heart of functionalism. Frazer was superseded by both a new kind of method and a new kind of *book*. The monograph was an intensive, concerted description and analysis of routine life collected (and in this respect Radcliffe-Brown's *Andaman Islanders* did not qualify) in the native language during a protracted visit to an intact society. It was offered neither as a handbook for colonial functionaries or missionaries nor as evidence supporting a theory about classification, evolution, or diffusion of particular traits (physical, customary, linguistic, or otherwise) but as pure description with a dash of humanistic hopes:

Perhaps as we read the account of these remote customs there may emerge a feeling of solidarity with the endeavors and ambitions of these natives. Perhaps man's mentality will be revealed to us and brought near, along some lines which we never have followed before. Perhaps through realizing human nature in a shape very distant and foreign to us, we shall have some light shed on our own. In this, and in this case only, we shall be justified in feeling that it has been worth our while to understand these natives, their institutions and customs, and that we have gathered some profit from the Kula. [Malinowski 1922/1961:25]

Again, the extravagant aim recalls Frazer, but the monograph genre does not.[6]

The monograph remained the ultimate means prescribed by Malinowski for realizing that "science of Man" whose "most refined and deepest version" would produce "the understanding of other men's point of view" (1922/1961:518). Echoing developments in literary realism and naturalism, monographs underscored the earthy activities of native populations to counteract rival images of vapid otherworldliness. The author as fieldworker was always implicitly present; the author as author was usually implicitly absent – a standard convention of realist fiction. Monograph readers presumably share the observer's experience as he or she documents a working social machine that is seen through evocations of the practical and emotional lives of the individuals who operate it.

As with any revolutionary leader, Malinowski's freshness, so "lively and stimulating" to Richards and others, withered as his followers routinized it. A stylistic taboo on authorial viewpoint helped rigidify the monograph format. Its order of contents – physical surroundings firmly first, religion vaguely last, kinship and social organization determiningly at the core – became so unquestioned that any departure from convention, such as Bateson's *Naven*, was instantly conspicuous. Because the proper fieldwork method was presumed equal to solving any problems, the genre provoked little self-consciousness. In an oft-cited rule of thumb, Evans-Pritchard allowed ten years for producing a first monograph, after two or three years' fieldwork (cf. J. Fox 1977:viii). Yet, increasingly methodology was formulated for fieldwork alone, with writing left to occur, one supposes, commonsensically – that is, in accordance with implicit monograph conventions. The meticulously standardized *Notes and Queries* on the proper collection of field data were agonizingly circumspect; functionalists responded with automatic adherence to the monograph's prescribed order of contents. In part the emphasis on "social structure" developed by Radcliffe-Brown and others reinforced the tendency to conformity. Radically differing cultures were paradoxically inscribed in disarmingly similar books. If anthropologists are to generalize, we may never quite overcome this paradox; yet we ought at least to bear witness to it: What subtleties of other cultures has the discourse of the normative monograph obscured?

Functionalist monographs portrayed cultures as functionalists assumed them to be: islandlike, space–time isolates of interlocking, reinforcing systems of relationships. When this preconception is duly acknowledged, there is nothing wrong with it; and structural functionalists and structuralists alike (with Durkheim's help) moved beyond atomistic views of societies and cultures as agglomerations of evolved traits, sometimes accelerating, sometimes lagging in the process. Many functionalists, however, would resist my suggestion that the preferred form of the monograph itself accounts for some of the success of the functionalist school. They would wish monographs to *re-present* what societies are, as an entity apart from how they can be inscribed.

One path to constructive semiotic doubt about the functionalist monograph entails pondering what it routinely, or perhaps strategically, omitted. The standard average monograph characteristically lacked several chapters:

1. Chapters on relations between a particular culture and others and on that culture's own sense of others. Evolutionists, "conjectural historians," and students of migration and diffusion – despite their storied excesses – conveyed a truth functionalists avoided: No society is, culturally, an island. Monographs need not have neglected evidence of alternatives to a society's beliefs and practices. Such alternatives can often be investigated indirectly next door (as in Leinhardt's work on Dinka [1961], which complements Evans-Pritchard's Nuer [1940, 1956] material). In functionalist approaches, even restudies of a given society could not give attention to dialectics: We need only recall the disputes between Redfield and Lewis about Mexican villagers or debates about Zuni ethos and character in tribal studies (see Murphy 1980:27–31). Even in investigations of acculturation, the fiction of a stable space–time isolate with a singular set of key social mechanisms remained the guiding image of standard accounts.

2. Chapters on the history of the tendency to conceptualize the population as a "culture" and on the ultimate fact of fieldwork: the significance of a stranger's inserting himself into the routine context of a face-to-face population. Although this last "chapter" pervaded Malinowski's first Trobriand accounts, it never became an integral component of monograph writing. *Argonauts* contains protracted confessions:

I would get out from under my mosquito net, to find around me the village life beginning to stir, or the people well advanced in their working day according to the hour and also to the season, for they get up and begin their labors early or late, as work presses. As I went on my morning walk through the village, I could see intimate details of family life, of toilet, cooking, taking of meals; I could see the arrangements for the day's work, people starting on their errands, or groups of men and women busy at some manufacturing tasks...Quarrels, jokes, family scenes, events usually trivial, sometimes dramatic but always significant, formed the atmosphere of my daily life, as well as of theirs. [1922/1961:7]

Not only did this sort of information become a mere token in later functionalist monographs, but Malinowski's early candor was eliminated altogether: "It is very nice to have a base in a white man's compound for the stores, and know there is a refuge there in times of sickness and surfeit of native" (1922/1961:6). Unfortunately Malinowski's sense of the irony of his own situation was also eliminated: "In fact, as they knew that I would thrust my nose into everything, even where a well-mannered native would not dream of intruding, they finished by regarding me as part and parcel of their life, a necessary evil or nuisance, mitigated by donations of tobacco" (1922/1961:8). "Surfeit of native" – and, reciprocally, surfeit of anthropologist!

It was necessary for people to forget these strengths in functionalism's founder at least in part before the posthumous publication of Malinowski's field diary could create a stir (1967). His diary expresses the ethnographer's "surfeit of native" in earthier terms (Trobrianders had doubtless voiced their own sense of nuisance in comparable ways). Professionals disturbed by Malinowski's private inscriptions apparently still believed that the champion of fieldwork was less fallible, less human – more objective – than his subjects of study, a brand of arrogance by no means confined to social anthropology (see Chapter 2). To Malinowski's credit, we can imagine that had he been stranded several years in the traditional courts of Versailles or in the Escurial, to which he favorably compared Trobriand life (1922/1961:10), these natives, too, would have been derided in his diary, although with different epithets.

But my point is that functionalism increasingly resisted self-awareness. Developed as a normal science, it eliminated any sense that the investigator's position was absurd, even after the collapse of colonialism meant that the absurdities could no longer be avoided. Functionalists neglected to acknowledge that all cultural traditions interrelate, British empiricism and confident "common sense" included. In addition, most ironically, they failed to look for the counterpart of "anthropology" in the whole-societies they observed. The promise of complexity and full vision in Malinowski's *Argonauts* became a routine neoutilitarianism that extended even to the bizarre Trobriands. Functionalism became an anthropology without irony.

Let us set aside the ideological clarion call for open-air fieldwork and turn from functionalist *books* back to Frazer's opus, which they replaced. *The Golden Bough*, more systematic than monographists would later admit, demonstrated that primitive, archaic, and contemporary religious rituals and institutions were variations on the theme of the legend of Aricia. The organic argument was a matter less of evolution or history than of allegory. For Frazer, human ritual diversity bore empirical witness to the fundamental paradox behind kingship and perhaps any system of social authority: It is necessary to kill the *person* filling the *office* of priest-king (thus vividly distinguishing the institutional component from the individual) in order to regenerate the nature base that sustains the society. This "strange and recurring tragedy," so conspicuous against "the polished Italian culture of the day," enabled Frazer to interrelate complex social and ritual usages: from the link between periodic licentiousness and abundant harvests to dissociable souls and the amalgamation of temporal and ecclesiastical power. To cite just a fragment of this once-famous beginning:

No one who has seen the calm water of the Lake of Nemi, lapped in a green hollow of the Alban hills, can ever forget it. Diana herself might still be lingering by this lonely shore, haunting these woodlands wild. In antiquity this sylvan landscape was the scene of a strange and recurring tragedy...The lake and the grove were sometimes known as the lake and grove of Aricia. In that grove grew a certain tree round which, at any hour of the day and probably far into the night, a grim figure might be seen to prowl. In his hand he carried a drawn sword, and he kept peering warily about him as if at every instant he expected to be set upon. He was at once a priest and murderer; and the man for whom he was watching was sooner or later to murder him and hold the priesthood in his stead. For such was the rule of the sanctuary: a candidate for the priesthood could succeed to office only by slaying the incumbent priest in single combat, and could himself retain office only until he was in turn slain by a stronger or craftier. Moreover – and this is especially significant – he could fling his challenge only if he had first succeeded in plucking a golden bough from the tree which the priest was guarding.

The post which was held by this precarious tenure carried with it the title of King of the Wood: but surely no crowned head every lay uneasier or was visited by more evil dreams...we picture to ourselves the scene as it might have been witnessed by a belated wayfarer on one of those wild autumn nights when the dead leaves are falling thick, and the winds seem to be singing the dirge of the dying year. [Frazer 1959:31–32]

An implicit theory of social contract and role differentiation (though it was never quite phrased in this way), linked to the ritual recognition of nature's cyclical rhythms, guided Frazer's quest through ethnographic whatnots. At a time when the empire was just past its prime, he managed to convert aspects of colonialized populations (human sacrifice, fertility rites) that were abhorrent to Victorian–Edwardian public sensitivities into an acceptable specialty for Britain's first chair of social anthropology (at Liverpool). Frazer rendered tawdry ethnographica palatable; and he challenged the standard civilizational prejudice for *lettres* by proclaiming the significance of all people's religious practices:

The position of the anthropologist of to-day resembles in some sort the position of classical scholars at the revival of learning...And as the scholar of the Renaissance found not merely fresh food for thought but a new field of labor in the dusty and faded manuscripts of Greece and Rome, so in the mass of materials that is steadily pouring in from many sides – from buried cities of remotest antiquity as well as from the rudest savages of the desert and the jungle – we of to-day must recognize a new province of knowledge which will task the energies of generations of students to master. [Frazer 1959:xxv]

"Rude savages" had fascinated natural scientists throughout the century, as evidenced by the voyage of Darwin's *Beagle* in 1831 and the famous Toda expedition in 1899 by W. H. R. Rivers and his colleagues. Malinowski only eventually dismissed Frazer's vision, but he immediately converted the expedition format into the fieldwork format. Malinowski inscribed native practices not as exotic specimens but as straightforward human experience. Frazer, on the other hand, neither expeditionist nor fieldworker (and really not much of an evolutionist), represented the culmination of traditional compilations of "fardles of fashions" and cabinets of curiosities (cf. Hodgen 1971:chap. 4). His inspired connoisseurship of exotic rites was never geared to the rites' practitioners, whether tribesman or archbishop. Tomes by Frazer and others working in his image (such as A. E. Crawley) were books of records, with rites transposed, commended to the reader's imagination for empathetic response. An expandable interpretive catalog of the worldwide range of human ritual usages had first appeared in English in 1625 in Samuel Purchas's *Hakluytus Posthumus; or, Purchas His Pilgrimes* (see Chapter 5); it last did so in the fullest edition of *The Golden Bough*.

Malinowski made Frazer's books of records obsolete by writing books purportedly of the people: Trobriand garden magic is presented, we are to assume, as experienced. But the functionalist revolution required the people to be inscribed *in monograph form*, and it would be hard to prove the constraints on monographic discourse any less conventional, and indeed any less "literary," than Frazer's allegory. Functionalists, after all, write realism, a discourse as "tropic" as any other.[7] Frazer wrote sometimes sentimentalized neoromance. Frazer's implied savages suffer (along with the civilized religions succeeding them) the consequences of building societies "on the sands of superstition rather than on the rock of nature" (1959:xxvi). In contrast, functionalist natives go about their sometimes peculiar businesses – subsistence, navigation, magic, myth, burial – simply to reinforce their social teleology. Malinowski replaced Frazer's allegory (less abruptly than many functionalists insist) with a metaphor of mechanics not celestial but mundane, psychological, and everyday. This "world's vision" is indeed like that called for by Malinowski but is not quite credited with being such by functionalists themselves and lacks the "love of the variety and independence of the various cultures" that the earlier, still Frazerian, Malinowski had professed.

As J. B. Vickery (1973) stresses, Frazer (like Proust) must be read with Renan and Chateaubriand. If we place him in such company, we are more likely to savor "his prose style of pellucid grace touched with an irony suggestive of Anatole France" (Baugh 1967:1590). But Frazer's vision as well as his prose may have been touched with irony – romantic irony? – which perhaps further explains the increasing disdain of functionalists.

Leach has alluded unflatteringly to parallels between Lévi-Strauss and Frazer (1970:65); such is the fashion. Yet not even Lévi-Strauss's foreshadowing of the twilight of man in the postnihilist finale of *Mythologiques* (see Chapter 7) surpasses Frazer's concluding scene (following a thin evolutionary metaphor) of crepuscular Christianity; perhaps Frazer never quite relinquished intermittent suspicions of phoenixlike, rather priest-king-of-Nemi-like, ritual resilience:

> Without dipping so far into the future, we may illustrate the course which thought has hitherto run by likening it to a web woven of three different threads – the black thread of magic, the red thread of religion, and the white thread of science, if under science we may include those simple truths drawn from observation of nature, of which men in all ages have possessed a store. Could we then survey the web of thought from the beginning, we should probably perceive it to be at first a chequer of black

and white, a patchwork of true and false notions, hardly tinged as yet by the red thread of religion. But carry your eye further along the fabric and you will remark that, while the black and white chequer still runs through it, there rests on the middle portion of the web, where religion has entered most deeply into its texture, a dark crimson stain, which shades off insensibly into a lighter tint as the white thread of science is woven more and more into the tissue. To a web thus chequered and stained, thus shot with threads of diverse hues, but gradually changing colour the farther it is unrolled, the state of modern thought, with all its divergent aims and conflicting tendencies, may be compared. Will the great movement which for centuries has been slowly altering the complexion of thought be continued in the near future? or will a reaction set in which may arrest progress and even undo much that has been done? To keep up our parable, what will be the colour of the web which the Fates are now weaving on the humming loom of time? will it be white or red? We cannot tell. A faint glimmering light illumines the backward portion of the web. Clouds and thick darkness hide the other end...

Our long voyage of discovery is over and our bark has drooped her weary sails in port at last. Once more we take the road to Nemi. It is evening, and as we climb the long slope of the Appian Way up to the Alban Hills, we look back and see the sky aflame with sunset, its golden glory resting like the aureole of a dying saint over Rome and touching with a crest of fire the dome of St. Peter's. The sight once seen can never be forgotten, but we turn from it and pursue our way darkly along the mountain side, till we come to Nemi and look down on the lake in its deep hollow, now fast disappearing in the evening shadows. The place has changed but little since Diana received the homage of her worshippers in the sacred grove. The temple of the sylvan goddess, indeed, has vanished and the King of the Wood no longer stands sentinel over the Golden Bough. But Nemi's woods are still green, and as the sunset fades above them in the west, there comes to us, borne on the swell of the wind, the sound of the church bells of Rome ringing the Angelus. *Ave Maria!* Sweet and solemn they chime out from the distant city and die lingeringly across the wide Campagnan marshes. *Le roi est mort, vive le roi! Ave Maria!* [1959:741–2]

Many anthropologists have never experienced this text! Nowadays, whatever ethnographers do, they seldom read Frazer. The discipline that strives to understand principles by which cultures communicate is in a pretty state of affairs: Frazer as scapegoat, buried (alive?) with Crawley and "all the rest of them," abandoned in the name of functionalist science.

Functionalists would have been more consistent had they not disowned Frazer but contextualized him and mechanistically explained his corpus. This task, however, might have proved difficult, because Frazer's work seems antithetical to its own context. To explain how Edinborough rationality produced Frazer or how British academia sustained his somewhat deviant work requires us to confront the very paradox that functionalists avoided: how cultures, perfectly commonsensical from within, nevertheless flirt with their own "alternities," gain critical self-distance, formulate complex (rather than simply reactionary) perspectives on others, embrace negativities, confront (even admire) what they themselves are *not*. However faulty its allegory, Frazer's *Golden Bough* both conveyed and exemplified, both described and epitomized, a profound motive force throughout human cultures: Rituals, myths, and religions (and in Frazer's own case rites *written*), mutually exaggerate, reciprocally radicalize, their meanings. The lowest common denominator of cultures in the prose of *The Golden Bough* is something less like mechanism and more like antithesis.

One trait of symbolic anthropology is the re-recognition that ethnographic description and ethnological comparison occurs *as writing*, that is, at a symbolic remove from whatever immediacy or presence ethnography presumes to recall. The fact of this distance helps us constructively to beg the difference between ethnography-ethnology and literature. I have suggested that functionalist monographs are as conventional, as unnatural, as un*representational* as Frazer's allegory. Similarly, ethnographic monographs are as figurative as literature. Do we need both a kinship theory of epics, romances, lyrics, and novels and a stylistics and discourse theory of ethnographies? How can ethnography and literature shirk each other as long as ethnographers write? Can both be set into one critical perspective, so that our glib confidence in the boundary between two equally problematic entities may be shaken?[8]

To start, we could join Frazer in deeming Malinowski anthropology's Shakespeare (I would prefer, however, to call him a Balzac or a Zola) by way of the Trobriands; would functionalists then accept Lévi-Strauss as anthropology's Proust by way of tribal myth (cf. Boon 1972: chap. 6)? Unlike Frazer, I seek an anthropological Molière as well, since comedy is the most difficult of all cross-cultural achievements, especially in our ponderously solemn age. Science-minded anthropologists would doubtless charge that my analogies make living cultures themselves secondary (oddly enough, however, the same anthropologists are always awaiting anthropology's Newton or Einstein!). Not at all; rather, the literary analogy acknowledges that living cultures in anthropology are inherently written, inscribed; how else could we "know" them? What anthropologist, furthermore, would deny that writing – literature, ethnographic detail, ethnological generalization – is constrained by conventions that at their fullest extent we call cultures?

But many people will understandably object; if anthropology is as genre-laden as literature, what becomes of the issues of falsifiability and accuracy? One answer: They are, like cultures and languages themselves, complexly conventionalized. The fact that functionalist fieldwork and monograph writing were standardized into "normal" anthropological science does not mean that the standards were natural or objective; it means, rather, that they were consensual: disciplinary "social facts." By the same token Frazer's writing might have endured as the norm of a collective endeavor. By the grace of God and Malinowski, it didn't. I make this comment seriously, because if forced to choose one or the other exemplar, I, too, would vote for Malinowski, even though Frazer's allegory of perpetuated ritual–role differentiation plus nature base may surpass functionalist mechanism in clarifying certain phenomena. But my question is: Need we choose? Must we have either anthropology according to a lot of would-be Frazers *or* anthropology according to a lot of would-be Malinowskis? Why not consolidate the differences: anthropology according to a lot of would-be Hocarts!

Or better yet, why not a pluralistic system? There are standards of "convincingness" in various cross-cultural styles and genres, just as there are canons of verisimilitude in realist-ethnography. To assess the accuracy of either Malinowski-like or Frazer-like (or Geertz-like or Lévi-Strauss-like) interpretations, we must plumb the complexities of convergent data – theirs and ours – and renounce the Enlightenment faith in analytic "simplicity," assumptions of direct determinacy, and hopes for unmediated communication, cross-cultural or otherwise.

In the meantime the analogy between literature and ethnology deserves to be pursued further. Most symbolic anthropologists could, I imagine, name their current Dante, especially if I add, "by way of Ndembu." But this question is too easy, since Victor Turner has himself commented on Dante in light of Ndembu symbology (1975:17). (Dante lovers who cringe at the thought are beneath anthropological contempt – they are right down in Ndembuesque Inferno.) Nearer home, we might pose Clifford Geertz by way of Indonesia and Morocco as our James (William and Henry?); or is he our Trilling? Is Raymond Firth anthropology's Trollope by way of Tikopeia? Are there any candidates for Melville?

Once these nominations have been made, what about the other side? Who is the Edmund Leach (by way of what) of literature? Or, to extend the metaphor to Leach, should we select an author-critic-philosopher: the Wilde, the Wilson, the Taine (Marvin Harris?), the Sainte-Beuve, the Leo Spitzer, the eventual always-already Derrida of anthropology? Text-involved litterateurs may show little interest in the analogy – all the more reason, then, for commending the anthropologist in whom litterateurs (Joyce, Yeats, Lawrence, and all the rest of them) *were* interested: Sir James Frazer, our Spenser, Scott, *and* Tennyson by way of everywhere. *Le roi* est *mort*.

Anthropos, the meanings of

With a sublime sense of superiority, man persists in seeing his name at the very top of Linnaeus' address book, with even the apes leagues beneath him, never for a second suspecting that by far the vastest part of his race, according to another and probably more sensible classification, is located somewhere below the huntsman's hound and the miller's ass.

Lichtenberg, "Commentaries"

I have argued that the descriptive monograph is more convention-laden than is ordinarily acknowledged; the same is true of a standard style of anthropological generalization. The discipline's findings are typically presented in two kinds of formulations: (1) details of personal fieldwork ("I know, because I was there"); (2) abstractions of cultural data into "Latinized" primates (*Homo* this or that). Neither kind of formulation – the first presumably particular, the second general – attains the comparative circumstantiality (recalling Weber) that will concern us in subsequent chapters.

Taxonomic labels for the human species are most prevalent in (and are most appropriate to) physical anthropology. We recognize *Homo sapiens sapiens* in contrast to predecessors: *Homo erectus, Homo habilis* – all based on physical traits, sometimes with hypothetical correlations in mental capacities adduced from tool-flaking and other evidence. This taxonomic style from physical anthropology can spill over into cultural anthropology. Through the centuries authors have introduced us to *Homo rationalis, Homo ridens* (scholastics could sound Enlightenment-like before the fact), *Homo ludens, Homo thanatos*, and recently *Homo absurdus*.[9] Humanity so titled – reasoning, lying, joking, reflecting on death, being philosophically ridiculous – can be redivided into provocative subtypes: *Homo hierarchicus* versus *Homo aequalis; Homo religiosus* opposed to both *Homo magicus* and *Homo saecularis*; and many, many more, each quality purportedly the redounding attribute of humankind or of one of its species.

Monolithic-sounding, quasi-naturalistic labels have flourished lately in derogatory brands for humanity, or at least for its worse half: *Homo* as naked ape, or as ruthless defender of territory, or as strategic maximizer of protein, or as selfish perpetuator of his gene pool, or as hunter forced by demography and technology beyond species-specific limitations. Such formulations can trigger heated debates; the last-mentioned label (*Homo venator*), for example, has provoked this retort: "For Robert Ardry evolution has no purpose, it is a response to necessity; he sees modern man as a fish out of water, trying to cope with elements beyond his ken, ill-adapted to the world he has created, unable to go back but doomed if he goes forward" (Turnbull 1976:26). Quarrels about human survivability generally have an evolutionary or otherwise teleological ring to them. We can rightly question whether anthropologists, archaeologists, or sociobiologists are in better position to judge these matters than anyone else. But the point to notice is that those coining sensational labels and passing judgment often fail to acknowledge that their labels, whether derogatory or rosy, are caricatures.

There is nothing wrong with caricatures recognized as such. In fact, cultures continually fabricate such ideas of each other and of themselves; when the caricatures are believed, we call them ideologies. Cultures are, so to speak, self-labeling; and any culture appears distorted when it is viewed in terms of all possible configurations: this was the famous insight, phrased psychologically, of Ruth Benedict's pattern theory. Labels for humankind should be regarded playfully, because cultures, just like anthropology, appear to be comprised of makers of exaggerated labels, and we should recall in this context K. Burke's "terministic screens" (1966: chap. 3). *Homo*-whoever is never thoroughly true to his (her?) own sobriquet – even, I hasten to add, under ideal fieldwork conditions. The singular pigeonholes implied by the designations – endemic warfare, proverbial laughter, preferential hairlessness – hinder the portrayal of human thought and action in its characteristic complexity. Contrary to the labels, abstract *Homo* is more of a humanist *anthropos*: intrinsically both comic and tragic, selfish and philanthropic, capable of asceticism and hedonism, and as likely to turn enthusiastically vegetarian as to wallow in the bathos of an atavistic hunter lacking game. I would deem this critical cultural license human *variability* rather than *adaptability* (which tends to imply known parameters) or *relativity* (which implies boundless freedom). The investigator attuned to variability seeks not what *Homo* (singular, direct, transparent, knowable) means but how anthropos (plural, evasive, darkling, paradoxical) "means." If in the end one is left confronting cultural indeterminacy, it is not a bland aspect of humankind but a highly specific one.

Still, even the anthropologist of ambiguous anthropoi cannot resist labels (a point that I will confirm shortly). The fashion remains most conspicuous in France: *l'homme rational, l'homme fou, l'homme sémiologique* – characterized by *raison, folie, pensée sauvage*. Posed properly (symbolically), however, these labels are rhetorical exaggerations, devised to engage rival arguments, not literally to index human nature. The labels are figurative, with powerful implications.

One last Enlightenment-like sobriquet deserves special attention. Anthropos is often typed as *Homo loquens* (or something similar), the speaking creature, the animal with language. Wherever this quality might situate our species with regard to other primates and porpoises, the label can prove misleading for intrahuman matters. Empirically, anthropos is the animal not with language but with language*s*. That plural morpheme encompasses all the grandeur and tomfoolery in human communication, and it signals the potential for misunderstanding and misinterpretations at the heart of theories of meaning. "Language" is an abstraction drawn from "languages," and languages are abstractions from performance and competence, speech and writing, and related dimensions of communication.

I join most modern linguists and anthropologists in assuming that all languages represent differential manifestations of an identical capacity called language, although any proof of the matter is hard to imagine. Moreover, one may stop short of a transformationalism that anticipates scientific (actually mathematical) verification of the "deep" grammatical identity of all languages. The very idea that such a proof is possible remains questionable for a semiotic reason: Languages are diverse. At some level this diversity itself may be the key to language systematics, just as it is the basis of any sense of, or consciousness of, "language" in the first place.

To construe diversity as a secondary, surface aspect of universal language is to short-circuit studies in language and culture. Certain philosophers, translators, linguists, and anthropologists – Herder, W. von Humboldt, Saussure, Peirce, Boas, Sapir and Whorf, Jakobson, to name a very few – have conceptualized languages as systems whose variance is fundamental. In our own day linguistics has become the exemplary multideterministic, or perhaps even nondeterministic, discipline; it largely abandoned both idealism and materialism by the early twentieth century. George Steiner has reviewed philosophical foreshadowings of this development. I here condense his florid, time-lapse backdrop for contemporary views of translation and interpretation:

In 1697...Leibniz put forward the all-important suggestion that language is not the vehicle of thought but its determining medium. Thought is language internalized... Tongues differ even more profoundly than do nations. They also are monads, "perpetual living mirrors of the universe."...No two languages construe the same world. Yet...Leibniz made suggestions toward a universal semantic system, immediately legible to all men...

A comparable coexistence of monadist and universalist concepts may be found in Vico. Philology is the key to the *Scienza nuova* because study of the evolution of speech faculties is a study of the evolution of mind...All nations most probably traverse the same major phases of linguistic usage, from the immediate and sensory to the abstract. Simultaneously, however, Vico's opposition to Descartes and to the extensions of Aristotelian logic in Cartesian rationalism made of him the first true "linguistic historicist" or relativist...

It is doubtful that Vico really influenced Hamann. Kabbalistic speculations and the pregnant muddle of Hamann's remarkable intellect were obviously more important ...Hamann's *Versuch über eine akademische Frage* of 1760 marks the decisive move towards a relativistic language theory...[with its] axiom that each language is an "epiphany" or articulate embodiment of a specific historical-cultural landscape...

Though indebted to certain of Hamann's suggestions, Herder's work marks a transition to genuine comparative linguistics. Calling for a "general physiognomy of the nations from their languages," Herder asserted that national characteristics are "imprinted on speech" and, reciprocally, carry the stamp of the particular tongue...

The short years between Herder's writing and those of Wilhelm von Humboldt were among the most productive in the history of linguistic thought [Sir William Jones, Schlegel, Mme de Staël]..."Die Sprache ist das bildende Organ des Gedankens," says Humboldt, using both *bildend* and *Bildung* in their forceful, twofold connotation of "image" and "culture." Different linguistic frames define different world-images. "Every language is a Form and carries in itself a Form-Principle."...Humboldt conjoins the environmentalism of Montesquieu and the nationalism of Herder with an essentially post-Kantian model of human consciousness as the active and diverse shaper of the perceived world...

There is no need here to do more than indicate the lines of continuity from Humboldt to Whorf. Via the work of Steinthal (the editor of Humboldt's fragmentary texts), linguistic relativity enters the anthropology of Franz Boas. From there it reaches the ethno-linguistics of Sapir and Whorf. A parallel movement takes place in Germany. Cassirer's doctrine of the unique "inner form" which distinguishes a particular tongue from all others, derives immediately from Humboldt's *Form-Prinzip*...

Edward Sapir's formulation, in an article dated 1929, summarizes the entire line of argument as it goes back to Leibniz: "The fact of the matter is that the 'real world' is to a large extent unconsciously built up on the language habits of the group. No two languages are ever sufficiently similar to be considered as representing the same social reality. The worlds in which different societies live are distinct worlds, not merely the same world with different labels attached."...

The work of Benjamin Lee Whorf can be seen as an extension and refinement of Sapir's statement. Whorf's "meta-linguistics" are currently under severe attack by both linguists and ethnographers. [Steiner 1978:138–143]

Tracing these semiotic impulses, Steiner rejects any singular and general comparativist vantage or solid, enlightened footing from which to translate everything, so to speak, equidistantly. He distrusts Chomsky's transformationalism because it obscures an essential semiotic quality. Any sudden abstraction of "deep structures," not to mention innate categories, relegates translation to a secondary significance, making it a known quantity that can, via one formalism or another, be discounted. Steiner, following Humboldt and Sapir, detects in language and poetics the same qualities that C. Geertz (1973), following Weber and Parsons, identifies in societies. Both writers abandon Enlightenment hopes that there will yet be found some uniformitarian common denominator behind cultural variation, some decultured foothold that affords readier access to different cultural systems than comparative scholars could have if they were beginning afresh each time. But we are doomed to, or rather, privileged to have, such fresh beginnings. Semiotically, passing from one culture to another does not *directly* facilitate moving on to a third. Similarly, interpreters who can translate language X into their own language might then be readier to translate language Y, but not because they have necessarily come any "closer" to language Y through language X, much less located a more abstract deep structure connecting the two. Rather, having once managed to dislodge themselves from their own language, they have perhaps decreased their resistance to doing so again. This lessened resistance is the only advantage, but a profound one, offered by the comparative–contrastive method.

Steiner celebrates limits of translation and interpretation grandly underestimated by Enlightenment logicians and their revivers. To anticipate Saussurian terms shortly to be discussed, we recognize other languages only from vantages of what they are *not*. Languages cannot be approached as if the observer stood beyond all of them; neither can cultures. A theory of language or culture that avoids the *s* in order to standardize some sort of universal thereby dodges the paradox of meaning in a world characterized by plural languages and cultures.

Upon closer inspection the paradox deepens. As languages can yield linguistics, cultures can yield anthropologies. (More paradox in the play of plurals!) Yet how can languages and cultures constitute conditions not-themselves while remaining themselves? This dialectically inclined question (rather than any answer to it) suggests that anthropology itself has the qualities of structuralist "myth" (recoding codes through contrast) and interpretive "meta" (symbols of symbols). If – following Enlightenment philosophers and their many successors who formulate taxonomic labels for humankind – we could abstract and objectively and directly compare cultural qualities, the paradox would not exist. Nor, I should think, would cross-cultural studies require fieldwork, since cultures could then simply isolate representative samples and could fair-mindedly communicate themselves to each other around a conference table. In contrast, fieldwork takes place on that unsettling middle ground (language*s*, culture*s*) between patent ethnocentrism and the would-be universal: short of innateness, yet beyond external determinisms, where each message mediates others. In such a cross-cultural terrain dwells anthropos: *faber symbolarum symbolarum*.

By avoiding taxonomic simplifiers and by inscribing cultural extremes – institutionalized extremely in diverse societies and experienced extremely in fieldwork – anthropologists of symbolic forms transpose and extend a process central to the tribes that have long been our subject of study. Hocart (digressing from Evans-Pritchard's insights into blood brotherhood) summarized the process with customary trenchancy. Throughout his work Hocart emphasized:

the pattern of behavior between two moieties: mutual aid combined with playful hostility, intermarriage, interburial.

The Fijians call such a reciprocal relation "mutual ministry" (more literally "facing one another," or "worshipping one another")...It means that if the deceased belongs to one line, the other buries him (Winnabagoes), or mourns for him (Trobriands), or otherwise plays the *vis-à-vis*. [Hocart 1952:186]

Through inscription, all cultures may stand as moieties, each playing to another the vis-à-vis. Toward this end anthropologists write, with increasing intensity as hope loses out to the day and age. Anthropology thus generates books of cultures by fieldworkers who become figures of and for the always-stylized, sometimes sluggish exchange of remotest meanings. Symbolically, fieldwork must occur because communication in universal "language" doesn't. The fieldwork ideal and imperative has materialized in light of this limit. Fieldwork keeps one half (*they*) of two communicating cultures fairly intact – full of ordered conflict, tension, and provisional resolutions. In the meantime a presumably (diaries aside) self-denying emissary from the other half (*we*) undertakes to write what happens. What could be more extreme or theatrical and less standardized or objective? Ideally, all cultures should be *we*s and *they*s to each other in turn. Politics, however, intrudes.

Experience across cultures, like communication across languages, is neither unique nor universal. Its advantage lies rather in the sense of exaggeration it ensures. Every culture appears, vis-à-vis every other, exaggerated (just like every language), hence the exhilaration of the imperfectible effort we call translation. I propose, then, that ethnographic writing about other cultures consists, like cultures themselves, in an exaggeration of differences. We start with the exaggerations (the language*s*, the culture*s*), and only certain kinds of theories – each itself an unwitting exaggeration – and attempt to compromise the mutual exaggerations into cozy universals. Standard anthropological genres – "objective" description (reportage), taxonomic labels (by-lines), realistic monographs (naturalism) – overlook their own symbolic nature and hyperbolism. As a counterbalance, this book champions instances of cross-cultural discourse that acknowledge the hyperbolic nature of perceived cultures and their comparison. This discourse of cultures confesses its own exaggeration and seeks to control and assess it by becoming interpretive, at times even literary, while remaining both systematic and dialectical.

2. Shades of the history of ethnology

The adequate record of even the confusions of our forebears may help, not only to clarify those confusions, but to engender a salutary doubt whether we are wholly immune from different but equally great confusions.

Arthur Lovejoy, *The Great Chain of Being*

As we have seen, Clifford Geertz urges anthropologists to "leave the garden" of the Enlightenment's "uniformitarian view of Man" and to navigate the perilous philosophical waters of cultural theory:

Man is to be defined neither by his innate capacities alone, as the Enlightenment sought to do, nor by his actual behaviors alone, as much of contemporary social science seeks to do, but rather by the link between them, by the way in which the first is transformed into the second, his generic potentialities focused into his specific performances. [1973:52]

Geertz warns us of the dangers of relativism and advises us to face human diversity squarely. I would make this addition to his observations: One component in the range of cultural diversity is that very uniformitarianism that I join Geertz in doubting. Paradoxically, when cultural anthropologists turn to history, we must attempt to understand among all other traditions one that would thwart our own enterprise. An anthropological critique of Enlightenment uniformitarianism cannot simply reject it but must dutifully compare it to the positions of other sciences and/or magics in other times and cultures.

This chapter employs two strategies to characterize and question the abstract conversion of cultural diversity into uniformity that became routine during the Enlightenment. In Chapter 1 we glimpsed the style in those formulaic *homo* thus-and-so's. Here I go on somewhat contentiously to contrast this approach with some of its often denigrated predecessors. I then trace the changes in such styles as they interacted in one disturbing case, full of incongruities and ironies, in the history of ethnological images.

Perhaps the most extreme *surestimation* of Enlightenment anthropology has been that of Marvin Harris: "All that is new in anthropological theory begins with the Enlightenment" (1968:9). According to Harris, Locke and Montesquieu discovered that "the mechanisms responsible for sociocultural transformations" were "purely natural expressions of cause and effect relations," and he builds his own cultural materialism on this assumption.[1] In contrast, I seek neither to congratulate nor to condemn the Enlightenment itself or, for that matter, the Renaissance or the Middle Ages. The history of anthropology requires no such invidious comparisons between eras, just as the pursuit of anthropology requires no indivious comparison between cultures. Rather, I stress a particular aspect of Enlightenment assumptions that has been pinpointed by A. L. Lovejoy:

Assuming human nature to be a simple thing, the Enlightenment also, as a rule, assumed political and social problems to be simple, and therefore easy of solution. Rid man's mind of a few ancient errors, purge his beliefs of the artificial complications of metaphysical "systems" and theological dogmas, restore to his social relations something like the simplicity of the state of nature, and his natural excellence would live happily ever after. [1964:9; cf. C. L. Becker 1932]

I address neither the strengths of Enlightenment philosophy in natural science and political theory nor companion topics in the difficult works of Montesquieu and especially Diderot and Rousseau. Rather, I locate an *esprit simpliste* in cross-cultural formulations, which were limited in the Enlightenment as in previous eras. I would expect no such formulations – whether past or contemporary, including my own – to escape similar cultural–historical limitations.

I argue merely that the "presumption of simplicity" afforded no more adequate a means of cross-cultural knowledge than certain value-laden interpretations that *philosophes* disowned. I thus isolate and compare not the Enlightenment "itself" but the Enlightenment's "other" – that is, the antithetical other behind any culture's sense of itself – in particular its formulations of exotic comparisons. The simplistic style of ethnology persisted even after ethnographic description began in the eighteenth century to convey the circumstantial differences that characterized remote peoples. It has continued, with evolutionary embellishments, through the nineteenth century down to our own day. Because ideals of a uniformitarian nature behind cultural diversity are by no means the profoundest legacy of the Enlightenment, their tenacity grows all the more provocative.[2]

Let me foreshadow my concerns with a preliminary glance at the most ambitious history of preprofessional ethnology yet written, Margaret Hodgen's *Early Anthropology in the Sixteenth and Seventeenth Centuries*. Hodgen reviews works of the ancients, the church fathers, scholastics, missionaries, traders, collectors, discoverers, and philosophers in her quest for scientific objectivity about remote peoples and customs. Her important book is perhaps most interesting for not quite attributing such objectivity to philosophes. Nevertheless, Hodgen's hopes for "unencumbered observation" show that Enlightenment values underlie her entire effort. She sees a "scientific impulse" as the prime mover of anthropological research, crediting both Herodotus and Columbus with a kind of beginner's luck. Her standards of judgment can be glimpsed in this discussion of the fourteenth century:

> In some respects, all three of these men – Carpini, Rubruck, and Marco Polo – deserve to be compared with Herodotus. They were not mere compilers or copyists. They were not true believers in the strange creatures...with which medieval ignorance had peopled the margins of the world outside the narrow [?] confines of Christendom. Each of them was...a breaker of the spell of ethnological tradition, with its abundance of oral or written reiteration and repetition. What they lacked most was the old Greek's detachment and fundamental humor. Certain practices among Asian or Barbarian folk were utterly repugnant to the two friars...Absent also was the moral, philosophical, and historical breadth of Herodotus' horizon...
>   The accounts of the two missionaries were not motivated by scientific curiosity. They were practical intelligence reports...Marco possessed curiosity, but he lacked the scientific impulse to find out, if possible, why people were as they were. [1971:102–3][3]

We can, of course, sympathize with Hodgen's interest in healthy ethnographic curiosity: What motives would prompt the medieval European trader, dealing with an Arab in gestures, nods, and lingua franca, to wonder whether the Arab marries, much less whether he marries his father's brother's daughter? What, moreover, would justify not suppressing such information on foreign customs in order to guard commercial advantage?

But to credit Herodotus, and practically no other, with detachment and scientific curiosity begs vital questions in the history of anthropology. Hodgen proceeds to chastise more than two millennia of writers, particularly those who lived during the Middle Ages, for succumbing to a "hypnotic tide of ethnological fantasy." If, however, we check Hodgen's estimation of Herodotus against an actual account by him, the line between "the scientific impulse to find out" and medieval fantasy appears less distinct than she implies. Here, for example, is Herodotus on Egypt:

> Not only...[are] the rivers unlike any other rivers, but the people also, in most of their manners and customs, exactly reverse the common practice of mankind. The women attend the markets and trade, while the men sit at home at the loom; and here, while the rest of the world works the woof up the warp, the Egyptians work it down...In other countries the priests have long hair, in Egypt their heads are shaven...Dough they knead with their feet; but they mix mud, and even take up dirt, with their hands. They are the only people in the world – they at least, and such as have learnt the practice from them – who use circumcision. They practice circumcision for the sake of cleanliness, considering it better to be cleanly than comely. [Quoted in Kroeber and Waterman 1931:3–4]

Interweaving empirical fact (the direction of the Nile) and opinion, Herodotus views Greece and Egypt as perfectly opposed. Nor was he "unencumbered" in favoring civil societies, however diverse their conditions, over barbarian ones.

As we shall see, much medieval and Renaissance stereotyping worked in the same way (at some level all ethnology employs polar distinctions). Moreover, Hodgen's allusions to "narrow confines" notwithstanding, Christendom sanctioned among its expanding and diverse members customary usages as disparate as Egypt and Greece according to Herodotus. Whether the range of diversity across Christian sects was more or less than the range of diversity cataloged in Herodotus is impossible to measure. Culturally, a sectarian or ritual difference is as great as concerned parties perceive it to be. Circumcision, for example, may distinguish cleanly Egypt from comely Greece, Coptic Christians from Catholic Christians, or chosen from condemned. Historians of ideas in anthropology, rather than contentedly applauding disinterested Herodotus writing of curious Egypt and excoriating ignorant ecclesiastics who spoke of threatening Tartaria, must take note of the church's own diversity as well.

Hodgen poses a crucial issue in the history of ethnology: What enables outsiders to stay judgment rather than to ignore exotic customs, to reproach them, or to appropriate them for simple ends of profit or domination? But she subsumes the issue in hopes of "unencumbered observation," thus implying that observers can fully escape culture and history to gain, Enlightenment-like, rarified objectivity. If ethnology required mere uniform objectivity to advance, it would have culminated during the Enlightenment. That it did not indicates comparative anthropology's paradox and limits. This chapter attempts to embrace them.

Comparing eras crossing cultures

Pre-Enlightenment views of human variability revolved around ideas of diminished divinity. Medieval compilers and Renaissance cosmographers considered "similitudes" of Christian texts, sacraments, doctrines, and rituals discovered in remote populations to be evidence of a lost unity. Interpreters and translators sought to restore total intelligibility to the diversity of languages, alphabets, and customary usages documented in history and travel. Babel as a second fall (after sexual awareness) into a multiplicity of tongues, and Kabbalism as a means to repair it, are just two examples of "philosopher's stone" motives of and for translation. George Steiner has reviewed a host of related themes:

Theologians and metaphysicians of language strove to attenuate this second banishment. Had there not been a partial redemption at Pentecost, when the gift of tongues descended on the Apostles? Was not the whole of man's linguistic history, as certain Kabbalists supposed, a laborious swing of the pendulum between Babel and a return to unison in some messianic moment of restored understanding? Above all, what of the *Ur-Sprache* itself: had it been irretrievably lost? Here speculation hinged on the question of the veritable nature of Adam's tongue. Had it been Hebrew or some even earlier version of Chaldean whose far lineaments could be made out in the names of stars and fabled rivers. . .? Jewish gnostics. . .Paracelsus. . . seventeenth-century Pietists. . .almost all linguistic mythologies, from Brahmin wisdom to Celtic and North African lore, concurred in believing that original speech had shivered into seventy-two shards...Which were the primal fragments? [1975:59]

Ideals of the lost language of Paradise imbued interpretations of human diversity with a sense of plenitude and lapse.[4] Both connotations were rejected in subsequent Enlightenment views of human uniformity. For the universal grammar of Adam reapproached through translation, philosophes substituted a uniform grammar of abstraction constructed through analysis. The pre-Enlightenment imagined diversity as a broken mosaic of once-divine perfection. Later, Voltaire, in verses doubtless more playful than the views they summarized, could confidently assert:

> La morale uniforme en tout temps, en tout lieu...
> C'est la loi de Platon, de Socrate, et la vôtre.
> De ce culte éternel la Nature est l'apôtre.
> Cette loi souveraine en Europe, au Japon,
> Inspira Zoroastre, illumina Solon.[5]

Put so baldly, and considered in light of what it replaced, such uniformitarianism suggests assiduous anticlericalism more than scientific advance.

The contrast I wish to emphasize between pre-Enlightenment interpretation and uniformitarian analysis has been elaborated by the French intellectual historian Michel Foucault. In his controversial and difficult *The Order of Things*, Foucault characterizes medieval and Renaissance visions of a "full and tautological world of resemblance." Interpretation, as I understand it, proceeds by circling through diverse varieties of flora, fauna, languages, doctrines, rituals, metals, and elements to uncover similitudes with the texts of Scripture and the ancients, according to an image of perfection (Paradise, Golden Age) only temporarily obscured. Foucault radically opposes to such interpretation seventeenth- and eighteenth-century methods of knowing:

It is no longer the task of knowledge to dig out the ancient word from the unknown places where it may be hidden; its job now is to fabricate a language, and to fabricate it well – so that, as an instrument of analysis and combination, it will really be the language of calculation...

It was the sign system that gave rise simultaneously to the search for origins and to calculability; to the constitution of tables that would fix the possible compositions, and to the restitution of a genesis on the basis of the simplest elements; it was the sign system that linked all knowledge to a language, and sought to *replace all languages with a system of artificial symbols* and operations of a logical nature. [1973:62–3; emphasis added]

Earlier interpretations construed diversity as revealing traces of resemblance to divinity/diabolicalness. Enlightenment methods construed diversity as conforming to taxonomies of measures. In Foucault's terms, everything hinged on "the possibility of establishing an ordered succession between things, even nonmeasurable ones. In this sense analysis was very quickly to acquire the value of a universal method...So there first appeared general grammar, natural history, and the analysis of wealth."

Foucault develops the contrast between implicit epistemological structures (*epistémès*) of the Renaissance (roughly the fifteenth and sixteenth centuries) and the French classical period (roughly the seventeenth and eighteenth centuries). Foucault's epistemes convert historicist concepts of eras and epochs to more intellectualist and dialectical constructs. An episteme, which is something like a paradigm or even a grammar and is unquestioned from within its assumptions, comprises the "conditions of possibility" of interrelating knowledge under distinct historical circumstances. Epistemes are systematic, holistic and contrastive, each a thorough transformation of the other – like the linguist's "langue" and the anthropologist's "culture," but with respect to the history of ideas. In my reading, an episteme is a "culture" of time.

Some of the most difficult portions of Foucault's work concern preclassical modes of interpretation:

> Let us call the totality of the learning and skills that enable one to make the signs [thought to comprise experience of and in the world] speak and to discover their meaning, hermeneutics; let us call the totality of the learning and skills that enable one to distinguish the location of the signs, to define what constitutes them as signs, and to know how and by what laws they are linked, semiology; the sixteenth century superimposed hermeneutics and semiology in the form of similitude. [In this episteme] to search for a meaning is to bring to light a resemblance. To search for the law governing signs is to discover the things that are alike...."Nature" is trapped in the thin layer that holds semiology and hermeneutics one above the other...a dark space that must be made progressively clearer. That space is where "nature" resides, and it is what one must attempt to know. Everything would be manifest and immediately knowable if the hermeneutics of resemblance and the semiology of signatures coincided without the slightest parallax. But because the similitudes that form the graphics of the world are one "cog" out of alignment with those that form its discourse,...it is [the task of knowledge] to weave...across this distance, pursuing an endless zigzag course from resemblance to what resembles it... [Foucault 1973:30]

This hermeneutics of resemblance, this semiology of signatures that promises to realign diversity into total, divine–natural similitude stands opposed to the classical episteme. Doubtless Foucault's contrast between the Renaissance intellectual value system (with its trails of the late medieval) and the classical one (with its seeds of the Enlightenment) is exaggerated. The implicit transformation is less sequential than dialectical: For example, preclassical Pythagorean codes in music and cosmology are transformed when the classical consolidates number with "measure." Foucault suggests not that the classical and the preclassical were thoroughly divorced but that the set of interrelations that came to define the classical episteme were not integrated earlier. (This broad contrast should help us trace the eighteenth-century equation between cultural diversity and species diversity, both within a species [monstrosities] and between species [taxonomies of differences]).

In short, for Foucault the basic classical principles include: reducing to order, keying a taxonomy, and generalizing a theory of signs, divisions, and classifications. He opposes to these pursuits earlier interpretations seeking "the spontaneous movement of the imagination, of nature's repetitions."[6] The classical episteme entails probability rather than perfectibility; genesis (origins) on the basis of the simplest (metonymy or part for whole) rather than genesis (primacy) on the basis of the metaphorically total all in one; and generalization by measures and calculations (succession between things, even nonmeasurable ones) rather than by epitomization. I would gloss the classical/preclassical distinction (roughly Enlightenment/medieval-Renaissance) as the following contrast: standardization based upon a lowest common denominator *versus* perfectibility based upon an epitomized whole. Foucault himself ultimately condenses the opposition into order versus interpretation:

This relation of *Order* is as essential to the Classical age as the relation to *Interpretation* was to the Renaissance. And just as interpretation in the sixteenth century, with its superimposition of a semiology upon a hermeneutics, was essentially a knowledge based upon similitude, so the ordering of things by means of signs constitutes all empirical forms of knowledge as knowledge based upon identity and difference. [1973:56–7]

Thus Foucault helps clarify the classical (and Enlightenment) approach to the "order behind" any diversity whatsoever: "how to discover a *nomenclature* that would be a taxonomy" (p. 208).[7]

In Enlightenment anthropology, measuring nonmeasurable things entailed charting human differences by analogy with natural differences, like species diversity. I shall briefly characterize (actually stereotype) this brand of analysis. I shall then oppose it to previous traditions that read all diversity, both sectarian and what we would today call cultural, according to biblical and ancient subtexts.

The Enlightenment construed diverse customs as deviations from a natural norm, ultimately embodied in figures like Voltaire's "L'Ingénu" (1767), the native naif (incidentally and ironically Huron) ripe for reasonable enlightenment (Voltaire 1960). Buffon on human kinds, Condillac (following Locke) on language and sensations, and other philosophers fabricated tabular arrangements of cultures as if all pertinent differences, even moral ones, could be physically measured. Consider, for example, Helvétius's response to Buffon, discussed by Michèle Duchet:

For Helvétius man differs from animal not through a spiritual substance, but through particular physical characteristics. A flexible hand and fingers, a longer life, a grander natural weakness, a more constant society, a plasticity of species that lets him be born and live in all climates: these are the distinctive traits of the human species. We see that Helvétius takes over most of Buffon's observations on *le physique* of man . . .: for Helvétius the human animal is a *homo faber*, and what distinguishes him from animals is the use he makes of his faculties thanks to their organization. While Buffon grants animals only material "interior sense" and a kind of very inferior memory he calls "reminiscence," Helvétius considers physical *sensibilité* or the faculty for receiving different impressions produced by external objects, and memory or "continued sensation" as faculties common to man and animal; and he considers them "the productive causes of our thoughts." [1971:377–8, 381; my translation]

In *De l'esprit* Helvétius outlines a uniformitarian materialism and a standardized mechanism by which passions operate (still calling nature "God"): "It seems that in the moral universe as in the physical universe, God has put but a single principle in everything that has been. That which is and that which will be is but a necessary development." Helvétius can then analyze human varieties – from Hottentots and Caribs to Fakirs and Brahmins – as so many gradable divergences, through political and religious corruption, from natural moral laws.

Such views finally identify uniformitarian nature with reason itself. Reason, ultimately philosophical rationality, is situated at an abstract remove from any particular customs, languages, or mores. Buffon again illustrates the tendency: He analyzes traditionally sensational cross-cultural topics – eunuchs, harems, human sacrifice – by charting them as innocuous, physiological correlations between sexual forces and vocal range, long before modern anatomy and hormone theory (1971). The notion of a neutral analytic locus, equidistant from (and unscathed by) all cultural extremes, was the most enduring simplification in Enlightenment comparative studies.

In a moment I will provide further examples of Enlightenment taxonomies versus Renaissance emblems in other cultures. But even this brief mention of Helvétius and Buffon raises a question fundamental to the history of ethnology: What is the difference in objectivity between writers who reveal a scriptural similitude that grounds diverse customs and writers who construct an artificial platform across them? Does a secular analysis of harems and human sacrifice as abstract variables mark an epistemological advance over pre-Enlightenment interpretations which, for all their value ladenness, often contained as much ethnographic information? Is the difference a matter of increased rationality, as Enlightenment philosophers needed, culturally, to think? Or is this difference, too, a kind of simplification?

The Enlightenment formulated abstract measures of cultural features to replace the religious doctrines they rejected. Their secularism persists in standard anthropology textbooks, which even today echo the antimedieval topos; to cite just one instance: "Medieval minds most often were turned inward to matters of theological concern, and for this reason non-Europeans were seen as souls to be saved and infidels to be conquered, rather than as peoples with customs to be described. The more distant a people were from Europe the more monstrous they became" (Oswalt 1972). It was never so simple; Enlightenment concerns produced their own credulous copyists. By uncritically repeating the charge that theology was narrow and the medieval mind closed, current scholars perpetuate two fictions perhaps initiated by philosophes themselves: (1) They project an integral European identity back into medieval (and Renaissance) times, and (2) they assume that exotic customs were inherently shocking before and during the Age of Discoveries. Both myths dissolve if we examine pre-Enlightenment sources in accordance with their own conventions. Here I mention only a few.

Before the uneven rise of a European identity during the seventeenth century, sectarian factions were rife. Religious and partisan interests and the civic/rustic distinction meant that commentators could easily feel as remote from doctrinal opponents or illiterate compatriots as from exotics. Distance from Europe was not yet a relevant factor in ideas of monstrosity. L. E. Huddleston reminds us that neither the idea of "Europe" nor that of the "New World" explained Columbus's reactions to his discoveries: "Columbus did not question the existence of men in the New World because he did not know it was a New World. The realization of this fact was a gradual one not fully made until the reports of the Magellan Expedition of 1519–1521 became available. There was, therefore, no reason to marvel at a New World filled with New Men because neither phenomenon was recognized as such" (1967:5). Moreover, Columbus first described Caribs almost prosaically: handsome, generous, and cleanly; displaying language, ingenious fishing technology, and monogamy; hence potential converts to Christianity. They were, in short, Indians, not cannibals. His earliest reports alluded to the natives' childlike simplicity when receiving trinkets, without, however, generalizing that Caribs represented the "childhood" of mankind. After these rather straightforward descriptions, Columbus's fuller interpretations later followed medieval and Renaissance styles of cross-cultural generalization. He advanced lively stereotypes of America that mingled the innocence of Adam and Eve (prior to sexuality, shame, and clothing) with classical idylls and antique monstrosities. Subsequent arguments about New World conditions identified them with both Paradise and biblical images of degradation: bedevilment, Nebuchadnezzar, and so forth.[8]

Such interpretations, then, were not ignorant and superstitious first impressions but overwrought second thoughts. For purposes of generalization, which required situating all populations in the Christian web of sin and salvation, Scripture was useful at home and abroad. We shall see that, after Magellan, ethnological marvels reflected Protestant/Catholic rivalry rather than any lingering medievallike confusion and awe over aboriginal practices. The more elaborate style of stereotyping practiced by Columbus flourished in the Reformation as well. Moreover, sectarian divisions meant that a clear and exclusivistic dichotomy between the European and the exotic was not formulated until religious reformism had been transformed into nationalism and Enlightenment secularism.

Medieval and Renaissance views of cultural diversity appear merely superstitious and "theological" only if we forget, with philosophes, that ritual and doctrine occupied a special place in less "territorialized" pre-Enlightenment traditions. Adequately to compare earlier views of *others* to Enlightenment views would require us to contrast the Middle Ages or Renaissance to the Enlightenment as total cultures. We would have to peruse the entire complex of institutional values and contrasting modes of citizenship, perhaps beginning with observations like R. W. Southern's:

The identification of the church with the whole of organized society is the fundamental feature which distinguishes the Middle Ages from earlier and later periods of history.
At its widest limits it is a feature of European history from the fourth to the eighteenth century – from Constantine to Voltaire. In theory, during the whole of this period only orthodox and obedient believers could enjoy the full rights of citizenship [an orthodoxy itself evolving] . . .
In a word, the church was a compulsory society in precisely the same way as the modern state is a compulsory society. Just as the modern state requires those who are its members by the accident of birth to keep its law, to contribute to its defence and public services, to subordinate private interests to the common good, so the Medieval church required those who had become its members by the accident (as one may almost call it) of baptism to do all these things and many others. [1970:17–18]

Hence the perceived threat of Anabaptists. Yet apart from baptism and re-lated, evolving sacraments, theologians admitted extensive variation within Christendom, including a diversity of vernaculars. We could contrast to this broad-mindedness the sort of Enlightenment uniformitarianism manifest in American rules of naturalized citizenship that demand strict "conversion" to American English. Given two cases of relative "sacramental intolerance" on the one hand and relative "linguistic intolerance" on the other, which is the more doctrinaire, the less objective? Christian ethnology, of course, stigma-tized certain categories of mankind, including Ethniks, Tartars, and the al-ways special Jews, identified as "licensed enemies" who were implicated in principles of heresy. No question of tolerance here; yet it was not mere monolithic intolerance, either. To overlook the diversity admitted even in negative medieval ethnological imagery is to ignore the social, political, and cultural context of church history and theological exegesis – not a very an-thropological policy.

It is true that in many cultural domains, the so-called medieval mind – like any "mind," or rather *mentalité*, or rather culture – rejected certain possibilities. Concealing momentarily my ulterior comparativist motive, let me mention just three items the Middle Ages tabooed: specific intervals of the musical scale (*diabolus in musica*), simultaneous polygyny, and serial polygyny (divorce) as well. But against these restrictions, we must consider what was allowed: polyphony, a trichotomy of monastic–ecclesiastic–temporal modes of authority, property, and legitimacy; a changing cosmology of love, including love of church, love of lord, and eventually romantic love and/or sacramental marriage; and communal ascetic renouncers (anchorites), who stood in contrast to the solitary renunciation that came to dominate some Eastern reaches of related Indo-European religious traditions. My choices are prompted by a crucial comparative fact: These very cultural complexities, amalgamated within the theology of medieval Christendom, could as well serve to set apart distinct cultures; in fact today they *do* distinguish variant cultural patterns of Indo-European religions and societies.[9]

If one were to select an age to brand inward turning and Europocentric, the Reformation and the Enlightenment would possibly be better candidates than the Middle Ages, which resisted singular modes of authority, singular types of love, and singular, uniform standards of national languages and legal codes. Several generations ago A. L. Kroeber championed medieval pluralism in extradoctrinal matters: "[During the Middle Ages] conformity to the Christian doctrine was exacted, but little else. In fact, controlled acculturation came late. Not until well into the modern period of European history, along with the rise of consciously nationalistic programs, did the inclination become strong to improve people of other culture and speech by inducing or forcing them to accept one's own" (1963:242). We might say, then, that one basic difficulty with comparing Enlightenment views of different cultures to medieval views of different cultures is that more than the uniformitarian Enlightenment, the medieval period *was* different cultures – like Herodotus's Egypt and Greece together, provided that both were baptized.

What, though, of medieval and Renaissance recourse to superstitious monstrosities versus Enlightenment skepticism and caution? Did not the lumières at last outgrow that "tide of ethnological fantasy" bemoaned by Hodgen? Our case study will reveal as much evidence of exaggeration and nonobjectivity in Enlightenment formulaic generalizations as in those of the Renaissance (I leave aside the issue of internal credulity for all eras). Furthermore, the same instance of monstrosity serves to exemplify two different styles of expressing cross-cultural diversity, both of them limited, but – and herein lies their anthropological interest – in different ways.

Patagonian marvels: Pigafetta, Darwin, Sagan

In 1520 Magellan's chronicler Pigafetta inscribed the natives of Tierra del Fuego as Patagonians ("big feet"), thus initiating a major legend in the history of ethnology.[10] Pigafetta's giants entered English in R. Eden's translation, edited by the Jacobean scholar Samuel Purchas in 1625:

They . . . sayled toward the Pole Antartike, where they found a great River of fresh Water, and certain Canibals. Of these, they saw one out of their ships, of stature as big as a Giant, having a voyce like a Bull . . .
This Giant was so big, that the head of one of our men, of a nice stature, came but to his Waste. He was of good corporature, . . . painted with divers colors, but for the most part yellow . . .
Shortly after, they saw another Giant . . . he layd his hand on his head, and pointed up toward Heaven, and our men did the like . . . This Giant was very tractable, and pleasant. He sung and danced, and in his dancing, left the print of his feet on the ground. Hee remayned long with our men, who named him John. Hee could well speake, and plainely pronounce these words, Jesus, Ave Maria, Johannas, even as wee doe, but with a bigger voyce.
[Later when the Giants] saw how they were deceived they roared like Bulls, and cryed upon their great Devil Setebos, to helpe them . . . They say, that when any of them die, there appeare ten or twelve Devils, leaping and dancing about the bodie of the dead . . . painted with divers colours . . . One of these Giants which they tooke,

declared by signes that hee had seene Devils with two hornes above their heads, with
long hayre down to their feet; and that they cast forth fire at their throats both before
and behind. The Captaine named these people Patagoni. [1625/1907, vol. 2:86–89]

No less than Columbus, Pigafetta's interpretations blended Old Testament
antediluvian conditions, ancient Cacotopian legends, and perhaps medieval
satanic hybrids to generalize the image of Patagonians. I am concerned,
however, less with the chronicler's sources than with his successors.

Sixteenth- and seventeenth-century Protestant scholars turned interpretations of diabolical gigantism back against their Catholic originators. To legitimate their own discovery, trade, and later colonization, Protestants identified
cannibalism and other traits with Antichrist embodied in the pope. Pigafetta's
account, for example, was edited and annotated by Samuel Purchas, who in
1625 associated giants, sodomy, and Devil worship with the league between
the Spanish and Pope Alexander VI. Similar ideas were elaborated in De
Bry's *Grand Voyages*, published between 1590 and 1634. Bernedette Bucher's
study *La sauvage aux seins pendants* (1977) has recently decoded De Bry's
iconography, which construed New World discoveries in Protestant (Huguenot)
terms of successive Falls and prelude to the Apocalypse – a kind of counter-
Counter-Reformation ideology. If Amerindians were Edenic innocents before
European contact, they afterward sustained a condensed version of Old World
human tribulations. For De Bry's illustrators, the vehicle of this belated Fall is
the pope-backed Spanish conquest: a Devil-Serpent come lately. Prior to the
Second Coming, a purge of these Spanish-engendered diabolical conditions
would be effected by the settlement of Protestants in self-sufficient communities:
orderly food producers and consumers and endogamous. To ardent Protestants
nothing remote could appear more monstrous than the very proximate papacy.

Although it was coined in the Renaissance, the image of Patagonian giants
thus persisted in late Reformation elaborations of New World History. Revisionist
Protestants converted scriptural similitudes to their advantage: Pigafetta's
reports; Benzoni's accounts of Tupinamba cannibalism; notorious episodes in
Acosta of Balboa's hurling Indian sodomists to ravenous dogs. Legends of
giants and devils confirmed other signs of antediluvian sin presumably in-
flicted on prelapsarian Indians by the forces of Spain and pope.

Physical gigantism among Patagonians was explicitly discredited and empirically disproved in 1670 by John Narborough. Yet legends of giants re-
emerged the next century, this time framed within Enlightenment scientific
generalizations rather than within medieval or Reformation sectarian ones. H.
Wallis helps us follow the complex episodes after Byron's famous visit in
1765:

The first report of the encounter reached England on 22 June 1765 in Byron's
letter to Lord Egmont written at Port Famine. This showed the Patagonians to be a
race formidable indeed: "The stoutest of our Grenadiers would appear nothing to
them... Our People on Board, who were looking at us thro' their Glasses, said we

looked like meer Dwarfs to the People we were gone amongst," Byron wrote, summing them up as "People, who in size come the nearest to Giants of any People I believe in the World." The Admiralty kept this remarkable information to itself. It was not until Byron's return in May 1766 that the sensational news of Byron's giants became the talk of Europe. The report that Byron had encountered men "of extraordinary bigness," "nine feet high," when passed on through French intelligence drew from the French Minister of Foreign Affairs, Praslin, the dry comment that Byron must surely have seen them through a microscope. The Royal Society Club discussed the news of the giants at one of its weekly dinners at the Mitre in July 1766, and Dr. Maty hastened to report the facts in a letter to M. de La Lande, President of the French Académie de Sciences. All Paris was amazed, as the Abbé Coyer sardonically reports, until on 1 August 1766 the French naturalist, M. de La Condamine answered in a letter to the *Journal encyclopédique* that the story of the Patagonian giants was a fable, and that the English government had put the story about to conceal the real objective of the fleet of four ships then being made ready for South America – Wallis's ships and the *Swift* – the exploitation of a mine which the English had discovered.

We need not presume to judge whether the "Enlightenment mind" actually believed in the reports; gullibility or credulity (even of the "medieval mind"!) is perhaps impossible to prove from documentary evidence. I only want to emphasize how giants settled readily into an eighteenth-century style of comparative generalization:

> The sudden outburst of news on Byron's return and the reticence of the crew do suggest that the British Government used the giants to divert attention from the more serious and controversial episode of Byron's voyage, the visit to the Falkland Islands. How far the Government actually believed the reports of the giants is not known, but the Royal Society under Maty's auspices apparently did, and publicized the reports with uncritical zeal. It is significant perhaps that when the crew did break their silence, the pronouncement came in the form of a letter to the Royal Society. [Wallis 1964:186–8]

Patagonian giants rematerialized in an implicit taxonomy of physical measures. A Renaissance–Reformation similitude of diabolical conditions was converted to an Enlightenment scheme of abnormal (unnatural) physicality. Like eunuchs, harems, and human sacrifice, giants, too, could be transformed, "with uncritical zeal," using Enlightenment methods of generalization through uniform measure.

The eighteenth century not only revived an old ethnological fantasy; it paved the way for a host of subsequent distortions and exaggerations by converting allegorical medieval–Renaissance–Reformation emblems to the style of visual representation developed in neoclassical aesthetics. Recall that in 1764 Byron had conveyed the "gigantic stature" of a Patagonian chief in prose and illustration. Our tale resumes in 1768, when Captain Cook embroidered Byron's account, deeming Fuegians "perhaps as miserable a set of people as are this day upon Earth." While verbal inscriptions leave open the question of whether a people is circumstantially or typologically miserable, visual inscriptions (in the conventions of Enlightenment representation, as opposed to those of medieval–Renaissance emblems) seem intrinsically typological and complete. It was according to neoclassical conventions that Cook's comment was incorporated into a drawing by Buchan, who offers a visual scheme of Fuegian types: squalid but symmetrical.

Later the explorer Hawkesworth construed "misery" as "austerity"; he described the people as hard primitives, contemporary paragons of Spartan virtue (more Enlightenment similitudes!); and his illustrator followed suit. From this point the plot could only thicken. Bernard Smith helps us trace the transformations in visual conventions:

If Hawkesworth's and Bank's accounts were colored by their classical learning and neo-classical romances like *Télémaque*, then, equally, Buchan's original drawing was falsified by the conventions of neo-classical artists. Buchan's drawing answers closely to a description of a Fuegian village written by Banks. Both men, doubtless, visited the village at the same time.

Cipriani made extensive alterations in redrawing Buchan's sketch evidently to bring it into line with Hawkesworth's interpretation of the Fuegians. He has made the six squalid figures in the sketch more comely and graceful...transformed... into the state of primitive elegance imagined by Hawkesworth...Falsified as the engraving was, it provided none the less a model for later illustrators of Pacific voyages. A degraded form of Cipriani's design appears, for instance, in an 1843 account of Cook's voyages. The two little naked amorini have been discreetly removed as befitted an account written with an eye upon evangelical opinion. And the landscape setting has been transformed from [Salvatore] Rosa's picturesque sublimity to the coconut palms of a tropical Elysium, despite the fact that the latitude corresponded to Britain's, that it was a land of beech...and birch..., and the weather so severe when Cook was first there that snow fell in January and two ...servants perished from exposure to the cold. [1960:23]

Yet half a century later Cipriani's figures still served to represent the shivering inhabitants of Patagonia, who had perhaps been better off interpreted as giants.

Distortions generated by the Enlightenment persisted through the time of Darwin's famous visit to Tierra del Fuego in 1832. Taxonomic schemes and "naturalized" models of cultures shifted smoothly from Enlightenment charts of savage/civilized into evolutionary sequences that began with a primitive state.

Foremost among the victims of this embellished Enlightenment style were the Patagonians and Fuegians themselves. Darwin's portrayal in 1871 set a tone of "scientific" cultural comparisons for the next century and beyond:

The astonishment which I felt on first seeing a party of Fuegians on a wild and broken shore will never be forgotten by me, for the reflection at once rushed into my mind – such were our ancestors. These men were absolutely naked and bedaubed with paint...their expression was wild, startled, and distrustful...He who has seen a savage in his native land will not feel much shame, if forced to acknowledge that the blood of some more humble creature flows in his veins. For my own part, I would as soon be descended from that heroic little monkey, who braved his dreaded enemy in order to save the life of his keeper; or from that old baboon who, descending from the mountains, carried away in triumph his young comrade from a crowd of astonished dogs – as from a savage who delights to torture his enemies, offers up bloody sacrifices, practices infanticide without remorse, treats his wives like slaves, knows no decency, and is haunted by the grossest superstitions.

Man may be excused for feeling some pride at having risen, though not through his own exertions, to the very summit of the organic scale; and the fact of his having thus risen, instead of having been aboriginally placed there, may give him hopes for a still higher destiny in the distant future. [Darwin 1859, 1871:919–20]

To argue the descent of man from monkey, Darwin posed a radical disjunction between Fuegian and European, between (*their*) past and our present, and between (*our*) present and some standard ameliorized future.

Darwin's optimism, and his post-Enlightenment uniformitarian standards (presumably natural) for measuring cultures, survived, whether fit or not, in evolutionist thinking; they are still influential. To take a recent example, the passage just cited from *The Descent of Man* forms the initial epigraph of Carl Sagan's celebrated study of the nature and future of human intelligence, *The Dragons of Eden*. The book, which ends with designs for extraterrestrial scientific communication, begins with Darwin on Fuegians. Sagan's later acknowledgments of inadequacies in the view are themselves inadequate:

Darwin was, of course, a man of his times and occasionally given – as in his remarks on the inhabitants of Tierra del Fuego quoted above – to self-congratulatory comparisons of Europeans with other peoples. In fact, human society in pretechnological times was much more like that of the compassionate, communal and cultured Bushman hunter-gatherers of the Kalahari Desert than the Fuegians Darwin, *with some justification*, derided. [Sagan 1977:6; emphasis added]

What justification, even partial, was there to Darwin's derision? His information on Patagonians and Fuegians stemmed from a Renaissance similitude (biblical giants) eventually converted into an Enlightenment taxon (species-giants) and subsequently transformed into neoclassical images of everything from Spartan to Italianate. Darwin's description merely echoes the stereotype of *natural* wretchedness (adding, it seems, a dash of diabolicalness) that we traced above. By reading further either on Fuegians or in Darwin, Sagan might have discovered abundant reason for denying any objective justification whatsoever for Darwin's evolutionist opinions of these primitives, which were reinforced by a distinctly nonempirical source:

While going one day on shore near Wollaston Island, we pulled alongside a canoe with six Fuegians. These were the most abject and miserable creatures I anywhere beheld...[they] were quite naked,...stunted in their growth, their hideous faces bedaubed with white paint, their skins filthy and greasy, their hair entangled, their voices discordant, and their gestures violent. Viewing such men, one can hardly make one's self believe that they are fellow-creatures, and inhabitants of the same world. We often try to imagine what pleasure in life some of the lower animals can enjoy: how much more reasonably the same question may be asked concerning these barbarians!

The Fuegians of Good Success Bay are a very different race from the stunted,

miserable wretches farther westward; and they seem closely related to the famous
Patagonians of the Strait of Magellan. . . Their skin is of a dirty coppery-red color.
Their chief spokesman, an old man, had a. . . face. . . crossed by two broad bars: one,
painted bright red, reached from ear to ear, and included the upper lip; the other,
white like chalk, stretched above the first. . . His two companions. . . were ornamented
by streaks of black powder, made of charcoal. The party altogether closely
resembled the devils which come on the stage in plays like "Der Freischütz."
[1873:99–100, 93–94][11]

Here Darwin interprets the taller inhabitants of Tierra del Fuego drawing on
similitudes from romantic drama and opera. Pre-Enlightenment methods lingered on. Perhaps neither Sagan nor any of us can finally escape them; but we
can avoid mistaking the bases on which we conceptualize about others as
nature, objectivity, or uniform reason.

Finally, the unacknowledged complexities behind the cross-cultural stereotypes that begin Sagan's book might even cast an anthropological shadow
over the extraterrestrial stereotypes concluding it. Having commenced with
Darwin, *The Dragons of Eden* ends with the highly publicized illustration of a
man and a woman *au naturel*, duly measured, his hand raised in greeting to
some unknown recipient of their intended message (p. 246). This is the visual
representation of the human species that NASA mailed to aliens anonymous,
to inform them about ourselves. Sagan made a token comparison of the man's
gesture across cultures (the Sioux) to confirm that, terrestrially speaking, it is
standard. Pausing to wonder, "Could the significance of the man's gesture be
deduced by beings with very different biologies," Sagan never questions
whether the whole image – part of the "first artifact of mankind to leave the
solar system" – would communicate as intended even to different cultures or
eras.

The picture of earthlings transmitted by the *Pioneer 10* and *11* spacecraft
was fabricated with Enlightenment-like simplicity, "in what is hoped is easily
understood scientific language," to convey "some information on the locale,
epoch, and nature of the builders of the spacecraft." Let us imagine, however,
that the message, devised in Enlightenment-style conventions, is received
according to conventions no more alien than those that have divided earthlings
(with the same biology). Imagine that extraterrestrials resemble the natives of
NASA in all respects save one: they employ pre-Enlightenment interpretation.
If we imagine as well that subtexts are shared (unlikely, I confess), Sagan's
message would communicate clearly that earthlings are, of all things, inno-
cent, nonprocreating prelapsarians (evidently childless and naked). Imagine
now *their* surprise, if ever they should land! Or in the more likely event that
(biologies aside) subtexts also differ, understanding, however it occurs, won't
be "easy."

I have toyed with Carl Sagan's assumptions and designs in order to high-
light the crux of comparative anthropology: Earth's own diversity of cultures

(and eras) is as mind-bending as a speculative diversity of natures. Moreover, can we imagine with contemporary philosophes that communication across galaxies might be simpler, more direct, less symbolically contorted than communication across cultures? "Shades," snorts the anthropologist, "of science fiction."

Chiaroscuro

Because the Middle Ages, and often the Renaissance, have been derided in standard histories of anthropology, I have attempted reciprocally to debunk an Enlightenment method of cross-cultural reductionism still very much with us. The exercise readily calls to mind Herder's early romantic insistence that

assimilation to a single universal pattern, of laws or language, or social structures, as advocated by the French *lumières*, would destroy what is most living and valuable in life and art... Hence, too, the attack on Sulzer for demanding a universal philosophical grammar, according to the rules of which one would be enabled to judge of the degree of the perfection/standardization of a people's language, and, if need be, correct its rules in the light of the universal rules... It is terrible arrogance to affirm that, to be happy, everyone should become European. [Berlin 1976:196]

But taken no further, romanticism remains reactionary: an apotheosis of diversity that had yet to become a theory of variation or a method of comparison. Nineteenth-century modes of description were enriched through romantic interest in local color and remote regional and historical life-styles. But its scientific generalizations retained abstract taxonomic schemes, shifting, for instance, a savage/civilized distinction to the child–savage theme pervasive in social Darwinism and Victorian paternalism; as B. V. Street recalls:

[Despite] later nineteenth century accounts of "savages" and the Darwinian struggle of primeval man..., the comparison of the savage with the child lived on with a new meaning. If, as anthropological theory held, the primitive races represented a previous stage in the development towards "civilized" man, then the model of a child growing into a man could be applied to human evolution, with the European races as the mature and fully developed men and the primitive races as "children." Thus, the "parent" races are obliged to treat their child-like charges with the care and control of a Victorian father. [1975:68]

Evolutionism embroidered Enlightenment abstract contrasts into a texture of fantastic stereotypes. Had the images not been thought to chart natural differences, one might almost call them ultramedieval:

That natives can't make logical short cuts, that savage people and jungle-beasts alike have an ability to sleep at will, that natives have cunning infantile minds, that they are fatalistic and have a sixth sense... And Wallace describes the natives Sanders encounters as "having a liking for forbidden fruit, a penchant for triviality, a prescience which is every aboriginee's birthright, and a sense of telepathy." [Street 1975:75]

Childlike or subhuman? Wretched or Spartan? Prophetic or superstitious? Whichever designation they chose, evolutionists, like certain philosophes, assumed that the complex, exaggerated impressions produced by cultures and languages in contact could be charted as natural, measurable differences. Against such assumptions Franz Boas would direct his antievolutionist theory of culture, continued in the anthropology of Robert Lowie, Alfred Kroeber, Edward Sapir, Ruth Benedict, and their successors.

A shadow of the pre-Enlightenment enriched Benedict's unsurpassed *Patterns of Culture* (1934). Although she was moralistic in tone, her vision was more paradoxical and self-ironic than it was later reputed to have been. Doubting a simple future of enlightened tolerance through universal conformity to a uniform human nature, she professed resignation, unsparing and prophetic:

Primitive man never looked out over the world and saw "mankind" as a group and felt his common cause with his species. From the beginning he was a provincial who raised the barriers high...

So modern man, differentiating into Chosen People and dangerous aliens groups within his own civilization genetically and culturally related to one another as any tribes in the Australian bush are among themselves, has the justification of a vast historical continuity behind his attitude. The Pygmies have made the same claims. We are not likely to clear ourselves easily of so fundamental a human trait, but we can at least learn to recognize its history and its hydra manifestations. [1934/1961:7–8)]

Benedict implied that all cultures and eras can foster both unwarranted esteem and undue contempt for portions of mankind, themselves and others. From the high moral arrogance of the Enlightenment, which eventually separated each type of the human species measurably from the other, she advanced to a cross-cultural chiaroscuro extending to ourselves.

Comparative anthropology is caught between eras – or epistemes – just as it is caught between cultures. Extracting ourselves from Enlightenment-style formulations lands us in pre-Enlightenment interpretation; and circumspect distance from the latter reintroduces Enlightenment abstraction. The Enlightenment fabricated a geographically and "naturally" remote *other* as exotic antithesis to itself. The pre-Enlightenment argued both the best and the worst – the perfected and the damned – wherever the sectarian brethren and enemies were perceived, exotically or intimately: Patagonian or pope.

Michèle Duchet touches a vital issue in Enlightenment anthropology: "For a society which doubts its own values and powers the occasion arises to put itself in question, to think of itself as other than it is, to invent its own negation, so better to measure its alienation" (1971:11; my translation). My questions then become: Did the Enlightenment actually put its society in question against its own uniformitarian abstractions? How does this view compare with that of interpreters who put their society in question against values of divineness/diabolicalness? Is the Enlightenment to be distinguished from other eras, anthropologically, less for its dialectical self-doubt than (taking Duchet more literally than she perhaps intended) for its confidence that its own alienation could be measured, uniformly removed from all cultures and all times? Was that article of faith, at least, inalienable?

After Herder, romantic ideals of translation revived interest in hermetic codes, lost languages, Ursprache, and related pre-Enlightenment concerns. Yet evolutionary science continued Enlightenment traditions of charting cultural differences as naturalistic taxons. For all its excesses and faults, medieval–Renaissance interpretation – culminating in a "Theater of the World" of ritual and religious rarities and varieties – avoids the particular type of reductionism that links Enlightenment philosophes with our current scientific optimists.

We have traced European misconceptions in our tale of Patagonia. Reciprocally, it is just as certain that Patagonians and Fuegians misconceived Europeans: Again, neither we nor they "are likely to clear ourselves easily of so fundamental a human trait."[12] A less obvious complication is that Europeans retrospectively misrepresented themselves in the act of encountering Patagonians. That French illustration of 1789 on the frontispiece of this book depicts Byron and his men (1764) as orderly, symmetrical observers of natives more shadowy and diversified (and larger!) than they themselves. Europeans inscribed Patagonians as, of all things, giants, and themselves as, of all things, Enlightened. Both sides of the inscription are equally distorted, because cultures, like historical styles, interpenetrate symbolically.

A tragically literal fact is that by the 1870s and 1880s, when long-term contacts were beginning, the inhabitants of Tierra del Fuego, now designated the Yaghan and the Ona, had been largely eradicated by European disease. Yet even under happier circumstances, it would have been the symbolic facts that influenced views of Patagonians and Fuegians from Pigafetta on through Darwin and others.[13]

The history of anthropology and the anthropology of history happen symbolically. Had American aboriginals – some taller than others but all naturally normal-sized – lived fully clothed, they could still have been viewed as exotic. (We must remember that they were only eventually construed as such, although many went naked; assuming that the message on the *Pioneer* spacecraft is received by some infinitely remoter *other*, next time it may be our turn!) Or, setting our sights at a more mundane (terrestrial) level, we may ask: Isn't it time for the Enlightenment to appear equally as exotic to us now as Patagonians appeared to Europeans then?

Knowledge of other cultures and eras depends on the cultures and eras doing the knowing. This fact should not obstruct but inform comparative anthropology throughout history. Because these limits cannot be transcended, they must be incorporated in our theories – and what better place to acknowledge them than in the history of cultures that imperfectly understand each other? The same limits might also give pause to message senders of all eras, including our own, by allowing us to recognize ourselves as not-inevitable. It is the mysteriously durable Enlightenment dream of direct, uniform knowledge communicated easily – independent of cultures, eras (or galaxies) – that certain schools of anthropological interpretation salutarily doubt.

Enlightenment simplicity imagined an unencumbered view of cultures and eras, a lookout external to all of them. It imagined as well that Patagonians were measurable, rather than scriptural, giants; or naturally symmetrical; or intrinsically wretched. If Enlightenment objectivity did no better by Patagonians and Fuegians than did the Renaissance, why should we voice confidence in one more than the other? Patagonians and Europeans alike were masters and victims of historical cultures, both exaggerated with reference to each other, and neither exaggerated with reference to nature's norms. (We may say the same of the Renaissance and the Enlightenment.) Anthropologically, there's the marvel.

By cutting both Patagonians and the Enlightenment down to comparative size, we may (Enlightenment-like?) outgrow superstitions of uniform, unadulterated objectivity across cultures. But even as I profess this symbolic hope, I feel its historical culture slipping out from under it; it is no more likely to survive than Patagonian giants or Patagonians themselves – whatever they might have been, had we known.

De-Enlightenment

The feeling of gratitude and humility that every member of a given culture can and must feel toward all the others can only be based on one conviction: It is that other cultures are different from his own in the most varied way [*les autres cultures sont différentes de la sienne, de la façon la plus variée*]; this remains the case even if the final nature of these differences escapes him or if despite all attempts one only succeeds in penetrating it imperfectly.

Lévi-Strauss, *L'anthropologie Structurale 2* (my translation)

The extent to which Enlightenment expectations persist in anthropology is apparent from high hopes (1) that our thus-far inferior science shall soon achieve paradigm breakthrough into genuine experimental falsifiability, firm correlations, prediction, and sound application; and (2) that anthropology and history will one day merge into regnant objectivity – and its moral equivalent "tolerance" – in human affairs. Well-meaning visionaries go so far as to anticipate, through anthropology, emancipation into "empathetic and comparative appreciation of human solidarity in cultural difference": "The comparative understanding of others contributes to self-awareness; self-understanding, in turn, allows for self-reflection and (*partial*) self-emancipation; the emancipatory interest, finally, makes the understanding of others possible" (Scholte 1973: 448; emphasis added). Although I share Scholte's will toward empathy and understanding, I underscore that parenthetical "partial" gratefully. Cultures in communication – like moieties – properly leave a little mutual mystery to each other: chiaroscuro. Cultures that became totally accessible, too clear, extraparadoxical – are doubtless not cultures at all. Paradoxes by their nature must be entered into, scrupulously, not solved.[14]

The two stock assumptions – anthropology is inferior science, and its mission is objective tolerance – are intertwined. Those who bemoan anthropology's scientific shortcomings underestimate its characteristic accomplishments: discovering subtlety, pattern, dialectics, and innuendo in human matters that, viewed by agencies of analysis outside anthropology, appear merely misguided, laughable, or simply transparent. Anthropology forestalls any culture's sense of its own inevitability. Culturally all peoples are capable of comparing each other with relative disinterest, but politically there is rarely the opportunity and almost never the prescription to do so. Professional anthropology safeguards convictions – often contrary to the *amour propre* of nation states – that cultures can and ought to encounter.

It is, I suppose, conceivable that anthropology might one day stumble onto a formalist solution for the uniform comparison of cultures. Yet we need not believe this prognosis in order to pursue cross-cultural knowledge (or cross-cultural doubt!). I personally feel that to parry the more obvious self-interests that motivate the comparison of cultures, we require more than "normal science," even if we ever properly formulate our paradigm and even where, as in British functionalism, approaches have been somewhat standardized. Again, visions of scientific convention echo hopes of objective tolerance. Yet how do we reconcile such noble aims with the fact that anthropologies themselves are embedded in cultures? If they were not, *cultural* anthropology at least would be fundamentally in error about its principal subject of concern. Does anthropology truly produce blushless Promethean observers, inured to the shock of other cultures, bravely protecting a spirit of tolerance? I doubt it. Any brand of tolerance reflects values tipped toward one type of society: hard-working peasants, leisurely hunters and gatherers, rugged pastoralists – to the implicit detriment of the others. Short of utopian conditions like Hodgen's "unencumbered observation" – and it is short of them that cultures both happen and communicate – the beacon of total tolerance becomes oblique. By diminishing ambitions while accelerating efforts, by striving more practicably to avoid today's narrowness rather than aspiring to absolute emancipatory tolerance, we advance toward pluralisms. So resigned a policy admits as well the possibility that rival, or superior, "anthropologies" might exist in non-Western and nonmodern peoples (cf. L. Dumont 1977). It acknowledges the inherent limits of *any* anthropology, which necessarily derives from the cultural system sustaining it. Culturally, then, one properly doubts the strident claims of anthropologists and social theorists who declare themselves – Enlightenment-like – radically *dépaysés*.

In a quiet moment Lévi-Strauss portrays tolerance as not a contemplative attitude dispensing indulgences but a dynamic attitude; and he poses anthropology's task as a continually expanding humanism:

Classical humanism was restricted not only with respect to its object but with respect to the privileged class which benefited from it. The exotic humanism of the nineteenth century found itself linked to the industrial and commercial interests that supported it and to which it owed its existence. After the aristocratic humanism of the Renaissance and the bourgeois humanism of the nineteenth century, ethnology notes the appearance – for the closed world (*le monde fini*) that our planet has become – of a humanism doubly universal.

By seeking its inspiration among the humblest and most scorned of societies, it proclaims that nothing human can be estranged from man, and thus establishes a democratic humanism opposed to its two predecessors created for the privileged and based on privileged civilizations. And by mobilizing methods and techniques from all sciences we advance the understanding of man and nature in a generalized humanism. [1973:322; my translation]

I would revise this vision of anthropology: Its humanism is less expanding than shifting – always disturbed, suffering setbacks, picking itself up again to extend an image of anthropos to those most recently excluded. Lévi-Strauss's "democratic humanism" itself must be regarded as relative, to be adjusted whenever democratic interests begin in turn to grow tyrannical.

Anthropology's appropriate feeling-tone – its inky ethos – lurks (for me) somewhere in our tale of Patagonia and in *Tristes tropiques*, Frazer's *soupirs*, Forster's *Passage*, Geertz's Weberian tonalities, and the cross-cultural laments in which other authors inscribe the wealth of human grandeur and tomfoolery, at times ironically. Edmund Wilson is an example. Wilson devoted a bookish lifetime both to capturing his own kind in words and to relating the customs of races *Red, Black, Blond, and Olive*, apologizing *amicus curiae* for White Man's sins against his neighbor Iroquois, and pursuing the history of romantic social hopes of utopian revolution through to their death knell as Lenin (about to dash vision on the shoals of political actuality) prepared to disembark at the Finland Station. At last Wilson returned *Upstate* to regain a Montaignesque sense of self, to peer back through his own experience or interpretation of Dead Sea scrolls, symbolist texts, Civil War literature, and Pushkin (and everything else to which his many languages, occasional travels, and constant reading exposed him).[15] He peered as well into the world's shadowy future: *Que sais-je*? Still chuckling, perhaps at his own undying curiosity, his sentences sighed:

Greece and Rome and classical France left behind them much more durable monuments than our old [New York] mansions gone to ruin and our broken-off fragments of old canals; but the aeons of time required for the mammalian plantigrades of the human race to achieve what we can now see to be a very moderate and partial degree of civilization has been coming to discourage and bore me. I look at the creatures on the street and think, well, we have begun to walk upright and our toes, now more or less impractical, are shrinking like the toes of elephants' feet. We have now arrived at a skill of uttering and writing sounds that can convey rather special meanings. But our problems of future development are still absolutely appalling...We have spent no one knows how many million years, as have the black widow spider, the hammerhead shark, the deadly amanita and the leaf-nosed bat, building up or assembling or creating – we do not know how to put it – what we call our bodies and brains, our consciousness. Only now are we beginning a little to understand how

these organs and members work. The process of finding out more is going to
be very tedious. At least, that is how I feel toward the end of a fairly long life
that has left me with the feeling – illusion? – that I have seen or sampled many
kinds of experience, that I know what this planet is, what its climates in
different places and at different seasons are, what its flora and fauna are, what
both its more primitive men and more mechanized men are like – so that, not
expecting any real novelty. . . [1971:384–6]

Ending in doubt, his faculties fading, Edmund Wilson continued to learn
Hungarian.

Part II
Systematics notwithstanding

We must not allow ourselves to be frightened away by the timidity of the specialists, who are often notably lacking in the sense of what I have called "contrastive perspective."

E. Sapir, *Language*

We have seen that certain Enlightenment theories of society and diversity, geared to simplicity of formulas and grammarlike abstraction, avoid recognizing the interplay of ideal/actual/negative in social orders, both their own and others. An evolutionary (or even a developmental) view denies complexity and dialectics to the (early) end of its spectrum; a mechanistic view dissolves them altogether. Even Marx, with his compelling portrait of societies in dramatic contradiction with themselves, necessarily imagined a classless utopia in utter conformity to itself, which he projected as history's own, so to speak, future.

In Part II, I shall oppose to such views arguments that the apparently simplest and the most exotic societies are, like all systems of signs and symbols, self-contradictory – not in the same way as capitalism, perhaps, but self-contradictory nonetheless. Chapter 3 argues the case from the vantage of comparative social theory, Chapter 4 from the vantage of issues in communication and translation and the science of signs and symbols. Again, even an "elementary" system with minimal specialization remains in other respects as differentiated and dialectical as the more conspicuous historical systems. In fact, supposedly simple systems, like tribes, are better designated "generalized" – their ideals and actualities neither simply confirm each other nor revolutionarily conflict with each other; rather, each stands in meaningful contrast to another, consistently.

In the terms employed by structuralists, social facts represent selections from larger sets of possibilities of which societies keep symbolic track, whether consciously or unconsciously, explicitly or covertly. Societies conceptualize themselves as select (in both senses) arrangements, valued against contrary arrangements that are in some way "objectified." Members of societies who subsist, cohere, expand, and reproduce at the same time make themselves "cultures" by imagining utopias past or future; by dividing into clans, classes, castes, or clubs (a central theme of Robert Lowie's anthropology); by performing rituals that both delineate "ordinary" time and activity and define the commonsensical as opposed to the sacred or taboo; by producing myths (and sometimes literatures); and by living different religions, each of which is

52

involved in the division of labor and the differentiation of society and culture. The views of Durkheim and Weber on religion helped prepare the way for a concept of culture in anthropology that emphasizes both integration and contrast (as did Boas's theories of language and art and Lowie's theories of social organization). Thus "culture" becomes the empirical and philosophical recognition that all symbolic *prises de conscience* of human populations are interrelated and are susceptible of comparison the world over. Cultures themselves are at base dialectical.

3. Social theories with a difference

Robert Murphy's important work *The Dialectics of Social Life* reminds us that "there were two Emile Durkheims": the positivist and the "almost-dialectician" charting the "relationship between society and states of consciousness" (1980:170). Yet Murphy's own readings of Durkheim emphasize the positivist half of his corpus. This chapter opens with a reading of Durkheim less according to the anthropological functionalism his positivism helped consolidate (particularly as exported to Britain) than according to the structuralism his almost-dialectical side presaged at home. I then move to Weber, Mauss, Lowie, and others, pursuing each corpus as something in its own right dialectical: a becoming. I emphasize those portions of their works that incline toward the meanest of tribes and the full range of historical states and religions. In fact, this chapter's movement from one theorist to another is mediated by various exotic institutions – by Indic *jajmani*, by tribal cross-cousins, and by sodalities. Thus, social practices themselves provide synapses between comparative theories, each of which may be reread in light of the others.[1]

From Durkheim's *Division* to *jajmani*

Durkheim became the Plato of the Australian Blackfellows in order to emerge as the Angelic Doctor of consensual society.

Dominick LaCapra, *Emile Durkheim*

Images of social solidarity are not always pretty.[2] The more brutal images help remind us that Durkheim's famous distinction between mechanical and organic solidarity isolates not two separate kinds of society but rather twin aspects, apparent if a social solidarity is fully conceptualized from both external and internal vantages. Consider a particularly brutal image, paraphrased from the movie *Serpico*: "I remember this [police] department when the only way to be hired was if you had an uncircumcised shamrock hanging between your legs." The image suggests that earlier cops were mechanically solidary (identified by likeness) for having, as it were, uncircumcised shamrocks. But the total system, complete symbolically regardless of actual ethnic and religious composition, operates implicitly as an organic solidarity (or, more

54

precisely in Durkheim's terms, as a negative solidarity). At this level, the noncop is likewise implicitly classified by occupation, religion, or ethnic identity, coded in a kind of "primitive classification" in urban U.S. culture. Any mechanical solidarity by likeness implies that a certain set of symbols has been selected from a larger sociosemantic field. The shamrocks and circumcisions in my example are at another level part of an "organic solidarity" of concepts (one might call it, with Lévi-Strauss, a totemism). The old-style police force actualized just one symbolic possibility. To comprehend such subtleties of solidarity, we must review certain lessons that Durkheim learned from Australian aboriginals who, I might add with a wink, happen to subincise, at least certain divisions of them.

Australia influenced Durkheim's theories without his going there. He placed data reported from non-Western, nonliterate, nonstratified, nonagricultural peoples at the center of a general model of society. After he had developed the mechanical/organic contrast in *The Division of Labor* (1893), Durkheim learned more about tribes whose practice seemed to fall into both categories. Australian ethnography did not simply refine Durkheim's theories, it restructured them. Aboriginals of Australia (and America) manifested not simple mechanical solidarity, as an earlier semievolutionist Durkheim had half-supposed, but a complex of solidarities. Their totemic classifications, spatial arrangements, and social units implemented an organic solidarity of ideals and rituals, beyond simple needs of subsistence. Ethnographic reports helped Durkheim transfer his view of representations and *conscience collective* into areas of both affect and intellection, ritual and classification. That aboriginals transcended mechanical solidarity – that dulling sameness of lifeways where every social unit replicates another, with no mutual mystery separating them – helped Durkheim adjust his view of social facts and their religious perpetuation. He came to see tribal "simplicity" more as a generalized organization.[3]

As we saw in Part I, many early compilers of exotica had considered aspects of primitive life as evidence of a lost paradisiacal condition. Later, for Frazer, tribes became a readable, allegorical, and perhaps ironic commentary on crown and miter; and according to functionalism tribes presented an image of everyday social engineers. But in Durkheim's school, tribes became exemplary in a peculiar way. They revealed an irreducible basis of solidarity/divisions and thus illuminated the sort of integration that France and modern Europe had lost. Hence Durkheim's and Mauss's interest in Australian details: "Though he may be essentially Wartwut and partially Moiwiluk, the Wotjobaluk described by Howitt is above all a Krokitch or a Gamutch" (1903/1963:84). Such data confirmed their view of the symbolic basis of social units, arranged according to ideals of mutual differences. The "division of labor," which pathologically degenerated into an alienation of individuals, elsewhere remained the key to integration of a divided social whole.

Durkheim's initial typology of social solidarity derived from a principle of altruism, the moral label for the extraindividual, the *social* basis of human experience. He derided social Darwinism as a false theory of egoism:

What gives this hypothesis authority in the eyes of certain persons is that it appears to be the logical consequence of the principles of Darwinism. In the name of the dogma of struggle for existence and natural selection, they paint for us in the saddest colors this primitive humanity whose hunger and thirst, always badly satisfied, were their only passions; those sombre times when men had no other care and no other occupation than to quarrel with one another over their miserable nourishment. To react against those retrospective reveries of the philosophy of the eighteenth century and also against certain religious doctrines, to show with some force that the paradise lost is not behind us and that there is in our past nothing to regret, they believe we ought to make it dreary and belittle it systematically. Nothing is less scientific than this prejudice in the opposite direction. If the hypotheses of Darwin have a moral use, it is with more reserve and measure than in other sciences. They overlook the essential element of moral life, that is, the moderating influence that society exercises over its members, which tempers and neutralizes the brutal action of the struggle for existence and selection. Wherever there are societies, there is altruism, because there is solidarity. [1983/1964:196–7]

To challenge Spencer's *Principles of Sociology*, which reduced solidarity to agglomerations of private arrangements, leaving no autonomy to the social whole, Durkheim criticized notions of contract that overlooked social constraints on individual interests: Social solidarity entailed more than economic relations and free initiative where "individuals exchanged the products of their labor" (1893/1964:203). In particular, Rousseau's identification of sentiment with nature was felt to obscure the importance of the social; in 1901 Durkheim insisted:

We are not in a position to see the perfect continuity in Rousseau's thinking from the second *Discours* to *The Social Contract*. The *state of nature*, as described in the former, is a kind of peaceful anarchy in which individuals, independent of each other and without ties between them, depend only upon the abstract force of nature. In the *civil* state, as viewed by Rousseau, the situation is the same, though in a different form. The individuals are unconnected with each other; there is a minimum of personal relation between them, but they are dependent upon a new force, which is superimposed on the natural forces but has the same generality and necessity, namely, the *general will*. In the state of nature, man submits voluntarily to the natural forces and spontaneously takes the direction they impose because he feels instinctively that this is to his advantage and that there is nothing better for him to do. His action coincides with his will. In the civil state, he submits just as freely to the general will because it is of his own making and because in obeying it he is obeying himself.

Here we can see the similarities and differences between Rousseau and his two predecessors, Hobbes and Montesquieu...

In Hobbes' view...societies are formed because men submit voluntarily to an absolute sovereign in order to avoid the horrors of the state of war, and they are maintained because the sovereign prevents them from breaking up...Montesquieu's view was quite different. Though only a legislator can establish the law, he cannot promulgate any law he pleases. A proper law must be consonant with the nature of things...Rousseau is perhaps even more categorical in this point. The social system is based on an objective harmony of interests and on the state of public

opinion, manners and customs. . . The general will cannot be represented by an individual. . .
    Though the three thinkers agree that the social and the individual are dissimilar, we observe an increasing effort to root the social being in nature. But therein lies the weakness of the system. While, as we have shown, social life for Rousseau is not contrary to the natural order, it has so little in common with nature that one wonders how it is possible. . . And just as he fails to explain how social life, even in its imperfect historical forms, could come into being, he has great difficulty in showing how it can possibly cast off its imperfections and establish itself on a logical basis. [1960b:135–7]

Durkheim's resistence to Rousseau most clearly distinguishes his *sociologie* from the *anthropologie* of Lévi-Strauss, his "inconstant disciple" (Lévi-Strauss 1963b). Lévi-Strauss returns to the nature-sentiment of Rousseau, in modes of both exquisite *rêverie* and empathetic *pitié* (a sentiment quite close to the altruism Durkheim himself underscored). Lévi-Strauss cradles the logical bases of cultures in the logical basis of nature (insofar as we can comparatively *know* it) in the rapprochement between Durkheim and Rousseau that he advanced after Mauss had converted notions of individual contract to principles of *exchange*, which were the clearest evidence of Durkheim's "social."
    Yet the subsequent shifts in the traditions of *L'année sociologique* arose from Durkheim's typology of solidarities and related concepts of "elementariness." Durkheim restricted his discussion to positive solidarity, because so-called negative solidarity "does not produce any integrations by itself." Today we might say that negative solidarity requires "scapegoats," out-groups who contrast with, and so consolidate, an in-group; negative solidarity is perhaps best understood as an incompletely detected system of organic solidarity (cf. the *Serpico* example just cited). Regardless:

Since negative solidarity does not produce any integration by itself, and since, moreover, there is nothing specific about it, we shall recognize only two kinds of positive solidarity which are distinguishable by the following qualities:
1. The first binds the individual directly to society without any intermediary. In the second, he depends upon society, because he depends upon the parts of which it is composed.
2. Society is not seen in the same aspect in the two cases. In the first, what we call society is a more or less organized totality of beliefs and sentiments common to all the members of the group: this is the collective type. On the other hand, the society in which we are solidary in the second instance is a system of different, special functions which definite relations unite. *These two societies really make up only one. They are two aspects of one and the same reality, but none the less they must be distinguished.* [Durkheim 1893/1964:129; emphasis added]

The last sentence contains the kernel of Durkheim's interest in comparative studies of tribal populations. In *Division of Labor* he concluded: "Social life comes from a double source, the likeness of consciences and the division of social labor." By the end of *The Elementary Forms of the Religious Life* (1912/1965), he had highlighted populations whose social life, although emerging from the same double source, could better be described as a division of consciences and a likeness of social labor. That is, social units identical and redundant in their organizational aspects (hordes) defined themselves antithetically in their categorical schemes (clans) through rituals that expressed the mutual "scarcity" of each and thus the ultimate reliance of one on the other.[4]

In the *Division of Labor* Durkheim had already considered ideas of *Naturvölker* suggesting an amorphous mechanical solidarity: families grown into clans, with no internal organization, "held together only by external circumstances and through the common habit of life" (p. 178). But even the early Durkheim quickly qualified an image of unregenerate mechanical solidarity. Although he posed a pure-type mechanical solidarity in his typology, he postulated the clan as well to introduce a different axis of solidarity across the mechanical units:

> If we try to construct intellectually the ideal type of a society whose cohesion was exclusively the result of resemblances, we should have to conceive it as an absolutely homogeneous mass whose parts were not distinguished from one another. Consequently, they would have no arrangement; in short, it would be devoid of all definite form and all organization. It would be the veritable social protoplasm, the germ whence would arise all social types. We propose to call the aggregate thus characterized, *horde*.
>
> It is true that we have not yet, in any completely authentic fashion, observed societies which, in all respects, complied with this definition. What gives us the right to postulate their existence, however, is that lower societies, those which are most closely akin to primitivity, are formed by a simple repetition of aggregates of this kind. We find an almost perfectly pure example of this social organization among the Indians of North America...In other cases, we are even nearer the horde. Fison and Howitt describe Australian tribes which consist of only two such divisions.
>
> We give the name *clan* to the horde which has ceased to be independent by becoming an element in a more extensive group, and that of *segmental societies with a clanbase* to peoples who are constituted through an association of clans. We say of these societies that they are segmental in order to indicate their formation by the repetition of like aggregates in them, analogous to the rings of an earthworm, and we say of this elementary aggregate that it is a clan, because this word well expresses its mixed nature, at once familial and political...
>
> Thus, the clan contains a great many strangers, and this permits it to attain dimensions such as a family, properly speaking, never has. It often comprises several thousand persons. Moreover, it is the fundamental political unity; the heads of clans are the only social authorities.
>
> We can thus qualify this organization as politico-familial. [1893/1964:174–6]

The horde/clan distinction is fundamental; and different views of what Durkheim meant by it came to distinguish different anthropologies: functionalism, structural functionalism, and structuralism.[5]

The Division of Labor already suggested shifting the locus of "divisions" (and differentiation) from the plane of social interaction to that of symbols: "But social solidarity is a completely moral phenomenon which, taken by itself, does not lend itself to exact observation nor indeed to measurement. To proceed to this classification and this comparison, we must substitute for this internal fact which escapes us an external index which symbolizes it and study the former in the light of the latter" (1893/1964:64). In this case Durkheim stipulated that the visible symbol was law; later he would address the subtle issue of societies where law and custom remain undifferentiated. Durkheim's concerns were motivated not by an interest in antecedents but by an interest in systematics. This fresh reason for scrutinizing the complex workings of primitive society and ritual systems was accentuated in the case of Australians (and Amerindians), whose institutions were not demonstrable forerunners of European ones. In such remote, generalized (but still "divisioned") societies, the "external index which symbolizes" solidarity was represented by religious ritual.

Durkheim turned to Australian ethnography for reasons that were not logical (as in Enlightenment traditions), hermeneutic (tracing biblical signatures), romantic or nostalgic, or colonialist or administrative but methodological. He investigated the operation of social solidarity in light of generalized systems (e.g., no formal distinction between law/custom) that were conveyed through both actions and ideals. Durkheim stressed aboriginals' systematic divisions (e.g., clans); emotive contexts for expressing those divisions, barely mentioned in *Primitive Classification*, were a later interest.

To illustrate difficulties with critics who forget Durkheim's priorities, we might consider a revealing summary of *The Elementary Forms of the Religious Life* (1912/1965) by Evans-Pritchard, which begins by reviewing Durkheim's clan/horde discussion accurately:

> [Blackfellows are] hunters and collectors, wandering about in small hordes in their tribal territories seeking game, roots, fruits, grubs, and so forth. A tribe is composed of a number of such hordes. Besides being a member of a little horde and of the tribe in whose territory the horde lives, a person is a member of a clan, there being many such clans widely dispersed throughout the continent. As a member of his clan, he shares with its other members a relationship to a species of natural phenomena, mostly animals and plants. The species is sacred to the clan, and may not be eaten or harmed by its members. With each clan are classed other natural phenomenon, so that the whole of nature belongs to one or other of the clans. The social structure thus provides the model for the classification of natural phenomena. Since the things so classed with the clans are associated with their totems, they also have a sacred character; and since the cults mutually imply each other, all are co-ordinated parts of a single religion, a tribal religion. [1965:58]

We saw above in *The Division of Labor* (1893/1964) that the horde/clan distinction was more than a mere caveat in mechanical solidarity. Durkheim and Mauss's *Primitive Classification* (1903/1963) went on to set out moieties, clans, and marriage classes as additional axes of division:

> Each tribe is divided into two large fundamental sections which we shall call moieties [Needham's replacement term for "phratry"]. Each moiety, in turn, comprises a certain number of clans, i.e., groups of individuals with the same totem. In principle,

the totems of one moiety are not found in the other. In addition to this division into clans, each moiety is divided into two classes which we shall call "marriage classes." [1903/1963:10]

That is to say, divisions are themselves differentiated (a structuralist notion of "axis" always implies a differentiation). Later Durkheim and Mauss trace classifications analogous to this social divisioning:

> Even though the members of each moiety are dispersed over a multitude of local groups, within each group they are opposed to each other in their camps. But these dispositions, and the orientation resulting from them, are apparent above all in the gatherings of the entire tribe. This is particularly the case among the Arunta. Moreover, we find among them the idea of a special orientation, a mythical direction assigned to each clan. The water clan belongs to a region thought to be that of water. The dead are oriented in the direction of the mythical camp thought to have been lived in by the legendary ancestors, the Alcheringa. The direction of the camp of the mother's mythical ancestors is taken into account at certain religious ceremonies (nose-piercing, extraction of the upper incisor). [1903/1963:64]

The significance of these whole-tribe gatherings (later characterized as effervescent and cohesive) is that relations correspond to ideal classifications, a kind of intellectual division of labor. The attachment of totemic emblems to clans is crucial for *L'année sociologique* approaches because clans represent one division of the whole, also otherwise divided into subsistence hordes. (Later Lévi-Strauss will underscore how "primitive classifications," or totemisms, articulate sociosemantic fields through such contrastive relations.)

Evans-Pritchard acknowledges that for Durkheim totemic emblems expressed both the unity and the exclusiveness of each clan. He also notes that Durkheim's "sacred" is society itself, represented in symbols to its members. But his statement is misleading unless we remember that organic solidarity remains Durkheim's touchstone, and that society is less "corporate group" than "divisioned whole." Evans-Pritchard then directs us to the tribal level, where total systems can be perceived:

> In each territory many clans are represented, each with its distinctive totemic emblems and cults, but all alike belong also to the tribe and have the same religion, and this tribal religion is idealized in the gods. The great god is simply the synthesis of all the totems, just as the tribes are syntheses of all the clans represented in them; and it is inter-tribal also in character, mirroring social relations between tribe and tribe, especially the assistance of members of other tribes at tribal ceremonies of initiation and sub-incision. So while souls and spirits do not exist in reality, they correspond to reality and in that sense they are real, for the social life they symbolize is real enough. [1965:61]

Indeed, the importance of ritual subincision is that it is performed by clans, a social distinction cutting across local hordes. Through its emotive rites, the society represents itself not as a simple cohesive unity but as a system that is horde divided for certain purposes and clan divided for others. The horde/clan distinction is a harbinger of the full social/cultural differentiation in less "generalized," more "complex" systems.

Evans-Pritchard distorts Durkheim's arguments in concluding: "Fundamentally Durkheim elicits a social fact from crowd psychology" (p. 68).[6] Elsewhere Evans-Pritchard admits that for Durkheim the real significance, as opposed to the stated purpose, of totemic rites is "firstly that they draw clansmen together, and secondly, that enactment of the rites on these occasions of concentration renews in them a feeling of solidarity." Indeed, even when a category (the clan) becomes momentarily a group, the rite heightens distinctions rather than collapsing them.

Durkheim stressed that totems worked through interrelated differences and that organic solidarity depended not on circumstances of proximity but on symbolics of nomenclature:

> Each clan has its totem, which belongs to it alone; two different clans of the same tribe cannot have the same. In fact, one is a member of a clan merely because he has a certain name. All who bear this name are members of it for that very reason; in whatever manner they may be spread over the tribal territory, they all have the same relations of kinship with one another. Consequently, two groups having the same totem can only be two sections of the same clan. Undoubtedly, it frequently happens that all of a clan does not reside in the same locality, but has representatives in several different places. However, this lack of a geographical basis does not cause its unity to be the less keenly felt. [1912/1965:123]

Yet, to make a case against Durkheim, Evans-Pritchard speaks of unity as if it were not a part of systematic solidarity:

> With regard to the Australian evidence cited: one of the weaknesses of Durkheim's position is the plain fact that among the Australian aboriginals it is the horde, and then the tribe, which are the corporate groups, and not the widely dispersed clans; so if the function of religion is to maintain the solidarity of the groups which most require a sense of unity, then it should be the hordes and tribes, and not the clans, that should perform the rites generating effervescence. Durkheim saw this point, and tried to elude it by the answer, which seems to me to be inadequate, that it is precisely because the clans lack cohesion, having neither chiefs nor a common territory, that periodic concentrations are necessary. [1912/1965:66]

Evans-Pritchard elides ritual unity and social solidarity; he finally accuses Durkheim of perpetrating a just-so story of the origins of totems, concluding rhetorically: "What is the point of maintaining through ceremonies the solidarity of social groupings which are not corporate and which do not have any joint action outside the ceremonies?" It is as if the *Division of Labor* had never been written. This rhetorical question is to be directed not against Durkheim but against human society. Evans-Pritchard converts what is irreducible in *sociologie* to something empirically problematic; yet, calling it into question, he offers no answers.

There have been two typical functionalist responses to Durkheim: (1) to turn him into a believer in the unificational capacity of group assemblies or (2) to reduce him to the sort of substantive social determinism that he was, as his work developed, gradually escaping. Neither view is thoroughly mistaken, yet each overlooks the general thrust of Durkheim's corpus. I am not denying

Durkheim's persistent evolutionist tendencies, basic positivism, or frequent reifications of the distinction between group and thought. Indeed, R. Needham has reviewed *Primitive Classification*'s lapses into pseudohistorical formulations and tautological correlations. Nevertheless, the consistent theme running from *Division of Labor* to the *Elementary Forms* and extending to all the methodological and ethnological endeavors in between is solidarity/ differentiation. Durkheim and Mauss's goal was to demonstrate how both social divisions and natural divisions are knowable, re-cognizable, attributes of *conscience* in both senses, cognitive and moral. Occasionally they even glimpsed ways to surmount the society-versus-thought dilemma that many functionalist successors would force back into the work: "We have seen, indeed, how these classifications were modeled on the closest and most fundamental form of social organization. This, however, is not going far enough. Society was not simply a model which classificatory thought followed; it was its own divisions which served as divisions for the system of classification. The first logical categories were social categories" (1903/1963:82). Here, then, neither society nor thought is independent of "category" itself, a formulation already verging on structuralism.

Durkheim's *Elementary Forms* must be read in its entirety and in concert with the themes of *L'année sociologique* (themselves an organic solidarity).[7] Consider, for example, Durkheim's famous definition of religion: "*A religion is a unified system of beliefs and practices relative to sacred things, that is to say, things set apart and forbidden – beliefs and practices which unite into one single moral community called a Church, all those who adhere to them*" (1912/1965:62; italics in the original). This does not make a church a homogeneous community throughout its various levels of organization. If beliefs and practices are a unified *system* relative to sacred/profane things, then they are unified in divided fashion. The moral community invoked corresponds neither to mechanical solidarity nor, of course, to fragmentary *anomie* but to organic solidarity.

Elementary Forms culminates in symbolic analysis: The "social" is completed through "systematic idealization," often termed "religion": "Men alone have the faculty of conceiving the ideal of adding something to the real. Now where does this singular privilege come from?" (1912/1965:469). Durkheim's famous answer to this question – society – is often construed as reductionist; yet it is as much a critique of the question, whose individualistic and atomistic undercurrents Durkheim had so long refuted. We can follow Durkheim as he increasingly situates the axiomatic notion of "society" in the details of social organization and ritual practice emerging from a continent of aboriginals who traditionally knew no cultivation, property, or other civilizational "complexities":

For a society is not made up merely of the mass of individuals who compose it, the ground which they occupy, the things which they use and the movements which they perform, but above all is the idea which it forms of itself. It is undoubtedly true that it hesitates over the manner in which it ought to conceive itself; it feels itself drawn in divergent directions. But these conflicts which break forth are not between the ideal and reality, but between two different ideals, that of yesterday and that of to-day, that which has the authority of tradition and that which has the hope of the future. There is surely a place for investigating whence these ideals evolve; but whatever solution may be given to this problem, it still remains that all passes in the world of the ideal. [1912/1965:470]

In the world of the symbolic, ideals are divided just as society is divided – two sides of the same coin. Ideals as a whole contrast with (are differentiated from) actualities as a whole (we might call them mutual "alternities") just as one social division contrasts to another: male versus female, generation versus generation, clan versus clan.

If we construe social differentiation as a division of divisions, Australians are fully "religious":

> It is the same with religious universalism as with this individualism. Far from being an exclusive attribute of certain very great religions, we have found it, not at the base, it is true, but at the summit of the Australian system. Bunjil, Daramulun or Baiame are not simple tribal gods; each of them is recognized by a number of different tribes. In a sense, their cult is international. This conception is therefore very near to that found in the most recent theologies. So certain writers have felt it their duty to deny its authenticity, howsoever incontestable this may be. [1912/1965:473]

Here and elsewhere Durkheim probably misconstrued many facts of Australian worship, but his use of the term "international" should preclude any charge of sociological reductionism. Neither mystical nor transcendental, he argues that religion and society are equivalent evidence for the differential basis of solidarity. Durkheim reinforces the point with what we would now consider a pseudohistorical theoretical narrative:

> Neighboring tribes of a similar civilization cannot fail to be in constant relations with each other. All sorts of circumstances give an occasion for it; besides commerce, which is still rudimentary, there are marriages; these international marriages are very common in Australia. In the course of these meetings, men naturally become conscious of the moral relationship which united them. They have the same social organization, the same division into phratries, clans and matrimonial classes; they practise the same rites of initiation, or wholly similar ones.
>
> Mutual loans and treaties result in reinforcing these spontaneous resemblances. The gods to which these manifestly identical institutions were attached could hardly have remained distinct in their minds. Everything tended to bring them together and consequently, even supposing that each tribe elaborated the notion independently, they must necessarily have tended to confound themselves with each other. Also, it is probable that it was in inter-tribal assemblies that they were first conceived. For they are chiefly the gods of initiation, and in the initiation ceremonies, the different tribes are usually represented. So if sacred beings are formed which are connected with no geographically determined society, that is not because they have an extra-social origin. It is because there are other groups above these geographically determined ones, whose contours are less clearly marked: they have no fixed frontiers, but include

all sorts of more or less neighbouring and related tribes. The particular social life thus created tends to spread itself over an area with no definite limits. Naturally the mythological personages who correspond to it have the same character; their sphere of influence is not limited; they go beyond the particular tribes and their territory. They are the great international gods. [1912/1965:473–4]

But behind the conjectures (recalling Freud's narrative of patricidal primal hordes, Frazer's Aricia allegory, and other theories in the shape of just-so stories), we can still understand how these "international" tribal gods clarify Durkheim's famous equivalence of society and church, in fact society and God. To call society a church is first to call it a church rather than a cult: A church has a diversified organized membership; a cult has a homogeneous body of enthusiasts. As Durkheim insisted, "there is no church of magic" (1912/1965:60).

Ultimately, then, Durkheim converts neither religion to society nor society to religion; rather, he collapses the distinction – one arising only with the development of secularism. Most important for anthropology, the distinction collapses in light of generalized tribal systems where it does not obtain. The society/culture distinction can be similarly collapsed, throwing into relief those systems (such as our own) in which this distinction has become "native." As Talcott Parsons summarized this fundamental analytic and historical issue:

> It seems to have been Durkheim's view, a strongly defensible one, that the more primitive the society and the culture, the less differentiated they are from each other. He extensively analyzed the case of the Australian aborigines on the strength of this theory: the phenomena of the integration of culture and society could be seen there in their "elementary forms." But his interest in these elementary forms does not mean that Durkheim did not have a broad understanding of the possibility and importance of differentiating conceptually between cultural and social systems, even though, as Bellah points out (Bellah 1959), he somewhat obscured this vital point by using the term "social" for both. Unfortunately, he never worked out a thorough analysis of the place of religion in a highly differentiated society – a task that might well have led him to clarify his conception of the relations between "representations" and social structure.
>
> . . . An important semantic point is that just because a relatively undifferentiated complex is called "religion" for an earlier stage of development and only one of its two or more differentiated derivatives retains that name for a later stage, it is not legitimate to assert that "religion has declined." [Parsons 1974:lx, lxii]

Critics who accuse Durkheim of either secularizing the sacred or sacralizing the secular miss Parson's points. Plentiful philosophes before Durkheim had debunked religious institutions and ideals, and countless clerics had denied the ultimate value of temporal arrangements. Durkheim did neither because he did both, proclaiming the ideal/actual irreducible. Durkheim's detractors – whether prosecular or proecclesiastical – frequently cite his famous equation between God and society. They would do well to add a crucial footnote from the *Elementary Forms* that pursues implications of institutional differentiation seen against the limiting case of generalized systems: "At bottom, the concept of totality, that of society, and that of divinity are very probably only different aspects of the same notion" (1912/1965:490).[8] Here Durkheim approaches the purely relational–structural (indeed dialectical) principles of his direct successors. Of course, Durkheim's explicit formulations remained quasi-developmental and substantivist; and he never fully abandoned a sense of palpable mechanical solidarity (cf. Traugott 1978:13–15). Yet Mauss and others would prove society/culture to be as differentiable for tribal systems as for historical ones, thus complementing Durkheim's own insistence on the horde/clan distinction and fulfilling the potential significance of his view of the division of labor better than he himself could.

Below we shall see how Mauss helped refute any *basic* mechanical solidarity in actual societies, thus placing in question nostalgia over its loss or utopian dreams of its return. But with Durkheim's typology of solidarities fresh in our minds, it is worth considering Louis Dumont's extension of Durkheim's insights into Indic studies and into areas of comparative epistemology and methodology.

Emphasizing tribal kinship and marriage and Indic caste, Dumont advances Durkheim's implication that, if anything is relatively abstract, it is the "individual" that is abstracted from an irreducible "social." According to this structuralist outlook "social" stands to "individual" as "language" would stand to "speaker" (see Chapter 4). He attests the primacy of structural systems in all institutions: "We [Westerners] conceive of a unilineal group as a line, a continuous flow of generations maintaining a substantial unity; in short, a kind of collective, and thus permanent, *individual*. . .in Australia. . .instead of a line, there is an alternation of two kinds of generations" (L. Dumont 1966:237). "Generation" is in Australian conventions a complementary opposition perpetually interrelated. Here Dumont, like Durkheim, Mauss, and Lévi-Strauss before him, adduces tribal evidence to support *socio-logie*.

Dumont's most elaborate studies employ Indic traditions to correct individualistic distortions in standard Western views of social, political, and economic systems. His work on caste achieves precisely what Parsons would have wished from Durkheim: "a thorough analysis of the place of religion in a highly differentiated society." Dumont argues that caste hierarchy encompasses economic organization, that the whole informs more specific action, that a totalized division of labor is logically prior to particular occupations. Dumont thus confirms the priorities earlier suggested by Hocart, provided we eliminate suggestions of temporal sequence (as opposed to logical priorities) from Hocart's formulation: "Comparative evidence then shows that caste is older than occupation and is the cause of specialization in work, not the consequence. It has made necessary a certain specialization that was not there before. This specialization has broken up the caste system that gave rise to it"

(Hocart 1970:297; cf. 1950). In structuralist terms, then, caste is a system encompassing occupational specialization. From the start, such specialization is dialectical, playing out its inherent contradictions. This approach has implications for general epistemology: "[We Westerners would be] well advised to reverse our inherited view and to suppose that structure or complementarity is necessarily and historically prior to substance and individuality, and in that sense complexity is prior to, and more explanatory than, simplicity" (L. Dumont 1966:238).

It is in accordance with this view that Dumont analyzes the prestations and counterprestations composing India's jajmani system – ideals of a village-level, premonetized, closed economy of goods and services:

> A Hindi dictionary gives for *jajman* "he who has religious (*dharmik*) rites performed by Brahmans by giving them fees, etc." (Note the mention of the counter-prestation immediately evoked by the notion); for *jajmani*: "the privilege (*adhikar*) of performing the function of domestic priest (*purohit*), barber, *bari*, (a helper) on the occasion of a marriage, etc." Everything in this definition should be remembered: it is a question of family ritual, and above all, of marriage. It is a privilege to take part, even in the capacity of preparing the humble ceremonial materials, cups made from a leaf pinned together (the *bari*). [1970a:98]

Dumont stresses the hereditary, personal relationships that organize specialized services in a holistic division of labor. Moreover:

> [*jajmani*] regulates prestations and counter-prestations in a way which accords with custom: for the usual tasks repayment is in kind: it is not made individually for each particular prestation but is spread over the whole year, as is natural for a permanent relationship in an agricultural setting: a little food may be provided each day, and there is always the right to a fixed quantity of grain at harvest time, and finally there are obligatory presents (often of money) on the occasion of the main festivals of the year and, above all, at the major family ceremonies, which are advantageous occasions for the *praja* of the house. A fact which underlines the limited but effective solidarity which is thus set up between *jajman* and *praja* is that in many regions those who are considered the main servants of the village enjoy a gift of land from the communal funds which are at the disposal of their patrons collectively.
>
> Here the division of labor, which forms an integral part of the caste system, may be most clearly understood. [L. Dumont 1970b:98–9]

Homo hierarchicus relates *jajmani* to the codes of purity/pollution that inform various Hindu traditions: (1) ideological *varnas*: Brahman, Kshatriya, Vaishya, Shudra, plus Untouchables; (2) local endogamous divisions as they contrast with tribal exogamous traditions; (3) caste mobility; (4) hypergamy: Women marry only equals or betters; (5) dominant caste (primary landowners); and so forth. But his comments on *jajmani* alone suffice to demonstrate complementary opposition (among ritual specializations), where other observers perceived substantive unity of each division and simple coercion between them.[9]

In Dumont's controversial interpretation, *jajmani* ideals make the lowest task as indispensable as the highest. Here hierarchy implies the kind of or-

ganic solidarity that Durkheim sought in European guilds and Australian rites
alike. Yet Dumont never, as some critics charge, prettifies Indian society or
ignores its political and economic victims. Rather, he insists that the harsher
realities must be understood in the social and cultural context of economic and
political orders. Ideally *jajmani* worked to the exclusive interest neither of
dominant landowning castes nor of the hierarchy's apex, the Brahmans. In a
vital passage Dumont pauses to imagine the system as it might have operated
ideal-typically, in order to contrast the egalitarian West which long found
jajmani incomprehensible. Notice that his conjectural voyage to the past
opens in the subjunctive mood:

> Were we to travel in our imagination to a threshing floor in traditional India, we
> would see there the farmer measuring one after the other the King's share, that of
> the person who is found to have a superior right over the land, then the shares of
> the Brahman who serves as domestic priest, the barber, and so on, until perhaps he
> reaches the untouchable ploughman. Would we not have the impression of a
> phenomenon where, as in a market, qualitatively different prestations are in fact
> measured in the same units, and thus reduced to a common element, an element
> which clearly extends beyond religion? One would then speak of the "value" of the
> various prestations.
>
> In my opinion, such a view would be a mistake, for in bringing the two phenom-
> ena together in this way, a vague exterior likeness is allowed to conceal profound
> differences between them. This fact did not escape Max Weber. In a market all buyers
> and all sellers are as such identical, each after his own profit, and needs are adjusted
> unconsciously, by the market mechanism. But this is not the case here: not only are
> the majority of the relationships personal, but this is so in virtue of an organization
> which is to some extent deliberate and oriented towards the satisfaction of the needs
> of all those who enter into the system of relationships. What is effectively measured
> here is, so to speak, interdependence. Whilst directly religious prestations and
> "economic" prestations are mingled together, this takes place within the prescribed
> order, the religious order. The needs of each are conceived to be different,
> depending on caste, on hierarchy, but this fact should not disguise the entire
> system's *orientation towards the whole*. Thus we shall say that distribution on the
> threshing floor is essentially different from a market in that it takes place in
> virtue of the fact that everyone is interdependent. . . In the one case, the reference
> is to the *individual* pursuing his own gain, in the other to the *hierarchical
> collectivity*.
>
> . . . in short, the caste system should be seen as less "exploitative" than democratic
> society. If modern man does not see it this way, it is because he no longer conceives
> justice other than as equality.
>
> The conclusion to be drawn from this for the *jajmani* system is that it eludes
> what we call economics because it is founded on an implicit reference to the whole,
> which, in its nature, is religious or, if one prefers, a matter of ultimate values.
> [L. Dumont 1970b:104–6]

Traditional *jajmani* values presumably implemented what Durkheim found
lacking in the anomic West, which he hoped to restore to a sense of the
contrastive whole through *sociologie*. Social theorists before Dumont have
underscored the nonmarket nature of India's local economies. To name two:

In the *Theory of Social and Economic Organization*, trans. Henderson and Parsons, Max Weber classified the various types of the division of labor. The market economy corresponds to the type having autocephalous and autonomous elements: the agent acts of himself and in his own interest. In the Indian village, by contrast, the elements are autocephalous but heteronomous: they provide for the needs of the members of the group (p. 228), and a little later this type is called a "demiurgic liturgy." Marx had already emphasized two points in a rather similar way: the produce is for the immediate consumption of the community and does not become merchandise; and "The law that regulates the division of labor in the community acts with the irresistible authority of a law of Nature" (*Capital*, Eng. trans. Moscow, 1954, I sec. 4, Chapter 14, p. 358). [L. Dumont 1970b:294–5]

Dumont goes on to relate these exotic embodiments of premarket economy to Durkheim's typology of solidarities and to Mauss's principles of exchange as well, marrying anthropological fieldwork (L. Dumont 1957) to comparative theory, political economy, and intellectual history (1977).

Durkheim consolidated the organized pursuit of a discipline called *sociologie* according to hopes and ideals that on the other side of Indo-European traditions can be called *jajmanic*. That both *sociologie* and *jajmani* take on full significance not in isolation and substantively but complementarily and relationally – in reference to an implicit whole (call it comparative anthropology) – fulfills the science Durkheim envisioned insofar as conditions of variation and diversity allow.

Weber's typologies, to music

The comparative institutions approach has been less frequently pursued, partly because Weber tends to frighten anthropologists.

C. Geertz, *The Interpretation of Cultures*

Let us extend Dumont's formulations further than he himself might wish by merging his hierarchical/egalitarian poles of culture as the combined extremes of Indo-European ideology (here we take a cue from the great comparative mythologist Georges Dumézil, 1966–71). In this scheme of things, the eventual emergence of a *sociologie* (dialectically opposed to individualism) in the modern West would itself represent a transformation of Indic values such as caste-*varnas* and *jajmani*, dialectically opposed in India to principles of renunciation (cf. L. Dumont 1970b, 1975). In this way the Indic system and the European system could be posed together as variations on and negations of principles of hierarchy/equality. To gain a full contrastive sense at this grandiose level of cultural differentiation and integration would require contrasting the Sinic, the Pacific, the Semitic, and whatever else remained beyond the Indo-European. This worldwide, panhistorical level of macrocomparisons in light of microdescriptions points toward the province of Max Weber.[10]

Weber's massive works on religious sociology, history, and "economic ethics" palpably contrast specific systems of institutions and values. The opening of his *Religion of India* is characteristic: "India, in contrast to China, has been and remains" (1916–17/1967:3). Weber commences his 1915 study of religious-based world rejection in identical fashion:

> In strongest contrast to the case of China, Indian religiosity... is the cradle of those religious ethics which have abnegated the world, theoretically, practically, and to the greatest extent. It is also in India that the "technique" which corresponds to such abnegation has been most highly developed. Monkhood, as well as the typical ascetic and contemplative manipulations, were not only first but also most consistently developed in India. And it was perhaps from India that this *rationalization* set out on its historical way throughout the world at large. [1958a:323]

The broad distinction between India and China extends to India's emphasis on the village and on social organization by principles of birth. It is in contrast to India that China's bureaucratic traditions – idealizing a "national" level and organization based on talent – become so conspicious. Moreover, the two major cases of bureaucratic dominance – traditional Chinese and the modern European – will remain for Weber an ideal-type with a difference. Indeed, Weber's major anthropological achievement is to articulate ideal-types (like bureaucratization) without reducing all instances to uniform abstraction.

Weberian ideal-types are perhaps better termed logical-types (Parsons 1971:38) or constructed-types, since the types are never context-free; rather, they appear in interpretation from juxtaposing contexts. Yet Weber's work portrays the world succumbing, its rich historical and cultural variations notwithstanding, to disenchanted, rationalized, bureaucratic homogeneity:

> Weber attributes the slide towards bureaucratic fossilisation neither to demagogues nor to plutocrats, neither to taxes nor to the necessity to pander to electoral clienteles – Pareto's description or caricature of the Italian regime under Giolotti. He sees it as a perhaps irresistible movement resulting from the very nature of work in industrial enterprises of social relations, irrespective of the ownership, whether private or public, of the means of production. Rational planning, stemming from the need to make enterprises financially viable as well as from State management, is gradually encroaching on the whole of social life. In Weber's view, socialism threatens to push the tendency towards planning to the verge of bureaucratic fossilisation. But this threat exists in any case, inherent in the rationalisation imposed on all producers or managers interlinked with one another with a view to effective cooperation. [Aron 1976:48]

Reinhard Bendix conveys the resonance with prophetic traditions in Weber's complex and reflexive "preoccupation with the reciprocal effects of society and polity" (1962:454). Bendix's splendid summary is a moment in Weberian criticism that rivals Weber himself:

> For Weber, the events and ideas recorded in the Old Testament initiated the uniqueness of Western civilization. Against the ancient worship of many gods who must be placated each in his own domain, ancient Judaism developed over many centuries the worship of one infinitely powerful God, who had created the world. Judaism also transformed the ancient idea of divine rewards and punishments into the belief that every act in the here and now accounts for man's fate in this world

and that the practice of virtue would redeem the "chosen remnant" of the people in the historical future. Against the Oriental and Greek image of the world as an ever-recurring cycle of events, Judaism conceived of a radical contrast between the world as it is and as it will be.

These familiar beliefs were the creation of the Old Testament prophets, and Weber's singular contribution was his sociological analysis of this fact. Since the Bible refers to oracle-giving in many different ways, Weber sought to develop a typology in order to isolate the distinctive traits of the men who had formulated the beliefs of ancient Judaism. Among ascetic warriors, ecstatic war leaders and kings, professional magicians, and royal oracle-givers, there had emerged after the eleventh century B.C., under the reigns of Saul, David, and Solomon, a new group of prophets. These men were prophets of doom – from the early figure of Elijah to Isaiah and Ezekiel. They were distinguished from all others of their kind in materialistic terms, because they did not accept gifts and practical men will not pay for oracles that consistently predict disaster. The prophets spoke to the public at large when the spirit moved them, whether or not their counsel had been solicited and whether or not it suited the authorities. In Weber's view, they were the first demagogues and pamphleteers, who glorified the tribal confederacy of the past in pointed contrast to the abominations perpetrated under the United Monarchy. Yet the prophets were exclusively religious men, who were so otherworldly in their attitude toward politics that some of the prophecies were treason by secular standards. This independence from political considerations greatly enhanced their prestige. [Bendix 1962:479–80]

Bendix notes Weber's insistence on the patrician origins of prophets, paradoxically connected to lofty ethics, isolation from family, passionate loneliness, yet mass appeal based on "the rejection of all magic and the almost unwitting adoption of quasi-magical signs of authentication." Prophecy, moreover, became routinized in the "interest groups" it produced, even as it demonstrated the essential place of asocial and transcendent ideals in social life:

Most important of all, perhaps, was [Weber's] demonstration that the Old Testament prophets came to constitute an "interest group" of their own, because their opposition to the secular authorities, the credulous masses, and the vested interests of other holy men forced them to distinguish genuine from false prophecy and mark themselves off as a group with ideas, and hence with interests, of its own . . .

In this way, Weber transformed the great insight of Marx by showing that material interests are linked to man's inveterate quest for meaning and idealization, and that neither can be understood apart from the other. [Bendix 1962:480–81]

Hence Weber, whose work stands like an analogue of prophecy in a rationalized secular period, has proved resistant to simple discipleship!

Weber was most concerned with those dimensions of ancient Judaism that had been restored to the religious motivations embedded in economic activities from the Reformation onward: Calvinist legitimation of acts in the "here and now" as a kind of best evidence of being "chosen" – no longer in a world of "an ever-recurring cycle of events." Weber analyzed the transformation of diverse religious motivations into rationalized economic pursuits ultimately consolidated into bureaucracy. Yet he emphasized the range of religious sources for what, nevertheless, appears a worldwide slide toward disenchantment. The dimensions of different religioeconomic orders, even different bureaucracies, must be analyzed and empathetically understood (*verstehen*) by contrast; and contrast comes from outside the uniform (e.g., the Prussianized) community. Weber's *own* prophecy in light of diversity represents a paradoxical fatalism: History appears both convergent and plural. G. Roth conveys Weber's counterevolutionist verve in interpreting the development of institutions:

> Against the Romanticist notions of those mourning the passing of Community, but also against the apostles of Progress, Weber endeavors to show that "communal" and rationalist, capitalist and communist, traditionalist and modernist elements appear in ever new combinations – in short, that history is not the progression from *Gemeinschaft* to *Gesellschaft*.
>
> . . . Weber particularly stresses the pluralism of group affiliation in relatively undeveloped societies before the emerging political community gradually monopolizes the use of force – contrary to the view that modern society is more pluralist than traditionalist society in this respect.
>
> Weber sees no evidence for a universal stage of matriarchy . . . Weber likes to move back and forth, often with ironic undertones, between the ancient origin of a phenomenon and its survival into modern times . . . [Concerning monogamy, dowry, etc.] Weber points to an historical twist: a "later" economic stage, such as capitalism, may perpetuate or recreate an "earlier" communistic family structure . . . Weber takes obvious pleasure in outdoing the dialectic of historical materialism. [1968:lxviii]

These remarks should be recalled when we turn to Robert Lowie.

Swooping from his broad typologies (traditional/rational) into contextual details, Weber reveals the interrelationship of all institutions – economic, political, religious, artistic. His most famous argument is that in the development of Western capitalism, Protestant ethic and "rational" economic spirit are, as I would put it, an undifferentiated complex, each an aspect of the other. *In fact the religious/economic distinction is itself an aspect of rationalization.* Similarly, Weber demonstrated that Indic *jajmani* illustrated generalized order in the religious "division of labor" articulated in *varna*–caste concepts, thus recalling Durkheim generally and foreshadowing Dumont specifically:

> Economically, the traditionalism of the professional castes rests not only upon a mutual segregation of the various branches of production, but also, and today very often, upon the protection of the livelihood of caste members against mutual competition. The artisan belonging to the ancient "village staff" who was settled on garden land or who received a fixed income was absolutely protected in this respect. However, the principle of patronage protection, the guarantee of the *jajmani* relation went much further and still is strictly enforced by numerous occupational castes. We learned of the principle in connection with the Brahmans, and the meaning of the word *jajmani* ("sacrifice giver") suggests that the concept originated in the conditions of the Brahman caste. It could, perhaps, best be rendered by "personal diocese." The status etiquette of the Brahmans secures their dioceses among some other castes. They are by the caste organization and indeed – as always in India – hereditary (clan charismatic). [1916–17/1967:105]

Weber, a masterful thematic translator, renders *jajmani* as "economic diocese," with the qualification that unlike a diocese, *jajmani* is hereditary. Yet
the compound term (nearly an oxymoron) suggests the lines of difference
from exploitative democratic arrangements. Furthermore, as always, when
Weber injects the generalization "as always in India," we should understand
"in strongest contrast to China" or something comparable. (Just as here, in
reading "as always in Weber" we should understand "in strongest contrast to
Marx" or something comparable.)

In a sense then, Weber's theoretical ideal-types are themselves "organic
solidarities" by way of implied negatives. Systems of attributes are parceled
across variant traditions: "Diocese" becomes religious and nonhereditary in
the West; economic and hereditary in India, and so forth. Weber produces a
cinemascope of comparative social–religious–economic–political complexes;
yet his tone remains foreboding, sepia. It is the scope that dazzles, the tone
that saddens. To read Weber's comparative corpus is to enter a mirror house
of contrasts: India, not China, not Protestantism, not Judaism, not China, not
India. The only thing substantive is the Prussian-like bureaucratization thereby
delayed.

Listen awhile to the negative echoes and reverses in these Weberian webs
of world religion and cultural history:

> For Asia as a whole China played somewhat the role of France in the modern
> Occident. All cosmopolitan "polish" stems from China, to Tibet to Japan and outlying
> Indian territories. Against this India has a significance comparable to that of antique
> Hellenism. There are few conceptions transcending practical interests in Asia whose
> source would not finally have to be sought there. Particularly, all orthodox and
> heterodox salvation religions that could claim a role in Asia similar to that of
> Christianity are Indian. There is only one great difference, apart from local and
> pre-eminent exceptions – none of them succeeded in becoming the single dominating
> confession, as was the case for us in the Middle Ages after the peace of Westphalia.
>
> Asia was, and remains, in principle, the land of the free competition of religions,
> "tolerant" somewhat in the sense of late antiquity. That is to say, tolerant except
> for restrictions for reason of state, which, finally, also for us today remain the bound-
> ary of all religious toleration only with other consequences. [Weber 1916–17/
> 1967:329]

Weber weaves his contrasts and analogies by viewing all institutional levels,
historical periods, and interpretive themes simultaneously; he could endure
this. The symbolic dimension of comparison arises from the fact that the
boundaries of any unit shift as we move across systems. Again, "diocese," a
unit of territory and officialdom, is ecclesiastical in the case of Europe,
economic in India. Thus the boundaries of the "economic" and the "ecclesiastical" themselves shift. This dialectical rhythm recalls Durkheim only in his
more anthropological, less positivistic moments.

To savor such movement across cultures and history, consider Weber's
ideal-type of "tolerance" in the above passage stretching from Asia to medi-

eval Europe; let us stretch even further in a spirit of pastiche. How do we "measure" tolerance/intolerance in America? According to its own Enlightenment values of nationhood, America tolerates diverse sects and religions, save those advocating overthrow of the state or those whose religious practices interfere with civic standards deemed the province of the state (e.g., polygamy versus monogamy). Outside these parameters, American religion appears "tolerant" of religious diversity. Leaving aside all the issues this view begs, we can still compare relative intolerances by shifting our vantage from politics and religion to politics and language. Whether or not tolerant and pluralist in matters of religion, sect, and ethnicity (outside the color bar), America has been by doctrine intolerant in matters of language. Ours was the first national identity to project itself as a mechanical solidarity of citizens speaking the same language and required to prove it if they were born outside our sacred territory. America's partial religious heterodoxy should be considered together with this peculiar linguistic orthodoxy, perhaps even dogmatism. Indeed, recent demands concerning the rights of non-American-English speakers have registered with the impact of heresy in other cultures and times.

A shift into "language" from "religion" to interpret tolerance would be one way of effecting a Weberian roll into the New World from China, India, and the issues of Westphalia that I have cited. Space, divisible to the anthropologist, and Time, divisible to the historian, became transformable through Weber's ideal-types of "heredity," "charisma," "tolerance," and so forth. Ideal-types isolate extreme value components systematically; they form the semiotic underpinnings of Weber's studies that are both deliriously comparative and hauntingly specific.

The comparative dimension of Weber reveals as well that *verstehen* is more than intentionality or subjectivity, even in issues of "meaning." Weber demonstrates that systems of meaning pervade politics, economics, and arts just as they do religion. Here Weber resonates with the anthropologist's "culture": "Believing, with Max Weber, that man is an animal suspended in webs of significance he himself has spun, I take culture to be those webs, and the analysis of it to be therefore not an experimental science in search of law but an interpretive one in search of meaning" (C. Geertz 1973:5). Moreover, meaning is not merely the sum of subjectivities of "believers." Weber's interpretations of *verstehen* attach subjectivities to institutions, comparatively. His sprawling organic typologies of contrasts scan systematic variants for clues to more local meanings. Even for the closest description of concrete cases, Weber keeps in tune his operationalized ideal-types: "Thus for substantive reasons, we may hope to facilitate the presentation of an otherwise immensely multifarious subject matter by expediently constructed rational types," he insists, just after stipulating that these "substantive reasons" involve typology itself:

Such constructions make it possible to determine the typological locus of a historical phenomenon. They enable us to see if, in particular traits or in their total character, the phenomena approximate one of our constructions: to determine the degree of approximation of the historical phenomenon of the theoretically constructed type. To this extent, the construction is merely a technical aid which facilitates a more lucid arrangement and terminology. Yet, under certain conditions, a construction might mean more. For the rationality, in the sense of logical or teleological "consistency," of an intellectual-theoretical or practical-ethical attitude has and always has had power over man, however limited and unstable this power is and always has been in the face of other forces of historical life.

Religious interpretations of the world and ethics of religions created by intellectuals and meant to be rational have been strongly exposed to the imperative of consistency. The effect of the *ratio* . . . [1958a:324]

Here Weber postpones discussion of the parallels between the "rationalities" of so-called religious and so-called objective (or even scientific) interpretations of the world. He proceeds, rather, to confirm the value of ideal-types by investigating the most evasive aspects of religious systems: asceticism and mysticism. Elsewhere Weber demonstates how ideal-types penetrate areas of religious life more obviously content-laden and institution-bound; consider, for example, the comparison of theodicies:

One can explain suffering and injustice by referring to individual sin committed in a former life (the migration of souls), to the guilt of ancestors, which is avenged down to the third and fourth generation, or – the most principled – to the wickedness of all creatures *per se*. As compensatory promises, one can refer to hopes of the individual for a better life in the future in this world (transmigration of souls) or to hopes for the successors (Messianic realm), or to a better life in the hereafter (paradise).

The metaphysical conception of God and of the world, which the ineradicable demand for a theodicy called forth, could produce only a few systems of ideas on the whole – as we shall see, only three. These three gave rationally satisfactory answers to the questioning for the basis of the incongruity between destiny and merit: the Indian doctrine of Kharma, Zoroastrian dualism, and the predestination decree of the *deus abscondidus*. These solutions are rationally closed; in pure form, they are found only as exceptions. [1958a:275; cf. 358–9]

Any positivist history of religion can analyze the contents, doctrines, and institutions associated with explicit theodicies. The more dialectical dimension of Weber appears in "Religious Rejections of the World and Their Directions," which detects sociological space where it is least expected. He enters the specificities of diverse religions by placing in the forefront the nearly negative (asceticism) and the nearly vacant (mysticism). His achievement, here recalling Marx, was to discern social and cultural form amid doctrinal absences: Even mystics and ascetics are interest groups.

Weber's comparative typology of religions thus commenced with components ostensibly the most rarified and contextualized them by "treating the terms asceticism and mysticism as polar concepts" (1958a:325). He charted the variant ways society and institutions are believed to be circumvented by selflessness in direct touch with divinity (see Weber, 1914–20/1968, vol. 2:541–51). The paradoxical result is a richer sense of actual social and historical contexts than any single study of specific institutions and doctrines could supply. Weber never reduces mysticism or asceticism to mere compensatory reflexes to external social or historical conditions. Rather, he conveys a sense of something like an "organic solidarity" of social, religious, economic, political, and artistic forms as so many "cultural systems" posed against their denial – negatives like asceticism and mysticism. Here we glimpse, I think, the "elective affinity" between scholars like Weber on the one hand and Dumont or Hocart on the other (see Chapter 6). Weberian ideal-types are never simply imposed on the flux of time and cultures in some mechanical fashion. Instead, ideal-types emerge from juxtaposing dimensions such as asceticism/mysticism and from allowing the relative form they lend each other to reverberate through substantive creeds (e.g., theodicy). All dimensions of culture or history, even bureaucratization and rationalization, are dialectical. Ultimately, rationality is posed not as a natural reason producing inevitable Enlightenment but as a religious value, one that has a history, or rather histories. Weber then reveals its varying tonalities, both within a tradition and, most important for our purposes, across widespread historical and cultural cases.

Anthropologists' relative neglect of Weber may stem in part from his concentration on literate cultures and historical states from biblical to industrial times (but cf. Weber 1914–20/1968, vol. 2:367–9). To appreciate Weber's place in comparative anthropology we must trace an ideal-type, such as routinized bureaucracy, across its variations. Consider again China. In strongest contrast to the case of India, Weber emphasizes Chinese values of achievement and talent, gentleman-ideals, education, and the authority of literati. To a point, then, Chinese bureaucracy amalgamates ideals associated in the West with humanism and rationalism, Reformation, and Enlightenment. But Weber, ever the anthropologist, concludes his 1914 account of Chinese literati not on a note of convergence with Western developments but with a curious pattern that for centuries animated Chinese politics. Chinese literati may represent a self-serving status group of interested advisers, selected (ideally) by talent but to serve traditional ends, rational insofar as they promoted the gradual adjustment of an improved officialdom. But what literati are *not* is equally important. Weber's ultimate emphasis is unmistakable:

There remained only one major and permanent enemy of the literati: sultanism and the eunuch-system which supported it. The influence of the harem was therefore viewed with profound suspicion by the Confucians. Without insight into this struggle, Chinese history is most difficult to understand.

The constant struggle of the literati and sultanism, which lasted for two millennia, began under Shi-Hwang-Ti. It continued under all the dynasties, for of course energetic rulers continually sought to shake off their bonds to the cultured status group of the literati with the aid of eunuchs and plebeian parvenus . . . Every drought, inundation, eclipse of the sun, defeat in arms, and every generally threatening event at once placed power in the hands of the literati. For such events were considered the result of a branch of tradition and a desertion of the classic way of life...the result was always the cessation of the unclassical form of government, execution or banishment of the eunuchs. [1958a:442–3]

Literati, not eunuchs. In a few paragraphs Weber traces the literati/eunuch competition behind Chinese political dynamics to the close of the nineteenth century:

The harem system was of considerable danger because of the way in which successorship to the throne was ordered. The emperors who were not of age were under the tutelage of women; at times, this petticoat-government had come to be the very rule. The last Empress-Dowager, Tsu hsi, tried to rule with the aid of eunuchs. We will not discuss at this point the roles which Taoists and Buddhists have played in these struggles, which run through all of Chinese history – why and how far they have been natural coalitionists, specifically of the eunuchs, and how far they have been coalitionists by constellation...

In the conviction of the Confucians, the trust in magic which the eunuchs cultivated brought about all misfortune. Tao Mo in his Memorial of the year 1901 reproached the Empress that in the year 1875 the true heir to the throne had been eliminated through her fault and in spite of the censor's protest...Also the belief of the Empress and of numerous princes in the magical charisma of the Boxers, a belief which alone explains her whole policy, was certainly to be ascribed to the influence of eunuchs. On her death bed this impressive woman left as her counsel: (1) never again to let a woman rule in China, and (2) to abolish the eunuch system forever. [1958a:443]

The case of China is crucial because of the dominance of a rationalized officialdom in a traditional system. But the subtler typological point is whether a bureaucracy that emerges from competitions between literati and eunuchs can precisely be said to converge with bureaucracies developing from other values.

In the history of China eunuchs represent a social category marked by a form of abnegation (chastity, asexualism) that is put to very different use from ideal-type abnegation familiar in India or in the history of social divisions eventuating in Western bureaucracy. To follow Weber, we must contrast the social and cultural use of other sorts of nonprogeny or asceticism, whether in India-not-China or in medieval-Europe-not-India-not-China. M. Jay recalls Weber's "neo-Kantian skepticism about the irreconcilability of practical and theoretical reason" and contrasts his views with Marxian and romantic hopes alike: "Although recognizing the replacement of what he called 'substantive' reason by its formal counterpart, Weber was unable to entertain the possibility of its restoration. The 'rationalization' of the modern world was meant solely in a nonsubstantive sense. Weber, unlike some of his more romantic contemporaries, did not hope to turn the clock back, but it was clear that he greeted the world's disenchantment with little enthusiasm" (1973:260). Indeed, Weber resisted fossilizing bureaucracy, and he possibly regarded disenchantment with ironic resignation. Yet paradoxically, his detailed comparisons reinforce the impression that Weber would be among the last to admit that two systems superficially similar were profoundly so. He was ever the semiotic anthropologist.

Commentators' sense of Weber's pessimistic gloom has doubtless been intensified by rereading his work after the horrors of National Socialism. To appreciate the complex twists and turns in his view of cultures and history, we must locate rationality as both a religious value and a differential one. After reviewing this issue, I shall consider the solidarity such rationalism sustains in the process of social change: Durkheim may help here. Finally, I shall detect nonrational underpinnings of rational forms, linking Weber's work on music to comparative typologies. Indeed, Weber possibly considered *Religionssoziologie* itself a device to rescue Western institutions, intellectual life, and values from their own bureaucratization. This is the Weber invoked by Parsons, in a characteristic spurt of boosterism:

[Weber's] resolution of the trilemma [the historicistic aftermath of German Idealism: atomistic, sometimes rationalist utilitarianism; socialist thought; and Marxism] pointed in the direction of a new pattern of thinking in the area, of which an autonomous theoretical sociology was an essential ingredient...

I would go farther to suggest that Weber's "fourth position" could not be absorbed simply into another ideology, to compete on the same level with the other three. It is...impossible to classify Weber politically as a "conservative" in the older German tradition, as a "liberal" in the economic individualist sense, or as a "socialist." His intellectual breakthrough meant, however, more than a "neutral" personal position as among these ideological positions it was an implied assertion that the time would come when these old alignments would no longer be meaningful. To use the phrase made current in the United States recently by Daniel Bell, Weber heralded "the end of ideology."...

He understood, as hardly any of his contemporaries did, the fact and nature of the break-up of the older system...I cannot refrain from feeling that the emergence of the science of [comparative] sociology, of which I regard Max Weber as one of the very few true founders, is a harbinger of these great changes, and that our science may well be destined to play a major role, not only in its primary task of understanding the social and cultural world we live in...but...in actually shaping that world. [Parsons 1971:46–50][11]

Religion and rationalism

For Weber the rationalism of bureaucratic institutions remains a religious value. The disenchantment behind rationalism is itself a kind of asceticism, organized into what we might call the "mechanical solidarity" of a reactionary sect, rallied round a charismatic leader. We underread Weber if we confuse rationalism with secularism or rationalization with secularization. Rationalism implies an extra level of differentiation of religious legitimacy: prophet over and against establishment priest or humanist against cleric. The result can hardly be called secular, even if the agents of rationalization claim it so. Here, then, is Weber's famous ideal-typical account:

When religious virtuosos have combined into an active asceticist sect, two aims are completely attained: the disenchantment of the world and the blockage of the path to salvation by a flight from the world. The path to salvation is turned away from a contemplative "flight from the world" and towards an active ascetic "work in this world." If one disregards the small rationalist sects, such as are found all over the world, this has been attained only in the great church and sect organizations of Occidental and asceticist Protestantism...Partly the social environment exerted an influence...Partly, however – and just as strongly – the intrinsic character of Christianity exerted an influence: the supra-mundane God and the specificity of the means and paths of salvation as determined historically, first by Israelite prophecy and the thora doctrine. [1958a:290]

In Weber's interpretation, active asceticism takes wing both as an internalizable value and as an ideal-type that parcels out the world religions and their historical epochs as well. I cite his panoramic vision panoramically:

No matter how much the "world" as such is religiously devalued and rejected as being creatural and a vessel of sin, yet psychologically the world is all the more affirmed as the theatre of God-willed activity in one's worldly "calling." For this inner-worldly asceticism rejects the world in the sense that it despises and taboos the values of dignity and beauty, of the beautiful frenzy and the dream, purely secular power, and the purely worldly pride of the hero. Asceticism outlawed these values as competitors of the kingdom of God. Yet precisely because of this rejection, asceticism did not fly from the world, as did contemplation. Instead, asceticism has wished to rationalize the world ethnically in accordance with God's commandments. It has therefore remained oriented towards the world in a more specific and thoroughgoing sense than did the naive "affirmation of the world" of unbroken humanity, for instance, in Antiquity and in lay-Catholicism [contrast Durkheim's eventual sense of essentially "broken," that is, divided, humanity, even at the most primitive level]. In inner-worldly asceticism, the grace and the chosen state of the religiously qualified man prove themselves in everyday life. To be sure, they do so not in the everyday life as it is given, but in methodical and rationalized routine-activities of workaday life in the service of the Lord. Rationally raised into a vocation, everyday conduct becomes the locus for proving one's state of grace. The Occidental sects of the religious virtuosos have fermented the methodical rationalization of conduct, including economic conduct. These sects have not constituted values for the longing to escape from the senselessness of work in this world, as did the Asiatic communities of the ecstatics: contemplative, orgiastic, or apathetic. [Weber 1958a:291]

Thus far it sounds as if Weber were reifying rationalism and identifying it with everyday life, as Calvinists themselves might have. (We have cited scholars like Dumont who subsequently would find more sociological implications in the fact of contemplative renunciation.) But simply by pursuing Weber's own reflections, we can see that he never really reifies, at least not for long; because he always retypologizes. What sounds like a singular form is actually varied forms; what sounds like a convergence in history always trails threads of its contrastive pasts:

We have to remind ourselves in advance that "rationalism" may mean very different things. It means one thing if we think of the kind of rationalization the systematic thinker performs on the image of the world: an increasing theoretical mastery of reality by means of increasingly precise and abstract concepts. Rationalism means another thing if we think of the methodical attainment of a definite given and practical end by means of an increasingly precise calculation of adequate means. These types of rationalism are very different, in spite of the fact that ultimately they belong inseparately [*sic*] together. Similar types may be distinguished even within the intellectual comprehension of reality; for instance, the differences between English Physics and Continental Physics has been traced back to such a type difference within the comprehension of reality. The rationalization of life conduct with which we have to deal here can assume varied forms. [1958a:293]

(The next paragraph treats Confucianism, utilitarianism, and Renaissance artistic canons with their *naturalis ratio* that ultimately prevailed over partial Platonizing mysticism!) Finally, how Weber's views of rationalism themselves relate to a religious philosophy of history is suggested by Parsons in a posthumous publication on the "intricate parallelism between the Christian myths and both the economic myths of Marxism and the ideology of liberal economies":

In the Marxian analysis, the capitalist or the bourgeois class are curious, robot-like human beings. They seem to be conceived as actuated purely by the rational pursuit of self-interest defined in terms of the profit motive. But anything so human as "labor," especially with its presumption of suffering, is denied to this capitalistic robot. What Weber did was through his concept of the calling and its imputation to the Puritan doctrine, radically to change this situation. Precisely the capitalist was actuated by the motive to work, and to work not for profit but for disinterested achievement, in the background of which lay the obligation to contribute to the building of the Kingdom of God on Earth. Since Marx had lent the members of his working class a monopoly of not merely the necessity to work but the ethical virtues of the attendant suffering, Weber threw a kind of bombshell into the Marxian camp by depriving the proletariat of their monopoly of the all-important virtue. From his point of view, proletarians and bourgeois were "all in the same boat." Exploitation, instead of being the act of the impersonally mechanistic operation of profit-oriented self-interest through the market, would have to be dealt with in a much more complicated and "human" setting as a function of more complicated social variables than the highly simple Marxian formulae could deal with...for Weber, whoever lived in the capitalist society, in *whatever* class status, was to be condemned to suffering, that is, the kind of suffering entailed in the commitment to work. However that may be, work as a human fate was no longer the monopoly of the exploited proletariat but was general to all members of society. [Parsons 1979:451–2]

"Prophets," I would add, "included." This penetrating commentary reveals in Weber (and in Parsons himself) a more dialectical philosophy less limited to structural-functionalist mechanism, than critics – including the most insightful ones (e.g., Murphy 1971:12–13) ordinarily allow. In sum, even the famous end-specific, goal-oriented *Zweckrationalität* type of rationalism – in which Weber's own research and sense of *Beruf* ironically is implicated – conforms to religious values (cf. Peacock 1975). Value-freedom itself does not escape this fact.

Rationalism through social change

These points may be clarified by focusing on a basic organizational context of rationalization: the sectlike cult. It is here, I think, that Durkheim and Weber can be brought to bear on each other (at the risk of oversynthesizing certain strands of their texts).[12] Weber argued that social change is produced by a reformed community of actors, bound by a religious sense of homogeneity, who implement the message of a charismatic leader. Functionaries and routinization come later. Weber's preferred historical cases entail reactionary movements which may be either fraternal (monastic) or familial (Puritan, bourgeois); but they are all relatively ascetic (celibate, monogamous or, at least, "faithful"): more regulated than hedonistic. Their members become status groups with interests as much economic as religious. Whether entrepreneurs or utopianists, they routinize prophetic charisma in institutional forms, ultimately producing bureaucracy itself, which joins asceticism in rational ends (e.g., profit rather than expenditure) with asceticism in stratigraphic values. Bureaucracies homogenize goals and values differentiated only by simple grades. All members may aspire to the same highest rank or mark; there are ideally no vertical divisions. Moreover, the uniform aim of all sectors is efficient maximization of a simple end without ambiguity, which is analogous to victory in military strategy or increased profits in capitalist enterprises. A member advances by leaving the ranks unruffled. A bureaucracy can imagine conflict of goals within its ranks no more than a Protestant group could imagine nonconformity within its community. Thus, just as reformed sects are the most mechanically solidary of communities (and are initially constituted reactionarily), so a bureaucracy is the most mechanically solidary – orthodox? – of stratifications.

As we saw in the earlier Durkheim of *The Division of Labor*, mechanical solidarity binds individuals through their sense of sameness to some organizational mechanism. In anthropology this theme was developed by Radcliffe-Brown and others who considered the basic "problematic" of society to be how members cohere in corporate groups. Durkheim eventually recognized that the solidarity required a collective representation that organized the sense of sameness in a system of contrasts; this theme was accentuated by his French successors. Now, Weber likewise posed a mechanical solidarity; but instead of making it the basis of stasis (stability in positive terms, or stagnation in negative terms) as functionalists and structural functionalists building on the early Durkheim were inclined to do, Weber made it the crux of historical change. Something like mechanical solidarity characterizes the identity of the reformed community whose leader embodies the thrust of meaning and values available to dissidents of this time and place. The capacity to forge a mechanical solidarity for an enthusiastic, reactionary community is for Weber a dynamic, in fact a dramatic, process. In Weber's theory of action, religious symbols can legitimate a leader's charisma because they relate to the entire repertory of meaningful motivations; and it is this repertory that Weber continually "tracks" at the typological and comparative level.

I would tie Weber's vivid sense of dynamics to Durkheim's acute view of consensus as follows: Weber's typological level of interpretation recalls Durkheim's organic solidarity level of social systems. Weber's typologies differentially order the possible sources of mechanical solidarity activated by groups as history unfolds. Weber used the concept of prophet and of (biblical) tribes to epitomize the history of cultic communities surrounding charismatic figures. Durkheim, on the other hand, used the concept of (aboriginal) tribe, divided into clans, to epitomize the organic solidarity that is the systematic backdrop to any mechanically solidary component. Having corrected mistaken views on the solidarity of *Naturvölken*, the Durkheimian tradition stretches from tribal clans (generally exogamous and totemic) to caste ideals that imagine divisions of labor as an organic solidarity (of purity/pollution inequalities). Within a single clan, or within a single occupational caste, cohesion appears mechanical; but this fact is intelligible only in light of the system of different positions that lends all clans or castes reciprocal value. In short, such systems of economic ethics entail a process of mutual valuation. As one recent scholar has put the matter: "What it implies is that economic value is Saussurean, it is the differential standing of a given object in a system of meaningful relationships. (This would only be fair, since Saussure understood linguistic value by the economic.) The effect of the process is to establish structures of differentiation between goods [and between services] which are isomorphic with, as they substantialize, the categorical distinctions among men" (Sahlins 1976a:36). Weber, too, posed so-called traditional societies as something like organic solidarities: enchanted, occupationally divided, harboring mutually complementary status groups. For Weber religious reformism's universalistic, everyday rationalism runs contrary to traditionalism. Moreover, like Weber, Durkheim opposed idealism, utilitarianism, and socialism alike; both men rejected the latter outlook in particular for similar reasons: "Advocacy of the interests of the working class as opposed to those of the bourgeoisie, Durkheim states, is in fact secondary to the prime concern of socialism to realize the centralized regulation of production" (Giddens 1971:100, 97). Both feared the portent for social life of any Hegelian dimensions of the state that resulted in a bureaucracy subordinating the individual, with no secondary groups (such as Durkheim's "occupational associations") intervening.

Once we have acknowledged that Durkheim and Weber shared anxieties about the state yet resisted socialism, we can extend Parson's project of interrelating their theories by stipulating a basic contrast of their comparativist research: reformist (and prophetic) views of society and change on the one hand versus "divisioned" (whether in tribal clans or occupational castes) views of society and change on the other. Weber's ethical, ascetic reformism embodies something like Durkheim's mechanical solidarity and an ethos of homogeneity. It assumes different religious guises: Jewish, Protestant, Islamic, Confucian, Hindu-bhakti, Democratic nation-state, Marxist; and it can arise in nonliterate tribal situations as well, in the form of revitalistic movements or other reactions. Weber considers reformism to be most thoroughgoing in ascetic cults of the Book associated with world religions. Thanks to Durkheim, we can see that what is reformed away is organic solidarity – ideals by which systems persist as interrelated divisions – so conspicuous in tribal exogamy or in caste occupations.

It is thus Weber who perceives the force of mechanical solidarities in history. For all Durkheim's scruples about modern states, Weber is obliged to question more profoundly the fate of the temporary, charismatic vitality of reformist communities as rational pursuits become routine, ultimately concentrated into bureaucracies, sometimes totalitarian ones. Mindful of the strengths of traditionalist systems, Weber traces rationalism wherever it occurs, most intensively in homogenized communities professing universalistic ethics that would level all human differences (marginally preserved, however, in the contrasting interests of status groups). The hopes of such groups are utopian: beautiful dreams; their fate, Weber proves, is bureaucracy.

Natural irrationalism: Weber on Western music

In strongest contrast to Marx, whose historical optimism equated ultimate rationalism with classlessness, Weber's irony assumed all the qualities of prescience. Yet it strikes me that, like Durkheim, Weber maintained, if little hope, at least a little suspicion that the whole of human history might not pass altogether out of enchantment. We recall that Durkheim's prescriptions for revived organic solidarity played against a specter: *anomie*, rabid, egoistic individualism – not the originality of social institutions (per Hobbes), but the pathology. Durkheim's plans to restore occupational groups suggest a *jajmani*like system minus exclusivistic rankings; a totality of tasks with each group reciprocally and perhaps cyclically serving the other: Brahmin today, barber tomorrow. So Weber too, despite his forebodings, saluted a rational order that appeared like an organic solidarity of differences neatly arranged, bureaucratized, yet charismatically led and continually reenchanted. The example stems from one exceptional sector of experience: Western music. I shall argue that, for Weber, nonrationality underpinning even rationalized Western music is analogous to the nonrationality behind the historical and cultural variations of ideal-types, which is the rhyme behind the reasons why he proclaimed *comparative* interpretation the promise of the West's intellectual future.[13]

Weber's concern with music is familiar to readers of *The Protestant Ethic*, where it is introduced with art and architecture as a colorful digression from a discussion of rational legal canons:

The musical ear of other peoples has probably been even more sensitively developed than our own, certainly not less so. Polyphonic music of various kinds has been widely distributed over the earth. The co-operation of a number of instruments and also the singing of parts have existed elsewhere. All our rational tone intervals have been known and calculated. But rational harmonious music, both counterpoint and harmony, formation of the tone material on the basis of three triads with the harmonic third; our chromatics and enharmonics, not interpreted in terms of space, but, since the Renaissance, of harmony; our orchestra, with its string quartet as a nucleus, and the organization of ensembles of wind instruments; our bass accompaniment; our system of notation, which has made possible the composition and production of modern musical works, and thus their very survival; our sonatas, symphonies, operas; and finally, as means to all these, our fundamental instruments, the organ, piano, violin, etc.; all these things are known only in the Occident, although programme music, tone poetry, alteration of tones and chromatics have existed in various musical traditions as means of expression. [1904–5/1958b:14–15]

For Weber there is no Enlightenment mathesis behind either canons or harmonics, nothing natural that they directly code. In fact, at the base of Western music lies a fundamental nonrationality that produces the tensions, indeed the meaning, in even the most rationalized harmonics, orchestral organization, and so forth. The nonrationality – and I do not mean mere emotionalism – is inescapable. Significantly, Weber alludes to it when he outlines varieties of rationalization in world religions. Obviously, religions themselves envision irrationalities: Asceticism and mysticism are prime evidence of this fact. But Weber's point here is that religious organizations are built on nonrational foundations; this critical passage requires studious rereading:

Many more varieties of belief have, of course, existed. Behind them always lies a stand towards something in the actual world which is experienced as specifically "senseless." Thus, the demand has been implied: that the world order in its totality is, could and should somehow be a meaningful "cosmos". . .

The general result of the modern form of thoroughly rationalizing the conception of the world and the way of life, theoretically and practically, in a purposive manner, has been that religion has been shifted into the realm of the irrational. . .On the one hand, the calculation of consistent rationalism has not easily come out with nothing left over. In music, the Pythagorean "comma" resisted complete rationalization oriented to tonal physics. The various great systems of music of all peoples and ages have differed in the manner in which they have either covered up or bypassed this inescapable irrationality or, on the other hand, put irrationality into the service of the richness of tonalities. The same has seemed to happen to the theoretical conception of the world, only far more so; and above all, it has seemed to happen to the rationalization of practical life. The various great ways of leading a rational and methodical life have been characterized irrational presuppositions which have been accepted simply as "given" and which have been incorporated into such ways of life. . .

Furthermore, the irrational elements in the rationalization of reality have been the *loci* to which the irrepressible quest of intellectualism for the possession of supernatural values has been compelled to retreat. That is the more so the more denuded of irrationality the world appears to be. [Weber 1958a:281–2]

Here in 1915 Weber's prose sweeps on until we are not sure whether he is discussing specific irrationalities in the contents of particular religious systems or that Pythagorean comma: the prime nonrationality that prevents any musical rationalization from converging with a natural mathematical system. In 1922, posthumously, Weber's writing went on to address music proper. It is here that the Pythagorean comma comes to represent the guarantee, in music at least, of a dramatic tension between rationality and nonrationality:

> Weber called attention to the fact that harmonic chord music resting on a scale permitting a maximum of ordered relations does not in the diatonic scale have a closed logical system. From the very beginning a nonsymmetric division of sounds is evident. The octave is unequally divided into the fourth and the fifth. Harmonic division of the fourth is omitted and the interval of the seventh is left aside.
>
> When one ascends or descends in rows or circles of octaves, followed by rows of fifths or other intervals, these divisions can never meet on the same note...When in accord with harmonic rules one forms the seventh,...the entire logical structure tends to come apart at the seams. A suppressed sense of excitement attaches to Weber's discussion of this problem that transcends any mere passing curiosity over the fact that there is an uneliminatable logical looseness which appears at the heart of harmonic chord music. It cannot be dismissed, apparently, with the question, What's the difference? [Martindale and Riedel 1958:xxv]

A similar excitement appears whenever Weber traces an ideal-type, such as the dread bureaucracy, toward its richer tonalities (whether literati or eunuchs). The image of music's fundamental illogicality, even in Western harmonics and the increasingly rational Western orchestral and sonata forms, is the last metaphor Weber offers to characterize the historical and cultural variation of ideal-types. I am simply suggesting that, for Weber, religious–economic institutions reveal – through the comparison of their particularities – their own Pythagorean comma:

> In Western music the drama of the experience of Western man is re-enacted...
>
> Thus, harmonic chord music rests on a rationally divided system of basic tone relationships, but basic to the system is a residual irrational division the consequences of which form a primary object of theoretical reflection for Occidental musical theorists.
>
> The intervals of the diatonic scale have been decided by tonality and harmony. While sounds may be perfect according to the pythagorean theory of acoustical laws, when sounded together they may produce unpleasant effects. The introduction of harmony led to a change in the intervals established by the Greeks. That between the D and E and between G and A were lessened and that between E and F and A and C were increased. The diatonic scale with C as a keynote already had two semitones. The addition of the black keys of the piano or organ suggests a continuous succession of semitones. However, the semitones do not represent a continuous succession of regular tone distances. A given tone like A when counted downward from the tone above A, which is B, is not identical with the first. A-sharp will be a little below the second, B-flat. This difference is a pythagorean comma. [Martindale and Riedel 1958:xxvii]

Adopting the hermeneutic terms sampled in Chapter 2, we might say that the "Pythagorean comma" is the name of the irreducible fact that ascending–

descending tones and formal–logical harmonics are out of cog. No table of conversions can directly eliminate their constitutive difference. Similarly, there is a discrepancy between any "harmonics" and the "tonalities" of contrasting cultures. Western intellectuals must thus systematically compare social, economic, and religious meanings – ourselves included – in order to sense, if not to understand, our own Pythagorean comma. Or have I simply appropriated Weber into symbolic anthropology? If so, I can only say the door has been opened by others:

> It lay in Weber's nature to master all material which was observable for the construction of ideal types in the sociology of culture and history, and there is no doubt that if he had lived longer, he would have mastered the ethnographical material too. He had already begun to do this in the analyses contained in the second and third volumes of the *Religionssociologie* and in his amazing writings about the rational and sociological bases of music. These are lines for further research. [Muhlmann 1971:251]

Weber's study of music (written about 1911) suggests that no ideal-type, even routinized bureaucracy, can ever quite collapse into one of its actualizations, because any ideal-type is less mathesis than Pythagorean comma. Moreover, the Pythagorean comma is, if anything, an absence. Rationality is removed from something it cannot encompass. This is the true source of science that is *wertfrei*. More sentimentally, is it too much to wonder whether Weber's work on music inserted a caveat even in the specter of historical fossilization? If disenchanted rationality appeared epitomized in institutions organized like the Prussian army, a variation on this theme was nevertheless the Prussian orchestra. In terms of regulated, ranked divisions of labor, orchestra and army appear nearly identical. But in terms of meaning, *verstehen*, and the source of their leaders' charismas: *There's* the difference.

Of Mauss and Marx

Weber never wrote a well-wrought book.

> Guenther Roth, *Introduction to Weber*

Lest this talk of religion and music sound ethereal, we should recall that praxis, infrastructure, and the hard realities of social existence are themselves symbolic, replaceable, convertible, underdetermined. Even what appears to be sheer survival is symbolic. For example, the natural reason for wearing a coat appears to be to conserve body heat. But there is no natural reason for wearing a *mink* coat rather than a *cloth* coat, or for *wearing* a coat and not *moving* south, or for *everyone* to desire the heaviest coat rather than to divide labor so that only a *few* souls need venture out in extreme weather. For everyone to need to wear (as against some other act) a coat (as against some other item) is conventional. "Coats," moreover, are never abstract but always good or bad, men's or women's, of different styles, colors, cuts, and so forth.

I shall trace the conviction that essential items of production (enmeshed in basic social relations) partake of the ideal-symbolic to Mauss's theory of exchange inspired by exotic institutions. Finally, I might note that as symbols, coats can be supercharged with meaning, as in Gogol's "The Overcoat."

I mention coats less because Gogol did than because Marx did.[14] Few would quarrel with deeming an elaborated metaphorical overcoat symbolic; but many would deny that coats are symbolic in and of themselves. Yet here is Marx on commodities, in particular, on coats:

At first sight a commodity presented itself to us as a complex of two things – use-value and exchange-value. Later on, we saw also that labor, too, possesses the same two-fold nature; for, so far as it finds expression in value, it does not possess the same characteristics that belong to it as a creator of use-values. I was the first to point out and to examine critically this two-fold nature of the labor contained in commodities. As this point is the pivot on which a clear comprehension of Political Economy turns, we must go more into detail.

Let us take two commodities such as a coat and 10 yards of linen, and let the former be double the value of the latter, so that if 10 yards of linen $=$ W, the coat $= 2W$.

The coat is a use-value that satisfies a particular want. Its existence is the result of a special sort of productive activity, the nature of which is determined by its aim, mode of operation, subject, means, and result. The labor, whose utility is thus represented by the value in use of its product, or which manifests itself by making its product a use-value, we call useful labor. In this connection we consider only its useful effect.

As the coat and the linen are two qualitatively different use-values, so also are the two forms of labor that produce them, tailoring and weaving. Were these two objects not qualitatively different, not produced respectively by labor of different quality, they could not stand to each other in the relation of commodities. Coats are not exchanged for coats, one use-value is not exchanged for another of the same kind. [Marx 1867/1967:41]

Now, whether "particular wants" satisfied even by use-values are at base culturally *constituted* (and thus symbolic) or natural, utilitarian *givens* remains an issue dividing theories of exchange, including various Marxist and Marxian ones. But here let us pass directly to the exchange-value of commodities which, in Marx's *Capital*, is not secondary to use-value but its opposite and complement.

Commodities come into the world in the shape of use-values, articles, or goods, such as iron, linen, corn, etc. This is their plain, homely, bodily form. They are, however, commodities, *only because they are something two-fold, both objects of utility, and, at the same time, depositories of value*. They manifest themselves therefore as commodities, or have the form of commodities, only in so far as they have two forms, a physical or natural form and a value-form. [1867/1967:47; emphasis added]

(This twofold nature of commodities is as irreducible as Saussure's twofold nature of linguistic signs, to be discussed shortly.) Here in Marx the plain and homely is *completed* as value-form. Marx then injects the famous equation between a "purely social reality" (with reference to which exchange-value is determined) and labor:

Turn and examine a single commodity, by itself, as we will, yet in so far as it remains an object of value, it seems impossible to grasp it. If, however, we bear in mind that the value of commodities has a purely social reality, and that they acquire this reality only in so far as they are expressions or embodiments of one identical social substance, viz., human labor, it follows as a matter of course, that value can only manifest itself in the social relation of commodity to commodity. In fact we started from exchange-value, or the exchange relation of commodities, in order to get at the value that lies hidden behind it. We must now return to this form under which value first appeared to us.

Every one knows, if he knows nothing else, that commodities have a value-form common to them all, and presenting a marked contrast with the varied bodily forms of their use-values. I mean their money-form. [1867/1967:47]

Here Marx implies that exchange-value is autonomous; he points out the noncoincidence between use-value and money-form, which latter measures commodity against commodity. But Marx feels he must preserve a substantive homogeneous reference – "labor" – behind exchange-value. The view of human labor as "one identical social substance" is the modicum of Enlightenment philosophy and classical economics concealed in Marx that explains his approach to the division of labor. (Like Chomsky's idea of deep structure, which I will consider later, Marx's idea of labor is uniformitarian.) This aspect of Marx's views has been challenged in subsequent critical theory:

Not only did the Frankfurt School leave the vestiges of an orthodox Marxist theory of ideology behind, it also implicitly put Marx in the Enlightenment tradition. Marx's overemphasis on the centrality of labor as man's mode of self-realization, which Horkheimer had questioned as early as *Dämmerung*, was the primary reason for this argument. Implicit in the reduction of man to an *animal laborans*, he charged, was the reification of nature as a field for human exploitation. If Marx had his way, the entire world would be turned into a "giant workhouse." [Jay 1973:259]

What Durkheim would later view as differential specializations in light of an ideal totality of skills and tasks, Marx viewed as camouflaged coercion and distorted expropriation. No one, I think, would deny that coercion and expropriation pervade many economies, including the old factory system. But the more general question is what this fact has to do with tailors/weavers. In Durkheimian terms tailoring and weaving are not two distortions of an "identical social substance"; rather, they are opposed skills that would have no value (or use!) without a cultural insistence on fitted clothes. This value establishes their reciprocity; this reciprocity constitutes their value. In the matter of coats, then, neither weaving nor tailoring is sufficient or complete; at this level the division of labor guarantees a share in production for two specializations; because *culturally* coats are what must be worn. With ponchos no "need" for tailors; with hides, no need for weavers. *"Coats" are a commodity that integrates weaving/tailoring into a scheme of mutual necessity.* Though the means of their manufacture, distribution, and conversion into money-form may introduce many bleaker dimensions, even these do not reduce labor to "one identical social substance."

When Marx occasionally set aside his uniformitarian sense of labor, he precociously formulated the systematic basis of commodities as exchange-values. But he at once purged the very thought from his prose:

A commodity appears, at first sight, a very trivial thing, and easily understood. Its analysis shows that it is, in reality, a very queer thing, abounding in metaphysical subtleties and theological niceties. So far as it is a value in use, there is nothing mysterious about it, whether we consider it from the point of view that by its properties it is capable of satisfying human wants, or from the point that those properties are the product of human labor. It is as clear as noon-day, that man, by his industry, changes the forms of the materials furnished by Nature, in such a way as to make them useful to him. The form of wood, for instance, is altered, by making a table out of it. Yet, for all that, the table continues to be that common, every-day thing, wood. But, so soon as it steps forth as a commodity, it is changed into something transcendent. It not only stands with its feet on the ground, but, in relation to all other commodities, it stands on its head, and evolves out of its wooden brain grotesque ideas, far more wonderful than "table-turning" ever was.

The mystical character of commodities does not originate, then, therefore, in their use-value. [Marx 1867/1967:71]

(What does the ideologist do? – he writes. What does he write? – rhetoric. What does he desire? – action. What does the ideologist still do? – he writes.) This sequence of ideas brings us to Mauss.

Like Durkheim's "division of labor," Marcel Mauss's "exchange" principle assumes that "societies" are total systems wherein items *from others* (whether utensils, foodstuffs, spouses) are valued in light of prohibitions against each unit's producing for itself. This principle is embodied in Mauss's celebrated theory of "the gift" with its implicit corrective to earlier political economy. For Mauss the special attributes of items exchanged arise not from anything mysterious or irrational but from the irreducible value attached to exchange. Moreover, I would propose a corollary using Marx's own derisive terms quoted above: Use-value is as "mystical" as exchange-value. This fact becomes clear in the ethnographic cases examined by Mauss where no substantive, homogeneous "labor" exists independent of its socially divided forms.[15]

What, then, is the significance of Mauss's "archaic" economic institutions that lack markets and specialized economic roles? In such generalized systems the basis of political economy is not Marx's near-utilitarian theory of labor but something more like his despised specter of commodities. I shall insist on this point in Mauss's *The Gift* by substituting a single word in Marx's famous inscription, slogan, or "general formula" for bourgeois production. Proclaims Marx: *The circulation of commodities is the starting point of capital*. In light of Mauss we rewrite this statement: *The circulation of commodities is the starting point of culture*. Moreover in the revised slogan, the concept of commodities retains those twofold characteristics Marx himself emphasized. In this view, however, what Marx called exchange-value in the realm of commodities lies behind every item produced and every act of production and transaction underlying total social "prestations." The point appears in a central passage from *The Gift*:

In the systems of the past we do not find simple exchange of goods, wealth and produce through markets established among individuals. For it is groups, and not individuals, which carry on exchange, make contracts, and are bound by obligations; the persons represented in the contracts are moral persons – clans, tribes, and families; the groups, or the chiefs as intermediaries for the groups, confront and oppose each other. Further, what they exchange is not exclusively goods and wealth, real and personal property, and things of economic value. They exchange rather courtesies, entertainments, ritual, military assistance, women, children, dances, and feasts; and fairs in which the market is but one element and the circulation of wealth but one part of a wide and enduring contract. Finally, although the prestations and counter-prestations take place under a voluntary guise they are in essence strictly obligatory, and their sanction is private or open warfare. We propose to call this the system of *total prestations*. Such institutions seem to us to be best represented in the alliance of pairs of phratries in Australian and North American tribes, where ritual, marriages, succession to wealth, community of right and interest, military and religious rank and even games all form part of one system and presuppose the collaboration of the two moieties of the tribe. [Mauss 1925/1967:3–4]

Mauss, like Durkheim, was most concerned to challenge the principles of natural economy or utilitarianism:

We have repeatedly pointed out how this economy of gift-exchange fails to conform to the principles of so-called natural economy or utilitarianism. The phenomenon in the economic life of the people we have studied (and they are good representatives of the great neolithic stage of civilization) and the survivals of these traditions in societies closer to ours and even in our own custom, are disregarded in the schemes adopted by the few economists who have tried to compare the various forms of economic life . . .

Here is the answer to the question already posed by Durkheim about the religious origin of the notion of economic value. The facts also supply answers to a string of problems about the forms and origins of what is so badly termed exchange – the barter or *permutatio* of useful articles. In the view of cautious Latin authors in the Aristotelian tradition and their *a priori* economic history, this is the origin of the division of labor. On the contrary, it is something other than utility which makes goods circulate in these multifarious and fairly enlightened societies. Clans, age groups, and sexes, in view of the many relationships ensuing from contracts between them, are in a state of perpetual economic effervescence which has little about it that is materialistic; it is much less prosaic than our sale and purchase, hire of services and speculations. [1925/1967:69–70]

As we saw above, elements of "natural economy" characterized Marx's notion of substantive labor as well. Looking back at Marx from Mauss, one would almost call Marx's theory of labor a tenet of formalist economics and his insights into the exchange-value of commodities a promise of substantivist economics. Regardless, the tension between Marx's "twofold" nature of commodities has fueled many debates between Marxists, Marxians, structuralists, and others. For our purpose, Marx's sense of commodities provides an early glimpse of symbolic principles of exchange; only his need to decry the factory system precluded his sufficiently generalizing the principle. Rather, he insisted:

A commodity is therefore a mysterious thing, simply because in it the social character of men's labor appears to them as an objective character stamped upon the product of that labor; because the relation of the producers to the sum total of their own labor is presented to them as a social relation, existing not between themselves, but between the products of their labor. This is the reason why the products of labor became commodities, social things whose qualities are at the same time perceptible and imperceptible by the senses. [Marx 1867/1967:72]

Durkheim, Mauss, and their followers have argued that whatever such "mystery" may be, it is not precisely the invention of any particular social economy (e.g., capitalism), because a similar dimension characterizes exchange and production from the start. In fact, exchange and production ultimately cannot be distinguished, because everything is produced as a consequence of its value as an item of exchange (recall tailoring/weaving). Even in the most rudimentary economic system, needs are determined culturally and socially, not individually or naturally. Following this line of thought, we can credit Marx with having perceived a fundamental property of tribal consciousness without, however, being able to realize it:

There is a physical relation between physical things. But it is different with commodities. There, the existence of the things *qua* commodities, and the value-relation between the products of labor which stamps them as commodities, have absolutely no connection with their physical properties and with the material relations arising therefrom. There it is a definite social relation between men, that assumes, in their eyes, the fantastic form of a relation between things. In order, therefore, to find an analogy, we must have recourse to the mist-enveloped regions of the religious world. In that world the productions of the human brain appear as independent beings endowed with life, and entering into relation both with one another and the human race. So it is in the world of commodities with the products of men's hands. This I call the Fetishism which attaches itself to the products of labor, so soon as they are produced as commodities, and which is therefore inseparable from the production of commodities.

This Fetishism of commodities has its origin, as the foregoing analysis has already shown, in the peculiar social character of the labor that produces them. [Marx 1867/1967:72]

Had Marx consistently recognized the twofold dimension that characterizes products of labor as commodities, had he not yearned for use-value pure and simple, for commodities purged of their commoditiness, he might have seen "fetishism" more thoroughly as "totemism." Totemic schemes inject precisely this mediating code – social reactions between men conceptualized as relations between things (and I hasten to add, vice versa) – but with no intrinsic inequality and no distinction between use-value and exchange-value or between labor and life. In such schemes anything merely kept or private is valueless.

Mauss's concept of exchange thwarts Marx's simple view of commodity Fetishism as a mist-enveloped false consciousness. To appreciate the force of

John
Hawkins

this view, notice how Edmund Leach, in an interesting passage stipulating the proper locus for distinguishing functionalist from more dialectical theories of value, overlooks the fundamental distinction between Marx's and Mauss's sense of the sacred and religious:

Both Radcliffe-Brown and Malinowski tend to assume that economic value depends upon utility rather than scarcity, and they attempt to distinguish ritual value as something other than economic value. Radcliffe-Brown shows that the Andamanese attached "ritual value" to objects (including foods) that were scarce luxuries, but he makes an unnecessary mystery of this fact. Karl Marx had a much clearer understanding of what is, after all, our common experience. Marx observed that the value of commodities in the market is quite different from the value of the same goods considered as objects of utility. He distinguishes the extra value that goods acquire by becoming market commodities as "fetishistic value". . . This concept is closely akin to Radcliffe-Brown's "ritual value," though in Marx's argument the magical element is only an aspect of the commodity value, rather than the value as a whole. Furthermore, where Radcliffe-Brown urged that ritual is to the advantage of society, Marx claimed that it is to the disadvantage of the individual producer. The Marxist thesis is that in the activities of the secular market – where all values are supposed to be measured by the strictest canons of rationality – judgements are in fact influenced by mystical nonrational criteria. A full generation later Mauss [1867/1967] developing his general theory of gift exchange from an entirely different viewpoint, reached an identical conclusion. Exchanges that *appear* to be grounded in secular, rational, utilitarian needs turn out to be compulsory acts of a ritual kind in which the objects exchanged are the vehicles of mystical power.
[Leach 1968:522]

Leach's eliding of Marx and Mauss is itself quasi-functionalist, a fact that helps drive home the thoroughness of Mauss's concept of exchange. For Mauss, gifts are not irrational and mystical but religious and social. He fulfills Durkheim's arguments by showing that the elementary economy is a system of exchange, just as the elementary social organization and natural classification is a system of totemism. Economies, that is, exchange systems, are, from any individualistic vantage, prealienated. Their parties (divisions) stand in culturally defined, mutually contrastive need of each other's specialization – like moieties. In Mauss's economies, unlike Marx's, there is no oneness, no whole-man, no uniformitarian rationality to be nostalgic for or to prophesy. An economic system's motive force involves such ideals, not in a longing for their actualization, but rather – Rousseau-like – in resignation to their ideality. Moreover Mauss's formulation helped deepen a basic issue in anthropological economics of how to compare societies not based on differential access to means of production to societies that, according to Marxist theory, are so based.

It is arguable that Mauss achieves rather than refutes Marx through a synthesis that obliterates the provisional (but necessary) thesis/antithesis necessarily posed as use-value versus exchange-value. This contention is fine. Each party will choose sides on the issue, depending on its visions, revisions, and divisions of Marxism, structuralism, cultural interpretation, and so forth. For symbolic analysis, deciding the question is less crucial than identifying it. But however we nowadays construe Marx, certainly Mauss's work refutes Engels. For it was Engels who temporalized Marx's twofold sense of commodities to advance a theory of state formation more evolutionary than dialectical. Hence the famous panorama:

> Production at all former stages of society was essentially collective and, likewise, consumption took place by the direct distribution of the products within larger or smaller communistic communities. This production in common was carried on within the narrowest limits, but concomitantly the producers were masters of their process of production and of their product. They knew what became of the product: they consumed it, it did not leave their hands; and as long as production was carried on on this basis, it could not grow beyond the control of the producers, and it could not raise any strange, phantom powers against them, as is the case regularly and inevitably under civilization.
>
> But slowly, division of labor crept into this process of production. It undermined the collective nature of production and appropriation, it made appropriation by individuals the largely prevailing rule, and thus gave rise to exchange between individuals – how, we examined above. Gradually, the production of commodities became the dominant form.
>
> With the production of commodities, production no longer for one's own consumption but for exchange, the products necessarily pass from hand to hand. [Engels 1884/1972:655–6]

Finally with the advent of money and merchants: "Commodities now pass not only from hand to hand but also from market to market. The producers have lost control of the aggregate production of their own life, and the merchants have not acquired it. Products and production become the playthings of chance." (Engels 1884/1972:656)

One of the many issues raised by this passage is whether a tribal exchange system – a Melanesian kula ring, matrilateral cross-cousin marriage rules, and, so forth – is under the "control of the producers" any more than an anonymous market would be. Indeed, all such systems, bourgeois or tribal, appear directed by "chance" only from the viewpoint of individual actors who need not conceptualize the total system to function correctly within it. Engels conjures an image of prestate economies where the motives of participants coincide with a model of the whole. From here he condemns both mercantilism and industrialism. To challenge Engels on this point is not to condone classical economics or to espouse the notion of "invisible hands" producing optimum general good as a sum of individual interests. Mauss's theory of exchange, for example, obviously is not advanced to justify either anonymous economic forces or impersonal market relationships. Indeed, Mauss celebrates the totality of social relations in tribal exchanges in a way Engels might have approved. But Mauss poses tribes as an *exchange* system, not as a communistic one. He thus challenges any implication that the sole alternative to becoming "playthings of chance" is a "collectively thought-out plan" such as that which Engels suggests. Mauss's archaic cases of "total prestation" reveal another path, and they undermine assumptions that even market economies are simply distortions from systems that should authentically be erected on their parties' expectations of direct, unmediated consumption of their own production. The latter ideal-type would not even qualify as a "society" in Durkheim's terms – a concept Engels would likely have regarded as "conventional hypocrisy," his construal of any division of labor. What kind of society, not to mention culture, would we call a case of each producing for himself, with nothing replaceable for anyone? Certainly a subsymbolic or, closer to Durkheim's terms, an amoral one.

Mauss's documentation of the principle of exchange sets aside developmental speculations like those of Engels. The "gift" is grounded neither in commodities and use-values (the supposedly "true value of labor") nor in labor and the surplus value that in Marxist terms renders exchange-values possible. The gift is grounded, rather, in a total system of reciprocity that, far from precluding competition, victimization, and power plays, rather situates these dimensions culturally. The values operating societies are systems of possible convertibilities – like economies, but without a natural base to conventions of scarcity – among different orders of relationship. To read Mauss according to the studies he fostered: A society is a motivated communication of messages (call it a culture). Every message is a complex set of replaceables – signs for concepts, responses for questions, spouse for sibling, currency for commodities (like coats), music codes for mythic codes, one language for another, and so forth. As developed in Lévi-Strauss's *Elementary Structures of Kinship*, for example, economics, linguistics, and marriage/descent are woven into a semiotic configuration – inherently variable – where everything cultural is convertible at its appropriate level. This notion brings us to the consummate example of models of social divisions implicit in values of "the gift."

Just as Durkheim had placed clan rituals (cutting across local hordes) at the center of human religion, Lévi-Strauss placed positive marriage rules cutting across exogamous units at the center of human kinship. The most general aspect of *Elementary Structures* is also its most Durkheimian aspect. If nuclear families (a set of parents and their children) are assumed to be the basic building blocks of kinship systems, then many tribal and "archaic" patterns seem abnormal. Lévi-Strauss, like certain ethnographers before him, turned his attention to these peculiar modes of tribal "organic solidarity" expressed as dual organization, formal moieties, cross-cousin marriage rules, or other variations on mutual exogamy. He argued that these apparently marginal systems best illuminate first principles of general human kinship and marriage. To totemic rites of the "elementary" forms of human religion we can now add bilateral/matrilateral/patrilateral cross-cousin marriage as the "elementary structures" of kinship. An "elementary" unit is not a simpler part that is eventually coagulated into a greater whole. Rather, it is the smallest part that contains all the dimensions that will, recombined, produce the range of (in Durkheim's case) religion and (in Lévi-Strauss's case) kinship. We cannot generate the full range of kinship and marriage systems from, say, spouses and their children, even if we admit into the domestic scene (with Freud) all the child–parent and sibling rivalries and ambivalences that can be projected into fundamental conflicts of human life and meaning. There is no way to move from such closed families, even perpetuated by an ideology of descent, to the types of systems that have been documented from Australia, Southeast Asia, the Americas, India, perhaps China, to name a few. To generate these systems requires an elementary unit that incorporates the contrary origins of two spouses and a rule distributing their children into the category of one or the other of them. Lévi-Strauss was not the first to insist on this fact, but he elaborated it into a comprehensive theory of social structure.[16]

The elementary condition of human kinship requires a distinction between two categories. One direct way to distinguish (and constitute) them is by a rule requiring each to marry the other. If we encode this requirement at the level of "family" formulations, then the basic family (Lévi-Strauss's "atom of kinship") must be said to contain an in-law relation as well as that between parents and childen:

> We reduce the kinship structure to the simplest conceivable element, the atom of kinship if I may say so, when we have a group consisting of a husband, a woman, a representative of the group which has given the woman to the man – since incest prohibitions make it impossible in all societies for the unit of kinship to consist of one family, it must always link two families, two consanguineous groups – and one offspring. [1963b:71, 43ff.]

We see, then, the importance of the avunculate, the mother's brother relation, which represents the category of the wife as a spouse rather than as a mother. In other words "families" contain so-called marriage relations as well as so-called descent relations; in certain types of tribal systems the two sorts of relations are undifferentiated: One set of distinctions divides the society at once into marriage categories and descent categories; one set of distinctions immediately maps the society into a divided solidarity. There is no way to generate a social structure of moieties (a society organized into a two-party system with exchanges, perhaps "sister exchange," required between the two), closed sets of exogamous clans, or cross-cousin marriage if one begins with nuclear families; hence the more complex, yet more basic, "atom of kinship."

The mysteries of *Elementary Structures* are profound and seductive. Here I want only to demonstrate their relation to Durkheim's types of solidarity. To do so requires artificially isolating one component from Lévi-Strauss's dialectical analysis. A society divided into categories articulated through sister exchange or bilateral cross-cousin marriage is in and of that rule a society

A   B

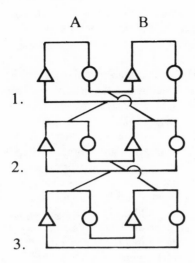

1.

2.

3.

divided into two and only two categories. That set of categories and their interrelation and perpetuation can be diagrammed (as shown in the figure).

What does the diagram mean? It organizes a society into a set of differences perpetuated through time by distinguishing sexes, collaterals, and genera-tions. This set of distinctions alone generates a society divided into two mutually necessary categories. An *A* man and woman of one generation may categorically be a brother and sister; thus they may not marry. By definition the spouse of an *A* man is a *B* woman; and the spouse of an *A* woman is a *B* man. Also, a *B* man and woman of one generation may be a brother and sister; thus they may not marry. The convenient solution: *A* marries *B* perpetually. This process could map an exchange of "sisters" (or "brothers," for that matter). *A* and *B* exchange "sisters" as spouses to produce the next generation. The point of the diagram is that it is irreducible; everything obtains whole cloth from the limited set of distinctions in play. Now consider that next generation, not as something subsequent to the first generation, but as some-thing implied in it from the start. Here cross-cousins (versus parallel cousins) enter into our gloss of the diagram. (We use these terms because of the history of eventually detecting this sort of system by peering out from our own genealogical conventions. The terms are misleading if we want to penetrate the universe of differentiation of this representation of a possible society; yet they are crucial if we want to compare systems.) Every figure on the diagram marries a figure that is the child of his mother's brother *and* his father's sister, still speaking in categories. The paramount fact is this: Every spouse is the child of someone categorized as both mother's brother *and* father's sister. In fact, mother's brother and father's sister are not two different entities in this system with few distinctions. Rather, they are undifferentiated, generalized.

Mother's brother's daughter *is* father's sister's daughter. These two varieties of "cross-cousins" are, at this level of minimal distinctions in elementary structures, an identity.

I have proceeded in this way in order to avoid the standard mistake in conceptualizing elementary structures from cross/parallel cousin formulations. It is easy to define a cross-cousin: either a mother's brother's daughter (MBD) or a father's sister's daughter (FZD) is my female cross-cousin. The connection in the prior generation contains both sexes: The connection is either a mother's brother (man and woman) or a father's sister (woman and man). On the other hand, parallel cousins are mother's sister's children or father's brother's children: The connection in the prior generation contains one sex. But the crucial fact is that the cross-cousins distinguishable in other kinds of systems are undifferentiated in a bilateral cross-cousin marriage system. The diagram reveals that every sibling in its categories is also a parallel cousin; that distinction, too, is inoperative at this elementary level, but it is available implicitly, a possible transformation to generate other elementary structures.

Here, however, we should note simply that this social scheme is a perfect organic solidarity, divided yet necessarily interrelated. There is no *A* perpetuated without *B* and vice versa. A single rule ("marry your bilateral cross-cousin") is a gloss from outside this system that implies everything about its totality.

All of this conceptualization is the easy part of *Elementary Structures*, among the most debated works in the history of anthropology and even of modern social science. To enter the work's maze, one must move to systems that admit a distinction inoperative in the above diagram: the distinction between mother's brother's daughter (MBD) and father's sister's daughter (FZD) (genetically equivalent). The category MBD is defined against FZD and vice versa; they are not an identity and may even be a polarity. To marry MBD (matrilateral cross-cousin marriage or one variety of asymmetrical exchange) is precisely *not* to marry the FZD. There are systems that stipulate MBD as ideal spouse; and there are perhaps systems that stipulate FZD as ideal spouse or at least valorize such a preference. Simply by considering these labels, we can glimpse certain complexities of such systems, the subject of perhaps the most acrimonious debates in recent anthropology. If I live in a system where I marry someone who stands to me as MBD (male viewpoint now), my wife comes to me from the same category that provided my mother to my father. My mother's brother, as the sibling of my mother, shares her natal category; I am taking a wife (his daughter) from the natal category of my mother. The fact, then, that the *M* and the *D* in the MBD marriage rule are both female means that in the system wives are moving consistently in one direction. (This movement contrasts to ideal bilateral cross-cousin marriage that I have diagrammed.) But it also contrasts to ideal FZD marriage, in which the *F* is male and the *D* is female. If I marry my FZD my wife comes from the category that in the prior generation took a wife (my father's sister) from my category. In this system, exchanges of spouses change direction from generation to generation. The type of solidarity articulated in and of the marriage rule is radically different for each of these varieties of alliance. One (MBD) is compatible with hierarchy, another (bilateral cross-cousin) with equalitarian relations. One sets up a contradiction and discrepancy in and of the rule (FZD); the others do not, and so forth. The permutation of these features in light of tribal and "archaic evidence" constitutes *The Elementary Structures of Kinship*, which reads at some levels like Durkheim plus algebra and at other levels like literary desire (see Chapter 7).

Kinship and marriage are complicated because we approach systems from both internal and external vantages, and we try to enter an exotic system in a way that enables us to exit from it as well. An additional complication in Lévi-Strauss's work is his view of the way positive categorical marriage rules limit tribal societies, which somewhat parallels Marx's view of the way means of production limit class societies. Moreover, Lévi-Strauss's later mythological analyses place limiting infrastructures – such as those disclosed by kinship and marriage analysis – among all conceivable systems from which they are necessarily selected. Nevertheless, throughout these enterprises an economic-cum-communication model is found to be manifest in the operation of societies themselves: The very thing produced by *us* (children) is already earmarked for *them* (as spouses), and it is valueless if retained. Production constitutes "the other."

Thus in tribal systems that have become exemplary in several schools of anthropological discourse, a sister-daughter is released from her domestic unit only in the expectation of her guaranteed replacement as a wife by the *trusted* exchange partners, at least indirectly. This is the symbolic foundation of societies that our own market economies, monetary systems, class consciousness, property laws, and negative marriage restrictions obscure without quite obliterating. Such is the sense of tribal exchange as inscribed first by Mauss, then by Lévi-Strauss: a social principle against which our own individualist values stand out in strongest contrast.

Lowie and others

Neither morphologically nor dynamically can social life be said to have progressed from a stage of savagery to a stage of enlightenment.

R. Lowie, *Primitive Society*

The most sustained anthropological attack on evolutionary views of society and culture came from Franz Boas and his followers who, rejecting the bolder assumptions of Lewis Henry Morgan, turned to fine-grained description and analysis of tribal populations. Boas is sometimes regarded as an empiricist whose approach was too inductive to advance social theory. Yet anthropological linguistics, monumentalized in Dell Hymes's *Language in Culture and Society* (1964), and cultural theory as well have developed in part from the kinds of contrastive generalization always implicit in Boas's work, particularly in his studies of language, art, and myth (1911/1965, 1927, 1916). Moreover, George Stocking reminds us of Boas's roots in a German "romantic, historicist, intellectual tradition" (1974:408) – a tradition filled with systems and would-be synthesis (cf. Stocking 1968). Recently Marshall Sahlins has insisted on a Boasian basis of structuralism (often acknowledged by Lévi-Strauss). Sahlins brings Boas to bear on the structuralist/Marxist issue in France, the philosophy of history, political theory, and symbolic analysis as well:

As opposed to a fundamental appreciation on Marx's part that men transform nature, produce, according to a construct . . . all conception now tends to be banished from the infrastructure to reappear as the construct of its material transformations. The anthropological objection would be that Marx arrives in this way at a truncated view of the symbolic process. He apprehends it only in its secondary character of symbolization – Boas's "secondary" formation – the model of a given system in consciousness, while ignoring that the system so symbolized is itself symbolic. There is again the fault, shared by Marx with certain functionalist-dualists, of limiting symbol to "ideology," thus allowing action to slip into the kingdom of the pragmatic. [1976a:139]

In the more properly social domain, it was Robert Lowie who advanced Boas's call for careful mappings of neighboring systems. Lowie's interrelated works on *Primitive Society* (1920/1961), *Social Organization* (1948), and *The Origin of the State* (1927) revolve around his low-key but high-power concept of contrastive social forms. Lowie lacked the academic theatrics and the eye for the sensational necessary to forge a distinctly Lowiean approach. Yet, carefully scrutinized, *Primitive Society* and subsequent works reveal a concept of social organization as intrinsically mediational and varying. I shall close this chapter's rereadings of comparative social theory with a nod toward Lowie and several contemporaries and successors in anthropology and related disciplines.[17]

It is characteristic of Lowie never to mention a social trait, even of the Crow, without tracing its contrastive manifestations. Consider the following vintage passage, which also permits us to review issues of exogamy and cross-cousins just discussed. (Notice how true to Lowie's *Primitive Society* Lévi-Strauss's *Elementary Structures of Kinship* remained. The latter work basically clarified the kind of dialectics implicit in Lowie's nonevolutionist social comparisons:)

It is easy to apply the principles used in comparing sibs [read "clans"] of different tribes to sibs of different order in the same tribe and prove that they are units of quite distinct character. Take exogamy, for example, as one of the most important and widespread functions. If the greater unit is exogamous, any of its parts must be so by logical necessity; hence it is possible to argue that the lesser unit is not really exogamous, accordingly differs in essence, hence in origin, from the larger group. Contrariwise, the large unit might be found wanting in point of exogamy and be ruled out as a phenomenon distinct from the exogamous sib. . .

Where there are only two exogamous divisions, there follow by logical necessity certain consequences that sharply differentiate a moiety organization from one with more than two exogamous sibs. Where the number of exogamous sibs is greater (unless special rules are superimposed) a man may marry a woman from any sib not his own. Thus, a Crow may marry a woman from any one of twelve sibs; twelve-thirteenths of the marriageable women of his tribe are his possible spouses. But with only two exogamous divisions a Winnebago is restricted to half the women of his people, a very considerable difference. There is still another implication of social significance. Among the [matrilineal] Crow a man has special relations with members of two sibs, of his own (i.e., his mother's) and his father's; but the number of individuals in both relatively [sic] to the total population is small [alienation?]. Given a moiety system, a man may have specific relations with all tribesmen, for one half of them belong to his own moiety, the remainder to the moiety of that parent through whom descent is not traced.

A striking feature of moieties is the development of reciprocal services. At an Iroquois burial the functionaries are always selected not from the deceased person's but from the opposite moiety. . .On the coast of northern British Columbia certain festivals are never arranged except in honor of the complementary moiety. It is a puzzling question how this reciprocity is to be interpreted. Is it fundamentally a matter of the moiety or merely incidentally so because either moiety includes one of the parents? [1920/1961:133]

Lowie's question strikes at what would later become the basic difference between structuralism's emphasis on total systems and structural functionalism's emphasis on social relations. He continues:

The Hidatsa case is illuminating because there we find that in burial it is not the non-exogamous moieties that function but the sib of the deceased person's father. It is thus possible that the Iroquois and Northwest Coast phenomena belong in the same category, and that in these matrilineal tribes reciprocity merely signifies social recognition of the father. Other functions of moieties have already been cited. Those of the Iroquois are characteristic of the Eastern Indians. At such games as lacrosse, members of opposite moieties are pitted against each other. At feasts and ceremonies there is a corresponding spatial grouping; one moiety faces the other, each being represented by a speaker. . .

Still more common [than appropriate nomenclatures] is the classification of cousins into parallel and cross-cousins. As Tylor pointed out, this, too, is admirably consonant with a dual organization. . .if a man belongs to moiety A, his brother will also belong to that group; both must marry women of moiety B and [in matrilineal systems] their children will all be B. Correspondingly, two sisters of moiety A must marry men of moiety B, and their children will all be A. That is to say, parallel cousins, the offspring of several brothers or of several sisters, will always be of the same social group. Not so with cross-cousins. For though a brother and a sister of moiety A must both marry individuals of the opposite moiety, the brother's children by maternal descent become members of B while the sister's retain their mother's affiliation. Thus, cross-cousins are bound to belong to different moieties [of course, in patrilineal systems as well].

But if we add only one sib, the situation changes. A man of sib A may then marry either a woman of sib B or of C; hence the wives and consequently also the children of several brothers will belong partly to sib B and partly to sib C, and there will be no reason in the sib alignment for classing them together. Thus, the presence of more than two sibs does not explain the most common form of the Dakota terminology nearly so well as does the dual organization. [1920/1961:133–35]

Lowie proceeds to cast doubt over all historicist interpretations of this disjunction between nomenclature and social structure. He sets the stage for analysis of matrilateral cross-cousin marriage, Crow–Omaha systems, and so forth (cf. Buchler and Selby 1968). Even Lowie could not always avoid reification: his analyses of teknonymy (1920/1961:107ff.), the sororate and the levirate, and other traits occasionally isolate and reify. Yet more often than not the fulsome praise of Rodney Needham applies:

The central advantage of Lowie's method is that in any analysis it dispenses with a crude substantive class and concentrates instead on the operation of classification. Instead of relying upon a paradigm case, and a class of other cases bearing more or less attenuated resemblance to this, the method investigates the intricate combination of classificatory principles by which any particular terminology may in fact be constituted. The craving for generality is checked, and the quest for essential features is given up.

In the study of relationship terminologies as well, therefore, we find that analytical advance is blocked by the familiar conceptual habits which have so much hindered the study of descent systems. The remedy is not only urged by Wittgenstein, but has actually been put into prior effect by Lowie. [Needham 1974:60]

Lowie's method leads him to investigate the role of voluntary associations in tribal populations. He confirmed Boas's rejection of Morgan's view that nonliterate life was centered exclusively on kinship; and he, too, denied any single chronological sequence underlying the "exuberant variety of phenomena" (1920/1961:430). Lowie's studies of the vision quest – perhaps the foremost topic in American ethnology – dislodged individual Indians from a group imposing fixed social constraints. A far more artful writer than was generally supposed, Lowie paused to visualize, almost sentimentally, the "multiplicity of social relations" characterizing Crow life. To accentuate elements of Lowie's style – its parallelism, antitheses, and syntactic reversals – I shall pull the first part of the passage out of its block-paragraph format:

In the Mountain Crow band,
some eighty years ago,
a woman of the Thick-lodge sib
gives birth to a boy.

Her husband summons a renowned warrior of his sib, the Badleggings, who dubs the child Strikes-three-men in memory of one of his own exploits. As Strikes-three-men grows up, he learns how to act towards the relatives on either side of his family and what conduct to expect in return.

The female Thick-lodges makes for him
beaded shirts and moccasins,
on the male members he can rely
for aid in any difficulty.

His father he comes to regard as the natural provider and protector of the immediate family circle; to all the other men of the Bad-leggings sib he gives presents when he can and treats them with respect.

On their part they become his official eulogists as soon as he distinguishes himself by skill as a hunter or by bravery in battle; and the bond between him and them is so close that when one of them commits an offense against tribal etiquette an appropriate nickname is attached to his own person.

With the children of his "fathers"
a curious reciprocal relationship unites him.
They are his mentors
and he is theirs.
They throw in his teeth his foibles and misdemeanors,
and he retaliates in kind.

To these various relations based on family and sib ties associational ones are soon added. He enters a league of playmates mimicking the warrior societies and tries to gain glory by striking deer and buffalo as the older braves count coup on Dakota or Cheyenne foemen.

As he grows older, Albino-bull, one of his companions,
becomes a bosom friend.
Together they go courting
and share each other's mistresses;
together they set out on war parties,
each shielding the other at the risk of his own life;
together they join the Fox society
to which Albino-bull has been invited;
and together they leave it
when the rival Lumpwoods,
impressed by the young men's war record,
bribe them into their fold.
[1920/1961:427–30]

Following these stately rhythms and rhetorical repetitions the pace quickens as Lowie projects quick shots of the manifold social possibilities with short phrases and conditional auxiliaries ("fancy may seize") in nervous juxtaposition with the narrative present and conspicious literary devices ("no strangers in the strange land"):

Now a novel set of relations ensues. Strikes-three-men aids his fellow-Lumpwoods as he aids his sib-mates; he and his comrade participate in all of the society's feasts and dances; and they while away leisure hours lounging and smoking in the tents of their new associates and singing Lumpwood songs. When Strikes-three-men buys a wife, still another unit is added to his social groups; added rather than substituted for the old family group because the tie that links him with his brothers and sisters remains not only unsnapped but in full force. About this time a fancy may seize our hero to cast in his lot with the band hunting about the Yellowstone confluence. Henceforth its political relations become his. With his new fellows he pays visits to the friendly Village tribes of the upper Missouri, with them he pursues a gang of Dakota raiders, and when the Mountain Crow decline to join a punitive war party against the hereditary enemy he is as vociferous as any River Crow in denouncing the pusillanimity of the band of his nativity. From the start he has been no stranger in the strange land: there are Thicklodges on the Yellowstone who greet him as a brother, and he mingles without formality with the Lumpwoods there resident. The illness of one of his children may evoke a vow: on its recovery he pledges himself to seek admission into the Tobacco order. Four-bears, of the Weasel chapter, is willing to initiate him, and so Strikes-three-men and his wife become members, privileged to join in the annual planting of the sacred weed and in all other ceremonial activities of their branch. A special bond of intimacy unites them henceforth with their sponsor Four-bears, from whom an occasional horse may be expected as a token of paternal affection. [1920/1961:428–9]

Finally the grandiloquent ecumenical imagery ("pusillanimity of the band of his nativity") accumulates into a macaronic prose almost Melvillean:

Thus our Crow comes to be a member of some half-a-dozen well defined groups. . .Doubtless some obligations sit more lightly than others. If one of two comrades were affronted by their military society, both would leave it and seek entrance into another. It is also safe to infer that regard for one's wife would be readily sacrificed either to one's blood kin or to one's club. *Not in the real life of the Crow bourgeois, but by that swashbuckling standard of honor to which he is content to make public obeisance*, a woman is only a woman and to show overmuch solicitude on her account would mean a loss of face. But the occasions for such demonstrations are not over-numerous and the average tribesman does not suffer much distress from the variety of his memberships. [Lowie 1920/1961:429–30; emphasis added]

We shall see that such swashbuckling standards – be they Thicklodge, Lumpwood, or more ominous ones – portend Lowie's theory of the state.

This descriptive synthesis that rings down the curtain on *Primitive Society* contains in a nutshell the positive theoretical thrust – not just antievolution or counterkinship – of Lowie's emphasis on voluntary clubs. Such "sodalities" reveal a tribe's capacity to sample alternate social forms, without necessarily adopting them as the central components of its social machine. Each tribal population appears almost to toy with patterns that are fundamental to its neighbors. Lowie presents the Crow themselves as self-contradictory: one thing in public, another interpersonally. Most important, through their diverse memberships the Crow are somewhat "cross-cultural," intertribal. Social organization itself embodies a playlike component of "alternicity." Tribal sodalities seem to institutionalize something like a dialectical remove from their own organizational centers – suggesting (to anticipate Lévi-Strauss) a kind of myth in practice.

Lowie's *Primitive Society* was in advance of functionalism before the fact. Yet over the years Lowie himself gravitated toward structural functionalism. For example, in *Primitive Society* chapters on marriage and exogamy precede kinship; this sequence is reversed in *Social Organization*, which tends to substantivize sets of social relations as corporate and not to precipitate contrastive social organizations out of a field of possibilities. Lowie, moreover, continued to consider families primary and clans (exogamous and interlocal) secondary elaborations – an assumption perhaps induced by his early contacts with

Shoshone bands (cf. Murphy, 1972). Clans remain for Lowie a halfway organization between families on the one hand and associations on the other.

Yet in *Primitive Society* it was the variable principles of clan structure that advanced the comparative sweep. The clan/sodality distinction underlay Lowie's theory of the state. In *Primitive Society* and *Social Organization* he samples the lush array of associations throughout the world's cultures:

In Oceania the Banks Islands parallel West Africa in the multiplicity of their sodalities, but other Melanesian groups, as well as Polynesia, have a very meager assortment. America yields similar contrasts. It is true that in the rudest tribes, those of the Basin and Plateau, sodalities dwindle down to nothing, whereas the Pueblos and coastal British Columbia spawn them. But the Plains Indians are hardly inferior to the Pueblos in this respect...To draw comparisons in Europe, Germany – notwithstanding a mania for founding and joining all sorts of voluntary associations that precipitated a special word, *Vereinsmierei* – never paralleled the development of upper-class clubs, often with political aims, so characteristic of England in the seventeenth and eighteenth centuries. The lack is, of course, to be traced to the total structure of social life in Germany, which inhibited such growth. In primitive areas we must also look for the explanation of corresponding differences in the surrounding social atmosphere. [Lowie 1948:294-5]

He suggests that modern pathological forms of state organization arise when the voluntarist component, inevitably androcentric, comes to dominate in the absence of social structures like clans. (This view is not unlike Durkheim's argument that individualistic anomie develops where intermediate-level organizations have atrophied.) Elsewhere Lowie alludes to Fascism as something like sodalities run rampant, loosed from the restraint of clans:

The broadest function of sodalities was clearly grasped by [Heinrich] Schurtz [1902]. By making cooperation a reality beyond the narrow confines of the blood tie they pave the way, in principle at least, for a wider integration, whether in the form of a state or of a supernational religion...
   Sodalities thus appear as a step toward territorial or political unification.
   However, there are sodalities and sodalities. The Dakota quill-embroiderers' guild is certainly not fit to found a state, nor are many masculine societies...
   Dual or multiple sodalities may coexist without strife, especially if there is some coordinating agency. The Arapaho, like the Crow, had military societies, but theirs formed one graded whole headed by the seven old men at the top who "embodied everything that was most sacred in Arapaho life." In these circumstances a flare-up between any two organizations could hardly develop into a serious conflict.
   "The monopoly of legitimate force" does not necessarily imply that all such force must be concentrated in a single individual or group for *all* purposes...It is only a totalitarian government, such as Nazi Germany's, that insists on controlling all of the social life of a people from a single center. [1948:316, 324]

In *Social Organization*, which looks back on *The Origin of The State* and forward to Lowie's postwar *Toward Understanding Germany*, Lowie returns to the Crow, this time from the woman's vantage, employing an artful blend of translated quotations and paraphrases:

Naturally, as in every militaristic culture, whether it be that of the North American Plains or of modern Prussia, the ideological superstructure bore heavily on women. It might thrill them to the core to hear how a son or husband had wiped out a whole tentful of Cheyenne, but it was not so pleasant when sooner or later retribution was visited upon a near kinsman. And it was not only the enemy that brought grief. How did Crow women feel about that fortnight's licensed libertinage in the spring, when Foxes and Lumpwoods broke up many happy homes?. . .Strikes-at-night gave a graphic account of the average woman's reactions:

> My husband was a great warrior. He was a Fox. The Lumpwoods and the Foxes were stealing each other's wives one season while my husband was on the warpath. Before I had married, another man had courted me with gifts of beef and horses, but I married Bull-weasel's father. Now this suitor came with other Lumpwoods to get me. I was afraid they were going to take me by force. . .My husband returned with Big-ox's war party, and I saw him looking for me. The people told him I had fled in order not to be taken away. . .He told me that if the Lumpwoods came for me while he was present he would let me go, but if I hid it would be well. . .I heard the Lumpwoods outside. They had taken the wife of a man who had been living with her peacefully for several years. He got furious and was going to kill her. . .The Lumpwoods all scattered. They took revenge on the Foxes by cutting up their robes into strips and pounding their horses' feet. . .the wife-kidnapping ceased, and I escaped. [1948:359–60]

Lowie ends by conveying the plight of woman and her complicity in "militaristic culture":

> Crow women of the old school, then, had a hard lot. They were forever mourning their husbands or brothers or sons; and at home they were exposed to the blatant virility of their tribesmen. Yet the women who had lived in the buffalo-hunting days preferred them to the pedestrian security of a modern reservation. The reason is clear: the old life had a tang that is drained out of contemporary conditions. . .Visions and ceremonial activity were open to both sexes. Muskrat. . .had visions that enabled her to doctor broken bones and other ailments. She had held the highest post in her branch of the Tobacco society and adopted many novices. For the old-fashioned Crow woman the days of the war parties and the military societies, for all their tribulations, had a rich content. "I know the songs (of the Goose Egg Dance)," Strikes-at-night told me, "and sometimes I sing them, and they bring back memories of the past that make me feel sad." [Lowie 1948:61]

(Might one translate "tang" as "Zauberung"?) Like Weber, the most disturbing aspect of Lowie's theory of the state (first outlined in 1920) – an overcentralization of sodalities that ought to remain plural and competitive – is how prophetic it proved.

Lowie's work on society and sodality clarified the contrastive systematics implicit in Boas's general view of cultures. Lowie, and perhaps Lowie alone of his generation of anthropologists, avoided those difficulties in German historicism that were, according to Talcott Parsons, "repeated a half century later in American cultural anthropology" (1971:30). His wary method eventually lost ground to the more substantialist views of social and psychological form developed in the school of culture and personality and to semisynthetic notions of superorganic culture tested by Kroeber and others. Lowie's intricate approach – avoiding pat paradigm cases and substantive classes of phenomena – was revitalized later by Fred Eggan (1950/1973, 1961), who incorporated Radcliffe-Brown's lessons in abstracting social structures in closely documented, historically informed "controlled comparison." Moreover, Lévi-Strauss – always expressing profound admiration for Boas, Lowie, and Eggan – developed his dazzling structuralism (a reconstituted, "depositivized" *L'année sociologique*) in light of their example. Although Lowie had barely mentioned Durkheim (Barnes 1966:171), in Lévi-Strauss's work they meet at last.

With these aspects of Lowie fresh in our minds, we might briefly turn to some related figures. Ruth Benedict, for example, as complex a writer as Lowie, was less reificationist and psychologistic than she was later reputed to be. Her work is often associated with the shift toward thematic wholes in the 1930s in light of psychoanalytic concerns – developments epitomized in Margaret Mead's remarkable career. Mead was the first professional American anthropologist to devote her primary fieldwork to non-Amerindian populations. The geographical remove of Samoa and her subsequent field sites from the mainstream of New World comparative research doubtless strengthened her already considerable determination to divert the discipline from diffusionism and close variations and to turn it toward psychological themes. The tenor of Mead's views is apparent from the advice she wrote Benedict from New Guinea, urging her to revise the manuscript for *Patterns of Culture*; Mead counseled her own teacher (Benedict) to disavow what she herself had been taught:

So here goes, and try to see me saying it, wrinkling my brows and making awful faces to get it clear...
The Zuni chapter is grand...And that chapter and the Northwest Coast will be the most important, of course. But the order and arrangement of the rest worries me. It's written to some four or five audiences...The result has had a bad effect on your style, the texture is all uneven and choppy, sometimes intimate, sometimes heavily formal, sometimes colloquial or journalese, sometimes in the jargon of anthropology and sometimes in the phrases of good literature...It would be a bad accident if your feeling for style and texture were to be spoilt by an accident of assembling of miscellaneous source materials, plus an evident consciousness of trying to write so that Papa Franz [Boaz] and Lowie will approve...Of course I am not sure whether you are writing an essay in social theory, or an essay in the philosophy of cultural temperament, or a book which, under the guise of dealing with this point is to put over a lot of other points also. I am afraid that it is the latter and I don't think it is best. The point is too fine to be muddied about with diffusion and evolution and race prejudice and all the rest of it. I'd scrap the first chapter forever...I'd write a short introduction along the lines of the "arc of human experience and the sounds in language" – but omitting the further illustrations as too slight to carry the point – for it needs a whole culture to do so.
And I'd leave out all the adolescence point and the war point – for as Reo [Fortune] says it's just a Lowie "they do and they don't" point while what you want to say is "they do and they don't incredibly" and it takes a whole culture to do that.

...make it a single theme essay – all in your own style – scrap all the other articles – don't ever look at them, and aim at a high audience. It will then be a fine thing, consistent in itself and with you, with no Boasian-Lowie-ish-Germanic scraps in it. [Mead 1959:335–7]

With that combination of subtle insight ("they do and they don't incredibly" – actually Reo Fortune's comment on *Patterns*) and diluting compromise (simplify! simplify!) that became her trademark, Mead demands of Benedict an interpretation more integrated than Benedict wished to make. Happily, on this occasion Benedict was a match for Mead's will; in 1933 she wrote in her response: "Classes are over and I'm working on the book. I'm distressed that you don't like it, the part you've seen. But I've consulted everybody I can think of about omitting the first two chapters, and they are strong against it...Well, I hope you won't think it's all awful...The blanket disapproval I can't do much with, but I've tried to bring the first chapters closer to my own standards" (Mead 1959:337–8). Moreover, she left Lowie (and Boas) in. *Patterns of Culture* (1934) – one of the few classics of American ethnology – survived. In its final form it continued to speak from many vantages despite Mead's pleas that it be reduced to thematic conformity. The weeding out of Lowie would have undermined its contrastive essence. A Sapir-like linguistic analogy frames the entire study – a portion of which Mead, too, would have preserved:

It is in cultural life as it is in speech; selection is the prime necessity. The numbers of sounds that can be produced by our vocal cords and our oral and nasal cavities are practically unlimited. The three or four dozen of the English language are a selection which coincides not even with those of such closely related dialects as German and French. The total that are used in different languages of the world no one has even dared to estimate. But each language must make its selection and abide by it on pain of not being intelligible at all. A language that used even a few hundreds of the possible – and actually recorded – phonetic elements could not be used for communication...

The great arc along which all the possible human behaviors are distributed is far too immense and too full of contradictions for any one culture to utilize even any considerable portion of it. Selection is the first requirement. Without selection no culture could even achieve intelligibility, and the intentions it selects and makes its own are a much more important matter than the particular detail of technology or the marriage formality that it also selects in similar fashion. [Benedict 1934/1961:23, 237]

Benedict used psychological labels to situate the relative position of certain cultures along her arc of configurations. More precisely, the labels pertained to the ritual emphases in each culture's self-exaggerations. She selected her two primary examples for their heightened contrast: pacific, ceremonious, prayerful, priest-controlled Zuni versus orgiastic, exhibitionist, shaman-bedazzled Kwakiutl. When Benedict appends psychological labels – "monomaniacal" Kwakiutls – she seems to be posing intrinsic traits. When she phrases the matter in distorted borrowings from Dilthey, Spengler, and Nietzsche as

contrasts in *Weltanschauungen* – Faustian/Apollonian or Apollonian/Dionysiac
– her argument sounds more relational, with neither quality representing a
lapse from some standard norm. Finally, when Benedict introduces more
cautious Boasian historical notes or Lowie-like particular contrasts, *Patterns
of Culture* avoids artificial, substantive reification altogether. Her suggestions
might be paraphrased in the following way: The Zuni, in strongest contrast to
the Apache (their neighbors and rivals who engage in vision quests and
individualistic warfare rites), organize themselves ritually around nonvisionary
ceremonies, more so even than the Hopi; and, compared with the Haida and
other neighbors, the not yet matrilineal Kwakiutl are property obsessed,
accentuating the mother's brother tie through transmission of status objects.

Patterns of Culture began and remained a contrastive study of the vision
quest and the ritual and social uses to which it was put; but, unlike Lowie's
work, it compared the most extreme cases, not the entire field of minute
contrasts. Moreover, one of the extremes, the Zuni, was a culture that seems
to have selected against the trait, that appeared almost to style itself ritually in
counterdistinction to violent visions. The book also revolved around matrilineal
variations, including both the Zuni and the Dobu and extending to the Kwakiutl
who, although nonmatrilineal, both typologically and historically must be
assessed in light of matrilineal possibilities displayed by their neighbors.
Benedict's third case, the Dobu (a Melanesian people described in Reo Fortune's monograph [1932/1963], who participated in the kula trade with the
Trobriands and other islands), was matrilineal as well, but residence alternated
between husband's and wife's natal groups, which fact produced an exaggerated, "paranoid" effect in Dobu social life. The combination of the Dobu and
the ambitious Kwakiutl helped Benedict point out parallel extremes in our
own culture.

Patterns of Culture quivers with the tension between diversity and integration. The Boasian chapters (1–2) are juxtaposed to the thematic treatments of
Zuni, Dobu, and Kwakiutl in a way that reinforces a sense of integration
arising from a field of contrasts, whether in the book (Zuni/Dobu), or in the
actuality of tribal contacts (Zuni/Apache, Dobu/Trobriand), or in the forgotten
history of tribal diversification (Kwakiutl/Zuni). Benedict's book does not
replace Boas–Lowieish scraps of detailed diversity with more comfortable
integration; rather it strikes integration off against diversity to vitalize both.
"You know," she wrote to Mead concerning cultures, "I like them scandal-
ous" (Mead 1959:331).

To read Benedict in continuity with Lowie is not to overlook her distinctive
achievement. She managed to "polarize" Zuni/Kwakiutl plus the Dobu as a
kind of odd culture out. It is important to recognize how fundamental this
methodological strategy of interpretation (to be discussed further in Chapter
4) remains in anthropology today. Louis Dumont, for example, in a Durkheimian
register polarizes "Indian civilization and ourselves", counterposing

hierarchy/equality as principles of cultural order, although at another level both are variations on Indo-European possibilities. Dumont even wonders whether individualistic–egalitarian views of social order do not preclude thorough comparisons:

We are separated from traditional societies by what I call the modern revolution, a revolution in values, which has taken place, I believe, through the centuries in the Christian Occident. . . how and why has this unique development that we call "modern" occurred at all? The main task of comparison is to account for the modern type in terms of the traditional type. For this reason, most of our modern vocabulary is inadequate for comparative purposes: *the basic comparative model* has to be nonmodern. (On a different level, is it not a reason why his *Formes élémentaires* is relatively so seminal in Durkheim's work?) [L. Dumont 1977:7; emphasis added]

Or Clifford Geertz in a Weberian register polarizes Java/Bali in terms of economic entrepreneurship (1963), Bali/Morocco in terms of cultural aspects of irrigation (1971), and Java/Bali/Morocco in terms of native viewpoints (1979). Indeed, even Geertz's first book about Java alone (1960) polarized Javanese religion and culture against itself, so to speak, by articulating a threefold distinction among the folk–ritualistic/reformist–Islamic/aristocratic–courtly variants of Javanese religion (*abangan/santri/priyayi*). Geertz thereby reoriented views of Java away from simple historical sequences and from any singular center of folk, reformist, or elitist principles, to point up the dramatic pluralism, highlighted in ritual and politics. Geertz's subsequent works demonstrate how this process of interpretation facilitates less reductionist comparison. That Islam in Java and Morocco is actualized so differently – standardized around neither an orthodoxy nor an orthopractice – allows (indeed requires) anthropologists to constitute "Islam" contrastively (C. Geertz 1968). That both Morocco and Bali irrigate, but in vividly contrasting ways, enables subsistence to be situated culturally. Characteristically Geertz begins with what might appear at first blush a singular entity: "Javanese religion," "irrigation technology," "Islam"; but through his interpretations, ethnographic particularities themselves emerge as subtle, operational ideal-types. Benedict, on the other hand, beginning with the vivid contrast Zuni/Kwakiutl/Dobu, sought some level of institutions or values that would lubricate the comparison of the relative integrations. She opted for clumsy psychological glosses, when what she really required was a theory of differentiated ideal-types. But she did not take Durkheim seriously (Benedict 1934/1961:231), and she read Dilthey and Spengler, rather than Weber.

Finally, would it be going too far to say that Lowie's distrust of centralization and related Enlightenment values rivals that of contemporary social theorists who challenged such assumptions more directly, although more narrowly? Consider, for example, Horkheimer and Adorno's resounding *Dialectics of the Enlightenment*, written in America after their departure from Frankfurt. M. Jay reminds us: "Marx of course was by no means the major target of the

Dialectic. Horkheimer and Adorno [1972] were far more ambitious. The entire Enlightenment tradition, that process of allegedly liberating demystification that Max Weber had called *die Entzauberung der Welt* (the disenchantment of the world), was their real target" (Jay 1973:259). Indeed, Horkheimer and Adorno trace disenchantment to the bourgeois philosophy consolidated in the seventeenth and eighteenth centuries:

In the most general sense of progressive thought, the Enlightenment has always aimed at liberating men from fear and establishing their sovereignty. Yet the fully enlightened earth radiates disaster triumphant. The program of the Enlightenment was the disenchantment of the world; the dissolution of myths and the substitution of knowledge for fancy. Bacon, the "father of experimental philosophy," had defined its motives . . .
    The disenchantment of the world is the extirpation of animism . . .
    Bacon's postulate of *una scientia universalis*, whatever the number of fields of research, is as inimical to the unassignable as Leibniz's *mathesis universalis* is to discontinuity. The multiplicity of forms is reduced to position and arrangement, history to fact, things to matter . . . Formal logic was the major school of unified science. It provided the Enlightenment thinkers with the schema of the calculability of the world. The mythologizing equation of Ideas with numbers in Plato's last writings expresses the longing of all demythologication: number became the canon of the Enlightenment. The same equations dominate bourgeois justice and commodity exchange . . . Bourgeois society is ruled by equivalence. It makes the dissimilar comparable by reducing it to abstract quantities. To the Enlightenment, that which does not reduce to numbers, and ultimately to the one, becomes illusion; modern positivism writes it off as literature. [1972:3–7]

This view is not unlike that of Foucault's characterization of the classical episteme, built around abstract measure rather than interpretive similitudes (see Chapter 2). Horkheimer, Adorno, and their companions in the Frankfurt School were able to perceive the Enlightenment (and certain vestiges of it in Marx) as a set of political rather than natural values. Foucault manages to pose the classical episteme as a set of historical–cultural values as well. One interesting aspect of Horkheimer and Adorno's *Dialectics* is the anthropological evidence it enlists: Robert Lowie on language, Hubert and Mauss on primitive mana, Durkheim and Mauss on classifications. Such sources lead them to surmise:

When language enters history its masters are priests and sorcerers . . . The dread which gives to *mana*, wherever it is met with in ethnology, is always sanctioned – at least by the tribal elders. No sector of language or society has monopolized conspiracy.
    Just as the first categories represented the organized tribe and its power over the individual, so the whole logical order, dependency, connection, progression, and union of concepts is grounded in the corresponding conditions of social reality – that is, of the division of labor. But of course this social character of categories of thought is not, as Durkheim asserts, an expression of social solidarity, but evidence of the inscrutable unity of society and domination. [1972:20–21]

I think they here misconstrue Durkheim; as we saw above, his achievement was to make such "unity" scrutable, after all, by attending to the institutional specifics of varieties of solidarity. Moreover, Lowie was doubtless making subtler arguments about individual autonomy versus tribal dependency than they imply. A careful reading of Durkheim, Hubert, and Mauss and of Lowie's evocation of actual social systems in *Primitive Society* would indeed have supported a suspicion that the seeds of domination are with society from the start, but not in any simple conspiratorial fashion. Lowie's sombre view of history, we recall, poses women implicated in militarism, bourgeois Crow, and so on: Is there no lost pure state to be regained? Thus, Lowie was in advance of Horkheimer and Adorno's lingering sense of some prior, essentialist–animist condition, perpetuated in and as systems of exploitation by elders. No sector of language or society has monopolized conspiracy.

An elective affinity between social theorists like Weber, with his paradoxical sense of rationality, and ethnologists like Lowie and Benedict resonates in the latters' ironic response to centralized authority and standardized states. To conclude on an extreme note of this kind, about 1925 Benedict extracted from the ethnographic record a ritual means of salvaging humanity's fate from its History:

We have already had recourse to many quaint primitive customs our fathers believed outmoded by the progress of mankind. We have watched the dependence of great nations upon the old device of the pogrom. We have seen the rise of demagogues, and even in those countries we consider lost in a mortally dangerous idealism we have watched death dealt out to those who harbor the mildest private opinions. Even in our own country we have come to the point of shooting in the back that familiar harmless annoyance, the strike picketer. It is strange that we have overlooked cannibalism.

Mankind has for many thousands of years conducted experiments in the eating of human flesh, and has not found it wanting...Secret societies of the men were all-important on Vancouver Island; the whole winter was given over to their rites. And they were sufficiently aristocratic; membership was limited to first sons of noble birth...the noble youth returned to the village with the Spirit of the Cannibal upon him...But when he had bitten the corpse, the ecstasy left him, and he was "tamed." He drank the emetic, and retired again to solitude in a state of great sacredness, where for months he observed the endless taboos of the newly initiate.

It is obvious that nothing could be more harmless to the community; one useless body per year satisfactorily satisfied the craving for violence which we have clumsily supplied in modern times in the form of oaths, blood-and-thunder, and vows to undertake the death of industrious households. [In Mead 1959:44–8]

Benedict proceeds to notorious cases from Malaya and the Maori; then she concludes her "modest proposal": "Our well-proved methods of publicity give us a new assurance in the adoption even of unfamiliar programs; where we might at one time well have doubted the possibility of popularizing a practice so unused, we can now venture more boldly. While there is yet time, shall we not choose deliberately between war and cannibalism" [Mead 1959:48]. Lowie, on the other hand, runs his 1920 masterwork into the sands of its data:

It is true that social organizations differ in complexity, but that difference fails to provide a criterion of progress. When the Andamanese evolved or borrowed the notion of segregating bachelors from spinsters, and both from married couples, their social culture gained in complexity, but it is not easy to prove that it experienced either improvement or deterioration. If our enlightened communities coped as successfully with, say, the problem of maintaining order as ruder peoples in a simpler environment, then it might be conceded that our complex administrative machinery represents an intellectual advance. But the condition is contrary to fact, and our cumbersome method of preserving the peace and the more elegant solution of the same problem in simpler circumstances remain incommensurable. [1920/1961:439]

Lowie's characteristically uncaustic prose ends by confronting the outer limit of incommensurability, after calmly proclaiming us, morally speaking, sub-Andamanese.

4. Assorted semiotics and dialectics

Following Mauss, we [take] "cultural phenomena" to mean phenomena common to several societies in contact. For the sociologist, these are also of course social phenomena. Only, while social phenomena are internal to one society, phenomena called here "cultural" are taken as external (to one society)...A somewhat narrow exegesis by Radcliffe-Brown of Durkheimian sociology may be responsible for the exclusive emphasis on the first.

L. Dumont, *Religion/Politics and History in India*

In his recent defense of the concept of culture against all varieties of "practical reason," M. Sahlins insists that each culture conforms to material constraints "according to a definite symbolic scheme which is never the only one possible. Hence it is culture which constitutes utility" (1976a:vii). Indeed, were any such scheme the only one possible, it would in and of that fact not be symbolic. Human beings living in social systems direct their lives according to meaningful values and images. These values are mutable, but they cannot seem thoroughly so from within. Responses to external conditions – to natural events, demographic factors, and biological needs – are mediated by symbolic schemes experienced as received knowledge that (as in language) *contain the conditions for their own reformulation.*

We can designate "a culture" the set of interrelations between a symbolic scheme and the diverse concerns, conscious and unconscious, of some population. Even to isolate a culture in this way requires encounters across different sets of interrelations, different cultures: Comparison is primary. Furthermore, societies, or more precisely social systems, are not simple empirical entities readily identified en passant by any investigator. Social systems are themselves abstractions (and thus symbols), made by an anthropologist according to his own culture, which orders his own social system and happens to include the values we call "anthropology." As we saw in Chapter 3, social systems are every bit as symbolic as cultures; but the two need not coincide.

"Social systems" are a diverse category: (1) residents of an island who directly reciprocate each other's culturally fashioned needs and desires; (2) native-born or otherwise "naturalized" citizens most of whom interrelate indirectly;

(3) nonnationalized groups from different areas who partly rely on each other for economic exchange, or for mutual confirmation of religious values, or for reciprocal proof of the contradictory claim that each is superior to the other. Thus nomads may regularly exchange pastoral goods for products from settled villages and in so doing confirm to themselves their rugged autonomy over the soft villagers, just as the latter perceive their own civility over the nomads' rusticity. Related conflicts and resolutions would vary according to whether the exchange (the system of replaceables) involved goods and products, spouses, services, labor, epithets, or reputations.

Whatever its scope and complexity, a social system need not be happy, harmonious, or homogeneous; but it remains systematic. In Chapter 3 we saw that to qualify as a social system in Durkheim's sense of "organic solidarity," a set of contrasting identities and roles must be *regularly perpetuated* over the generations. This fact, however, implies neither tranquillity nor political conservatism. Nor are social systems merely reflected or mirrored by their "cultures." Again, the two analytic slices through living populations are at different levels. I would phrase the irreducibility of society/culture this way: Cultures are ideals and values situated between social structures, and vice versa.

As both culture theorists and structuralists have stressed, relations between cultures and social systems are indirect.[1] No culture, whether a postindustrial nation or a band of hunters, is a reflex of economic "necessity," since what is deemed necessary is always overspecified, given economic constraints. Nor are cultures simple reflexes of political strategy, since living social systems embed "power" in factions, generations, descent rules, legitimacy, role differentiation, and other cultural values that preclude reducing power to an abstraction. Cultures neither reflect specific environmental conditions nor record an increasingly efficient ecological adaptation that works to the long-term advantage of some social systems. Nor do cultures maximize sets of psychological satisfactions through the camouflaged "expression" or projection of needs that could be put more directly, simply, rationally, scientifically, positivistically. Cultures can be reduced to none of these dimensions; it would all be so much easier if they could. The argument that cultures are symbolic (as are the social systems they valorize) does not overlook political power, economic forces, psychological and environmental needs and conditions, pervasive human suffering, or occasional human grandeur. Rather, the argument insists that powers, forces, needs, and conditions are never brute; they are transformed, intrinsically replaceable, conceivably otherwise. The concept of culture does not ignore harsher realities, but situates them in their motivational complexity and manifold determinacies.

To put these points themselves otherwise, cultures are more than machines for surviving or living or oppressing or even, in the idiom of our day, coping. As the possibility of cross-cultural comparison itself proves, "culture" removes "society" from some presumed immediacy of social bonds and of any external conditions. If social systems contain machines for living, cultures imbue those machines with affect, belief, rationales, persuasiveness, and "conceivable otherwiseness." Like anthropology itself, cultures exaggerate each other. Cultures produce beliefs in metaphysical others (or if not, they produce beliefs in the ridiculousness of cultures that do so, making the believers in metaphysical others as "other" as are the metaphysical others in cultures that believe in them!). Furthermore, cultures produce beliefs in cultural others. Now, perhaps such beliefs are in some way "adaptive," but this seems too bland a tag for them. For one thing, we cannot clearly specify the object or end point of the adaptation any more than earlier scholars could substantiate the teleology of their evolutionisms. Moreover, cultures, in positing notions of "others" as alternatives to themselves, motivate members of society both to maintain and to question their own social mechanisms. The conditions that produce either social maintenance or social change can be specified for particular instances but never for the culture as a whole, because it is in the nature of culture to be able to recondition the conditions. If this were not so, *we* could never identify *their* culture in the first place.

Many symbolic and semiotic anthropologists (myself included), at first glance paradoxically, admire the achievements of functionalism. An important component in the discipline is to demonstrate that apparently bizarre institutions, practices, and beliefs in fact *do* things, such as stabilize social relations, organize power play, maximize productivity, and charter general social arrangements. Heated disagreements arise only over the implication that such mechanistic functions *explain* the institutions, practices, or beliefs in question or that the sole task of the discipline is to document these doings.

Functionalist arguments and demonstrations are a necessary means of questioning the exoticity that we project onto remote customs. Yet functionalists overstep their bounds when they imply that by mapping the mechanisms one captures the culture. Mechanism itself breaks down as explanation because, however detailed the contextual account, we cannot specify the external conditions necessary and sufficient to manufacture the cultural apparatus that works this way. Nor can we devise the recipe for the mechanism's successful functioning or the standards against which any failures would be reckoned such by those implementing the mechanism. Societies may look like machines and occasionally at particular levels may work like machines, but they are not analogous to machines. Nor are interpretations of something culturally complex, say irrigation or marriage policies, to be assessed according to their machine likeness, whether mechanical or statistical. Although cultures can obviously accomplish ends, they always say more than they do. They cannot do things – even reproduce members, select spouses, produce subsistence, vent aggression, react to death, and so forth – without saying in and of the way they do it something that is not merely implicit in its being done. So far, no marriage system is a simple reflex of anyone's – native or observer – idea of an incest taboo. No irrigation directly implements for all involved some objectively ideal water allocation for maximum production of a rationally designated foodstuff. No political system, despotic or democratic, implements unified, unambiguous relations of power.

C. Geertz has phrased all these semiotic negatives as a cultural plus: "The whole point of a semiotic approach to culture is . . . to aid us in gaining access to the conceptual world in which our subjects live so that we can, in some extended sense of the term, converse with them" (1973:24). Posing conversation "in some extended sense" as the goal of semiotics, Geertz leaves open whether we emphasize the *they* conversed with, the *we* conversing, or the limits and principles of such conversations. All, I think, are worthy. These options distinguish modes of cultural interpretation and structuralism. Yet no semiotic endeavor mistakes conversing with as collapsing into. Our locus is cross-cultural, the most "extended" sense of conversation imaginable. Finally, to facilitate such conversation, semiotics relies on symbols, devices that keep cultures (like languages) dialectically removed from deterministic mechanisms. Symbols are our sole means of access to or egress from "cultures," the highest order of semiotic replaceables.

Paradox over mechanism

It is easy for the positivist to dismiss metaphor as "unscientific," as a substitute for rational or scientific reasoning, as belonging to the enchanted areas of life – art, religion, and myth. But from metaphor proceed some of the dominating themes of Western science and philosophy, as well as art. I shall mention three only, but they will serve to to suggest the vastness of the influence of metaphor. They are *growth*, *genealogy*, and *mechanism*.

R. Nisbet, *Sociology as an Art Form*

Let me start with the apparently paradoxical and yet perfectly plain and absolutely true proposition that the words of one language are never translatable into another.

B. Malinowski, *Coral Gardens and Their Magic*

It is easier to list what semiotics is not – positivism, behaviorism, utilitarianism, idealism or materialism, routinized functionalism – than to stipulate what it is. Semiotics is, in a word, the science of "meaning." Yet this definition does little to restrict the topic; rather, it introduces philosophical and critical traditions concerning the manifold "meanings of meaning," as in these admonitions by Max Black:

A little reflection will show "meaning" and its cognates to be one of the most overworked words in the language: it is a very Casanova of a word in its appetite for association. Any "theory of meaning," any attempt to do reasonable justice to the ways in which "meaning" is actually used, will need to take account of this extraordinary shiftiness of the word. Any monolithic, "single-factor" analysis of meaning is so implausible as to deserve little respect. [Black 1968:163]

The word becomes most licentious of all in anthropological investigations not directed primarily at "interiorized" meanings or at cognitive registers of meaning. Durkheim's concept of social facts and Weber's implication that charisma itself is an aspect of roles, institutions, and motivation apart from particular individual attributes preclude such restrictions on "meaning's" meaning.

The comparative anthropology of meaning proceeds apace while issues in depth psychology and linguistic "deep structure" remain unresolved. Anthropologists can isolate and analyze relatively abstract structures – less variable forms and codes – without assuming that to do so is to plumb psychological, linguistic, or philosophical depths. In fact, the view of abstract regularities as "deep," which often connotes interiorization, reflects a particular epistemology. Other epistemologies exist: Abstract regularities appear "high" from the vantage of Western religious cosmography; "elementary" from the vantage of Cartesian logic; "bloodless" from the vantage of empiricism; or for that matter "shallow" from the vantage of lived (*vécu*) experience. As I understand it, semiotics adopts no one of these attitudes but takes them all for what they are: possible variants. Finally, cultural meanings approached semiotically need reveal no purposive direction in history (whether for better or for worse) or permanent design. Resigning ourselves to forgo the ultimate meaning of cultural meanings can prove philosophically disturbing.

Semiotics, then, is the science of signs and symbols (two words no less promiscuous). Symbols and signs are *relatively* arbitrary, nonautomatic, optional, conventional, replaceable – at some level vis-à-vis some other level. Symbols and signs are improperly conceptualized in cause–effect relations. Moreover, any referential theory of meaning, which expects particular signs to bear singular relations with the things they signify, overlooks comparative complexities. Rather, a sign or a symbol (the latter will be our most inclusive term) *says* something. It is a selection from an implicit set of conceivable alternatives. Like Saussure's "sign" (the conjunction of a signifier and a signified, to be discussed), a symbol communicates positionally by what it is not. This fact precludes mechanical determinism.

I consider semiotics less an integral theory than a clearinghouse of issues in the complexities of communication processes.[2] It characteristically proceeds from careful observations about phenomena of language. Consider, for example, Martinet's points about linguistic arbitrariness:

A language is an instrument of communication in virtue of which human experience is analyzed differently in each given community into units, the monemes, each endowed with a semantic content and a phonic expression. The phonic expression is articulated in its turn into distinctive and successive units. These are the phonemes, of limited number in each language, their nature and mutual relations varying from one language to another.

This implies (1) that we must reserve the term language to describe an instrument of communication with this twofold articulation and vocal manifestation; (2) that outside this common basis there is nothing linguistic in the proper sense which may

not differ from one language to another. It is in this sense that we must understand the assertion that the facts of language are "arbitrary" or "conventional."
[Martinet 1966:29]

If everything properly linguistic differs from one language to another, language "itself" is essentially contrastive. This notion has been extended to the very smallest units of language and to the units of all activities that operate like language. Barthes, for example, characterized the structuralist object as simultaneously similar and dissimilar; only a resemblance at one level can make the difference at another level evident: The sounds *s/z* share the feature of dentality yet contrast according to the absence/presence of sonority; hence French has available the distinction between *poisson* ("fish") and *poison* ("poison"). What Jakobson and others would call the distinctive features behind the *s/z* contrast generate in French an entire field of possible semantic distinctions, only some of them actualized. Finally, with Lévi-Strauss one can explore the extent to which this sort of dialectical signification underlies all sorts of human activities, viewed comparatively:

Mais en est-il de même des autres aspects de la reálité sociale, tels que l'outillage, les techniques, les modes de production et de consommation? Il semblerait que nous ayons affaire ici à des objets, non à des signes – le signe étant, selon la célèbre définition de Peirce, "ce qui remplace quelque chose pour quelqu'un." Que remplace donc une hache de pierre, et pour qui? [Lévi-Strauss 1973:19]

Is a stone ax an object or a sign? To be a percept or concept, any object, even a tool or a means of production, must be understood as a relationship. Any relationship is implicitly selected from multiple possibilities; any relationship is a "structuralist object," a sign, "that which replaces something for someone."

Thus one way to develop a semiotic frame of mind is to extend principles of language to phenomena not so obviously languagelike by scrutinizing anything that appears pure, direct, or nonsymbolic. To take the simplest example I can imagine, consider the humble circle and line. This formal–logical antithesis, a seemingly pure type, conceals differential, ambiguous meanings if employed as representation. Taken together in their opposition, a circle and line may communicate a lollipop (φ), a yo-yo (ϕ), a spoon (─O), a severely amputated spider (○), or seven otherwise severely amputated spiders (○ . . .), with any arrangement equally capable of replacing any of the concepts or of replacing each other. Such ambiguity in symbolic representation is familiar from studies in psychological Gestalt theory and from the famous example of rabbit/duck (optional readings of an identical form, the latter's open beak becoming the former's ears) discussed by Wittgenstein, E. Gombrich, and many others.

Rabbits/ducks can shed light on cultures. Conventionally one culture's lollipop (φ) is another culture's balloon (φ). Or, more subtly, one culture's lollipop (♀) is another's "inverted" yo-yo (♀), in terms of the other's conventions of representation. Again, objects, forms, even tools are culturally meaningless independent of conventions of relationships. Moreover, language, music, and other forms are perhaps nothing save relationships – which may also be true of tools and of circles and lines (but I am no mathematician). Once we have acknowledged these complexities, semiotics requires another step. Contrary to many theories of percepts and concepts, including certain Gestalt and phenomenological ones, a particular culture's circle/line may not be representational in another culture at all. A circle/line need not necessarily be *re*-cognized *as* anything. To admit that a circle/line present in one culture may represent an absence, a negativity, in another culture is to reject formalism and radically to emphasize meaningful relationships.

The semiotics of cultures investigates "meaning" but not necessarily positive–present meanings. Nor is semiotics necessarily concerned with internal meanings. The distinction between intentionality and other levels of meaning is perhaps clearest in the domain of written texts, a point stressed by phenomenologists, New Critics, and structuralists alike:

> The ambiguity of the French expression *vouloir-dire*, the German *meinen*, and the
> English "to mean," attests to this overlapping. It is almost the same thing to ask "What
> do you mean?" and "What does that mean?" With written discourse, the author's
> intention and the meaning of the text cease to coincide. This dissociation of the verbal
> meaning of the text and the mental intention is what is really at stake in the inscription
> of discourse. Not that we can conceive of a text without an author; the tie between
> the speaker and the discourse is not abolished, but distended and complicated . . . the
> text's career escapes the finite horizon lived by its author. [Ricoeur 1979:78]

What a speaker means to say (or an author means to write) is only a small part of what his or her saying means; nor are all intentions freely available in all circumstances, since speakers speak understandably only through "languages" and "cultures," the conditions enabling us to posit "senders," "receivers," and "messages" with their complexes of codes, contacts, and so forth in the models of communication devised by Jakobson (1960) and others. By stressing the systems through which any meaning must be transmitted, semiotics displaces autonomous individuals as privileged reference points; this displacement avoids reducing meaning to matters psychological. By accentuating the negativity behind any code or system (pointing us toward alternate codes or systems), semiotics avoids as well reducing meaning to reference.

None of these points implies that cultural meanings have no formal, material or psychological aspects but only that these aspects neither exhaust nor explain them. At base the psychological is not private, nor is the material "natural." Indeed, approaches we would today call semiotic typically begin by opposing one or another reductionist explanation. One traditional foe is environmental determinism, hence a remark by Steiner that lodges the semiotic basis of comparative linguistics in a disarmingly passing, Boasian comment: "Eskimo syntax [along with five to eight thousand other languages, give or take a thousand] is appropriate to the Sahara" (1975:55). Indeed, Eskimo syntax (rules governing the sequencing of units in speech) is part of Eskimo culture, yet transferable to non-Eskimos (and new Eskimos) while remaining a particular manifestation of something generally called "language." As a language, Eskimo is seemingly nonspecific to the Arctic Circle, however many words its speakers might apply to "snow(s)." Yet, paradoxically from the vantage of environment, an Eskimo can be fully Eskimo only in Eskimo and fully himself only in his own version of Eskimo. These points are the foundation of anthropological studies in language and culture.

The convoluted semiotic fact is this: Something that within a designated culture looks like a simple behavioral response to a conditioning stimulus appears across cultures as a conventional performance evoked by a conceptualized circumstance. "Fear," for example, is not an automatic response to "death," because there is no culturally constant index of fear. Nor for that matter is there a culturally constant index of death. Cultures place fear, death, and everything else within quotation marks. Cultures are, with respect to each other, discursive. All this is, as the saying goes, "Anthropology 101, Week 2: Relativity." But it bears repeating, because as beliefs and customs have come to appear less like behavioral responses and more like systematic statements, semiotics has burgeoned.

Today semiotics is vast beyond measure. Umberto Eco, who himself holds a professorship of semiotics, has conservatively listed multiple subfields: zoosemiotics, olfactory signs (codes of scents), tactile communication, codes of taste, paralinguistics (supplementary codes during speech events), medical semiotics, kinesics and proxemics (gesture codes), musical codes, formalized languages, written languages, unknown alphabets, secret codes, natural languages (same province as linguistics, much philosophy, anthropology, and psychology), visual communication, systems of objects, plot structure, text theory, cultural codes, aesthetic texts, mass communication, rhetoric (1976: 9–14).

While the contents of semiotics seem comically all-inclusive, certain principles can be stated succinctly. In keeping with Eco's last subfield, for example, semiotics approaches nothing as a simple fact of truth. It is less what is said that matters than how what is said can be taken arbitrarily or relatively according to certain conventions. This point recalls medieval rhetoric:

The Schoolmen said that the *proprium* of human beings is to be *ridens*. . . not only is semiotics the science of everything subject to the lie: *it is also the science of everything subject to comic or tragic distortion*. . . To explain the comic effect means to elaborate a complete intensional semantics, or a theory of content. To explain the semiotic import of the lie means to understand why and how a lie (a false statement) is semiotically relevant irrespective of the truth or the falsity of that statement. [Eco 1976:64–65; italics in the original]

Such relative arbitrariness underlies human abstraction – the means by which concepts are removed from an immediate stimulus.

Any content-laden image of humankind – *anthropos* as essentially power grabbing, or sexually repressed, or belief seeking, or intrinsically doubting – is finally nonsemiotic. Inspired by the multiplicity and variability of languages and languagelike systems, semiotics doubts bottom lines and inexorable fates ("alienation," "modernization"), and it questions explanations of cultural diversity – say, human dietary preferences and taboos – by ecologically specific adaptative benefits.

Putting the matter positively, semiotics ensures against (!) explaining away cultural variation. If something uniform or invariable is suggested, a semiotician maintains active skepticism, so as not to naturalize anything cultural. Yet semiotics posits not flaccid relativity or free-wheeling diversity but variations at one level of something less variant at another level. Now, the least variant level may ultimately be designated Nature (Enlightenment), or psychic unity (psychological anthropology), or human constants (pattern theory), or innate capacities (Chomsky), or generic potentialities (Geertz). Or it may be viewed less as ultimate invariance than as relative randomness, as in Lévi-Strauss's concept of a Nature against which the universe of rules (Culture) imposes selected orders. Regardless, this final level can never be reached semiotically, because as one approaches it, one's analytic apparatus emulsifies. One finds oneself relativizing the a priori by imagining its contrast or even its absence. Just as investigators are about to succumb to "positivize" a meaning, they notice themselves about to succumb, thus shifting a level and rendering meaning at the prior level relatively arbitrary once again. (E.g.: *En train de succomber a "menentukan" eine Bedeutung, le rechercheur se regarde comme prête à [menjerah, sterben, s'y soumettre] le faire, donc sich heissen sederajat lagi en rendant le früher sens encore relativement arbitraire*.) Little wonder that practitioners of semiotics grew queasy. On the one hand their endeavor is polyglot, recalling famous predecessors:

It is as if [Marx and Engels] had developed their special cutting comic tone, their detached and implacable attitude, their personal polyglot language ("Apropos! Einige Portwein und Claret wird mir sehr wohl tun under present circumstances;" "Die verfluchte vestry hat mich bon gré mal gré zum 'constable of the vestry of St. Pancras' erwählt") in proportion as they have come to realize that they can take in more and more of the world. [Wilson 1940/1972:251)

On the other hand semiotics is, or should be, both dialectical and reflexive, tricky concepts to which I will shortly return.

Semiotic methodologists are forever refining models of communication and meaning. Basic issues revolve around signs and symbols, and indexes, signals, signa, images, icons, and other message units, often qualified in degrees of conventional, arbitrary, and nonce, on down to habitual, motivated, and finally natural. Related issues include metaphor and metonymy and traditional "figures of speech," which imply principles of nonliteralness and thus covert conventions of understanding. Also important are the older denotative/connotative distinction and related notions of metaphorical "extension." The paradigmatic/syntagmatic contrast is pervasive (think of slot machines: One wins syntagmatically – three cherries [I think] in a row; but one knows the odds paradigmatically in terms of the set of possibilities for each position; suitably abstracted, language works the same way). Finally, semiotics traffics in genres, notations, scores, scripts, performances, and everything that transcends mere human (to borrow a term from Edmund Leach) "whim."

I like to categorize semiotic pursuits into two general divisions: the visual-spatial and the aural-durational. The one tends toward mappings, architectonics, taxonomies, and Neoplatonic seeming schemes; the other tends toward discourse, decentering, and contrastive remove. The one is in the broadest sense of the term iconographic; the other is Saussurian. Yet in any semiotic study constants are posited thanks to variation. "Symbols" in religion, myth, ritual, language, and so forth make experience sharable but not identical. Symbols in fact make experience paradoxical: same stimulus (presumably), variable responses (culturally). The paradox merits amplification.

Cultural meaning is both context-laden and context-convertible (by "context" I intend psychological, demographic, and environmental conditions). Symbols are devices in cultural systems by which this fact is assured. Thanks to symbols, cultural meanings are rich, deep, multivocal, many layered, highly wrought, and shared but also rarifiable, subject to abstraction, exportable, often communicated: thus not substantively shared but rather *exchanged*. Something nonsymbolic would be either perfectly context-specific, a reflex of an external condition, or absolutely context-free, a given fact, an a priori. Something symbolic is from different vantages perceived as both (recall Peirce's "replacing something for someone").

Cultural symbols reveal a literal duplicity: (1) they mesh the options and possibilities (both real and imaginary) provided for in social action with the intellectual schemes that both guide and respond to action; thus they weave, interrelate, and cross-reference diverse spheres of life in society: cultural symbols integrate; *and* (2) they establish formulas that remain internally consistent regardless of context; without such formulas there could be no communication across cultures, no relative abstraction of one culture by another, no self-stereotyping by one culture against its stereotypes of others and, heaven forbid, no anthropology. Thus cultural symbols differentiate, indeed sometimes alienate, the very integrities they integrate. "Semiotics," as the term is employed in this book, attests to this paradoxical duplicity; by "symbols" the paradox is sustained.

Lest we feel overwhelmed by such semiotic intricacies, it is well to recall a basic limit: However varied the anthropological approaches to symbolic forms across cultures, they are *less varied* than the cultures themselves. Yet the intricacies intensify when we acknowledge that cultures, as anthropologists abstract them, *are* symbolic forms, and so are anthropological approaches. This exponential symbolism precludes any positivistic view of "reality" or "experience" as directly apprehensible through unmediated ("lived") channels of stimulus-response, need-adaptation, or interior intuition.

To achieve a semblance of control, anthropological accounts of exotic symbolism often emphasize social meaning – not psychological meaning, not intuitive meaning, not linguistic meaning (although this last provides a near equivalent). Social meaning is significance registered in both feeling and intellection that intensifies the differentiation of populations into clans, classes, castes, lineages, generations, alternate generations, sexes, occupations, families, ritual specializations, speech communities, roles, "individuals," and so forth. Social differentiation and integration are heightened in the very processes by which humans symbolize themselves and their contexts and motivate collective activities through time and across space. Groups approached with primary reference to social meanings, rather than to social divisions per se, are better designated cultures. The hypothetical totality of all such meanings is "culture itself" – a too-fulsome concept perhaps best left aside.

With our semiotic paradox, which seems to me irreducible, freshly in mind, it is worth considering several endeavors that are in part semiotic but ultimately differ from a thoroughgoing comparative semiotics of cultures. I shall designate four such areas: symboling, generative models, protomodels, and transformationalism.

Symboling

Anthropological semiotics strives to catch cultures in the flagrant act of symboling. Yet certain influential theories of symbols remain largely mechanistic and, I would say, subsemiotic. Societies or groups are said to use symbols and to develop more complex symbol systems. For example, L. White's well-known "Symboling: a Kind of Behavior" offers these definitions:

A *symbol* may be defined as a thing or event, an act or an object, upon which meaning has been bestowed by human beings: holy water, a fetish, a ritual, a word. A symbol is, therefore, a composite of (1) a meaning, and (2) a physical structure. A symbol must have a physical form; otherwise it and its meaning can not enter our experience – unless we are willing to accept the claims to telepathy or clairvoyance. But there is no necessary relationship between the meaning of a symbol and its physical basis; the relationship between the two is purely arbitrary . . .

But there is another class of things or events whose meanings may be related in purely arbitrary fashion to their physical forms: a green triangle may mean food to a laboratory rat, or it may mean an electric shock, or something else. But this is a *sign*, not a *symbol*.

A *sign* is a thing or event that indicates something else. There are two kinds of signs: (1) those whose meanings are inherent in themselves and their contexts (steam issuing from the radiator of an automobile, geese flying south, jaundiced eyeballs), and (2) those whose meanings are not inherent in their physical structures and situations (the green triangle that means food, the yellow quarantine flag). One learns the meanings of signs by experience (observation, the conditioned reflex). [L. White 1962:26–7]

Semiotics opens the space between the essentially materialistic alternatives of patent physicality versus clairvoyance somewhat scoffingly posed by White and many predecessors. White views signs as conventions arising from statistical regularities or conditioned reflexes; and his phrase "bestowing meaning on" implies that meaning is merely attached to rather than constitutive of. This residue of positivism characterizes archaeological-development views of symbols as well.

Generative models

Other developmental approaches in semiotics, in particular generative ones, are a shade more dialectical. The influential works of J. Piaget provide a case in point. Piaget argues that human reasoning, not to be reduced to mere stimulus-response, occurs according to conceptual structures normally ordered in set stages of increasing complexity:

As soon as the semiotic function (speech, symbolic play, images, and such) comes on the scene and with it the ability *to evoke what is not actually perceived*, that is, as soon as the child begins to represent and think, he uses reflective abstractions: certain connections are "drawn out" of the sensori-motor schemata and "projected upon" the new plane of thought; these are then elaborated by giving rise to distinct lines of behavior and conceptual structures. [Piaget 1968:64; emphasis added]

No stage is ever quite left behind, because each new stage is implicit in the structure of the prior stage. The generative model contains a dialectics of emergence, whereas simple developmental or evolutionary models remain sequential, with the transformations between stages unclarified.

Generative models require a constant unit that persists as semiotic complexity increases. For Piaget it is the child. A child demonstrates emergent schemata for "evoking what is not actually present"; but at whatever stage, it remains the same child. Unlike native views of life-crises rites, for example, a generative view considers new structures merely as subsequent stages of the same being, not as evidence of new being or rebirth into a different social being (cf. Van Gennep 1909/1960).

Psycholinguistics and sociolinguistics apply generative models to problems in language development: Maturing speakers acquiring full language competence along with cognitive and motor skills. Normal language development reveals stages ranging from simple (some would say two-positional) grammars to the full elaboration of adult syntax. Issues in language development concern this emergent complexity: Some codes are simply repressed in subsequent stages; if stages are skipped, do the full consequences become evident only at much later stages? Abnormalities in development provide crucial evidence about normal workings of a "semiotic function," recalling Jakobson and Halle's celebrated study of aphasia (1956).

Development of competence in speakers of a particular language can be approached generatively, thanks to contrasts between different stages and between these and abnormal patterns produced by hearing and speech defects, brain damage, and so forth. But the relevance of generative models to language diversity is less clear. Modern linguistics seldom pose generative relations between present-day languages or any languages *as total spoken languages*. This fact strikingly distinguishes their aims from nineteenth-century philological motives (e.g., Sanskrit as the wellspring of German, both Aryan languages) and from both medieval and Renaissance interests in hermetics and Kabbalism (see Chapters 2 and 7). The relationship between modern linguistics and Enlightenment theories of signs is more complicated, because General Grammarians prefigured the modern tendency toward descriptive versus historical studies (with the emphasis of synchronic over diachronic and *langue* over *parole*) by posing an abstract, Cartesian locus of language order.

Protomodels

In these difficult linguistic issues, there is one important concept that appears somewhat generative: "protolanguage." Yet any identification of the historical linguist's "proto" and a semiotic "generative" would be misleading. A protolanguage is never formulated from the same order of evidence as contemporary speech. A protolanguage is constructed from contemporary evidence plus textual evidence. The latter may appear to carry us back to expressions of the protolanguage that are nearer to its originality. But the complex relationship between written texts and once-spoken language precludes direct evidence of the latter, even if we assume that it was in fact a spoken language (such as vulgar Latin) and not instances of refined, normative, rhetorical standards (such as classical Latin). A protolanguage is a different level of linguistic construct from its cognate spoken languages or from some archaized set of standards embodied in a literary standard. On the other hand, generative models like Piaget's are based on the conviction that uniform evidence can be adduced for each and every stage in the normal development from infant to adult cognition.

In other words a protomodel is precisely neither generative nor developmental. In a posited sequence from a protolanguage to a current language (even abstracted at a langue level), any stage may, taken alone, appear less complex than the relations between its entire range of successors. But as an abstracted language capacity (a langue) that presumably rendered possible the understood speech (parole) of a community of speakers, the protolanguage is no simpler than, however different from, subsequent cognates. Whatever was spoken back when paroles of the protolanguage were current was just as thoroughgoing as later cognate languages. This indirectness of evidence in the very idea of proto lends it a more dialectical flavor than a generative approach that hopes for direct laboratory evidence of all stages. Yet the concept of proto still imputes a kind of weight and authority to an earlier stage rather than operationalizing a perpetual analytic distance from any instance of variant systems unevenly evidenced in writing and speech.[3]

Transformationalism

I have implied that the diversity of languages is inhospitable to generative models. Yet many linguists hope to clarify all languages, at least one by one, with transformational models. The relations between generative and transformational approaches to grammar, syntax, and semantics are more complicated than I am qualified to explain. We should, however, consider briefly the type of transformational analysis associated for several decades with the name of Chomsky. To simplify radically: A transformational model is something like a two-stage generative model but with no stages, just levels – surface and deep. In a broad sense, analyzing one level of a system as the readout, or the performative realization, or the projection of a more profound level is transformational:

Various writers have pointed out its similarities in this abstract sense to the theoretical programmes of Chomsky, de Saussure and Piaget – all of them based on the analysis of surface phenomena derived from underlying structures through the interposition of transformation rules – in Freud's case, dream work and the distortions of ego defence mechanisms – were the principal transformations. Perhaps, as intellectual historians, we should take seriously the fact that this type of formulation has had so powerful an impact on common sense, on interpretations of the ordinary. [J. Bruner 1976]

From this vantage everyone begins to look fairly uniform (the Enlightenment is never far removed). Freud, for example, sees individual consciousness as a projection (a false projection) of subconscious desires. Marx sees class consciousness as an ideology (a false consciousness) of economic relationships. Lévi-Strauss sees myth as concrete–logical evidence of esprit. Indeed, commentators occasionally classify these three scholars together and lump them with Chomsky: just so many structuralists. But this reduction, which collapses both transformationalism and structuralism into fancy terms for analysis, obscures crucial differences among its victims. For both Freud and Marx the surface level is masked and emotively conflictual. But analysis can detect the truth; and therapy, whether through psychoanalysis or historical action, can bring the surface projections – consciousness, ideology – into genuine relationships with the deep level. I call this view utopianist. In contrast, Lévi-Strauss allows for logical contradiction and certainly does not preclude emotive conflict (although, as we shall see, he never grants it privileges).

But his resigned view of myth foresees no ultimate resolution between myth and the orders of social structure, marriage and descent, ritual, ecology, and so forth that it dialectically constitutes.

Compared with all the former, Chomsky's transformationalism seems practically puritanical. Surface structures mask nothing; they merely realize deep structure. There is little sense of conflict or contradiction, emotive, logical or otherwise. Moreover, in contrast to Lévi-Strauss, Chomsky need trace no transformations between language and anything else – or, more to the point, between different languages – except presumably to say that the deep structures of two languages would be closer than their surface structures. (Like Marx's idea of labor, considered above, Chomsky's idea of deep structure is uniformitarian – recalling Enlightenment ideals.)

Chomskian transformationalism is an extreme example of analyzing a language in a way that is completely internal to language itself. From the surface structures of grammatical sentences ("John hit the ball") paraphrased by competent speakers into variations ("The ball was hit by John"), one abstracts deep rules governing the relation of (in this case) active to passive constructions. The goal of analysis is to delineate the "transformations" that enable passives and actives to be understood by competent speakers as grammatically correct paraphrases. Transformationalism is important to semiotics for illustrating how analysis can remain internal to the phenomenon at issue. Transformational grammar enables a linguist to enable a language to elaborate something of itself in itself to itself without looking outside itself. Transformationalism, furthermore, recognizes that *unending* variability, at least syntagmatically, can result from the application of a *finite* set of rules – as in Chomsky's famous point about the recursiveness of language.

Yet the self-containedness of transformationalism sustains a uniformitarian hope of detecting the deep structure of all languages. This hope opens a wide gulf between transformationalism and both a semiotic view of cultures and a structuralist view of myths, whereby myths establish codes to articulate cultural and social values and distinctions, including the distinction between myth itself and other orders and levels. In strongest contrast to transformationalist ideals of general order, structuralist myths become metalanguages that establish the conditions of possibility of ritual paralanguages and vice versa.

I have introduced these allusions to developmental, generative, and transformational approaches to imply that the semiotics of cultures have not proceeded this far. Nor, I think, can they without again brushing against Enlightenment uniformitarian simplicity (cf. Chapter 2). Generative and evolutionary models of the rise and development of culture are, of course, commonplace in archaeology. But they require reading *entire* cultures according to *particular* institutional components rendered accessible by material evidence. Who would quarrel with the view that an administrative apparatus or an irrigation technology can increase in scale and efficiency? But this fact implies not increasing cultural or civilizational complexity but only an elaboration of one component while others – marriage alliance, familial authority, *science concrète*, and so on – diminish. Total "cultures," with their rules for perpetuating their own recognized divisions and distinctions in areas of kinships and marriage, power, subsistence, and ritual and religion, remain equally complex and mutable. How would I even presume to deem my culture more advanced than a Bushman's, I who cannot distinguish one variety of grub-worm from another, although they include the contrast poisonous/harmless. Such maladaptation on my part; such underdevelopment!

Eschewing an overspecified generative model, the semiotics of cultures also evades hermetic transformationalism. This, for a semiotic reason: All languages are equally complete, and none is an atavism of another. Anything can be communicated just as well (but not, of course, just as succinctly) in any language. Recall for a moment the famous hypothesis advanced by Whorf and Sapir that grammar constrains world view, that members of cultures conceptualize experience according to the rules governing how they speak. If Whorf was right in his celebrated work on Hopi (1964), the Hopi Indian language more readily articulates quantum physics than does everyday English. But this fact would not necessarily imply that the Hopi world view is any truer to quantum physics than is the world view of people who speak English. It means, rather, that Hopi *grammar* (covert, unconscious) is nearer the quantum physics *world view* (overt, formulated) than is English grammar. Semiotically, the notion that overt quantum physics is closer to covert Hopi than to covert English or German is less surprising. All this reasoning holds – if Whorf was right (cf. M. Black 1962a: chap. 14).

Yet right or wrong, the Whorf-Sapir hypothesis conveys a basic semiotic value: The wealth of attested human languages appear "merely" different ways of articulating what – in terms of any informational gloss external to the particular language in question – might as well not be in that particular language. Except that culturally, if it were not in that language, it just, well, wouldn't be Eskimo or Hopi (although it might be quantum physics!). That languages say differently what is ultimately different only because there are different languages (tied to different cultures but not tied one to one) is the semiotic centerpiece of language and cultural diversity.

Semiotically, no language is inherently more or less natural, true, adaptive, efficient, sublime, original, pristine, or decadent than another. Moreover, no whole-language is generatively more complex than another. Particular analyzable aspects may vary in complexity across languages. One spoken language may have a larger lexical set than others; or two spoken languages may differ in complexity of syntax, or affixing, or phonetic spectrum. But any relative simplicity may balance out with complexity in some other aspect.[4]

Contrary to commonplace notions, no whole-language is intrinsically easier than another. The question is semiotically provocative, because it cannot really be asked or answered "objectively." A speaker judges difficulty of other languages from his or her native speaking. Even the so-called bilingual or tri-lingual speaker has a "native language," a set of transformations that operate his or her performance across competences usually recognized as different languages. Moreover, it is uncertain that a bilingual's speaking capacity is any richer than a monolingual's, because the bilingual speaker might underelaborate various possibilities elsewhere highly elaborated. An English–French bilingual, for example, may rely inordinately on usages characterized by equivalent syntax, such as "not that I know of/*pas que je sache*."

The question of "easiness" cannot arise with respect to one's native speaking capacity, since there is nothing to compare except hypothetical nonlanguage. Any difficulty with native language that registers as a communication disorder (such as aphasia) is as much exaggeration as simplification. Disorder is a kind of order, a dis-order. English speakers can wonder if German or French is easier only with respect to English, or actually only with respect to their particular English, their "idiolect." An English speaker whose native competence hinges more on syntax (the metonymic pole of speaking-thinking) may find German easier, because Germanic principles of English register in our syntax. A vocabulary-oriented speaker (the metaphoric pole of speaking-thinking) should find French more compatible, thanks to our Norman loan words.

In all these issues the profound semiotic point remains: If languages are respectively neither true nor false, better nor worse, easier nor harder, nor reflexive of something external to them (environment, technology, divinity), what are they? They are systematically different, yet each is thoroughly integral. Each thus appears in itself immanently right and uniquely confirmed yet can be taken cognizance of only in contradistinction to others. In such respects, then, languages are highly reminiscent of cultures: Whatever appears internal to a culture is admissible *as cultural* because a case of its absence is likewise known or imagined. *Cultural interpretation poses relative integration across evidence of contrary cases.* Thus, short of generative models and outside mere transformationalism, stands the semiotic paradox of cultures: that arbitrary/motivated duplicity that I just saluted.

Peirce, Saussure, and Peirce

We had learned that each language is arbitrary in its classifications, but this traditional (particularly Whitney's and Saussure's) statement is subjected by Boas to an essential restriction: indeed, the Introduction [to his Kwakiutl dictionary] says each language may be arbitrary, but solely "from the point of view of another language" in space or in time. In a mother-tongue whether "primitive" or "civilized" no classifications are arbitrary for its speakers. Such classifications develop "in each individual and in the whole people entirely subconsciously" and build a kind of linguistic mythology which may direct the attention of the speaker and some mental activities of the given speech community in definite lines.

R. Jakobson, "Franz Boas' Approach to Language"

Comparative cultural semiotics – not mechanistic, generative, or transformational, yet keeping track of all such possibilities – accepts the limits of analysis associated with the theories of Saussure and Peirce. Aiming neither to reduce signs and symbols to simpler universals nor simply to regulate their interrelation, these scholars disclosed the diversity (variation) across generalized systems. To advance their project, it is important as well to compare the founders of semiotics and semiology themselves, whose legacy originated cross-culturally. What could be a more appropriate anthropological task than helping the conceptual worlds of Peirce and Saussure gain access to each other, albeit paradoxically?

Resisting a still murkier neologism – semiologics? – I call semiotics the insistence on relative arbitrariness of signs and symbols in systems of meaning. If the arbitrariness were absolute, it itself would not be arbitrary (I cannot even think about it). "Relative" arbitrariness implies that the very act of delineating a sign or symbol contains the capacity to negate the meaning, at that level. This point, less obscure than it sounds, merges Saussure's semiology and Peirce's semiotics: Each requires the other to become complete. Saussure managed to isolate "language" as systematic, but the only means of ushering additional data into an analysis was to collapse it into "language." Peirce's typology of signs helps surmount this dilemma by enabling us to elaborate Saussure's distinction of arbitrary/motivated (cf. Friedrich 1979: chaps. 1–2).

I begin with Saussure's "sign." A sign is one point in a system of connections between (1) a system of sounds (distinguished by a community of speakers-hearers) and (2) a system of concepts (understood by a community of speakers-hearers). *Systems*, then, are pervasive. Systems are arrangements of units such that a change in one automatically shifts all the others. Lengthen one side of a triangle and, to remain a triangle, the other sides must be lengthened according to precise formulas. Or a key signature in music is a system of relations between a selection of the possible positions on the scale. Change one note and either you have another system (key) or the other notes must shift.

Now, in Saussure the sound system and the concept system are both *systems of differences* rather than systems of substances. Again, a sign is a point of connection between the two systems of differences. Consider the sound half of a sign. A sound connects with a concept only by virtue of the systematically distinguished sounds that it is *not*. The sound *fad* connects a concept different from the concept connected to by *pad* only because the contrast *f/p* is heard (is phonological) in English. Were this contrast not heard (as it is not, e.g., in Indonesian), there would be no *f/p* sound to distinguish two concepts. I want to stress that this point could not be made if there were only one language; but there isn't.

The concept half of a sign (a connection) is also a unit in a system of differences. This fact is clearest in areas of obviously "scalable" concepts, such as colors, musical notes, and so forth. A particular color is distinguished by being *not* what other colors are, just as the notes of a musical scale. (Whether we could see or hear anything unscaled in these examples is beside the point; the issue is how we discriminate and scale light waves into colors and sustained tones into music.) Many followers of Saussure consider that this differential quality characterizes the whole of human concepts, the thought half of the language-and-thought issue (of course, it characterizes the language half as well). This view can seem very mysterious and Eastern, or very preliterate, or very Platonic: In fact it has reminded diverse commentators of any non-Aristotelian emphasis on the musiclike nature of experience.

The twofold entity "sign" is the heart of Saussurian semiology. An entire system of signs – an entire set of connections between a sound system (signifiers) and a concept system (signifieds) – is a language. In fact the sole means by which sounds or concepts are communicated (experienced?) is the system of signs. Yet for some reason we think signs are abstractions of sounds and concepts when our most immediate information is the signs themselves. Which is the ghost(s) and which the machine(s)? This is the unsettling implication of Saussurian epistemology:

> If, Saussure writes, the most precise characteristic of every sign is that it differs from other signs, then every sign in some sense bears the traces of all the other signs; they are co-present with it as the entities which define it. This means that one should not think, as logocentrism would like to, of the presence in consciousness of a single, autonomous signified. What is present is a network of differences. If I utter the word *brown* the "concept" present in my mind (if there is a concept present at all) is not some essence but a whole set of oppositions. Indeed, ultimately we could say that the whole notion of a linguistic system, the whole notion of *la langue* as Saussure defines it, is that of networks of differences at the level of both signifier and signified – networks which are already in place, already inscribed or written, as it were, in the mind of the subject. The act of uttering is simply a transitory and hence imperfect way of using one network of differences (those of the signifier) to produce a form which can be interpreted in terms of the other network of differences (those of the signified). The meaning of *brown* is not some essence which was in my mind at the moment of utterance but a space in this impersonal network of differences (the semantic system of the language).
>
> Attempts to challenge logocentrism involve a host of extremely complex problems and have so far appeared only in very abstruse discussions, of which the most intelligent are the writings of Jacques Derrida. [Culler 1977:122–3][5]

We can go further. The heard distinction in English between *blue* and *black* renders possible a coded difference between two areas of the color spectrum, and not every language codes this color difference. That is, some languages leave our *blue/black* concept distinction undifferentiated, just as in Saussure's famous example the English contrast "mutton/sheep" remains in French the undifferentiated "mouton" (cf. Boon, 1972:71). Moreover, where two concepts are distinguished, the similarity of the sounds *blue/black* (the common *bl*) implies no similarity between the percepts blue and black or the concepts blueness and blackness. Sounds are in this sense unmotivated with reference to concepts (and vice versa): The sign as connector is an arbitrary value. This arbitrary aspect might cloud over when, for example, the sounds *blue/black* (rather, *black/blue*) through their alliteration and a conventionalized reference to bruises acquire a sense of substantive similarity that seems to echo their heard similarity (the alliteration). But such poetic and metaphorical dimensions do not contradict the fundamental arbitrariness of sound with respect to concepts and vice versa. Saussure's breakthrough was to demonstrate arbitrariness by making reference not to some unmotivated "Nature" but to *other* languages, entities we know only contrastively, just as we know their constituent· units only contrastively.

Innumerable academic debates in semiotics and semiology have developed from Saussure's issue of arbitrariness. In fact pedantic-sounding shop-talk squabbles about the nature of basic units of meaning are the virtual trademark of semiotics. To illustrate the point, I shall take issue with a discussion of meaning by Eco, certainly a most circumspect semiotician, who generalizes as follows:

> What, then, is the meaning of a term? From a semiotic point of view, it can only be a *cultural unit*. In every culture "a unit is simply anything that is culturally defined and distinguished as an entity. It may be a person, place, thing, feeling, state of affairs, sense of foreboding, fantasy, hallucination, hope or idea. In American culture such units as uncle, town, blue (depressed), a mess, a hunch, the idea of progress, hope and art are cultural units" (Schneider 1968:2)...A unit of this type might also be recognized as an intercultural unit which remains invariable despite the linguistic symbol with which it is signified: /dog/ denotes not a physical object but a cultural unit which remains constant or invariable even if I translate /dog/ by /cane/ or /chien/ or /Hund/. In the case of /crime/ I might find that the corresponding cultural unit in another culture has a broader range or more restricted range; in the case of /snow/ it might be found that for the Eskimos there are in fact four cultural units which correspond to four different states of snow and which are conveyed by four expression-units. [Eco 1976:67]

It is mistaken to distinguish /dog/ from /crime/ or /snow/ in this regard because Schneider's "cultural units" imply that the "meaning of a term" is never constant or invariable across languages. Even /dog/ and /chien/ are not simply two different terms for an invariable reference. While /dog/ and /chien/ may conceivably serve as label for an identical set of quadrupeds, the exclamation "Dog!" would more likely appear in French as *Cochon!* than as *Chien!* and *mon petit chienchien* would probably translate "my little turtledove," whereas "my little doggy" might become *mon petit toutou*. We can add all the contrasting "associative sets" of synonyms and opposites that surround terms with such varied resonances across cultures, such as d-o-g as a mirror image of G-o-d, important in certain English poetics; with no equivalent n-e-i-h-c in French. As in so-called connotation, so in so-called reference. I take Schneider's semiotic point to be that a term as a *cultural unit* does not correspond at any level (even referential or denotative) to any cross-culturally constant reference, a fact obscured in functionalist theories of "metaphorical extension." The point holds not just for lexemes and the classes they are presumed to label but for all "cultural units." Although Eco ultimately confirms the point, his momentary capitulation to /dog/ = /chien/ as an invariable cross-cultural unit misses the fullest implications of a concept of arbitrariness, implications developed for culture theory by D. M. Schneider (1968, 1972, 1976a) and for "operational" semantics by John Lyons (1968, 1977).

Thus, whatever *chien* means is not necessarily packaged and coded by any term in another language. Saussure's sheep/mutton versus *mouton* proves as much. The importance of this point cannot be overstated, because it underlies the very contrast arbitrary/motivated. Arbitrariness is a principle of language that registers across languages, whether or not it registers between language and something presumably external to "it." Consider the privileged philosophical case of onomatopoeia. The proof that onomatopoeias are not "naturally motivated" (identical with nonlanguage sounds) comes in comparing so-called imitations across languages. The difference between the way two languages phonetically encode the same external sound situates a relative arbitrariness even in onomatopoeia. Yet the fact of "onomatopoeia" as a possibility that languages entertain suggests that motivation is also fundamental, not because any phonetic pattern can be identical with language-external sounds, but because there is a value on connecting language sounds with presumed nonlanguage sounds (and, I would add, there is a language-based system for positing "nonlanguage sounds"). In brief, if we trace out the implications of Saussure, "motivation" is not a property of sign systems just when they are viewed from inside; nor is arbitrariness the ultimate outsider vantage on any and all languages. Rather, arbitrary/motivated is a relational and dialectical pair, each side of which is necessary to posit the other (recalling Durkheim's organic/mechanical). The same holds for all Saussure's distinctions, most clearly signifier/signified (since he labeled their dialectical complementarity the "value" of the "sign"), but also synchrony/diachrony, langue/parole, and paradigmatics/syntagmatics. In such distinctions, to abstract one side is automatically to precipitate the other (cf. Boon 1972: chap. 3; Culler 1976: chap. 2).

I use "symbol" to designate a Saussurian sign – an arbitrary systematic connection between at least two systems of differences – that if likewise (from outside the language) arbitrarily motivated is nevertheless *intrinsically susceptible to motivation*. Signs are inevitably supportable by connections with other levels of signs (beyond the sound/concept distinction).

This point situates us at the threshold between semiology and semiotics and brings to mind Lévi-Strauss's aphorism on Saussure: "To simplify my argument, I will say that the linguistic sign is arbitrary *a priori*, but ceases to be arbitrary *a posteriori*" (Lévi-Strauss 1963b:90; cf. Boon 1972:70ff). Here, however, I must insist that the so-called a posteriori is implied from the start. If not, we fall into the unsemiotic position of positing some absolute arbitrary, a non-sense. In Lévi-Strauss's formulation the a priori/a posteriori becomes as dialectical (versus sequential) as other oppositions of the sort K. Burke calls 'polar terms': "By 'positive' terms would be meant terms that imply no direct 'logical opposite,' as distinct from 'polar' terms, that do imply logical opposites. Thus, a word like 'table' is 'positive' in the sense that it implies no contradictory term such as 'anti-table,' or 'non-table.' But 'polar' terms such as 'right,' 'true,' 'order,' 'yes' imply respectively: 'wrong,' 'false,' 'disorder,' 'no' " (1970:24n). Burke's "polar terms" approximate what Durkheim called "the moral." Burke's insight helps us appreciate how structuralism views "totemism," for example, as cultural conventions that in fact "polarize" ostensibly positive terms and categories. Burke's comment also helps us notice something overlooked in British versions (e.g., Leach 1976; Needham 1973) of Lévi-Strauss' structuralism: Structuralist oppositions internalize their own "polarity." The second side of a productive opposition conceals a dialectical thrust; the second side implies a potential elaboration absent at that level in the first side. This quality characterizes all the fundamentally polar structuralist oppositions: silence/sound, raw/cooked, colorless/colored, and indeed a priori/a posteriori. Here I would suggest that the last-mentioned opposition becomes in Lévi-Strauss's above formulation a polar set; in fact it perhaps merges into synchronic/diachronic.

That symptomatic Saussurian queasiness – the semiological sense of Burke's "polar" – eventuates in Derrida's operationalized and exponential sense of *mise en abîme* (cf. DeMan 1971:10). Yet the queasiness arises even in translating "sheep/mutton" to *mouton*, if one realizes from the outset that the point is not to translate positive to positive or even polar to positive; the point is to comprehend any two languages as *polar with respect to each other*. The same point holds in translating ostensibly positive "dog" to *chien*, but the point is accentuated in terms with a clear contrast in differentiation, such as differentiated sheep/mutton versus undifferentiated mouton. Queasiness increases as we proceed to surmount the a priori/a posteriori distinction attached to arbitrary/motivated, that is, to make each opposition internally polar and to make both components polar with respect to each other. Having habituated ourselves to such queasiness, we can perhaps now tolerate surmounting even the semiology/semiotics opposition by translating Saussure into Peirce and vice versa, an endeavor that places us once more on the verge of exponential semiotics.

Again, I call a symbol the concurrence of arbitrary and motivated, which implies multiple levels of determining meaning for any "sign." In brief, what

Saussure called a sign is necessarily apprehended within semiotic systems as what Peirce designates an Icon. This point brings us to Peirce's fundamental typology of signs.

Peirce outlines the first member of his well-known typology of signs (Icon, Index, Symbol) as follows:

> An Icon is a sign which refers to the Object that it denotes merely by virtue of characters of its own, and which it possesses, just the same, whether any such Object actually exists or not. It is true that unless there really is such an Object, the Icon does not act as a sign; but this has nothing to do with its character as a sign. Anything whatever, be it quality, existent individual, or law, is an Icon of anything, in so far as it is like that thing and used as a sign of it. [Peirce 1893–1910/1955:102]

Thus, Peirce presents the Icon as a type of sign that is taken as a thing-itself that is like something else (the Object it signifies) but this Object's thing-itself-ness, its essence, is nowhere implied in and of its resemblance to this kind of sign, this Icon. Thus just as for Saussure, for Peirce the sign (in this case his Icon-type) demonstrates a kind of primacy vis-à-vis its Object. If anything in communication is immediate, the sign is, not sensations, not ideas, not anything extralinguistic. If anything, the Icon is less abstract than the Object.

The difference between Peirce's and Saussure's concepts of signs remains a vital issue in semiotics and semiology. The problem is compounded by the fact that Peirce clarified his types more than his concept of sign, which is what the types are types of. Such is philosophy. Possibly however, Saussure's notion of sign approaches Peirce's Symbol. Peirce's Symbol is patently conventional, the connection between a sign and an Object "by virtue of a law, usually an association of general ideas, which operates to cause the Symbol to be interpreted as referring to that Object" (ibid).

I am not using "symbol" in this way, because Saussure's sign seems to me to include such a social, contractual, conventional, and general basis while simultaneously insisting on the fundamental negative quality of signs (they are what they are not) and the systems through which they are constituted. Still, Peirce's "Symbol" approximates Saussure's "sign" because Peirce characterizes the Symbol by *the relation with the Interpretant* (*and not with the Object*). To pursue this point we might recall with Derrida that Peirce collapsed logic into semiotic:

> Semiotics no longer depends on logic. Logic, according to Peirce is only a semiotic: "Logic, in its general sense, is as I believe I have shown, only another name for semiotics (*semeiotike*), the quasi-necessary, or formal, doctrine of signs." And logic in the classical sense, logic "properly speaking," nonformal logic commanded by the value of truth, occupies in that semiotics only a determined and not a fundamental level. As in Husserl...
>
> Peirce goes very far in the direction that I have called the de-construction of the transcendental signified, which, at one time or another, would place a reassuring end to the reference from sign to sign. I have identified logocentrism and the metaphys-

ics of presence as the exigent, powerful, systematic, and irrepressible desire for such a signified. Now Peirce considers the indefiniteness of reference as the criterion that allows us to recognize that we are indeed dealing with a system of signs. *What broaches the movement of signification is what makes its interruption impossible. The thing itself is a sign.* An unacceptable proposition for Husserl...[Derrida 1976:48–9].

Peirce, then, establishes semiotics on the triadic relation between sign, Object, and interpretant: "The triadic relation is genuine, that is its three members are bound together by it in a way *that does not consist in any complexus of dyadic relations.* That is the reason the Interpretant, or Third, cannot stand in a mere dyadic relation to the Object, but must stand in such a relation to it as the Representamen [the Sign] itself does" (1893–1910/1955:100; emphasis added).

The threefold classification of signs (Icons, Indexes, and Symbols) enables Peirce to weight the connections among the members of this triadic relation differently. Hence his central synopsis:

A sign is either an *icon*, an *index*, or a *symbol*. An *icon* is a sign which would possess the character which renders it significant, even though its object had no existence; such as a lead-pencil streak as representing a geometrical line. An *index* is a sign which would, at once, lose the character which makes it a sign if its object were removed, but would not lose that character if there were no interpretant. Such, for instance, is a piece of mould with a bullet-hole in it as sign of a shot; for without the shot there would have been no hole; but there is a hole there, whether anybody has the sense to attribute it to a shot or not. A *symbol* is a sign which would lose the character which renders it a sign if there were no interpretant. Such is any utterance of speech which signifies what it does only by virtue of its being understood to have that signification. [Peirce, 1893–1910/1955:104]

How, then, can we relate Peirce's Object-yet-Symbol (where the interpretant–sign relation prevails over any relation to Object) and Saussure's signifier/signified dichotomy of the "sign?" Peirce's Object is virtually out of the picture where his Symbol-type prevails, and with good reason, since Object is evidenced only through Symbol. Thus Peirce's Symbol-type most nearly approximates Saussure's general view of the sign. I suggest that the essential lesson of Peirce is that the Object is never obliterated but only absent (effaced?). This provisional absence or effacement of the Object is in turn the aspect of Peirce's semiotics that motivates the distinction between language and culture – which makes language/culture dialectically complementary – just as Saussure would have wished had he persisted in investigating what enabled him to posit *langue/parole* not just as a distinction but as an integrated distinction, an organic solidarity. It takes a higher-level distinction (e.g., language/culture) to motivate a distinction within one of its sides, such as *langue/parole* for language or idealization/actualization for culture.

Our point may be restated as follows: It is part of a sign's arbitrariness that it be construable as Icon, as motivated. Symbols, then, are not specialized signs or vice versa. Rather, signs and symbols are complementary abstractions of a whole. I designate the whole "symbol" and the two complementary abstractions "signs" and "symbols." Thus, as in many taxonomies, one term, "Symbol," occurs at two levels of the model. (The terms could be reversed or neologisms coined.)

The crucial analogy is this: Saussure's "sign" is the basis for *a comparative sense of "language."* (A language can only be known contrastively.) One's own phonetic or grammatical or lexical system would be confused with "primary reality" were it not apprehended contrastively. The abstraction language (subabstractable into *langue/parole*) is fundamentally contrastive, if only because "mutton" and *mouton* do not coincide, thanks to "sheep." Analogously, I pose the symbol – that is to say, the Iconizable (in Peirce's sense) sign (in Saussure's sense) as the basis for *a comparative sense of "culture."* How could it be otherwise?

Perhaps synthesizing a triad (Peirce's) and a dyad (Saussure's) yields a pentade (I am no mathematician). But this much is clear. Saussure needs a sign–Object–interpretant model to valorize his signifier/signified. Likewise, language needs culture. Also, Peirce needs a signifier/signified model to clarify the internal relationships of his scheme and to progress from triad to triad: language-cum-culture to language-cum-culture. The total triad of Peirce (language in action = culture) must be reduced to the double-dimension of Saussure's "sign" en route to constituting another triad (language in action = culture).

Saussure's signified (a concept that is senseless without the trace of signifier, since the only evidence of either is the *sign*, their state of connection) is the name of Peirce's Object from outside the system. Peirce's Object is the name of Saussure's signified elaborated in action – what Peirce elsewhere presents both as belief (versus doubt, each of which valorizes the other) and pragmatism ——➤ pragmaticism.

Earlier structuralism recognized that any presumed Object within a language-system is rather a signified from outside that system. Eventually structuralism implied as well that one must avoid the mistake of posing inside/outside itself as a positivistic distinction. Some poststructuralists (e.g., Donato 1975) overlook this development within structuralism; but it is the only way to explain or understand *Mythologiques*. In brief, every so-called inside vantage contains the conditions of possibility of approaching itself externally and vice versa. Whether this compromise obliterates what Derrida calls the "transcendental signified" remains open to question; if it did not remain open, the compromise itself might claim transcendence![6]

The criticism often lodged by sociolinguists (cf. Hymes 1970, 1971) against Saussurian approaches – that they insufficiently address context and performance – lacks epistemological bite, because context and performance, just like everything else, must be coded at the *langue* level (the level of the conditionally possible) if they are to be transmitted to the next generation, or to outsiders, including linguists or anthropologists. On this epistemological limit, Lévi-Strauss constructed his entire *Mythologiques*. Yet a similar limit is implicit in Peirce as well. Just as Peirce allows for a symbol-type of sign, he must allow for a symbol-type dimension of his whole triadic relation, his whole sign theory. That is, if Peirce's *theory of* signs is itself a sign, *it must occur at a certain level as a symbol* (one of his three types of signs). I see no reason why it shouldn't, and I would call this sign-theory-as-(Peirce's)-symbol just what Saussure suggested: semiology. In semiology the emphasis falls not on performance and context but on comparative/contrastive relations across systems, just as in Peirce's symbol-type. In sum, apply Peirce to Peirce and one produces Saussure; and vice versa.

We cannot accede to a final semiotics simply by ever elaborating models of communication events. Rather, playing Saussure and Peirce off against each other returns us to that fundamental paradox of context-laden (Peirce) *plus* context-convertible (Saussure) that underlies semiotic meaning, both deep and exportable. Would it be in keeping with the insights of Boas, Sapir, and Kroeber if culture theory (although Sapir would not have so named it) pointed away from generative and transformational linguistic models toward dialectics, or metacommentary, or whatever we call that cultural capacity for systems of meaning (language included) to keep one step removed from themselves and thus at base remain both beyond and behind (Weber) and above and below (Durkheim) anything that would be, from any vantage, unmediated? Saussure's semiology *plus* Peirce's semiotics suggest as much.

Lévi-Strauss/Geertz

I would like to add a confession. This kind of intimate relationship that I enjoy with Rousseau is one I also feel with Chateaubriand, who is the contrary of Rousseau, yet the same. So the person I feel closest to is neither Rousseau nor Chateaubriand but a kind of chimera, the Janus figure constituted by the Rousseau-Chateaubriand dyad, which offers me the dual aspect of the same man, though they made diametrically opposite choices...So it is not a particular truth, or the expression of a particular truth, which attracts me. It is, rather, the expression of a complexity, a body of contradictions in which we live – in which I live, at any rate. It is the feeling of this contradictory situation – contradictory within the *oeuvre* of Rousseau, contradictory when you put the *oeuvres* of Rousseau and Chateaubriand together – it is in this contradiction that I myself feel caught; and that is why I feel close to them.

Lévi-Strauss, "Claude Lévi-Strauss Reconsiders"

We conclude these comments on semiotic issues by setting structuralism against cultural interpretation (which I shall align with pragmatism and dramatism).[7] I shall pose the distinction between C. Geertz and Lévi-Strauss in the cultural domain in a way that echoes Peirce/Saussure in the linguistic domain. The writings of Geertz and Lévi-Strauss among all recent anthropologists seem to me most forcefully to pose the negatives set in abeyance by all cultures. Both endeavors are thus radically distinct from functionalism and from Enlightenment methods that avoid the language of the negative. Each in his own way seems partly compatible with preclassical hermeneutics and other interpretive pursuits (even Frazer) sampled in Part I, provided the pursuits be joined to theories of social systems and ideas of language reviewed in Part II. The programs of both Geertz and Lévi-Strauss underlie the interpretive excursion we shall undertake in Part III.

In the name of both Max Weber and semiotics, Clifford Geertz has inveighed against inadequate cross-cultural investigations of public, shaped behavior, or culture. He debunks superorganic reification, brute behaviorism, and "privatized" mentalistic theories of culture that, wedding subjectivism to extreme formalism, locate it exclusively in the minds and hearts (rather than the performances) of men (1973:11). Listen to Geertz's list of other escapist tactics in comparative interpretation:

> turning culture into folklore and collecting it,
> turning it into traits and counting it,
> turning it into institutions and classifying it,
> turning it into structures and toying with it.
> [1973:22; *I have blocked off the list*]

Then listen to William James profess his own calling in 1907–9:

> A pragmatist turns his back resolutely and once for all upon a lot of inveterate habits dear to professional philosophers. He turns away from abstraction and insufficiency, from verbal solutions, from bad *a priori* reasons, from fixed principles, closed systems, and pretended absolutes and origins. He turns towards concreteness and adequacy, towards facts, towards action and towards power. This means the empiricist temper regnant and the rationalist temper sincerely given up.
> [James, 1907–9/1960:31–2]

James says that pragmatism "converts the absolutely empty notion of a static relation of 'correspondence'. . . between our minds and reality, into that of a rich and active commerce. . . between particular thoughts of ours, and the great universe of other experiences in which they play their parts and have their uses" (p. 39). Pragmatism is no "bobtailed scheme of thought" but a "wide window upon human action" (pp. 63–4). Like Geertz, James notes: "Pragmatism insists that truth in the singular is only a collective name for truths in the plural"; and James, too, admonishes philosophies past for forming "whole universes of platonic ideas *ante rem*, universes *in posse*, though none of them," James insists, "exists effectively except *in rebus*" (p. 71).

I shall here provisionally brand as "pragmatism" a significantly American, continued resistance to any simple, particularistic empiricism yet mistrust of Continental schools of rationalism and idealism. I see a persistent pragmatism in American anthropology as part of a postwar refinement of Boas's concept of culture – one that acquired too many echoes of idealism when expanded into Kroeber's "superorganic." These pragmatist inclinations coincide with

Talcott Parsons's views of cultural systems as well: coordinated with social, psychological, and biological systems; neither idealist nor materialist but, as Weber demonstrated, engaged in action.[8]

Pragmatists are "not adherents to a doctrine but proponents of a method" (like structuralists?), and their ideas form a "corridor theory" for disparate interests (Konvitz and Kennedy 1960:7). Nevertheless, pragmatists (like structuralists) are more than mere nay-sayers simply wary of other methods. Now that we have heard what pragmatism does not think of man, what does it think? James gives more clues: "For the pragmatist. . . all discarnate truth is static, impotent and relatively spectral, full truth being the truth that energizes and does battle." In coping with this conflictual truth, man does something distinctive: "After man's interest in breathing freely, the greatest of all his interests (because it never fluctuates or remits, as most of his physical interests do), is his interest in *consistency*, in feeling that what he now thinks goes with what he thinks on other occasions" (1907–9/1960:72, 75). It is unclear whether James is here saluting "personality" or "culture," but in light of his prior emphasis on *in rebus*, we shall call it the latter. Thus, James characterizes man as establishing consistency – could we say pattern? – in the face of an energized, embattled truth. Or truths; for James's universe is plural, a view he attributes to Peirce and to Bergson as well:

Peirce's "tychism" is thus practically synonymous with Bergson's *"devenir réel."* The common objection to admitting novelties is that by jumping abruptly in *ex nihilo*, they shatter the world's rational continuity. Peirce meets this objection by combining his tychism with an express doctrine of "synechism" or continuity, the two doctrines merging into the higher synthesis on which he bestows the name of "agapasticism" . . . which means exactly the same thing as Bergson's *"évolution créatrice."* Novelty, as empirically found, doesn't arrive by jumps and jolts, it leaks in insensibly, for adjacents in experience are always interfused, the smallest real datum being both a coming and a going. . . the fatally continuous infiltration of otherness warps things out of every original rut. [James 1977:153]

At this juncture I would recall Sapir's articulation of language "drift." I would also signal the structuralist notion, properly construed, of diachrony: Synchronies are contrastive because the diachrony from which they are abstracted admits of continuous infiltration of otherness: "Every system, linguistic or otherwise, is in a constant unbalance (*déséquilibre*) with itself; this is the motor of its internal dynamism" (Lévi-Strauss 1975b:183; my translation).[9] James on the other hand, continues:

Peirce speaks of an "infinitesimal" tendency to diversification. The mathematical notion of an infinitesimal contains, in truth, the whole paradox of the same and yet the nascent other, of an identity that won't *keep* except in so far as it keeps *failing*, that won't transfer [translate!] any more than the serial relations in question transfer when you apply them to reality instead of applying them to concepts alone. . .
. . . If such a synechistic pluralism as Peirce, Bergson, and I believe in, be what really exists, every phenomenon of development, even the simplest, would prove equally

rebellious to our science should the latter pretend to give us literally accurate instead of approximate or statistically generalized [I think we would almost have to "translate" this as ideal-typical] pictures of the development of reality.

I can give no further account of Mr. Peirce's ideas in this note, but I earnestly advise all students of Bergson to compare them with those of the french [*sic*] philosopher. [1977:154]

Compared with these remarks by James, everything I have to say is easy.

Pragmatism understands man as spinning ever-altering webs of meaning about the conflictive, vital really-real. This really-real is, moreover, suffused with what Kenneth Burke calls negativity – one of his attributes of any symbol system. Burke's work, I think, helps clarify the pragmatist man of action. Readers of Burke may suspect that his principles relate to the ethics and aesthetics of Judaic prophets, to Protestant theology which makes Everyman his own prophet, and especially to New England transcendentalism. Also, with Burke one must always worry about how Augustine, Coleridge, and Aristotle fit in. But I propose here merely to contrast, through Burke, meanings pragmatist with codes structuralist.

Burke isolates as a major corollary in his dramatistic definition of Man: "Goaded by the spirit of hierarchy"; he then steps it back to "moved by a sense of order" to signal the "incentives of organization and status" in symbol systems: "Here we encounter secular analogues of 'original sin.' For despite any rule of good manners and humility, to the extent that a social structure becomes differentiated, with privileges to some that are denied to others, there are the conditions for a kind of 'built-in' pride. King and peasant are 'mysteries' to each other. Those 'Up' are guilty of not being 'down,' those 'Down' are certainly *guilty* of not being 'Up' " (1966:15). Burke sees significant forms as "negatively infused," as based on an implied "hortatory negative, 'Thou shalt not' ": "Laws are essentially negative; 'mine' equals not thine. . . The negative principle in morals is often hidden behind a realm of quasi-positives . . . think of monastic discipline." He summarizes the hortatory negative in dramatism as a theory of action: "*Action* involves *character*, which involves *choice* – and the *form* of choice attains its perfection in the distinction between Yes and No (shall and shall-not, will and will-not). Though the concept of sheer *motion* is non-ethical, *action* implies the ethical, the human personality. Hence the obvious close connection between the ethical and negativity, as indicated in the Decalogue" (1966:10–11). Significantly, Burke cites Emerson to illustrate this Mosaic principle. So I call all this pragmatism: What else is Emerson?

Elsewhere Burke proceeds to themes of scapegoats and vicarious victimage, "a special case of antithesis combined with another major source of symbol systems, namely substitution":

The intricate line of exposition might be summed up thus: If order, then guilt; if guilt, then need for redemption; but any such "payment" is victimage. Or, if action, then drama; if drama, then conflict; if conflict, then victimage.

A dramatistic view of human motives thus culminates in the ironic admonition that perversions of the sacrificial principle (purgation by scapegoat, congregation by segregation) are the constant temptation of human societies. [1968:450–1]

Geertz's interpretive theory – partly Weberian and Parsonian, developed in light of Kluckhohn, and often citing Burke as well – includes elements of negativity and victimage; for example, in the realm of ethos and sacred symbols: "Both what a people prizes and what it fears and hates are depicted in its world view, symbolized in its religion and in turn expressed in the whole quality of its life. . . its vices are as stylized as its virtues" (1973:131). Geertz's work "depsychologizes" many of the core themes of anthropology's culture and personality school. Psychology cannot explain culture, or vice versa; rather, psychology is among the set of properties constituting cultural systems. To Geertz religious symbols are cultural insofar as they attain "an aura of factuality" and seem "uniquely realistic" to their believers. Ideological symbols are cultural insofar as they are authoritative, "suasive images" by means of which (politics) can be firmly grasped (p. 218). Politics might be about brute power, but the culture of politics is about *shaped* power.[10] This model is all very intense; little is playful and nothing is trivial. Even cultural play is deep play – *about* (in Bali) obsessive status pride. This kind of committed meaning appears actively threatened – liable to be obliterated by a hortatory no. Geertz researched religion and ideology in Java, where social divisions and politicoreligious factions are intensely partisan and aware of their traditional antagonists. This is meaning versus "thou shalt not." I call it pragmatism, to have a tail to wag it with.

What about structuralism? Burke points our way when he chides existentialism for playing linquistic games with the paradox of Nothingness (*le Néant*). Children, says Burke, cannot grasp Nothingness, but they can grasp "no." "We can't have an idea of nothing, we can have an idea of no" (1966:10). Here, at last, we can elucidate Leach's offhand suggestion (1968a:344) that to understand Lévi-Strauss one must be initiated into existentialism, the dispute between Lévi-Strauss and Sartre notwithstanding. I see the matter this way: For pragmatism the opposite of meaning (the negation of significant form) is *no!* For structuralism – here it echoes existentialism and, I would add, French literary symbolism – the opposite of meaning (the negation of *sens* or *signification*) is *rien*: void, silence, indifference.

If Geertz's culture of politics, religion, status pride, and so forth breaks down, the result is presumably anarchy, atheism, war. These systems of action challenge the negative forces they are designed to withstand: James's consistency above the battle. Pragmatist meaning is shaped and formed above a chasm of fearful negation – much like that which Erich Auerbach (1957) suggests for the Old Testament. Structuralist meaning is selected and codified against a background not of pending, negativized chaos but of silence, mute undifferentiation – much like that which Auerbach suggests for Homer. Pragmatism infers a sculptural *significance* thrust over contrary forces. Structuralism infers a distillated *signification* etched against absence. To put the matter much more mildly, they are different levels of comparativist analysis.

The implications of this issue are most apparent in polemics that have arisen between Lévi-Strauss and scholars more concerned with the affective, multivocal experience of symbolic forms. To take one lively example, consider rejoinders by Lévi-Strauss to the criticisms of Victor Turner:

> From diverse sides, but especially in England (Fortes 1967); (Leach 1967, 1970) I have been accused of reducing experiences intensely lived (*vécues*) by individual subjects to symbols which are affectively neutral like those utilized by mathematicians, although the thought of preliterate peoples has recourse to symbols which are concrete and thoroughly impregnated with emotional values...In the words of another author sharing the same viewpoint, "symbols and their relations...are not only a set of cognitive classifications for ordering the universe...They are also, and perhaps as importantly, a set of evocative devices for rousing, channeling, and domesticating powerful emotions such as hate, fear, affection, and grief. They are also informed with purposiveness and have a 'conative' aspect. In brief, the whole person and not just his mind (*esprit*) is existentially involved in the life or death issues" (Turner 1969:42–43). All right; but having said all that and rendered a pious verbal devotional-duty (*devoir*) to affectivity, one has not advanced a single step towards explaining how the bizarre concerns to which ritual lends itself, and the representations related to them, are able to produce such pretty results...
>
> In the first place all these commentaries that aim to place affectivity at the center of ritual and epilogize the anxiety felt before taboos evoke irresistibly some ethnographer from another planet: in his monograph devoted to the earthlings, he would describe the superstitious terror preventing motorists from crossing the symbolic limit marked by a yellow line between lanes, even briefly to infringe on it (*même de mordre tant soit peu sur elle*); he would relate while shuddering in horror the punishments incurred by the profanators in the form of collision with another vehicle...But we really feel nothing of the kind; we respect the yellow line as a routine affair in which we invest no emotional value. As in so many ritual acts, conduct is perfectly automatic (*va de soi*) for those who conform, because any consciousness they take of it presents it to them already completely integrated in a conception of the world. [1971:597–8; my translation]

A gifted rhetorician, Lévi-Strauss nevertheless misses an opportunity here again to deny the untenability of a distinction between emotional/intellectual or affective/routine, an argument he elsewhere supports with the example of music. In cultural symbols intellectual and affective properties are consolidated: Lévi-Strauss's yellow line indeed takes on affective properties (like those he implies that Turner would overenthusiastically attribute to it) when a Frenchman takes the wheel on British highways integrated in an inverse (left/right) vehicular Weltanschauung. Turner's works on ritual suggest that symbols like the yellow line are *both* routine and supercharged under different circumstances; this fact emerges most clearly across cultures. Turner emphasizes the "monstrous" dimensions of sacred items in life-crisis rites (often accompanied by ritual inversion) that implement an emotional sense of otherness within the routine. Yet Turner sometimes glosses over intellectual dimensions by suggesting that liminal, emotive, status-confusing rites are "antistructural," implying a collapse of structure rather than an additional articulation of structure.

For Lévi-Strauss the fullest articulations of structures, including allusions to what is absent, occur in myths that tie intellectual/emotional order to institutions of marriage, inheritance, residence; cycles of seasonal, solar, and environmental events (*intelligence du milieu*); orders of space, time, and objects, including their manufacture and exchange; costume, sexuality, sensory codes, foodstuffs, and so forth. Myths, as they are repeated and gradually altered in community oral performances, afford models of what a society stretches its own values toward and of what it has possibly rejected in actuality but still poses intellectually. What has *not* been selected gives value to what has been. For Lévi-Strauss, then, mythic structure encompasses so-called anti-structure. This view recalls Durkheim, who saw religion as the affect-laden divisions and diversifications of space, time, and society itself. Moreover, both myth (at the intellectual level) and religious ritual (at the solidarity level) become privileged areas for comparing cultures, because each removes actuality, so to speak, from itself. Whether in intellectual myths or emotive rites, cultures re-cognize and remotivate themselves at a remove.

Throughout such debates Lévi-Strauss has remained true to a view informed in part by Saussure: As cultural forms take on significance, there is a lingering sense that their features are selections from multiple possibilities – reduced for the sake of systematicity and communication – a sense that is heightened in cross-cultural studies. I have elsewhere (1972) likened this appreciation of human meaning to French Symbolist aesthetics and poetics. Lévi-Strauss views myths as detemporalized, systematic constructions of sensory correspondences abstracted and interrelated from the ongoing, continuous bustle of preliterate groups. Only studied retrospectively, myth is nevertheless presented as constitutive. Likewise, certain symbolists viewed their literary creations as detemporalized intersensory correspondences, compositions of discontinuous materials of poetic discourse, abstracted from a perceptual continuity and systematically arranged. Of special note is Mallarmé: the symbolist poem is not a victory of meaning against either ignorance or untruth but a postponement of pending silence; a fragile, unexpected, sense-laden message, just barely articulated out of the bright white light, the deafened (not deafening) numb of non-sense: *nature*. The symbolist alternative to the interpenetrating synesthetic codes of a poem is not the doom of failure, but the absence of anything – sterile, spaceless void. This view is at least as existentialist as Camus and as structuralist as Lévi-Strauss's *Mythologiques IV*, in which the last note – its final term, what Burke calls a "sesame word" – is *rien*.

At the level of totalizing comparisons, structuralism downplays hortatory negativity – hence the reactions of scholars like Paul Ricoeur (1963, 1979) and René Girard (1973, 1977). Lévi-Strauss presents tribal totemisms, for example, as intellectual, oppositional codes; unlike Mary Douglas (1966), he investigates not the sense of disgust if dietary restrictions or other taboos are transgressed but the categories articulated by taboos in and of their operation. Unlike Freud, Lévi-Strauss says little of any emotional overkill surrounding incest taboos; rather incest is the negative name for the irreducible "motive" of nonisolationism: At some level divisions cannot provide for themselves; groups are fundamentally constituted and perpetuated when, with other groups, they exchange siblings for spouses.[11]

Similarly, as we saw in Chapter 3, Dumont (like Hocart) stresses the ritual occupational ideals in caste (*jajmani*) that require priests to employ lowly barbers for handling corpses and barbers to rely on priests for ultimate religious ceremonies. This organic solidarity distinguishes caste from mere stratification with its simple projection of up/down principles. Moreover, for Dumont, caste must be understood cross-culturally as a holistic, categorical system. To overestimate dimensions such as Burke's "guilt" would underestimate the reciprocity. Such views of Dumont, Lévi-Strauss and, to some extent, Mauss, have provoked accusations of antiseptic escapism. But readers of their extensive works will find that they do not sterilize cultures or history; their Durkheimian subject is how human societies, through their actions and ideals, perdure. Nor does structuralism deny the guilt component of social systems; rather, its emphasis on synchrony and reciprocity (echoing the marriage rules and mythic formulations it often investigates) is used as a corrective against oversimple assumptions about exploitation or master–slave relations. This situation recalls earlier arguments and quarrels in the history of interpretation. Kenneth Burke himself – who stresses guilt and victimage in rhetorical aspects of narrative and social dramas – nevertheless is alert to more structuralistlike options, as here, in the history of theological discourse:

> The ambiguous relation between the two styles of placement (the narrative and the logical) can be seen if we stop to consider again the way in which the Second Person of the Trinity is said to "proceed" from the First, and the Third from the first and second. Though we think of a Father as *preceding* a Son in time, and though we conceive of "generation" in temporal terms, orthodox theologians admonish that the process whereby the Father is said to "generate" the Son must *not* be conceived temporally...
>
> Note that the idea of personal relations involving two "generations" contains this ambiguity. Though there is a sense in which a Father precedes a Son, there is also a sense in which the two states are "simultaneous" – for parents can be parents only insofar as they have offspring, and in this sense the offspring "makes the parent." That is, logically, Father and Son are *reciprocal* terms, each of which implies the other. [Burke 1970:32][12]

(Teknonymy smiles.) This embedding of Father/Son in its mutually constitutive contrasts is a theological echo of the logic that Lévi-Strauss finds in tribal marriage and myth, that Dumont finds in ritual tasks of castes, and that both proffer as the basis for structuralist comparisons at the level of contrastive *langues*.

But my primary point is that Burke's and Geertz's interpretations of dramatic action and structuralist analysis of contrastive systems stand in decided contrast to each other. Let me couch the matter in a formula (itself, I confess, somewhat structuralist, but only for the moment). *Pragmatism (especially Burke) views negativity (in the sense of the hortatory "thou shalt not") positively; Structuralism (especially Lévi-Strauss) views positivity (Durkheim's "positive" categoricalness) negatively (in the sense of diacritically or oppositionally).* Pragmatism-dramatism's chosen specialty is overt, obsessive native rationales; its metaphors for systematic meaning tend toward the creative and plastic. Structuralism's select specialty is covert, hypothesized native categories; its metaphors for systematic meaning tend toward the relative and positional. Structuralism has difficulty decoding bitterness, disgust, politicized controversy, factious competition – which are pragmatism's forte (but cf. Detienne 1979). Pragmatism has difficulty interpreting empty metaphors, apparently nonsensical images, play for play's sake, inversion for inversion's sake – which are structuralism's forte. (Cultures, needless to say, abound in the components of both these lists). The pragmatist-dramatist prefers conflict, politics, and public performances; the structuralist prefers puzzles or, better, *jeux*. Pragmatism is not about *Ideen* (that is idealism) but about style: concrete ideas obviously wedded to world view. Structuralism turns as often to fashion or *mode* – concrete ideas not so obviously wedded to world view but, for that reason, as certain structuralists insist, all the more indicative of general half-conscious processes.

Now for the drama. Structuralism studies symbol systems as fragmentary trails of simultaneously concrete–abstract classification schemes. In the protostructuralism of *L'année sociologique* and in the Leiden school of ethnology, such fragments were considered reverberations of lapsed, perfected archaic schemes.[13] In the advanced structuralism of *Mythologiques*, the fragments provide evidence of persistent fields of metaphors and metonymies that reveal unexpected relationships in the "semantic universe" of traditional New World societies. In either case, however, structuralism thrives on forgotten connections. Pragmatism, on the other hand, studies symbol systems as vital synapses that join the roles of living actors to their social institutions and their beliefs. Pragmatism thrives on active connections. The dramatic–pragmatic image of the social scientist recalls Weber:

Instead of conceiving of the social scientist as a kind of bricklayer the Weberian image is much more heroic. There is an image of the dedicated scholar who must find his lonely way without well-charted rules . . .
Here there is no one overarching order or *Logos* in the world that awaits discovery or in which the sociologist, like others, participates. On the contrary, the world is one of cosmic conflict among divergent heteronomous values. It is a cosmos in which

good and evil are intertwined, and often mutually productive of one another. [Gouldner 1973:100]

In the anthropological variation on this image, the semiheroic ethnographer strides not through world religious history but through field sites. (Scholars like Clifford Geertz and Louis Dumont actually consolidate these two images.) We might immediately oppose Lévi-Strauss's image of the anthropologist as half antihero. In *Tristes tropiques* the overeducated, urbane, synesthesia-prone, intellectual salvages from a disheveled humanity enough evidence of reciprocal "bricoleuring" (cultural makeshifting) to rescue his own *esprit* from pending ennui.

The contrast between structuralism and pragmatism-dramatism should not obscure the features they share. Both challenge Enlightenment views of uniformitarian man: There is no simple universal under our costumes of culture. This point is less obvious in Lévi-Strauss because of resemblances between his analytic technique and certain schemes of *philosophes*. But documenting, translating, and transforming hosts of sensory–abstract structures is a far cry from projecting a rationalist scheme into the empty skies over Paris, presumed center of the universal (cf. Scholte 1970). This plurality of cultural orders distinguishes Lévi-Strauss from those philosophes he recalls only during his exercises of self-conscious pastiche. The distinction between Lévi-Strauss and uniformitarian ideas is as thorough as that between structural linguistics and General Grammarians.

In a profounder sense still, both pragmatism-dramatism and structuralism resist locating verification in material facts, idealist values, or more recondite versions of either. One situates persuasiveness of interpretation in the "active commerce" among loci and frames of action; the other situates convincingness of decodings in the mediations among levels of particular systems. Finally, both confront varieties of negativity and express resistance to direct determinism in paradoxical writings. Needless to say, it is in the paradoxes that their ultimate difference is revealed. Lévi-Strauss, like Durkheim and Mauss, relies on the French reflexive (cf. Boon 1972:203): *"Les mythes se pensent dans l'homme."* Few attacks on Lévi-Strauss have overlooked this notorious phrase from *Le cru et le cuit*. But it is not hard to demonstrate that nonstructuralists as well counter naturalistic, psychologistic, or associationist theories of meaning with paradoxical formulations. (They at least seem paradoxical from the vantage of any Cartesian mind/matter dualism.) Here's Geertz: "Without men, no culture, certainly; but equally, and more significantly, without culture, no men" (1973:49). If *that* bothers you, think how it would sound in French: *Sans hommes, pas de culture* [structure?], *certainement; mais également, et d'une manière plus significative, sans culture, pas d'homme.* In English it sounds antiatomistic and almost optimistic (although Geertz himself – in this respect more Weberian than Parsonian – is pessimistic). In French it sounds somehow pessimistic, even nihilistic. *But it says (means?) the same thing. (Mais ça veut dire [bedeutet?] la même chose.)*

Pragmatism-dramatism (call it cultural interpretation) and structuralism, even when their forms can be identified, remain distinguished by their implicit negatives. (Like literati-not-eunuchs.) Hence the semiotic paradox of cultures implies as well a semiotic paradox of methods. The contrast between such schools of exaggeration in the discourse of cultures is analogous to the contrasts separating (for translation) cultures themselves.

Part III
Essays in exotic texts

And the women of New Bedford, they bloom like their own red roses. But roses only bloom in summer; whereas the fine carnation of their cheeks is perennial as sunlight in the seventh heavens. Elsewhere match that bloom of theirs, ye cannot, save in Salem, where they tell me the young girls breathe such musk, their sailor sweethearts smell them miles off shore, as though they were drawing nigh the odorous Moluccas instead of the Puritanic sands.

Melville, *Moby Dick*

We other semiotic anthropologists are not alone in exaggerating and interrelating extremes. Such cross-cultural pursuits restore to Western traditions modes of interpretation and understanding that have flourished in systems of meaning under those very social structures – reciprocal exogamies of tribes, pervasive hierarchies of traditional religions – that the reformed, rationalized, and individualistic West has purged. Certain parties would wish to restore exotic principles (or reputed ones) to a hollow, disenchanted, modern social order: if not communal unity, then perhaps moietylike teams (for example, Democrats marrying, or otherwise playing the vis-à-vis with, Republicans); or perhaps sets of ritual specializations, each task assured its part in the whole (so much for sports). Others, like myself, hesitate over these hopes, fearing that to reintroduce such social structures might also restore the xenophobia of tribes or the segregation of occupational castes, even ritual ones (see Appendix C).

Still, vexed issues lurk behind fancies of retribalization or retraditionalization. Can tribal or hierarchical meanings be divorced from their social underpinnings and/or religious exclusivity? If not, how have they been exported; indeed, how have they been perceived from outside? If not, why encounter them; why compare? Or do our comparisons themselves unwittingly perpetuate either millenarian and apocalyptical dreams or hopes heretical to a standardized scientism? In our own age comparativists detect in others what past interpreters in the history of the West longed to achieve for themselves. Oddly, anthropology dwells on practices and beliefs like the very ones our rational order supposes it has discarded: all those monographs on tribal-brand hermetics, horticulturist esotericism, peasant cosmologists, and latter-day Neoplatonic states. What murmurs beneath our tolerance? How near does anthropology itself approach the view Melville inscribes in what is probably a parody of Christian apologists (such as Thomas Maurice) who from the 1790s enfolded unsettling findings of comparative mythology in a theological orthodoxy:

All things form but one whole; the universe a Judea, and God Jehova its
head. . . Away with our stares and grimaces. The New Zealander's tattooing is not a
prodigy; nor the Chinaman's ways an enigma. No custom is strange; no creed
is absurd; no foe, but who will in the end prove a friend. In heaven, at last, our good,

150

old white-haired father Adam will greet all alike, and sociality forever prevail.
Christian shall join hands between Gentile and Jew; grim Dante forget his Infernos,
and shake sides with fat Rabelais; and monk Luther, over a flagon of old
nectar, talk over old times with Pope Leo... Then shall we list to no shallow gossip of
Magellans and Drakes; but give ear to the voyagers who have circumnavigated
the Ecliptic; who rounded the Polar Star as Cape Horn. [Melville 1849/1970:12–13]

Are we, anthropologists, the apologist or the parodist?

Forswearing any answer, the following chapters carry on, interrelating
exotic symbolisms, our own and others. Professional anthropology and Balinese
culture, for example, originated at opposite extremes of the globe. Yet the
interpretations each professes are not for that reason unrelated – a fact I shall
argue by juxtaposing J. F. McLennan's *Primitive Marriage* and ideals behind
actual Balinese marriage practice. Indeed Balinese culture and McLennan's
book are in a way cognate. Moreover Chapter 5 (on a vital text in the
preprofessional history of ethnology) and Chapter 6 (on Balinese marriage
and myth) are intended as moieties, each acting vis-à-vis the other; the same is
true of Chapters 6 and 7 (on relations between Structuralism and Romanticism). While each chapter can be taken as an essay in its own right, there are
multiple connections among them; and the full significance of each only
appears by moving comparatively and contrastively across time and space –
and across this book.

Part III converts the dialectical systems and assorted semiotics of Part II to
more flowing, plural "textualities"; yet the same problems and principles
obtain. My own sense of cross-cultural discourse is informed by the late
Roland Barthes's movement "from work to text," which combined Marxism,
Freudianism, and structuralism to make relative the relations of writer, reader,
and observer (critic). "The work" is considered primarily as the property of its
author; its symbolic runs out at points presumed to refer to something external; and it is generally interpreted in a framework of filiation. Barthes contrasts to this concept "the text," which is radically symbolic; it is an activity of
production; it is subversive of old classifications and conventional genres; it is
always paradoxical and is regulated by metonymic associations and carryings
over. Barthes applauds the discovery by structuralism that structures of language (and derivatively of texts) are off-centered, without closure. Everything
Barthes says of the stereophony and fundamental "difference" of texts, I
would say of "cultures" as well: "The intertextual in which every text is held"
is itself "the text-between of another text." Barthes excludes from his profoundly playful sense of reading texts any hermeneutic course of "deepening
investigation." I would readmit hermeneutics as one component – but not a
privileged one – in the fragmented overlappings of text to text to text. Moreover, I would accentuate comparative institutions, social and cultural typologies, and various dimensions of so-called context as themselves textlike properties
that enrich the field of citations, references, and echoes constituting Barthes's

"very plural of meaning." Finally, and most importantly for our purposes, Barthes insists: "The Text requires that one try to abolish (or at the very least to diminish) the distance between writing and reading... the Text is that space where no language has a hold over any other, where languages circulate (keeping the circular sense of the term)." (1977:158–64).

Many are the theories of "text" other than Barthes's that could guide us. Many are the texts other than Jacobean tomes, Balinese rites and institutions, and Romantic and structuralist comparisons that we might transpose and interpret to implement hermeneutic-cum-structuralist cross-cultural readings, and reflexive ones at that. (In Chapter 2 we enlisted Patagonians, or their inscriptions, and the Enlightenment to similar ends). The endeavor now becomes to interpret both what we are interpreting and what we are interpreting with. Accordingly, Chapters 5 and 6 conclude with sections of reflexivity; and Chapter 7 ends by becoming a commentary on what it itself is doing, but not only that.

Epistemologies and methodologies can be variable, plural, reflexive – like texts, like cultures. Indeed, they must be, if Weber, Durkheim, semiotics, and all the others have anything to say of each other. Of course, methodologies are dialectical as well, in a sense recently made vivid by Jameson:

For insofar as dialectical thinking is thought about thought, thought to the second power, concrete thought about an object, which at the same time remains aware of its own intellectual operations in the very act of thinking, such self-consciousness must be inscribed in the very sentence itself. And insofar as dialectical thinking characteristically involves a conjunction of opposites or at least conceptually disparate phenomena, it may truly be said of the dialectical sentence what the Surrealists said about the image, namely, that its strength increases proportionately as the realities linked are distant and distinct from each other. [Jameson 1971:53–4]

This wedding of distinctness through distance and surrealist dialectics carries me back in turn to a moment in Lévi-Strauss's reflections where the ironies of inclining toward the other, with no epistemological certainty of having access, become reciprocal:

It is highly possible, indeed, that so-called ethnological knowledge is condemned to remain as bizarre and inadequate as that which an exotic visitor would have of our own society. The Kwakiutl Indian whom Boas sometimes invited to New York to serve him as an informant was indifferent to the spectacle of skyscrapers and streets lined with automobiles. He reserved all his intellectual curiosity for the dwarfs, giants, and bearded ladies which were at that time exhibited in Times Square, for automats, and for the brass balls decorating staircase bannisters... all these things challenged his own culture, and it was that culture alone which he was seeking to recognize in certain aspects of ours...

Of course, we have acquired direct knowledge of exotic forms of life and thought which our precursors lacked; but is it not also the case that surrealism – an internal development of our own society – has transformed our sensitivity, and that we are indebted to it for having discovered or rediscovered at the heart of our studies a certain lyricism and integrity? [Lévi-Strauss 1966c:121]

Finally, presaging our nod from Lévi-Strauss's structuralism (vis-à-vis Romanticism) toward Walter Benjamin (Chapter 7), we might recall the ancients and their like who read the "torn guts of animals, starry skies, dances, runes and hieroglyphs" (Demetz 1978:xxii). Like Benjamin, the serious surrealist (who, like Lévi-Strauss, was drawn to Baudelaire), in an age verging on disenchantment, we continue to " 'read' things, cities, and social institutions as if they were sacred texts." Comparative anthropology and semiotics help (cf. Bouissac 1979). For the fieldworker – like those gifted writers literally born fieldworking – even back home *everything* threatens to signify. With these precursors in mind – Melville, Benjamin, Boas's Kwakiutl transfixed on a banister ball – we here begin our own "Book voyage and Reading Navigation" (S. Purchas 1625/1907: vol. 15).

5. Jacobean ethnology:
An East–West intercourse

What would ye give now
To turn the Globe up, and find the rich Moluccas?
To pass the straights?

> Beaumont and Fletcher, *Loyal Subject*,
> 1618 (Theodore's query upon presenting
> his sisters to two loyal gentlemen)

This chapter explores a pivotal British text published in 1625 that consolidated symbols of exotic kingships and tribesmen. The works of Samuel Purchas extended and annotated Europe's most expansive endeavors in cross-cultural discourse, particularly those accounts dating from the Age of Discovery. Although technology had opened the way for regular circumnavigations and frequent exposure to a greater range of distant tribes and monarchs, the intercourse of Europe and remote cultures continued to be mediated by conventional expectations. Moreover, as European scholars produced a discourse inscribing remote kingships, their views of domestic monarchy and legitimate settlement were transforming.

By scrutinizing the historical context and complex symbols of one example of such discourse, we can better appreciate how conceptualizations of the exotic and the domestic – even their most basic institutions – are inextricably intertwined. In the case at hand, *Purchas His Pilgrimes* manages to dis-cover from the writings of history a Stuart royal symbology, a post-Elizabethan Anglican version of previous biblical, classical, and Catholic varieties. It simultaneously dis-covers from the writings of exploration an Indic royal symbology, a composite of Sumatran, Javanese, Balinese, and ultimately Mogul varieties. Serving as foil for the worldwide, divine stuff of kings are tribal vagrants that Purchas increasingly defames. Indeed, against these stigmatized subsocieties, Purchas's tomes celebrate a complementarity of monarchs in the Last Age: Thames married to Ganges – or rather, engaged.

The first concerted, literally global English language interpretation of the meeting of East and West appeared just after the death of James I and just

154

months before its author's own death. The scope of Samuel Purchas's twenty-volumed *Pilgrimes* recalls Iberian predecessors; its title reads:

containing a History of the World, in Sea Voyages and Lande-Travells, by Englishmen and Others, wherein Gods wonders in Nature and Providence, the Actes, Arts, Varieties and Vanities of Men with a world of the World's Rarities, are by a world of Eye Witness-Authors related to the world, some left written by Master Hakluyt at his death, more since added; his also perused and perfected. All examined, abbreviated, Illustrated with notes, enlarged with discourses, adorned with pictures, and expressed in Mapps.

Educated at St. John's College, Cambridge, Purchas became a curate, then a vicar, then chaplain to the archbishop of Canterbury, George Abbot, then rector of St. Martin's, Ludgate. Little is documented of Purchas's life, apart from his tireless interviews with world travelers. Earlier works, the *Pilgrimage* and the *Pilgrime* (1613, 1619) earned him the eventual designation of "probably the first collector of religious rites on a worldwide scale"; portions were reputedly read through seven times by his patron, King James (Hodgen 1971:195, 236).[1] *Hakluytus Posthumus; or, Purchas His Pilgrimes* (1625/1907) apparently commanded a broad readership for generations:

Purchas, with the stay-at-home reader in mind, began to cut away at Hakluyt's conservatively edited documents. Hakluyt's *Principal Navigations* had established a taste for closet travel: his literary legacy provided two-fifths of the 1625 edition of *Purchas His Pilgrimmes*, a vast and popular compilation extending to four million words. The documents curtailed by Purchas may make more lively reading, but they are prone also to mislead. . . Travel and exploration were being turned at his busy hands into national myth. Purchas was awarded 100 pounds from the East India Company, and in the two centuries that followed, being readable and romantic, his book was more highly regarded than Hakluyt's work of sober scholarship.
[Beeching 1972:25]

By 1905 when the work was reprinted, it had come to be valued mainly as an augmented collection of discovery literature gathered by R. Hakluyt but unpublished before his death. Subsequent "captious critics" have generally disparaged Purchas's tomes; typical remarks run as follows: "It is a work of greater bulk than Hakluyt's but infinitely less readable. . .He helps us to realize Hakluyt's greatness as an editor. But Purchas was Jacobean." E. G. R. Taylor, on the other hand, has recognized the fuller vision of Purchas's " 'omnibus' book of giant proportions": "The weakness of Hakluyt was that he never attempted any synthesis of the vast material at his disposal: Purchas, on the other hand, drew all his reading together in order to develop a single theme, a survey of the world from the point of view of its peoples and their religious practices" (1934:54–61). Yet Taylor goes on to stress Purchas's style of redundance, circumlocution, and excessive ornament and above all his shapelessness:

Had Purchas kept strictly in view the presentation of a picture of the world, he might have compiled a shapely and readable pair of volumes. But he did not view his task objectively; he was by turns the preacher, the publicist, the patriot. There were things that Englishmen ought to know, things that Englishmen ought to do, things that Englishmen ought to read: his volumes had a didactic purpose, or rather many such purposes, and so became swollen, disproportionate, unbeautiful. Purchas the preacher peeps out already in the Preface to the reader...

Purchas the publicist is seen in Book V, to which he was adding when the English clash with the Dutch in the Indies was brought to a head by the Massacre of Amboyna...

Finally, Purchas the ardent advocate of colonial expansion appears...[2] [1934:61]

Thus a fundamental problem confronts the modern reader of Purchas, especially the overwhelmingly "Jacobean" introductory volume. What do we make of a work that is at once a monarchist tract, church history, military area handbook, tour guide, prospectus for commercial investment, history of travel and trade, one-man promotional campaign for the merchant marine, and above all an early seventeenth-century Human Relations Area File? One anthropological strategy is to approach Purchas's work insofar as possible in its own terms. This essay offers a reading of Purchas that accentuates signs and symbols of Indic monarchies and their contrast with New World aboriginals presumed to be vagrants. These comparative aspects of Purchas's texts have been often overlooked in historical assessments and largely ignored in the history of ethnological ideas. Yet the signs and symbols revolving around kingship/vagabonds suggest interrelationships among Purchas the preacher, the publicist, and the patriot – and perhaps even Purchas the protoanthropologist. We are concerned less with Jacobean Britain itself than with Jacobean symbols of others, in particular Eastern kings and Amerindian tribes. Historical events and circumstances are pertinent to the extent they inform this ethnological symbology. In structuralist parlance, our topic is neither Purchas himself nor the Jacobean period as a past "presence," but the signs and symbols of "others" inscribed in an era which is itself equally an "other."[3]

The commerce of kings

The latter volumes of *Purchas His Pilgrimes* include translations of Linschoten on Portuguese Goa, Acosta on Mexico, and sundry accounts of exploration and colonization in the Far East and the New World. But it is the first five volumes, written under payment to the East India Company, that convey a kind of ethnological word drama, or rather masque: "hopefully promising Riches, Honour, Happie Successe and Long-Life, of the East-Indian Society, which we have also in a Scenicall History, or an Historicall scene (the Actors being the Authors, and the Authors themselves the Actors of their owne Parts, Artes, Acts, Designes) brought from the Cradle to the Saddle...[in]...this Booke-Voyage, and Reading Navigation" (vol. 3:356). First the West is epitomized in Elizabethan–Jacobean symbols of divine kingship. As successor to the Virgin-Astraea, James I becomes the Solomon-like sponsor of

Navigation and the ultimate Apostle ushering in the last Age.[4] Then the East is represented by Indic kingships, portrayed with increasing pomp, pageantry, and splendor. Purchas disrupts chronology and annotates documents of successive encounters with the sultans and rajas of Sumatra, Java, and Bali, building toward the Great Mogul of glorious Agra.

Before considering his arguments, it is important to remember that the hopes for a unified empire of Catholic peoples enjoyed by Purchas's Iberian predecessors had dissolved. J. H. Elliott reminds us, for example, that while sixteenth-century natural and moral historians of the New World – Oviedo, de las Casas, Acosta – differed in "sheer intellectual curiosity," they shared the belief that "the great line of division lay between the Christian and the Pagan": "For all their differences [Spaniards] were the products of a society united by certain strongly defined attitudes – Christian in its values, legalistic in its outlook, corporate and hierarchical in its organization" (1973:105–6). Equally important, any sense of united Protestantism, both at home and internationally, was, as Purchas wrote, a fading hope. Hakluyt's vision of England advancing under Elizabeth after the Spanish defeat, a vision we associate with Raleigh's heyday, had clouded with the aggravation of religious and political factions. Much of the anthropological interest of Purchas's text lies in its articulation of a royal British order, to the exclusion of Catholics and Dutch Protestants alike, which tied exotic courts to the monarch, over and above any companies, parliaments, or other forces of interest.[5]

Purchas celebrates Britain's perfected circumnavigators who mark the final chapter in human history as a peregrination. Appropriating rival puritanical themes of pilgrimage, he emphasizes monarchical legitimacy in a line with scriptural and classical *auctores*, complemented by new eye evidence. Every variety of prior argumentation is recapitulated, all joined in a culminating, English-language hermeneutics. If Portugal had been the Prophet of the arts of Navigation, Britain is to be the Savior: Witness the experiments of Doctor Gilbert, Britain's more numerous circumnavigations, and indeed Purchas's very books, apogee of Print:

> God Almightie pittying this Frailtie, intending better things to the last and worst Ages of the World (as in this fulnesse of time he sent his Sonne and the Spirit of his Sonne to prepare men for Heaven, so since, I hope to further the former) hath given the Science of the Loadstone and Astronomicall Rules and Instruments, applyed by Art to Navigation, that hee might give more ample Possession of the Sea and the Earth to the sonnes of Men. Let others applaud, admire, adore, the Stones called Precious: this shall bee to mee Pearle and Ruby, and Saphire, and Diamant, and more then all those multiplyed Names of Gemmes, which all are also made ours by helpe of the Loadstone. This magneticall vertue was hidden to the Golden and Silver Ages...
>
> Amongst all which helpes by humane industry, none (in my mind) have further prevailed then these two, the Arts of Arts, Printing and Navigation... For how were the learned and remoter Tongues buried and unknowne in these parts, till that Art brought in plentie, facilitie and cheapnesse of Bookes, whereby Languages became the Keyes, Bookes the Treasuries and Storehouses of Science; whiles by those men

found access into these; and Printing yielded admittance to both in plentie and varietie...?

And thus hath God given opportunitie by Navigation into all parts, that in the Sun-set and Evening of the World, the Sunne of righteousness might arise out of our West to illuminate the East, and fill both Hemispheres with his brightnes. [Vol. 2, 3–8][6]

In Purchas's prolonged commentary, "the whole Globe is epitomized, and yields an abridgement and summaries of itself in each countrie, to each man." He inscribes the show and exchange of diverse resources, commodities, languages, alphabets, seals, rituals, religious sects, and courtly processions and performances by highly theatrical monarchs.

Purchas's anthropology is couched in his approach to customs as "similitudes" (see Chapter 2). Certain notorious usages – polygyny and circumcision, for example – ran counter to Catholic sacraments (as they were developing) and to ideals of domestic and community life in Puritanism as well. Yet such usages pass muster in Purchas's commentary and marginal notes, provided they add luster to monarchs who remain unsullied by Spanish or papal influence.

As we shall see, accounts of the courts of Acheh, Bantam, Jakarta, and the supposedly maharajalike king of Bali – an island the British knew only through Dutch documentation – are edited into a pageant of reciprocal kingships, rid of pope and emperor, each enjoying comparative advantage in rare customs and commodities, each entertaining and sustaining the others. This panorama of legitimate monarchy appears explicitly as a succesor to the Catholic panorama of monastic orders that Purchas reviews in volume 1. Traditional modes of argument are turned against their Catholic originators to formulate a world stage setting with James I (or at the last moment Charles I) at its apostolic apex and center, thus implementing history's last age:

When so many Nations as so many persons hold commerce and intercourse of amitie withall; Solomon and Hiram together, and both with Ophir; the West with the East, and the remotest parts of the world are joyned in one band of humanitie; and why not also of Christianitie...?

Meanewhile, wee see a harmonie in this Sea-trade, and as it were the concent of other Creatures to this consent of the Reasonable, united by Navigation, howsoever by Rites, Languages, Customes, and Countries separated. [vol. 1, 56]

Eventually the splendors of the world's rarities and her natural and religious varieties are embodied in Purchas's prose, which registers all languages, scripts, and hieroglyphs attested through time and across the globe in an English universally enriched through "Japonian and China rarities"; through "Indostan, Arabike, Persian, Turkish, and other Letters"; through translations and collections "out of the Hebrew, Auncient and Moderne Greeke, Abassine, Tartarian, Russian, Polonian, Ægyptian, and innumerable other Nations Christian, Jewish, Mahumetan, Ethnike, Civill, Barbarian, and Savage, innumerable wayes diversified"; and even through the picture histories of Mexico, the famous Booke of the Indians with Mexican interpretations, described by

Acosta, collected for Charles V but undelivered, now translated for James I, the ultimate monarch (Vol. 15:413). Purchas forges the world's religions, languages, and alphabets, and the natural forces and diverse commodities they name, into rhetorical tropes revolving around James I, thanks to the Art (Navigation) he perfectly embodies; I quote at length to convey the sweep and pulse of Purchas's Jacobean prose:

Now for the services of the Sea, they are innumerable; it is the great Purveyor of the Worlds Commodities to our use, Conveyor of the Excesse of Rivers, Uniter by Traffique of al nations; it presents the eye with diversified Colours and Motions, and is as it were with rich Brooches, adorned with various Ilands; it is an open field for Merchandize in Peace, a pitched field for the most dreadfull fights of Warre; yeelds diversitie of Fish and Fowle for diet, Materials for Wealth, Medicine for Health, Simples for Medicines, Pearles and other Jewels for Ornament, Amber and Ambergrise for delight, the wonders of the Lord in the Deepe for instruction, variety of Creatures for use, multiplicity of Natures for Contemplation, diversity of accidents for admiration, compendiousnesse to the way, to full bodies healthfull evacuation, to the thirsty earth fertile moysture, to distant friends pleasant meeting, to weary persons delightfull refreshing; to studious and religious minds (a Map of Knowledge, Mystery of Temperance, Exercise of Continence, Schoole of Prayer, Meditation, Devotion, and Sobrietie): refuge to the distressed, Portage to the Merchant, passage to the Traveller, Customes to the Prince, Springs, Lakes, Rivers, to the Earth it hath on it Tempests and Calmes to chastise the Sinnes, to exercise the faith of Sea-men; manifold affections in it selfe, to affect and stupifie the subtilest Philosopher; sustaineth moveable Fortresses for the Souldier, mayntayneth (as in our Iland) a Wall of defence and waterie Garrison to guard the State; entertaines the Sunne with vapours, the Moone with obsequiousnesse, the Starres also with a naturall Looking-glasse, the Skie with Clouds, the Aire with temperatenesse, the Soyle with supplenesse, the Rivers with Tydes, the Hils with moysture, the Valleyes with fertilitie; contayneth most diversified matter for Meteors, most multiforme shapes, most various, numerous kindes, most immense, difformed, deformed, unformed Monsters; Once (for why should I longer detayne you?) the Sea yeelds Action to the bodie, Medita-tion to the Minde, the World to the World, all parts thereof to each part, by this Art of Arts [here the preacher presumably pauses], Navigation. [Vol. I, 46–7]

Purchas's wondrous rhetoric would require a study in its own right. Of inter-est to the anthropologist are those Jacobean efforts to usher all languages into an English universally enriched. These goals are clearest in collections and itemizations of alphabets, hieroglyphs, ideographs, and letters (Vol. 1, 492–3). But the host of loan words and lists of exotica likewise convey pre-Enlightenment themes of incorporating all languages, or signs of them, into one language, but hermeneutically rather than abstractly. The associated motives of and for translation submerged as Enlightenment theories of language developed; but they resurface whenever hermetic and hermeneutic interest in rarities and varieties of tongues and texts reappear.[7]

What Purchas calls the "allegorical, anagogical, and tropological" compo-nents of his arguments are themselves most multiform, numerous, and often cryptic as well, shifting prior Jesuit, Holy Roman, medieval, and Patristic themes to an Anglican register. Here we can consider only a few arguments that relate to a comparative scheme of human diversity, eventually valorizing proper kings (who serve no pope) and stigmatizing tribes. Like previous Portuguese accounts, English explorers report from the remotest regions the fame of their own monarchs. In earlier traditions observers had sought evidence of Christ's name among Heathens as tokens of apostolization and thus potential reconversion. Later Protestant ideas posed the direct, unmediated effects of Scripture in the process of proselytism, as in Hariot's late sixteenth-century report on Virginian Indians:

> Many times and in every town where I came, according as I was able, I made declaration of the contents of the Bible, that therein was set forth the true and only God, and his mighty works, that therein was contained the true doctrine of salvation through Christ, with many particulars of miracles and chief points of religion, as I was able then to utter, and thought fit for the time. And although I told them the book materially and of itself was not of any such virtue, as I thought they did conceive, but only the doctrine therein contained, yet would many be glad to touch it, to embrace it, to kiss it, to hold it to their breasts and heads, and stroke over all their body with it, to show their hungry desire of that knowledge which was spoken of.[8]

In contrast Purchas emphasizes not Scripture itself but the names of Elizabeth and later James as word evidence of Britain's ultimate historical role. Like some belated portolan system of coordinates allying worthy courts the world over, the names of monarchs thread out into a network of authoritative fame – or like veins of gold among the baser natural elements. In Purchas's hermeneutics:

> English circumnavigators have attained what they sought. And What Phaeton in his Vulcanian Chariot lost, these in Neptunian Chariots gained, and followed the Sunne round about the world; at once seeming to imitate the heavenly Orbes (as so many Terrestriall planets) and to rule the Elements, spurring the Ayre, bridling the Ocean, contemning the narrow limits of known Earth, and filling the world with their Fame.
>
> The English exploits in this kind are the subject of this Booke, especially theirs, which since the establishing of the East India Co. or Societie of Marchants, have traded those parts; which was begun in the happy and flourishing Reigne of that Glorious Elizabeth, whose Name could not end with her life, but as then it filled the Christian, Turkish, Persian, American, Indian, worlds of Place; so still it seemes to begin, renue, and flourish in glorious verdure, and to promise a perpetuall Spring throw all Worlds and Ages of Time. [Vol. 2, 286]

Repeatedly Purchas suggests not simply that explorers enhance Britain's renown but that upon entering exotic courts they discover that their monarch's fame has preceded them, virtually paving the way. Moreover, exotic monarchs themselves, including those of Malacca, Ternate, and Tidor, are credited with complementary fame in the globe-encircling system radiating out from James I.[9]

The more patently strategical side of royal *fama* is that it excludes the Dutch. "Yea the name of English-men were so famous in the East that the Hollanders in their first trade thither, varnished their obscurity with English lustre, and gave out themselves English." (Vol. 2, 288). Anglo–Dutch rivalry intensified when Dutch influence in world commerce surged after C. de Houtman's voyage of 1595–8, which reached as far as Java and Bali and established initial trade agreements. C. Goslinga reviews the advantages afforded the Dutch by their relatively rationalized policies of investment and trade:

> Indeed Houtman's voyage had given heart and nerve to the Dutch. They knew that the world was theirs.
> In 1598 at least eighty Dutch ships swarmed out of the home ports to sail in all directions...
> Both the provincial and federal governments understood the importance of this activity. And they supported it by giving exemptions from taxes, freedom from convoy duties, and sometimes by supplying guns and ammunition for the ships.
> ... more than one thousand ships with chartering contracts...left the port of Amsterdam between 1597 and 1602. [Goslinga 1971:19ff]

English gains in mainland India had occurred at Portuguese expense: elsewhere the Dutch were outstripping them:

> It was against this background of English victories over the Portuguese that Sir Thomas Roe made his celebrated embassage to the court of Jahangir at Agra in 1615–1618. As King James's accredited ambassador this courtly diplomat was cordially received by the Great Mogul and, after various negotiations, entered into a treaty with that monarch which eventually opened up western India to British enterprise. This was all the more fortunate because affairs in the English outposts of the Spice Islands had been going from bad to worse. Under the ruthless direction of Jan Pieterszoon Coen the Dutch company had built up a tight monopoly and would brook no intrusion from outside interests. This policy reached its peak in 1623, when the English factors and merchants throughout the Archipelago were rounded up on the Island of Amboyna by the Dutch, tortured, and slaughtered to a man. The savage "Massacre of Amboyna" caused a wave of horror throughout England, but it produced the calculated effect: the English Company relinquished all interest in the Spice Islands and devoted its efforts to the Asiatic mainland and Japan. [Penrose 1962:28]

With no charge of popery to level at the Dutch, through "Annotations dispersed" and "Marginall Notes with Dutch Epithetes," Purchas's text develops the episode at Amboin into a central emblem of Dutch policy (vol. 1:xlix–1). Yet the "sore [that] hath broken out by that terrible tragedie at Amboyna" only complements a more pervasive argument in Purchas: The trade in commodities, rightly executed, is a matter for monarchs. Purchas's notes emphasize resplendent grandeur as the basis of legitimate East–West exchanges. For example, his synopsis of the initial Dutch reports on Bali construes its royal sector as centralized and absolute: a semidivine king and benevolent ruler, fitting ally of James I. Compared with Dutch originals, Bali in Purchas appears mogullike or nearly so. (We might note with some satisfaction that while the "King of Bali" was in these respects not quite as Purchas depicted him, neither was James himself.)[10] Purchas presents evidence that the connections of realms effected through navigation and trade cannot be left to nonmonarchists, in particular the Dutch, a nation his compatriots regarded as Sea Beggars.

Anglo–Dutch rivalry, of course, persisted through the seventeenth century as efforts continued to formulate secular laws concerning the reciprocal rights of nations. The legality of commerce, access to the seas, and related issues earlier treated in Iberian compilations, Jesuitical tracts, papal edicts, and Mediterranean city-state policies now shifted north. Purchas embedded forerunners of these issues in symbols of monarchy; soon the symbols would transform in accordance with the values of commonwealth and the protectorate. Purchas's text continued past arguments and augured future ones: theories of Lost Tribes and New World eschatology; the place of the Apostles and of the Jews in world history. How far had the Gospels spread? Were Indians actually Jews as evidenced in certain similitudes: some Indians circumcising and, a few even argued, some Jews scalping? Or were these apparent similitudes misleading tricks of the Devil? Under Cromwell, when relations with Jewish merchants in the lowlands were cultivated and Rabbi Manasseh's *Hope of Israel* appeared, implications of such arguments changed, but the mode of argumentation endured. Some favored converting the New World Indians (identified with Jews) to Christianity, to fulfill biblical prophecies by proving them to be the Lost Tribes. Others wished to admit Jews into England so the Indians (still identified with Jews) would join the English against the Spanish and prepare for the millennium (see Chapter 2). In some respects, then, Purchas's argument was less convoluted and "Jacobean" than succeeding ones; moreover, it remained integrated by a complex image of Anglican monarchy (soon to be abandoned).

Meanwhile, in 1625 Dutch inferiority was everywhere signified by a lack of royal fame. Purchas acknowledges the similarities of region, religion, and navigation between the Dutch and the English, but he regards the latter as "the elder Brother, a Doctor, and Ductor, to the Hollanders in their Martiall feats at home, and Neptunian exploits abroad." Repeatedly, explorers' accounts are edited to emphasize Dutch ineptitude, often comic; from John Davis on Acheh:

The King asked a man of Flanders among us if he were English...He...answered that he was not of England but of Flanders, and at the King's service. I have heard of England, said the King, but not of Flanders; what Land is that? He further enquired of the King, State, and Government; whereof our man made large report, refusing the Authorite of a King, relating the government of Aristocratie...Again [the King] required to know if there were no Englishmen in the ships. [Vol. 2:313]

The Dutch reveal a different strategy before the king of Bantam:

The Flemmings gave a present which they can easily bragge off, small matters, they doe not spare to bragge very much of their King, meaning Grave Maurice, whom they call in all these parts at every word Raja Hollanda.

...we told them, that they were no English men, but Hollanders, and that they had no King, but their Land was ruled by Governors...so that ever after that day, wee were known from the Hollanders, and many times, the children in the streets would runne after us, crying, Oran Engrees bayk, oran Hollanda Jahad, which is, the English men are good, the Hollanders are naught. [Vol. 2:486, 457]

This last passage is from Scot's "Discourse on Java." Below I shall use Purchas's annotations of Java's "pompe and hommage" to suggest the sense of Indic monarchy that emerges in the course of his volumes. The reader has already visited Sumatra (identified with the biblical Ophir) through John Davis's account of 1599 (but placed by Purchas after later Dutch reports) describing the "Citie of Achien," with its "Archbishop and Spiritual Dignitaries," its people who "Boast themselves to come of Ismael and Hagar, and can reckon the Genealogie of the Bible"; and its sultan Aladin, a true king, elephant borne and awaiting, Purchas notes, the "promised return of Mahomet" (Vol. 2:321).

Later we find the East India Company's patent (1600) in full and then Sir James Lancaster's account, complete with the letters exchanged between Elizabeth and "our loving Brother, the great and mightie King of Achem, etc. in the Iland of Sumatra" – translated through Arabic – that illustrate procedures for establishing "factor-ies." Then comes the "entertainement and trade," mutual presents, cock-fighting ("one of the greatest sports this King delighteth in"), and so forth (Vol. 2:406-32). The same buildup will recur in the ultimate case of Agra. Sir Thomas Roe's accounts (originally intended to end the books financed by the East India Company) are presented in detail; a host of description and correspondence is included, all foreshadowed in the previous reports of Hawkins. Everything culminates in the conjunction of the seal of the Mogul, "contayning only the Mogols genealogie from Tamerlane, in several circles, with the English translation," and an emblem of the British court, together with a Latin inscription on the mutual power and greatness of *Monarchi* and *Mogol* (Vol. 4, chap. 16:432–3, 468).

But Scot's account of Java will serve to illustrate the extremes of usage allowed in proper monarchy, and it perhaps most readily reveals certain complexities in Jacobean symbols of diversity. (I place Purchas's marginal notes in italics and parentheses.)

The eighteenth of July, the King of Jacatra came in to present his shew before the King of Bantam, also to give his present, and to doe his homage. (*King of Jacatras pompe & homage.*)

The Javans, who cannot indure to have any stand over them, would remove a good distance from us, and many of the Kings Guard forsooke their Weapons, and would goe sit afarre off, neither can they indure that one should lay his hand on their head, the which is not for any point of Religion, as some will affirm, but only of mere pride.

About twelve a clocke came his shew and presents. (*King of Jacatraes Presents.*)

The Souldiers came in order as I have before declared, being about three hundred in number, then followed so many women with Cashes and strange Fowles both alive and artificiall, and likewise many strange beasts...

There was drawne in like manner a huge Gyant, which by our estimation, might bee some thirtie foote in height: also a Devill came in, in like order: more there was drawne in a Garden having many sorts of hearbs and flowers in it. (*A huge Gyant and a devill. A garden and fish pond.*) In the middle of which Garden, was a Fish-pond, wherein was divers sorts of small Fishes, and all sorts of Fishes which they doe know in those parts, were brought in either alive, or artificially made. Amongst these things, came in many Maskers, Vawlters, Tumblers, very strangely, and salvagiously attired, which did dance and shew many strange feates before the King. (*Maskers and Tumblers.*) There was drawne in likewise a very faire bedstead, whereon was a faire quilted bed: also eleven boulsters and pillowes of Silke, embroidered with Gold at the ends. The posts of the bedstead were very curiously carved and gilded, with a faire Canopy wrought with Gold: A number of other pretty toyes, were brought in and presented. Last of all, came in his youngest sonne, riding on a chariot.

The second day after this show was presented, being Friday, and their Sabboth, the King was carried on his Pageant to Church, where he was circumcised. (*King of Bantam circumcised*). His Pageant was borne by many men, it was reported to me by the Kings Nurse, foure hundred: but I think she lied, for me thought there could not stand so many under it. [Vol. 2:487–90]

An earlier part of the festivities is included as well, with Scot's even fuller elaboration of the revels, following a slur on Flemish captain Cornelius Syverson, a proud Boore with "neither wit, manners, honesty, nor humanitie":

But now I will leave this contemner of curtesie and hater of our Nation, with his rascall crue...and speake somewhat of the manner and order of the Kings Circumcision, and of the Triumphes that were held there every day, for the space of a moneth and more before his going to Church...(*Circumcision of the King of Bantam.*) There was a great Pageant made, the forepart of which was in likenesse of an huge devill, upon this Pageant was set three chaires of State, the middlemost was for the King, which was placed higher then the other by some two foote, on either of his hands were placed the sonnes of Pangran Goban, who is heire apparant to the Crowne, if the King should die without issue. This Pageant was placed on a greene before the Court gate, and rayled in round about. The manner of their Countrey is, that when any King comes newly to the Crowne, or at the Circumcision of their King, all that are of abilitie must give the King a present, the which they must present in open manner, with the greatest shew they are able to make.

Now a word or two in what manner the King was brought out every day, and what shewes were presented before him (*Beati Pacifici. The Kings triumphall pompe*): Alwaies a little afore the shewes came, the King was brought out upon a mans shoulders, bestriding his necke, and the man holding his legs before him, and had many rich tyrasoles carried over and round about him...First, a crue of shot beeing led by some Gentleman-slave, after followed the pikes, in the middle of which was carried their colours, and also their musique, which was ten or twelve pannes of Tombaga, carried upon a coulstaffe betweene two; these were tuneable, and every one a note above another, and alwayes two went by them which were skilfull in their Country musique...

After all which past, one within the Kings Pageant, speakes out of the Devils mouth, and commands silence in the Kings name. (*Revels.*) Then beginnes the chiefest of the Revels and Musiecke, and now and then the shot discharges a Voley.

. . . likewise amongst some of these shewes there came Junckes sayling, artificially made, being laden with Cashes and Rice (*Junckes and Juncates.*) Also in these were significations of Historicall matters of former times, both of the Old Testament, and of Chronicle matters of the Countrey, and Kings of Java (*Histories.*) All these Inventions the Javans have beene taught in former times by the Chinees, or at least the most part of them; for they themselves are but Blockheads, and some they have learned by Goossarats, Turkes, and other nations which came thither to trade. [Vol. 2:481–5]

Purchas annotates those very elements – Revels, Pompe, land and sea processions, Histories – jointly elaborated in Elizabethan and Jacobean courtly displays. (I think it not unlikely that he construed the "Chronicles and Histories" mentioned in such accounts as Eastern counterparts of the very books he was writing).

But a subtler aspect of Purchas's annotations possibly concerns that complex of circumcision and giantlike and devillike tumblers, all part of the *Beati Pacifici* of Java's monarchs. These very features were crucial similitudes in the ethnological understandings of Purchas's time. Consider, for example, his own selection and annotations of Cavendish's earlier report of royallike ceremonies in the southern Philippines:

The people of this island go almost all naked, and are tawny of colour. The men weare onely a stroppe about their wastes, of some kind of linnen of their owne weaving, which is made of Plantan-leaves, and another strooope comming from their backe under their twistes, which covereth their privy parts, and is made fast to their girdles at their navels; which is this. (*A strange naile in the yards of men to prevent Sodomy, for which purpose in Pegu they weare in the same part balls.*) Every man and man-child among them, hath a nayle of Tynne thrust quite through the head of his privie part, being split in the lower ende, and rivetted, and on the head of the nayle is as it were a Crowne: which is driven through their privities when they be yong, and the place growth up againe, without any great paine to the child: and they take this nayle out and in as occasion serveth; and for the truth thereof, we our selves have taken one of these nayles from a Sonne of one of the Kings, which was of the age of tenne yeeres, who did weare the same in his privy member. This custome was granted at the request of the women of the Countrey, who finding their men to be given to the fowle sinne of Sodomie, desired some remedie against that mischiefe, and obtained this before named of the Magistrates. (*Circumcision.*) Moreover, all the males are circumcised, having the foreskinne of their flesh cut away. These people wholly worshippe the Devill, and oftentimes have conference with him, which appeareth unto them in most ugly and monstrous shape.

Here Purchas's notes stipulate that circumcision is a similitude of sodomy, joined in Cavendish's account with "Devill-worshippe." It is likely that this interpretation applies, because these people are known to have been contacted, and in Protestant eyes contaminated, by the Spanish (Purchas notes in Cavendish's account finally that "the inhabitants of Capul. . . promise to ayde the English against the Spaniards" [vol. 2:177]). Symbols of Anti-Christ concerning the effects of the papal and Spanish alliance in previously unknown populations had become mainstays of inflammatory Protestant argument. As we saw in Chapter 2, De Bry's work possibly concealed an iconographic code representing New World populations as Edenic victims plunged upon Spanish discovery into a state of sin marked by postlapsarian and antediluvian conditions of giganticism, devil worship, and sodomy as well as cannibalism.[11] Notorious episodes in New World history, such as Balboa's punishment of native sodomists (he unleashed upon them ravenous dogs), are construed in a way to defame the Spanish, serpents of a belated New World Fall. For Purchas such Protestant symbology appears most explicitly in his traditional animadversion on the papal bull of Alexander VI:

And what right then had the Pope to propound that Method in his Bull, Vobis subjicere & ad fidem Catholicam reducere? Is any thing more free, then to beleeve? Else if Ethnikes had beene to be compelled to enter into the Church (for it is otherwise with the Children of the Kingdome) hee would have sent Captaines, Conquerors, Alexanders. . . not Fishermen, Tent-makers, Publicans, as Sheepe amongst Wolves, not Wolves amongst Sheepe.

. . .good men (sayth he) should be sent, by their Preaching and living to convert them to God; and not such as shall oppresse, spoyle, scandalize, subject, and make them twice more the Children of Hell, like the Pharises.

And this may be the cause of all those Misorders which happened in the Indies: the most by a blind zeale, thinking they did God service in punishing the Idolatries, Man-eating, and Sodomies, and other Vices of the Ethnikes, with Invasion and Warre. . .

And if I should shew out of Casas, a Spanish Bishop in those parts, the executions of this Bull, you would say, that the Brazen Bull of Phalaris, the Monster-Bull of Minos, the fire-breathing Bull subdued by Hercules, the Jewes Behemoth, and those of Aegypt were but Calves to this of Pope Alexander. . .How doth Acosta and others deplore these bloudie and therefore slipperie foundations of the Faith?

. . .and yet one clause of Baptisme is more Bullish or Hellish then the rest. . .That Christians, that Kings are obliged, by their very Baptisme obliged to the Apostolicall, that is, in their sense, the Popes Commandements. . .Protestants are generally beholden to his Catholike Keyes, which open Rome, the Catholike Mother Cite, to Strumpets, to Jewes, but locke out our Generation to the consuming flames.

. . .so Kings (which even amongst Heathens knew no Superiour but God) must in their Baptisme make a tacite renunciation of their Kingdomes. . .and his subjects . . .are at the Popes Bulls first lowing to depose him. . .It is no marvell that this Bull hath begotten such brutish Christians in America, as the Jesuites complayne; I hope in the East they teach otherwise. [Vol. 2:42–64]

To conclude his animadversion, Purchas in typical fashion recapitulates the anagogical and tropological argument behind all twenty volumes:

And. . .the argument of this great Worke, Navigations, English Indian Navigations exacted some Apologie, to shrowd themselves from this Bulls pushing and lowd bellowing Thunders. . .And long, long may his Majestie of Great Brittaine spread his long and just Arems to the furthest East and remotest West, in the gaineful Traffiques, in the painefull Discoveries, in the Glorious and Christian Plantations of his Subjects (maugre such Bug-beare, Bull-beare bellowings) Salomon and Hiram,

Israelites and Tyrians, all Arts and Religions concurring into one Art of Arts, the Truth of Religion, and advancing of the Faith, together with the glory of his Name, the splendour of his State, the love of his People, the hopes of his Royall Posteritie to the last of Ages. Amen. Amen. [Vol. 2:64]

In Chapter 2 we sampled similitudes between exotic peoples and images of sinful degradation – devil worship, giganticism, sodomy, cannibalism – that occurred in the Catholic interpretations of Columbus, Da Gama, and many predecessors. In the Protestant views represented by Purchas, however, such images are tied to papal–Spanish policies, thus yielding inverse readings of different customs. Where Holy Roman or papal influence is suspected, circumcision, for example, signifies sodomy, perhaps even a false kingship (assuming a pun on that "Crowne thrust through the head of their privy parts" in the example cited above of Spanish-influenced Capal south of Manila). In other circumstances of kingship, whatever the religious creed, traces of similitudes – circumcision (as a sign of sodomy), giants, devils – appear in orderly pomp and costume, harmonized, as in Java, among the rarities of the realm. In Purchas's portrayal of reciprocal monarchs serving no pope, similitudes of Anti-Christ become part of the splendid show of a regal pageant. As a final example, consider his annotations of the earlier texts of Cavandish on Java (after Capal):

There came two Portugals to us, which enquired of Don Antonio their King, then in England, and told us of the Javanes, as followeth. (*Raja Bolamboam.*) The name of the King of that part of the Island was Raja Bolamboam, who was a man had in great majestie and feare among them. The common people may not bargaine, sell, or exchange any thing with any other Nation, without special licence from their King; and if any so doe, it is present death for him. The King himselfe is a man of great yeeres, and hath an hundred Wives, his sonne hath fiftie. The custome of the Countrey is, that whensoever the King doth die, they take the body so dead, and burne it, and preserve the ashes of him, and within five dayes next after, the Wives of the said King so dead, according to the custome and use of their Countrey, every one of them goe together to a place appointed, and the chiefe of the Women, which was neerest unto him in accompt, hath a Ball in her hand, and throweth it from her, and to the place where the Ball resteth, thither they goe all, and turne their faces to the East-ward, and every one with a Dagger in their hand, (which Dagger they call a Crise, and is as sharpe as a Rasor) stab themselves to the heart, and with their hands all to be-bath themselves in their owne blood, and falling groveling on their faces, so ende their days. (*The wives kill themselves after their husbands deaths. A strange order.*) This thing is as true as it seemeth to any hearer to be strange...If their King command them to undertake any exploit...[the men] dare not refuse it, though they die every man in the execution of the same. For he will cut off the heads ...Moreover, although the men bee tawnie of color, and goe continually naked, yet their women be faire of complexion, and goe more apparelled. (*Faire women in Java. Don Antonio might be received as King in the East Indies*). They told us further, that if their King Don Antoni, would come unto them...[Vol. 2:180–1]

This account is interesting to the Indonesianist for its glimpse of royal practices later identified as widow burning and collective suicide (in

Javanese–Balinese traditions, *satia* and *puputan*). In Purchas, however, the widowless kings of Java, will all their extremes of custom and usage, are presented as legitimate rulers and – in a rejuvenated hermeneutics stretching back through accounts of the Philippines and the New World alike, on to Scripture – as circumcisors but not sodomites.

Precisely when Inigo Jones was elaborating the art of the Jacobean masque, Samuel Purchas was editing exotic lands into a masque of East–West kingship.[12] Nothing could seem less orderly than the texts he amalgamates: his own review of the religious authority of exploration and trade; thousands of pages of eye evidence; The East India Company patent; his animadversions on Alexander's bull; the bull itself, translated; Mull's profit margin analysis of trade; royal letters exchanged; commentaries on the Dutch; Brerewood's *Enquiries* of languages and religions; Strachey's *True Repertory* (whose manuscript perhaps inspired *The Tempest*); New World policy papers looking back to Hakluyt's *English Plantation*; and more. Yet behind this concoction appear standards geared to Jacobean sectarian disputes that placed the bizarre rites of Indic monarchs, especially the Great Mogul, in a favorable light (soon to dim).

The implicit message, if we read the first books of *Purchas His Pilgrimes* in Jacobean terms, is that Agra and comparable courts will complement Britain in a totality of trade and alliance. The pathos in reading Purchas today is that we know it did not happen and perhaps could not have. The British East India Company, like its Dutch rival, implemented an economics of profit and domination, sustained by symbols more Calvinist than "Jacobean." East–West relations would develop not as a splendiferous masque of reciprocal rarities but as monopolistic profiteering (first mercantilist, then colonialist), favoring and isolating the ideally homogeneous community of Europeans planted on exotic shores. Purchas's vision of reciprocity, perhaps never practicable, submerged with the succession of Charles I, with the increasing dominance of Parliament and Puritans, and with the Revolution. Yet as we shall see, his text's symbology perhaps contained, through omission, its own eclipse.

The victimization of vagabonds

Lo I the Man, whose Muse mus'd on Plantations,
New England, Virgin, Bermude, Newfound-landed,
Lawrell for Olive take, and make Relations
Of Armes, Harmes, Fights, Frights, Flights,
    Depopulations
Romes Buls, Spaines, broyles, Irelands ire, Traitors
    branded.
God, Angels, Winds, Seas, Men, Elizas Glory
Conspire; Shee outlives Death, in Heaven, in Story.

                                        Samuel Purchas

Construed in a certain way, there was as much variety of custom at Purchas's doorstep as in explorers' accounts. Sectarian differences among "Popery," Anglicanism, and other Protestant factions were conceptualized mutually with exotic varieties. Purchas's text both defames Rome and assimilates rival Protestant themes to an Anglican vision. What we would today call cultural contrasts remain embedded in a generalized system of liturgical, ritual, and scriptural signs.

Non-Anglican Protestants promoted rationalization of access to offices, strict family-based discipline, conformity in homogeneous congregations, and regular Sabbatarianism, so not to hamper daily work (all for the Lord) by a panoply of saints' days. Advocates of direct understanding of Scripture rejected "divine right" for both appointed bishops and hereditary kings. As related reformist attitudes came to dominate trade companies in England and Holland, views of foreign monarchs altered accordingly. British developments eventually crystallized into vivid Puritan themes: "The Puritan imagination saw the life of the spirit as pilgrimage and battle...[The individual's] soul was a traveler through a strange country and a soldier in battle. He was a traveler who, having been pressed to serve under the banners of the spirit, must enact faithfully his part in the unceasing war of the spiritual against the carnal man" (Haller 1972:145). Exported, this "Puritan imagination" would yield closed communities, ideally endogamous. In contrast, Purchas's earlier texts encompass pilgrimage and proselytization in an apostolic succession (corrected against papal versions) from hearers of Christ's word, bringing a world of rites and languages into the theater of human varieties revolving around Britain's monarch. Nevertheless, in a crucial area of ethnological understanding, the Puritan imagination and Purchas's Anglican imagination merged: The absence of settlement came to signify vagabondage both abroad and at home.

Jacobean social conditions found some four million inhabitants in plague-ridden England and Wales, a quarter of them receiving alms during the depressed 1620s, when many beggars were condemned for witchcraft (cf. Thomas 1971). To bolster a divine right of kingship, James I sold knighthoods and titles. The squirearchy broadened; the yeomanry waned; and members of the House of Commons, who managed to keep themselves undertaxed through the seventeenth century, continued consolidating estates, part of a long-term process:

The great age of enclosure for sheep-farming had perhaps come to an end by the seventeenth century; but enclosure and consolidation for improved arable farming, to feed the expanding industrial areas, was proceeding apace. Enclosure had long been attacked on the ground that it led to eviction of tenants and so depopulated the country-side. Tudor governments had tried, less and less effectively, to prevent it. 1597 saw the last Act of Parliament against depopulation. A proclamation of 1619 admitted that the laws for the protection of corn-growing and peasant proprietorship hampered agricultural improvement. They were repealed by Parliament in 1624, and so one obstacle to capital investment in agriculture was removed. The Parliament of 1621 had seen the first general bill facilitating enclosure.

If the English economy was to continue to expand, a more specialized division of labor was essential. More food would have to be grown to feed the industrial areas, food prices must be lowered and corn import ended. There were many ways to increase production. Consolidation of holdings assisted capital investment in improvements. Introduction of root crops led to reduction of fallow. Outlying areas of England still awaited colonization, as the internal frontier moved north and west. [Hill 1966:18]

Our interest in these events concerns the implications for ideas of exotic populations.[13]

In his important study *The Invasion of America*, Francis Jennings condemns Purchas's role in formulating "an elaborate and seminal rationalization for colonization [of North American Indians] by conquest":

Purchas' unique distinction was the invention of the nonperson-nonland qualities of savages and the world they lived in – the depersonalization of persons who were "wild." Turning away from his pre-war [i.e., Indian uprising of 1622] boasts of how Englishmen had conciliated the savages, Purchas justified (in 1625) the Virginians' retaliatory massacres of the Indians. He argued that Christian Englishmen might rightfully seize Indian lands because God had intended his land to be cultivated and not to be left in the condition of "that unmanned wild Countrey, which they (the savages) range rather than inhabite."

It is instructive to dwell for a moment on that last phrase. Purchas may have picked it up from the Jesuit missionary Pierre Biard, who had described the Indians living farther north: "Thus four thousand Indians at most roam through, rather than occupy, these vast stretches of inland territory and sea-shore. For they are a nomadic people, living in the forests and scattered over wide spaces as is natural for those who live by hunting and fishing only." But Purchas knew perfectly well that the Virginia Indians were sedentary and agricultural and that the Jamestown colonists had been preserved from total starvation by Indian farm produce. [Jennings 1975:80]

I suspect that Purchas's evaluation of American aboriginals, rather than a mere conspiratorial distortion by a scholar who presumably "knew perfectly well" the truth, reflected developments in the perception of "Vagrancy." The cultivated fields and game-stocked forests of Eastern Indians came to be considered local holdings that hampered formation of estates, in this case, in the New World. Jennings acknowledges that Purchas's stereotypes of Indians seem inconsistent throughout the volumes of the *Pilgrimes*. Purchas's own cosmological preface, not concerned with the nature of "settlement," expresses the sort of admiration for New World ethnics displayed by Las Casas and other "pro-Indian intelligentsia of Spain" (Sanders 1978: chap. 14). Only in the volumes on Virginia, when Purchas is moving toward the New England "solution" for New World plantation, are epithets of "nonperson-nonland" applied to Indians: "like Cain, both Murtherers and Vagabonds in their whatsoever and howsoever owne."

Jennings avoids the broader issue with his unsubstantiated claim: "Certainly

Purchas understood what he was doing, and he was never foolish enough to believe that Virginia was really virgin land devoid of natives" (Jennings 1975:81). He thus fails to situate the brand of Eastern Indians as "unnaturall Naturalls" within changing views on the rights of native "inhabitants" as rural smallholders, along with vagrancy, philanthropic obligations of the local parish, and related Tudor and Stuart "ideas of settlement." Such economic developments have been summarized by Raymond Williams: "Much of the actual purpose of the laws against vagrancy was to force the landless to work for wages, in the new organization of the economy. But this was rationalized through the organization of relief on a parochial basis, as the duty of people to care for their own. The idea of settlement, and then of paternal care, was counterposed to the ideas of mobility, of the wandering sturdy rogues, the free laborers" (Williams 1973). I would not explain the Jacobean view of tribes purely by domestic infrastructures but I would insist that cultures conceptualize their own diversity and the diversity of others, both positively and pejoratively, in related symbols. Signs of Amerindian vagabondage "communicate" with more proximate victims of the Poor Laws, with the 1621 prohibition on the propertyless dwelling in towns or cities and with the whole nation branded as vagrants:

England's principal colony in the seventeenth century was neither a West Indian sugar plantation nor an Indian fort struggling with the vagaries of the central administration thousands of miles from the capital, but an old English conquest across the St. George's Channel, warswept Ireland.

In 1607 King James I struck the gong by publishing a proclamation against Jesuits, and when in 1609 . . . he decided to plant Ulster with English and Scottish colonists, this was to introduce a new Protestant colony amid a predominantly Roman Catholic community. [Ashley 1973:226]

Contrary to Jenning's suggestions, Purchas's rationale for colonization was neither "seminal" nor his own invention; signs cannot communicate if they are "unique."[14]

I aim not to absolve Purchas's text but to implicate those forces establishing "the sacred rights of property" that "removed all impediments to the triumph of the ideology of the men of property – the Protestant ethic" (Hill 1975:12). Moreover, only against the stigma of vagabondage do the images of exotic kingships sampled above take on full meaning. Certain Indic monarchies annotated by Purchas as worthy trading partners were presented (in accounts, later than Cavendish, that mention production) as benevolent agrarian realms. The "king" of Bali, for example, appears both a divine ruler patronizing the display and commerce of rarities and varieties and the lord of domestic bounty.[15] In Jacobean domestic affairs, on the other hand, symbols of benevolent plenty were being appropriated by the new propertied class, the very segment that would soon stigmatize both their own king and Eastern ones as well.

Representative symbols of domestic production have been reviewed by Raymond Williams in *The Country and the City* (1973). Williams traces "the pastoral convention in poetic imagery which was drawn on over several centuries to idealize and glorify the increasing process of agrarian capitalism." (Williams seems to assume an intentional mystification by owners to mask class divisions; I would expect the propertied class, doubtless believing in the bliss of the house over the misery of vagabondage, to be convinced by their own symbols, whoever the laborer-victims.) Pastoral idylls of the propertied class were in full play in the Jacobean scenes of Ben Jonson's *Penshurst*:

In a conventional association of Christian and classical myth, the provident land is seen as Eden. This country in which all things come naturally to man, for his use and enjoyment and without his effort, is that Paradise:

> The early cherry, with the later plum,
> Fig, grape and quince, each in his time doth come:
> The blushing apricot, and woolly peach
> Hang on thy walls, that every child may reach.

Except that it is not seen as Paradise; it is seen as Penshurst, a natural order arranged by a proprietary lord and lady... What is really happening, in Jonson's and Carew's celebrations of a rural order, is an extraction of just this curse [of labor], by the power of art: a magical recreation of what can be seen as a natural bounty and then a willing charity: both serving to ratify and bless the country landowner, or, by a characteristic reification, his house. Yet this magical extraction of the curse of labor is in fact achieved by a simple extraction of the existence of laborers. The actual men and women who rear the animals and drive them to the house and kill them and prepare them for meat; who trap the pheasants and partridges and catch the fish; who plant and manure and prune and harvest the fruit trees: these are not present; their work is all done for them by a natural order. When they do at last appear, it is merely as "the rout of rurall folke" or, more simply, as "much poore," and what we are then shown is the charity and lack of condescension with which they are given what, now and somehow, not they but the natural order has given for food, into the lord's hands. It is this condition, this set of relationships, that is finally ratified by the consummation of the feast. [Williams 1973:31–2]

Purchas's arguments about Indic kingships recall such Jacobean idylls: they overlook work and labor (as did the explorers' accounts) to celebrate the bountiful feast and show. More important for our interests, in Purchas Indic kings still appear to unify what was already rent asunder domestically: They embody both commercial exchange and agrarian production. That Britain's monarch ultimately could not epitomize *exchange* seems prefigured in the fact that he could not epitomize *production*. The signs of kingship, integral in Purchas's treatment of the East, were already fragmented in the West.

Williams's study demonstrates from a different vantage the style of Jacobean interpretation – soon to be stigmatized by rising Baconianism – represented by Purchas: Social processes and categories – whether domestic factions or world religions – are interpreted across the range of biblical, classical, and exegetical authorities. Basic contrasts between proper kingships and pope-infected ones, and distinctions between manor/rustic, sedentary/wild, and inhabited/range applied universally. Purchas's symbols of exotics were no more "mystified" – if mystification it is – than owners' symbols of themselves. Such symbols are to be explained by neither ignorance (of *them*) nor familiarity (with *ourselves*). Nor are such exaggerated symbols of others/selves outgrown as scales of religious superstition at last fall from scholars' eyes. The signs and symbols merely shift to other political, religious, and cultural divisions. Frank Manuel has urged a reconsideration of great Western enterprises according to the literary and biblical images by which they were understood and promoted; he urges us to "view Western history as a paradise cult: in sacred texts, in commentaries upon them, and in their secular adaptation. Grand enterprises of Western man, among them the propagations of Christianity, the crusades against Islam, millenarian revolts during the Reformation, the overseas explorations of the sixteenth century, and the settlement of the American continent drew sustenance from the body of this myth" (Manuel 1974:83) We can add to these grand, international quests and missions a process as proximate and often covert as agrarian capitalism, itself part of the web of meanings – simultaneously domestic and exotic, we/they – articulating varieties of East/West kingship and Old World/New World vagabondage in the inseparable domains of ethnology and history.

Marriage symbology annulled

We have barely penetrated the historical and cultural underpinnings of Purchas's text and arguments. To appreciate the fact, we might consider as a text in its own right Christopher Hill's review of the "association of ideas" in Stuart politics and religion:

Finance and trade were the most obvious sources of disagreement between King and Parliament. But quarrels also arose over foreign policy. In the Thirty Years' War the Habsburgs were trying to reverse the effects of the Reformation...Nearly a century of history and propaganda lay behind the identification of Protestantism and English patriotism. The heretics burnt in Mary's reign had been popularized as the victims of Spain by Foxe's *Book of Martyrs*, of which there was a copy in many churches. The tortures of the Spanish Inquisition, the Netherlands Revolt, the Massacre of St. Bartholomew in France, the Spanish Armada, Gunpowder Plot, all had been skilfully exploited to build up a picture of cruel Papists striving to dominate the world, and of God's Englishmen bravely thwarting them...A papal victory, moreover, would threaten those who had acquired monastic lands at the Dissolution of the Monasteries, in England as in Germany. Protestantism, patriotism, and property were closely linked. The association of ideas was strong and popular. The danger from Catholicism was both real and imaginary. Few English Catholics were Spanish fifth columnists, and Cecil and Archbishop Bancroft had skilfully played on their divisions. Yet the Jesuits certainly wanted a forcible reconversion of England, and if the Catholic cause had prevailed in the Thirty Years' War they might have got it.

James was pacifically inclined, by temperament and from financial necessity. He disapproved of his son-in-law's acceptance of the Bohemian crown, since he regarded it as subversive of European order and of the rights of the Habsburg family. He, like Queen Elizabeth, had always thought of the Dutch republicans as rebels against the crown of Spain rather than as Protestant heroes. James and Charles both admired the Counter-Reformation monarchies of Spain and France. [Hill 1966:57]

In its variety and diversity, Hill's full-visioned itemization rivals the heady passages of Purchas himself. Other recent historians of Jacobean culture sound even more like their subjects of study: exponentially Jacobean. Why not; anthropologically, shouldn't the cultural texts contaminate our interpretive discourse?

Purchas's own texts are noteworthy less for any originality than for developing amid rival factions a monarchical ideal encompassing the world of human varieties, as diversified as sects themselves. Since the fourteenth century the known world had been mapped as a host of kings joined through a portolan system of coordinates. But only with Purchas was the circumnavigated globe "Englished": *Purchas His Pilgrimes* represents something like the King James Version of ethnological texts. Jacobean political and religious factions grew comically, tragically, enriched as James I shifted allegiances between the Protestant Palatinate and those Counter-Reformation monarchies of Spain and France. These complex historical conditions enhance the anthropological interest of arguments for a reciprocity of sultan, raja, mogul, and king: Anglican monarch with eastern counterparts, all consolidated to the relative deprecation of tribes that elsewhere (e.g., in sixteenth-century French reports) had themselves been considered to be monarchies.[16] Purchas's readers found exotic confirmation of the primacy of proper kingships and of the vagrancy of unsettled populations; the latter topic complemented interests of both monarchists and estate owners, temporarily.

Purchas's selective annotation of accounts of Indic kings may help to clarify notions of divine monarchy in James's own *Basilikon Doron* and in the Neoplatonic "theater of power" staged in Jacobean courtly ceremony (Strong 1973). Proper kings, East and West, convert to entertainment even those customs that elsewhere, through complex arguments, betoken Antichrist: for example, circumcision, associated with sodomy, explained by papal influence. Royal courts convert comic tumblers and tragic widow burnings alike – and ultimately even diabolical antisacraments – to theater. A provocatively anthropological aspect of "divine kingship" – clearer in certain Elizabethan and Stuart texts and performances than in their Holy Roman forerunners – is its sweepingly cross-cultural character.

As Jacobean kingship reflects outward, so the stigma of exotic vagabonds reflects inward on Jacobean economic interests. Purchas's convoluted tomes represent no mere degeneration of Hakluyt's clearer compilations. Their dramaturgical vision of the encounter of remote peoples reminds us that Purchas's contemporaries included John Dee, Robert Fludd, and other scribes (I name not Shakespeare) preoccupied with the world theater of rarities and varieties. I would ask historians to situate Purchas's signs and symbols – not just of James I but of Indic counterparts as well – in the tangle of Jacobean developments that Francis Yates reviews so provocatively:

> The unease of the later years of the reign of James, when the Elizabethan revival is unacknowledged and half-suppressed, introduces a twist into the history of thought which it is hard to disentangle. The masque in *The Tempest*, with its emphasis on chastity, belongs to the Elizabethan revival, and is like a complex Elizabeth-portrait now applied to Princess Elizabeth. The later Ben Jonson masques for James show a shift of emphasis, away from the tone of the Prince Henry masques, away from the discouraged Elizabethan revival, and towards the Jacobean absolutism. Jonson flatters James most fulsomely in these masques, as absolute monarch, an attitude more in keeping with Spanish-Hapsburg influence than with the liberal monarchy of Elizabethan tradition. Owing to this deflection of Elizabethan tradition into Jacobean absolutism, the Puritan trend in the Elizabethan tradition becomes lost to sight and is confused with the imagery of the Stuart monarchy. The Caroline absolutism was of a different tinge from the Jacobean, not pro-Spanish, an Anglicanism influenced by French revival of Platonism, favorable to Shakespeare. But it further discredited courtly chivalry in the eyes of the Puritans. [1975b:132]

As we saw in Chapter 2, historians of anthropology have neglected the place of such complexities in the records of ethnological imagery and ideals. Finally, Purchas's arguments epitomize the culture of Jacobean Britain as a kingship; and they interrelate other cultures through signs and symbols including kingship.[17] More than simply reactionary, the texts at once embody Jacobean culture and compare it. Both inside and outside their own cultural–historical "presence," they are in the fullest sense ethnological.

Yet ethnology, which helps us to appreciate a certain coherence in Purchas's texts, also reveals their profoundest limit. Viewed from within Jacobean history, Indic courts seem to fare very well in Purchas: The commerce of kings revolving around James reads like a primus inter pares. We must, however, expand the horizons of Jacobean East/West assumptions to wonder, ethnologically, why Indic kings did not fare even better. Purchas's signs and symbols imply a perpetuated alliance of monarchs, East and West. But comparative anthropology reveals that there is only one means (even in the world's Last Age!) to ensure this. Recall from Chapter 3 the classical ethnological statement of the matter, Mauss's *The Gift*, which investigates the cultural conditions for exchange as a total social phenomenon, "at once legal, economic, religious, aesthetic, morphological," reciprocal, motivated, and enduring. Mauss concentrates on two privileged cases from ethnography – Trobriand kula and Kwakiutl potlatch, but his conclusions are universal: "true not only of Melanesia but also, and particularly, of the potlatch of Northwest America and still more true of the market-festival of the Indo-European world . . . In order that these meetings may be carried out in peace, there must be roads or water for transport and tribal, inter-tribal or international alliances – *commercium* and *connubium*" (1925/1967:76–7). Commercium and connubium – the principle

is clearly acknowledged in distinct areas of Jacobean traditions.[18] We need
only recall the most famous alliance with a foreign land during the reign of
James I:

At last on 14 February [1613] came the wedding, in the royal chapel at Whitehall.
The bride [Princess Elizabeth] wore "a crown of refined golde, made imperiall by
the pearles and diamonds thereupon placed, which were so thicke beset that they stood
like shining pinnacles upon her amber-colored haire, dependently hanging playted
downe over her shoylders to her waste." They were married by George Abbot,
Archbishop of Canterbury. The bridegroom was a Calvinist but the ceremony was
Anglican, "the Prince Palatine [Heidelberg] speaking the words of marriage in English
after the Archbishop." This was important, that the day was a triumph for the Church
of England which was extending its influence into foreign lands through this
marriage...
    That night a masque was presented in the banqueting house at Whitehall before
the newly wedded pair and the whole court. The words were by Thomas Campion,
the production by Inigo Jones. The theme of the first scene was the power of the music
of Orpheus to charm away melancholy and madness. Choral episodes between
Orpheus, the "franticks," and poetic frenzy followed. Then the upper part of the scene
was discovered in which were clouds and large stars. The harmony of the spheres
blended with the harmony of the royal wedding:

Advance your chorall motions now,
    You musick-loving lights,
This night concludes the Nuptiall vow,
    Make this the best of nights;
So bravely crowne it with your beames,
    That it may live in fame,
So long as Rhenus or the Thames
    Are knowne by either name.
[Yates 1972:4–5]

This celebrated wedding of Rhine and Thames was star-crossed, a prelude to
prolonged "Winter" rather than regeneration. But my point is that, despite
Purchas's similar symbology binding different realms through the pomp and
homage in a masque of monarchs, the marriage of Thames and Ganges (plus
Indus) was not even imagined. Purchas did inscribe the meeting of East and
West with less insistence on the kind of proselytizing and conversion that he
condemned in papal policies. But Purchas's symbology of East/West reciprocal
relations remained incomplete and therefore transitory, regardless, I suspect,
of events. To endure, his ethnological drama would have required an ideal of
intermarriage at the top, capstone to any totalized alliance in Jacobean (and
Maussian) signs.
    That connubium was an available "totalizer" in Tudor and Jacobean symbolisms
is clear from certain hermeneutic traditions; I shall mention just one tantalizing
example:

In Grafton's *Chronicle of England*, written in 1559 and planned to run from the creation
to "the firste yere of the reigne of our most deere and sovereigne Lady Queene
Elizabeth,"...Grafton was susceptible to the charms of the more colorful legendary

accretions to Scripture which had been made available by fable-mongers [such epithets are common in Hodgen's search for "unencumbered observation" in early anthropology] and the Commentaries – especially those which contained demographical or technological supplements to Genesis. Thus Cain and Abel were presented with twin sisters, and these feminine siblings became obvious historiographical assets when, with the purportedly concurrent relaxation of the laws relating to the marriage of near kindred, the peopling of the earth had to be accomplished within what Grafton regarded as a reasonable span of time. [Hodgen 1971:239]

To a structuralist ear Grafton's "solution" to the historical flaws (actually the absences) of Scripture rings true to the sociological device of sister exchange: perfect connubium in the Maussian sense. Cain and Abel's hypothetical twin sisters, exchanged, would have interrelated and perpetuated both pastoralists and agriculturalists, as well as Good (descendants of Abel) and Evil (descendants of Cain). A dual organization in Genesis would have articulated a lasting integrated system of contrasts rather than an unfolding of History – like the cross-cousin marriage of Lévi-Strauss's *Elementary Structures* (see Chapter 7). This is the tribelike mythological "suspension" (see Chapter 6) that, precluded by biblical scripture *as written*, Grafton was nevertheless able to imagine.[19]

Purchas's symbology, on the other hand, avoids ultimate ideal connubium; it thus remains partial, foreshadowing the eventual dominance of an exploitative Society of Merchants. Whitehall rhetorically courted Indic realms as trading partners, all the while desiring commercial concubines.

Reflexivity

But let us for a moment, in Jacobean fashion – "and in profit to Thee Reader, whom in the Lord, I bid farewell" – imagine it otherwise: The harmony of the spheres (and of the rarieties and varieties of East/West economies and courtly cultures) blended with the harmony of the royal wedding:

> Advance your chorall motion now...
> This night concludes the Nuptiall vow...
> So long as *Ganges* or the Thames...

Realistically though, there would be no Whitehall daughters for *these* foreign lands. Only what Purchas failed to inscribe can reveal the fullest meaning of his text. Its ultimate sense materializes against an ethnological absence: East and West, even their reciprocally famous monarchs, remain unequal and estranged.

6. Balinese incest recaptured: A discourse

Don Quixote reads the world in order to prove his books.

Foucault, *The Order of Things*

In Chapter 5 we examined dated Western efforts to comprehend eastern cultures and ended by discerning exotic components of the West itself. Here we turn to a contemporary Asian population that in its complex social arrangements, myths, and rituals is likewise, so to speak, self-exoticizing. A direct textual link ties Bali to Samuel Purchas, who first "Englished" aspects of the original Dutch reports that viewed the island's institutions through Indic lenses (Boon 1977: Part I). But this fact is secondary. Our broader aim in scrutinizing first Purchas, then Bali, is to demonstrate a methodological parallel between (1) the West converting the world into a discourse of cultures and (2) cultures like Bali converting themselves into a discourse of ancestor groups, caste ideals, and distant deities. This theme will emerge gradually, as we explore specific properties of Balinese values, texts, and marriage practices. We proceed by routinely comparing standard Hindu doctrine of karma to what it has, and has not, become in Bali, taking our cue from the ideal-types of Weber sampled in Chapter 3. Additional earlier topics (e.g., Dumont, semiotics) are woven together with threads of Balinese texts and contexts both to convey what is distinctive about Bali (not-India) and to turn the investigation of that distinction back on itself. I finally compare (1) what Bali does with (2) what we do in comparing what Bali does to what others do. They are both sufficiently strange! To arrive, however, at such intensive reflexivity, it is necessary to proceed step by step, moving forward, then looping back.

Comparative karma

No true Hindu doctrine knows of a "last day." Widely diffused doctrines maintain that there are epochs in which the world, like the Germanic *Götterdämmerung*, returns to chaos, but only to begin another cycle. The gods are as little immortal as men...An especially virtuous man may, indeed, be reborn as a god...The fact that the devout individual Hindu usually did not realize the grandiose presuppositions of *karma* doctrine as a whole is irrelevant for their practical effects which is our concern.

Weber, *The Religion of India*

In his comparative sociology of religions Max Weber situates karma somewhere between his two fundamental types of civilizational values: (1) The traditional, cosmological, and ritualistic versus (2) the reformist, ethical, and world-disparaging. Unlike ultimate Indic ideals of renunciation, karma doctrine seems to blend a partial world-rejection with continued celebration of opposed and complementary deities, rites, occupations, and varnas. Modified ideals of social resignation and qualified benefits of metempsychosis keep the traditional panoply of categories whirling.

Weber isolated Indic karma concepts with characteristic boldness. Hinduism's sole dogmatism is, he insisted, "the *samsara* belief in the transmigration of souls and the related *karman* doctrine of compensation" (1916–17/1967:118). Moreover, in karma doctrine, "the idea of compensation was linked to the individual's social fate in the societal organization and thereby to the caste order. All (ritual or ethical) merits and faults of the individual formed a sort of ledger of accounts; the balance irrefutably determined the fate of the soul at rebirth." For Weber, then, karma partly rationalized the cosmos, but not the economy, hence its spectral aspect: "*Karma* doctrine transformed the world into a strictly rational, ethically-determined cosmos; it represents the most consistent theodicy ever produced by history. The devout Hindu was accursed to remain in a structure which made sense only in this intellectual context; its consequences burdened his conduct" (1916–17/1967:119,121). While karma provided Weber with a key to India's socioeconomic stagnation, he never reduced the whole of Hindu religion to this single dimension. Indeed, earlier he stressed that "if we look beyond the ritualistic prescriptions to the structured core of Hindu ideas, we fail to discover in the Vedas a single trace of such fundamental conceptions as the transmigration of souls and the derived *karma*-doctrine (of compensation). These ideas can only be interpretively read into some ambiguous and undatable passages of the Vedas" (1916–17/ 1967:28).

Subsequent scholars have argued that the "structured core" of Vedic rites contained seeds of karma in values of the transfer of merit through sacrifice. Moreover, W. O'Flaherty suggests that the "pre-rebirth, Vedic model of birth" – transformed and indirectly perpetuated in myths – posed a complementarity of extremes: both sacrifice and *Soma*, both asceticism and eroticism (1973, 1980). In this light ethical karma doctrine would appear less specter than compromise, blurring the vivid polarities of Hindu mythology. For Weber as well, the eventual karma–samsara doctrines represented a reformed, rationalized, diluted, traditional cosmology, more compromised than the Buddhist Middle Path even, which still accentuated extreme renunciation embodied in the various ascetic orders implementing the example of the Buddha.

Enter Bali. Extending this comparative typology to Balinese variations of Hindu-Buddhism, we find a contemporary *culture* that in certain respects recalls the structure of *mythic* transformations of Vedic traditions based on a complementarity of extremes. Balinese symbology, ritual, and social organization exaggerate two opposed factors: (1) the rampant, sexual-demonic *and* (2) the controlled, incestlike near-spouse. Balancing this double extreme, prospering groups ensure ancestral benefits by displaying a full array of social categories, ritual devices, and dramatic–literary performances. I shall argue that Balinese Hindu-Buddhism is incompatible with a full-fledged ethical karma–samsara doctrine because of the force of an Indonesia-style ancestor cult with its hierarchy of rites, vocabularies, social structures, and in particular marriage types. Balinese culture has long been exposed to karma theories, but they have never become central. Bali thus provides evidence of religious, ritual, and social possibilities that are suppressed where karma values become encompassing. The comparative study of karma requires a sense of both what it establishes and what it precludes. In ideals and practices of karma, Bali represents something of a limiting case.

Like the erotic/ascetic complements of tantric mythology (cf. O'Flaherty 1973), Balinese traditions conjoin polarities – in this case *kama* (lust, desire) on the one hand and *dharma-artha* (ancestral duty and political prowess) on the other. The related symbology envisions little compromise ethic of compensation that would imply a universalistic consequence of deeds next time round. Indeed any cyclic returns – whether future births or rebirths or future consequences of present action – are presumed to remain within an ancestral division attached to an origin point (*kawitan*). Thus, ethical karma–samsara doctrine has been hemmed in by Balinese culture. In religious action Balinese karma suggests Vedic ideas of "parental karma" or perhaps Smarta Brahmin beliefs "that children are incarnations of dead grandparents" (O'Flaherty 1980). How are doctrines like karma "localized" in places like Indonesia? What enables them to be borrowed without being embraced?[1]

These remarks would be disputed by one sector of Balinese literati. Religious functionaries attuned to Indonesian national policies now emphasize ethical karma in manuals that reform Bali-Hinduism into a moral creed to be propagated beyond Bali's cultural context. Here for example, in an influential Indonesian-language manual, *Upadeça*, Rsi Dharma.Kerti instructs his naive interrogator on *hukum karma phala*, the law of karma:

So the meaning of *karmaphala* is the harvest from human deeds (*hasil dari perbuatan seorang*). We believe that good deeds produce good results and bad deeds bad results. In other words, fast or slow, in this life or a future one, all the rewards from those deeds are definitely received. . . And so my child, the law of *karmaphala* does not cause hopelessness (*putus asa*) and surrender to fate, rather it is positive and dynamic. [*Upadeça* 1968:31–3; my translation]

Nor is *Upadeça* the most reform-minded publication of *Parisada Hindu Dharma*, the primary agency of Bali's religious rationalization.[2] For example, although *Upadeça* still glosses the key term of Bali-Hinduism (*agama*) as "motionless, precisely in-place, eternal" (*tidak pergi, tetap ditempat, langgeng*); the more scholarly *Pancha Çradha* abruptly glosses *agama* as "arrival" (*kedatangan*;

pp. 25, 6)! Moreover the *Pancha Çradha* construes Balinese ancestor obligations in terms of ethical karma rather than ritualistically:

> The law of karma which influences anyone will not be received by himself alone but will also be inherited by his children and grandchildren (*anak tjutju*) or by his descendants as well. We see many examples in this world in which, for example, someone leads a life of luxury because he obtains great wealth by illegitimate or evil means – through theft, lying to others, or exploiting others. Yet after such a man dies and his wealth is inherited by his children and grandchildren, often they have bad characters or unhealthy dispositions. For example, one may be mad, or arbitrarily throw away the wealth until the inheritance is depleted and the inheritors impoverished, along with all the inward sufferings. This is caused by the influence of karma from ancestors (*leluhur*) who can directly influence their descendants (*keturunannja*). [Punyatamadja 1970:60; my translation]

Similar views of karma appear in Indonesian textbooks on Hindu sociology published by the national department of religion (Gde Pudja 1963:22ff.), which follow philological precedents in equating Balinese religiosity with themes in cosmological texts and related traditions of the palace.[3]

I cite this sample of sources to suggest the availability of ethical karma–samsara doctrine to interested Balinese Indonesians, and diverse outsiders. But my argument remains that for ethical (versus parental?) karma to penetrate Balinese ideals and actions, radical transformation, or really reformation, of the culture's symbology would be necessary, especially where it articulates ritual, myth, and marriage. In these domains Balinese traditions conform to principles more tantric than karmic.

Vagina-foot in love

> Myths stick together because of cultural forces impelling them to do so: these forces are not primarily literary, and mythologies are mainly accepted as structures of belief or social concern rather than imagination. But it is the structure of myths that makes the process possible, and since folktales possess the same kind of structure they can stick together too.
>
> Northrop Frye, *The Secular Scripture*

Again, we stretch to Bali from India. In his Durkheimian study of Indian caste and culture, Louis Dumont reserves a special place for marriage. Dumont's emphasis on Brahmanic and royal idealizations of marriage enable him to relate the pattern to Dravidian terminology, cross-cousin alliances, and other South Indian principles of organic solidarity that perpetually join opposed categories. Whether for methodological or intrinsic reasons or both, L. Dumont stresses the absence of symbols of impurity in marriage rites:

> Thus one can observe a parallelism between the states which accompany the ceremonies of the ages of life, and even the main actions of everyday life, and caste ranking. A mourner not following the precepts and lacking the help of specialists would remain more or less untouchable. A menstruating woman may not cook for

her family. Marriage on the contrary, the only *rite de passage*, it may be noted, which is not accompanied by any impurity, gives the impression, by the prestige which it radiates and many other traits, that in it the Hindu finds himself symbolically and temporarily raised from the condition and assimilated to the highest, that of prince or Brahman for a non-Brahman, that of god for a Brahman. [1970a:53]

Even allowing for Dumont's aim to encompass North and South India in a single interpretation, his comment leaves one wondering if the complementary impurity has been reformed away. I raise the question not to answer it but to contrast Bali.

Although India is the source of much Bali-Hindu marriage symbology, Bali displays more totalized hierarchy here than Dumont admits in India itself. The impure, the licentious, the demonic-Rakshasa side of marriage is less sublimated in Balinese culture. Mythlike, Balinese marriage requires a coexistence of opposite extremes: the capturelike and the incestlike, both necessary to the complete hierarchical order.

Balinese marriage revolves around three basic options. Any ambitious ancestor group, whatever its caste-title, may enhance itself by accentuating first-son rights and obligations and by (1) making ancestor-group-endogamous marriages (some degree of patrilateral parallel cousin or father's brother's child), (2) facilitating favorable prearranged outside marriage alliances and, (3) allowing not-unfavorable mock capture marriages with individuals. I shall here outline this hierarchical system with notes on relevant symbolic correspondences (recalling that in a hierarchy the bottom is as essential as the top, and the middle is by no means the average).

Endogamous marriage

In cosmology: unions of gods, as in the Hindu consort motif, sun–moon spouses, hermaphroditic attributes, and so forth; in short, the conjunction of two differences that are halves of the same whole. *In social action*: unions of patriparallel cousins; second patriparallel cousins (grandchildren of brothers, *mindon*) are considered a diminished version of first patriparallel cousins (children of brothers, *misan*); the latter are in turn a diminished version of siblings, and siblings are a diminished version of opposite-sex twins. (One might call patriparallel cousins "genealogical gods" of social groups.) These versions of actual or ideal spouses can symbolize different levels of the cosmos (divine, earthly, demonic) of social *warnas* (Brahmanas and Satrias, Wesias, Sudras), and even of ancestor groups (as when elder sons by a father's higher wife are deemed most suitable to make first cousin marriages). Symbols of endogamy, most elaborate for the higher sectors of society, are complemented by principles of hypergamy (daughters may not wed inferiors). Rituals surrounding endogamous unions center on a group's ancestors, whatever its title-caste. (If one correlated Balinese marriage types with G. Dumézil's formulation of tripartite Indo-European ideology, endogamous unions would represent the *dharma* component, since duty in Bali is ancestor oriented, and patriparallel cousin marriages, if properly executed by auspicious members of the group and fertile, intensify ancestral essence in descendants.)[4]

Exogamous marriage alliance

In cosmology: unions of god with a god-in-earthly-guise, thus connecting two separate spheres; hypergamy would require the divine component to be male, the earthly female. *In social action*: unions between separate houses (ancestor groups) with elaborate arrangements concerning dowry, reciprocal title acknowledgments, mutual temple attendance, and so forth. Symbols of alliance are highlighted in the Satria palaces (*puri*) and in those sectors of the title–caste system (*Dewa* or *Gusti*, depending on the kingdom) most involved in the traditional state. Rituals emphasize the joint role of two separate groups and the power alliance of prestigious houses. (In Dumézil's formulations, alliance unions would correlate with Indic artha: force, worldly power.)

Capture marriage

In cosmology: abductions by demonic Rakshasas (to be discussed shortly). *In social action*: mock abduction, the ordinary marriage of commoners and auxiliary marriages of rajas or anyone else who is smitten; blurs with concubinage at upper social levels. Symbols and rituals revolve around the furtive escapade of two lovers, romantic allure, love potions, auspicious signs that stress the essential intrusion of passion in the total marriage scheme. Romantic attraction is an elaborate theme in Balinese literature as well. (In Dumézil's formulation, marriage by capture would correlate with Indic *kama*, sexual desire.)

In a previous work I related this set of marriage options to Balinese social change, political action, and title–caste dynamics (1977: chaps. 4, 6, 8–9). I also traced symbols of provisionally separated, incestuous twins and the sun–moon imagery of Panji tales – all pertaining mainly to endogamy and marriage alliance (as indicated above). Here we shall peruse texts underscoring the fundamental place of capture values in Bali's marriage hierarchy.

One example is *Windu Sara*, a romance that commences by distinguishing (1) sexual abstinence, (2) cousin marriage, (3) auspicious prearranged alliances, and (4) passionate allure that, in this case, eventuates in adultery. As in all Balinese romances, matters become very convoluted; but a summary of even the tale's first parts suggests the catalog of marriage motives emerging:

Windu Sara only cared about flowers and books, and took no interest in women. His mother was always urging him to marry, and one day she told him that she had chosen for his wife a cousin of his, named Mertadjadnya. He still protested that he had no wish to marry, and besides the girl in question had a dimple on her shoulder, a sure sign that she would be fatal to men. His mother replied: "If she is not to your taste, I have another choice for you; Navartna, a sister of Djagasatnu who is also of royal blood." But he explained that she was *ngelangkargunung*, i.e. her birthday was in an unlucky relation to his own; there was only two days difference between them. "Who then would you like to marry? You have only to say the word and I will get her for you, from wherever it may be." But Windu Sara said that he could see no reason for marrying any one; he did not want a wife.

His friend Djagasatru meanwhile married Mertadjadnya, and begged Windu Sara to come and help him to entertain the wedding-guests. The wedding-day came. Mertadjadnya was fetched in a litter; there was a great banquet and Windu Sara entertained the guests. Mertadjadnya was marvellously dressed, and as Windu Sara was helping her to descend from her litter he was so overwhelmed by her beauty that he fainted. And Mertadjadnya gave him medicine to revive him. But he left the feast and went home; and the wedding went on without him. When he got home he would eat nothing and his mother asked him what was wrong. At first he would not reply, but after long asking he confessed that he had fallen passionately in love with his friend's wife, and that he would die unless he got her for himself. His mother was angry, and reproached him for his former obstinacy. Now it was too late; but she promised to try and get him a *vidyadhari* in place of the wife he could not have [De Zoete and Spies 1939:314]

As episodes unfold, all the forces of nature and society bring the full range of marriage possibilities into play, set in relief against the possibility of celibacy.

Traditions with still richer implications for the capture side of Bali's marriage system surround the well-known tale of Lady Uma. A written Balinese–Javanese form dates from 1500; its episodes and themes recur throughout Balinese oral traditions to this day. Here is a summary of the story by J. Hooykaas, whose ear for popular Balinese traditions may have helped determine how she condensed and translated T. Pigeaud's Dutch translation of the courtly text *De Tantu Panggelaran*:

The mahasuras and kalas had been subdued and were afraid of the five gods. The five gods then waited upon the Lord Guru to ask for teaching. The Lord would not allow the Lady Uma to listen to the teaching. He, therefore, sent Her away, telling Her to fetch the milk of a virginal black cow. The Lady Uma obeyed and went on Her way. Peaceful was the teaching by the Lord Guru to the five gods...

Meanwhile, the Lady Uma wandered through the Heavens in search of milk of a virginal black cow: She went to the Underworld, but She did not find milk of a virginal black cow. Then She wandered on Earth and happened to bump Her foot against a rock. And the big toe of Her left foot was split and She had to walk with a stick.

The Lord Guru wished to test her and to try Her faithfulness. He, therefore, became Kumara Gopala, an extremely handsome young cowherd. His vehicle the white bull He turned into a virginal black cow when Uma came upon him.

"Cowherd," She said to Him, "I want to ask you for some milk."

"I will not give it to you."

"Well, if you will not give it, I will buy it for gold and jewels."

"Well, I will not give it. What is the use of gold and jewels to me?" So He spoke.

In the end Kumara Gopala asked for union with Her. The Lady Uma felt ashamed, which was the expression of Her faithfulness. . .However, She desired the milk of a virginal black cow, so She had union with Kumara Gopala. Nevertheless She remained faithful to the Lord Guru, for She had not united in Her vagina, but between her thighs, which She bent so that they became like Her vagina. . .The semen flowed on the earth. . .It dripped into the Lady's split toe, which then swelled up.

Kumara Gopala gave the lady the milk of the virginal black cow and then He flew away, and became the Lord Guru again. The bull also flew away at the same time. [J. Hooykaas 1960:267–8]

It takes little stretch of the imagination to diagnose the split big toe of Lady Uma's (inferior) left foot that swells up when Gopala's semen drips in. Who would dispute that three levels of vagina are implied: the actual vagina and two surrogates – the thighs explicitly "like her vagina" and, here inexplicitly, the split toe? This bizarre anatomy materializes amid Heaven/Earth/Underworld, where opposed categories manifest in virginal-black-cows-giving-milk *versus* rutty-white-bulls-ejaculating (Siva-Parvati's mount, transformed into a virginal-black-cow by the Lord Guru) play out the familiar Indo-Javanese-Balinese cosmography.

In this article and elsewhere, J. Hooykaas noted the pervasive influence of Tantrism in Balinese cosmology:

The religion which found its way from India to Java was a Siwaistic Tantrism. . .In this religion the sexual union of the Upper God Siwa and His spouse plays a prominent part. It is believed that a *yogin* who is able to effect in his body the intercourse of those two gods achieves liberation. In Java several images of the divine figure have been found in which is expressed this complete blending of male and female. They are called *Ardhanareswari* and have one male and one female breast. In Bali nowadays, when the Brahmin priest, to prepare the holy water, achieves this mystic union in his body, he mentions the divine couple (*dampati*) in his chant. . .

The influence of Tantric thought has played an important role in both Java and Bali. In a bride and groom the god and goddess of love are regarded as having entered. Even in Muslim Java bride and groom are still worshipped on their wedding day as if they were gods. . .We [find the literary expression of this Tantric belief] again in the introduction to "Tantri Kamandaka" [a version of the Indian *Panchatantra*]. Here the King decides to take a new bride every night; he justifies his desire with the words:
At the exact moment of the consummation of the marriage, the God Iswara and His spouse Ardhanari incarnate themselves in the bridal couple when they are on their couch. Batara Wisnu and His Spouse, Batari Sri – all the gods are there. This is the result of marriage: the daily worship to all the gods. Do not forget that. What is the result? The whole country is prosperous, the rainy seasons are long, all plants grow lusciously on earth and so there is plenty of food. That is why I want to marry daily. [J. Hooykaas 1960:276–7; cf. de Zoete and Spies 1939:97, 273; J. Hooykaas 1957; Boon 1977: chaps. 4, 6, 9]

(We should note that in these Javanese–Balinese versions of Indic themes, Uma, Wisnu's spouse, tends to merge into Sri, Siwa's spouse, yielding an arch-couple, like Gopa and Gopi.)

But important components of "Tantrism" – the very ones perhaps least sublimated by priestly formulations – go unmentioned in J. Hooykaas's observations on Lady Uma. Hooykaas clarified neither Uma's swollen toe, nor her vagina-thighs, nor the concrete specifics. Instead she followed precedents of reducing sexual imagery to vague fertility beliefs and a pan–Malayan–Indonesian harmony, static and archaic, between casually dualistic conceptions of Father Sky and Mother Earth evidenced in the rice-goddess cult of Dewi Sri. Was it for cultural and historical reasons that many Western interpretations of an earlier day – ethical, moralistic, and reformist in their own right – skirted the issue?

In interpretations, no less culturally and historically determined, of our day (my own interpretation included), it would be unthinkable to downplay "the semen...dripped into the Lady's split toe which swelled up" – unless one were tending to mold Balinese traditions into conformity with karma–samsara or with some other ethical doctrine. Recent less reformist philological work restores the emphasis on *kama salah* in translations and summaries of texts on Lady Uma (who eventually is transformed into the evil, corpse-stealing Durga, as J. Hooykaas stressed). For example, C. Hooykaas has consolidated all the priestly texts at his disposal that bear on Kama/Kala (love/evil), which some Balinese exegetes consider to be the essence of *wayang* shadow-puppet performances. He concludes in his account of texts on Lady Uma: "The sperm does spill (*kama salah*) onto the ground but some of it finds its way into the split in her left big toe. As a consequence she bears male triplets" (C. Hooykaas 1973:307).

While today's philology is, in matters of kama, less reformist than yesterday's, it still does not pursue the dimensions of Tantrism that concern us here. We are after not what lies in these texts but what lies between them and historical change, social action and complexities of rank and capture-marriage (hence the preference standard in anthropological structural-functional and structuralist accounts, for folk–"oral" versions over literati–"textual" versions even in a highly literate society). I suggest that the seamier side of traditions surrounding Uma-Sri, viewed in light of the system of social marriage options outlined above, may further our understanding of Balinese "Tantrism" at all levels of society and "cultural performance" (cf. M. Singer 1972). Uma's thrice-located vagina, epitomized in the vagina-foot extremity, could again allude to the total marriage system – which we might now consider a sort of "primitive classification" (Durkheim and Mauss 1903/1963), here, however, purged of any archaic overtones, or as a sort of "cryptotype" (B. Whorf 1964b) embedded in marriage symbology.[5]

If a vagina-part (metonymy) implies the hierarchical whole (metaphor), the institution of marriage reveals covert extremes. It becomes, like coitus, symbolically threefold. Heavenly marriage, explicitly coded as incest mythically, becomes vagina-located-in-the-vagina in anatomical symbols. In a sense the vagina situated naturally symbolizes "unnatural" (incestuous) intercourse. Underworldly marriage, coded as Rakshasa capture in myth, drama, and ritual, becomes vagina-footedness in anatomical symbols. Finally, the anatomical symbol for earthly marriage is vagina-thighs. Earthly marriage, then, is not an averaged type: It implies a complementarity of extremes like the other two types.

Earthly marriage does, however, point toward the "socioanagogic" (K. Burke 1966:108) dimension of this symbology: namely, that ambitious houses aspiring to prominence would most fully embody all three marriage types, with the accent on political alliance. Earthly marriage as well conjoins the three types: incestlike cousin marriage and romantic capture (partly illicit) with political alliance. Indeed, as the story of Lady Uma itself stipulates: "The milk of the virginal black cow was to be found neither in Heaven, nor in the Underworld, but on Earth" (J. Hooykaas 1960:276).

In these respects Balinese marriage diverges from Indic Laws of Manu that assign capture marriage (one of eight varieties) to the military sector of society. Balinese capture rites, as would be expected in a partly Pacific culture, characterize both the general populace and rajas and other polygynists whose spouses run the gamut. Yet as the arch-political category, rajas and nobles (*Dewa* or *Gusti*) are epitomized by alliance, just as priestly Brahmanas are epitomized by endogamy. Lady Uma helps expose the partialness of these two types emphasized in courtly traditions. She underscores how thrusting sexual escapades – the domain of Rakshasas and of capture rites – complement the political and endogamous dimensions.

Lady Uma's anatomy recalls the familiar equivalence of microcosm (body) and macrocosm (cosmology) basic in many Indic, Pacific, and other symbolisms. But the dislocation of her vagina reveals dialectical complexities often underestimated in standard-average microcosm/macrocosm analysis and always overlooked in sociologistic reductions of symbol systems.[6] What appears bodily most "normal" and human – the vagina where it naturally occurs – is associated with the divine–incestuous level of cosmography, leaving one abnormal vagina (in the foot) to the demonic-capture realm and another abnormal vagina (in the thighs) to the "ordinary" human realm. *Nowhere in such symbolic conventions is a naturalistic gloss appropriate.* All the realms – including the human political arena – are mutual extremes. This relational and shifting symbolism, dynamic and hierarchical, contrasts vividly with a stratificational symbolism – for example, head-Brahmin, shoulders-Satria, feet-Wesia – often assumed to exhaust macrocosm/microcosm equivalences. I suspect that the hierarchical-dialectical is compatible with Tantrism, whereas the stratificational-reflectionist already implies a tendency toward reformism.

The complete marriage scheme is simultaneously Divine/Human/Demonic and ancestral/political/romantic at the levels of cosmology, society, and actor motivation (Boon 1974). It helps broaden the significance of another surmise by J. Hooykaas, once Uma and the Lord Guru appear as analogues to Dewi Sri and Siva, ultimately returning to heaven astride their white bull:

So one may surmise that when the gods performed a *wayang* play as a means of exorcism, which showed "the true nature of the Lord and the Lady on earth," it was the kind of story as told above.

In conclusion: first I have compared the myth with ancient conceptions of the union of Father Sky and Mother Earth. This concept was widespread in pre-Hindu Indonesia. The XVth century form of it might have been modernized to suit the ideas of that period, which were dominated by Tantric thought with the union of Siwa and Uma as its kernel. The union described in the myth was probably thought of as an initiation, a parallel to that of the Half-One. The fertility myth in its new form brought in its train stories that were exorcistic in character, with the young cowherd and the little girl on the bull being victorious over the demon. The true nature of the gods was the very old one: that of fertility. [1960:278]

A countersurmise would be that the fertility involved entails not just an archaic–abstract union of Father Sky and Mother Earth but a conjoining of all marriage aspects, particularly the demonic-sexual. How else might one solve the riddle unanswered by the demon Kala elsewhere in these traditions: "There is a being with three heads, two horns, one female part and two males ones, one tail etc." (J. Hooykaas 1960:277)?[7] One possible solution, as certain texts confirm, is the united couple astride their bull: three heads (Siwa, Sri, bull), two horns (bull), two male parts (Siwa, bull), one tail (bull). The double male parts imply that Siwa's divine lingam is complemented by the bull's lusty one. Hence in a modern drawing depicting the riddle (J. Hooykaas 1960), the demon-giant Kala's arm penetrates the *galungan*, fundamental symbol of a balanced cosmos inevitably displaced from the screen by *wayang* episodes. Nothing could be more suggestive of *kama*'s thrust into incomplete dharma-artha (ancestral-duty-cum-political-prowess) essential in dramatic narrative.

Finally, we now know from Lady Uma that the "one female part" of the riddle (Sri's) is implicitly three, again completing the picture by confirming the tripartite values of marriage: not an ethical compromise but an interrelation of extremes behind Balinese life and imagery or, in terms to be adopted below, not a solution but a suspension. I submit that where such extremes remain hierarchically interrelated, ethical karma doctrine remains culturally "shallow" (cf. C. Geertz 1973: chap. 15).[8]

Hypergrammatically

The myth is certainly related to given (empirical) facts, but not as a *re-presentation* of them. The relationship is of a dialectic kind, and the institutions described in the myths can be the very opposite of the real institutions. This will in fact always be the case when the myth is trying to express a negative truth.

Lévi-Strauss, "The Story of Asdiwal"

Balinese culture enables me to put my argument otherwise, to elicit conver-gent data from different symbols. That karma-samsara has not become a central theme in Bali may in part be explained by the fact that incest remains, indirectly, exemplary. Balinese incest symbolizes the mutual desirability of extremes. Again, in Bali patriparallel cousin marriages appear as diminished equivalents of sibling marriages, which are diminished equivalents of twin marriages. (We should note that the separation between each simile in the sequence – second cousins, first cousins, siblings, twins – is itself a factor ultimately represented by "capture" as a bridging of distance between suitable spouses.) Ethical karma doctrines, like any reformism, would modify such extremes; incest imagery glorifies them and thus converges with Lady Uma and related traditions.

To gain perspective on this aspect of Balinese symbology, we shall stretch now toward not India but Oceania, in light of D. M. Schneider's argument that incest is a cultural code regardless of any naturalistic basis. Schneider's general thesis is confirmed by Bali, although its finer points require a profound twist. He summarizes:

"Incest" is symbolic of the special way in which the pattern of social relationships, as they are normatively defined, can be broken. "Incest" stands for the transgression of certain major cultural values, the values of a particular pattern of relations among persons.

For those who should be respectful "incest" signals the lack of respect. For those who should have responsibility and authority it is a sign that responsibility has been abrogated and authority misused or broken down entirely. "Incest" means the wrong way to act in a relationship: as father-son, as father-daughter, as mother-son, as mother-daughter, as brother-sister, as cousins, as kinsmen...

To act not merely wrong, but to act in a manner opposite to that which is proper. It is to "desecrate" relationships. It is to act "ungrammatically." And each particular definition of "incest" – as "cannibalism," as "animal," as "eating blood" – gives the special meaning of the "desecration," the meaning that is special to that particular system of symbols and meanings, the culture, that is, in which it is embedded...

...the meaning of "incest" as it appears in known societies where it is disapproved (without qualifications, without ambiguity), is that it is a "desecration", it constitutes "cannibalism." [Schneider 1976b:166–7]

In contrast to these Oceanic societies, Bali's incest prohibition is *not* unqualified; that is, the prohibition is qualified. One might even playfully deem Balinese "incest" not "ungrammatical love" but "hypergrammatical love." The grammar analogy collapses: we must shift from a linguistic metaphor of competence to one of poetics. Balinese incest represents the too-grammatical in a way that recalls K. Burke's principle of "perfectibility" in systems of rhetoric/poetics, systems ordered like some cultures themselves. Incest in Bali is like three perfect statements simultaneously, or better, like a triadic chord whose harmonics are more than the sum of its individual notes. Incest implies a surabundance of attributes – more in the marriage gamut than any given marriage may contain – yet the full gamut remains the cultural desideratum. Incest thus plays a double role symbolically. It epitomizes endogamy itself (stepped back to cousins in actual practice); and it symbolizes the conjunction of all three marriage types. The sister spouse (most extremely a twin) conceals three dimensions: Like actual cousin spouses, she is endogamous; like alliances she joins houses (in narratives twins are separated into different kingdoms; also, cousin spouses rejoin collateral lines); and like captured lovers, she is desired and desires, to the point of self-immolation. (Note as well that in Bali, captured outsiders are eventually cremated and elevated into ancestresses of their children's, and husband's, group.) The triple ideal symbolized in incest is in any given instance or at a given level unachievable. It is truly an ideal: cultural hyperbole. *Only the culture as a whole through time and throughout its differentiations, achieves the implications of incest.*

Yet hypergrammatical love, like the Oceanic ungrammatical love Schneider discusses, relates incest to other cultural domains. Consider, for example, cremation, the ultimate ritual and religious concern of Bali, derived from India, yet markedly different from South Asian practices. I am among the quickest to acknowledge the risks of interpreting Balinese traditions using South Asian texts or contexts (Boon 1977: chap. 9). But I want at least to raise the possibility in the matter of Balinese incest and cremation. In particular one secret of the Balinese variety of Indic *suttee*, or widow immolation (in Bali called *satia* and practiced at least into the second decade of our century), emerges in *Siva Purana* myths from India on the birth of Pippalada. In an analysis of Tantric components of Hindu myths, O'Flaherty summarizes certain variants as follows:

One text offers as a specific parallel to the myth of Siva and Parvati the story of Pippalada and Padma, who are considered to be incarnations of the god and his wife. Pippalada was born when a pregnant woman mounted her husband's funeral pyre; another version states that he was born when a woman wearing the loincloth of her brother, stained with his seed, bathed and became pregnant, whereupon, in fear of her husband, she deposited the child at the foot of a fig tree (*pippala*), whence his name. [1973:62]

We find here a striking case of mythic "multiforms." In the Pippalada–Skanda birth stories the husband's cremation implies the brother's semen.

Whether these multiforms existed as texts or even as oral versions in traditional Bali is beside the point; they could have been implicit in ritual forms just as well as in textual ones. I want merely to suggest that a code could not be better suited for Balinese ancestor ideology, in which brother and sister may symbolize ideal spouses for perpetuating houses. An equation between husband's ashes and brother's semen might even clarify the sensational satia at the end of a raja's reign, when his consorts could follow his corpse into the flames. Did the fires of satia ritually realize the full marriage ideal by converting all spouses into immolated widows, equivalents of incestuous wives whose progeny, as products of the highest union, would enhance the realm's future? Judging from Pippalada, perhaps.

If, following Schneider, we interpret incest and kinship culturally, incest does not necessarily represent the horrifying or the psychologically ambivalent, such as sons' hearts murmuring subconsciously for their mothers or sisters and vice versa. Nor, I would add, need incest exactly represent the ungrammatical. Rather, in Balinese symbology, incest implies the more-than-can-actually-happen and the complementarity of conflicting ideals: always oxymoron. "Incest," perhaps traditionally reiterated in satia, or suttee, means all the advantageous attributes of marriage at once: sister-cousin, political spouse, lover. So enhanced, the cosmos is complete, kingdoms would be perfect, and an ancestor group's ambitions could be achieved. Stylized, sublimated Balinese suttee is a far cry from the lusty details of Lady Uma – all semen, vaginas, misejaculations, and mixed-up categories. Yet both symbols run counter to ethical reformism. In Bali suttee and Uma appear to have become variations on the same ritual symbology: as imaginary as copulating twins and as real as a widow's suicide.

Finally, let me relate these data to basic issues in the history of religions. The types of religious reformism implying world rejection include renunciation, monastic celibacy, and various strains of rationalism, such as karma doctrine. Whether in Hindu, Buddhist, or Islamic traditions, reformism, accompanied by moralistic values of education and literacy, requires that kama either decline or be sublimated (as in Bhakti communal devotionalism). On the other hand, the Indo-Pacific culture of Bali (perhaps like Tantrism itself) gives kama, embodied in Rakshasas and capture–marriage escapades, coprimacy with dharma and artha. Dramatic narratives envision a recurrent, complementary standoff among all three. Again, the generalized symbology of love and marriage in Bali calls to mind Hindu mythology more than karma doctrine, particularly insofar as mythology is "solutionless":

These fleeting moments of balance provide no "solution" to the paradox of the myth, for indeed, Hindu mythology does not seek any true synthesis. Where Western thought [most of it, anyway] insists on forcing a compromise of or synthesis of opposites, Hinduism [that is, its mythology] is content to keep each as it is; in chemical terms, one might say that the conflicting elements are resolved into a suspension rather than a solution. [O'Flaherty 1973:317–18]

Similarly, extremes of incest/alliance/capture are suspended in the symbology implicit in Balinese ideals and action.

Rama redux

During an important temple-feast, a *Wajang Wong* festival may last for a week, different episodes of the story following each other on successive days without regard to their sequence. We may have, as it were, *Das Rheingold* interposed after *Siegfried* or even after *Götterdämmerung*; in terms of *Wajang Wong* the episode which led to the rape of Sita and the subsequent mobilization of the monkeys, on the last day of the festival instead of on the first, as epilogue instead of prelude. Ritual requirements are satisfied by the performance of scenes from the *Ramayana*, from which every episode in *Wajang Wong* is drawn.

[De Zoete and Spies, *Dance and Drama in Bali*]

To reiterate the fundamental significance of Lady Uma's nethermost vagina, we can turn to the ultimate text of the capturing Rakshasa, the *Ramayana*. Just as in its own texts, the Indic *Ramayana* never really concludes (consider the so-called supplemental episodes), so in Balinese culture the *Ramayana* never exactly commences but has always "already commenced" (consider the *Ragu* tales of *Arja* performances that treat Rama's Sudra ancestor). I hope to show that in a more profound sense still, the implicit order of the *Ramayana* in Bali is fundamentally recurrent.

As a preliminary we should note that Rakshasas figured in the original anthropological view of "capturing wives" as the foundation of exogamous marriage. In 1865, McLennan's *Primitive Marriage* cited Sir William Jones's translation of the *Institutes of Manu* to place India among the many areas revealing customs of capture:

In the Institutes of Menu we have marriage by capture enumerated among "the eight forms of the nuptial ceremony used by the four classes." It is the marriage called Racshasa, and is thus defined: – "The seizure of a maiden by force from her house while she weeps and calls for assistance, after her kinsmen and friends have been slain in battle or wounded, and their houses broken open, is the marriage called Racshasa." Elsewhere in the code it is mentioned as appropriated to the military class. [McLennan 1860/1970:34]

Before veering into comparative folklore, McLennan's inventive appendix on the *Probable Origin of the Name Racshasa* pondered the curious association of a high-caste martial-style marriage with a race of demons:

The story of the Ramayana may be said to be that of the carrying off of Rama's wife, Sita, by the Rakshasa, Ravana, and of the consequent war carried on by Rama against the Rakshasas, ending in their defeat and the recovery of Sita [McLennan cites sources]...Wilson...speaks of the Rakshasas as "a people, often alluded to, from whom the Aryas suffered much, and who, by their descendants, were transferred in idea to the most distant south, and treated by them as a race of mythical giants"...Lassen takes the same view. "The *Ramayana*...contains the narrative of the first attempt of the Aryans to extend themselves to the south by conquest; but it presupposes the peaceable extension of Brahmanical missions in the same direction as having taken place still earlier...The Rakshasas, who are represented as disturbing the sacrifices and devouring the priests, signify here, as often elsewhere, merely the savage tribes which placed themselves in hostile opposition to the Brahmanical institutions. The only other actors who appear in the legend, in addition to these inhabitants, are the monkeys, which ally themselves to Rama and render him assistance. This can only mean that, when the Arian Kshatriyas first made hostile incursions into the south, they were aided by another portion of the indigenous tribes." Dr. Muir can find no authority for saying that the word Rakshasa was originally the name of a tribe. At the same time...he inclines to hold the descriptions we have of them as having more probably originated in hostile contact with the savages of the south, than as the simple offspring of the poet's imagination...He quotes from the *Ramayana* a passage which represents them as cannibals – feeding on blood, men-devouring, changing their shapes, etc., and another, in which they are described as "of fearful swiftness and unyielding in battle"; while Ravana, the most terrible of all the

Rakshasas, is stigmatised as a "destroyer of religious duties, and ravisher of the wives of others." Dr. Muir adds, that the description of the Rakshasas in the *Ramayana* "corresponds in many respects with the epithets applied to the same class of beings (whether we take them for men or for demons) who are so often alluded to in the Rigveda," and that it is quite possible that the author of the *Ramayana* may have borrowed therefrom many of the traits which he ascribes to the Rakshasas.

But how came the name of a legal mode of marriage to be that of such a race of beings? The only answer that we can make is a surmise – viz., that while the system of capture had not as yet died out among the Kshatriyas, or warrior caste of the Aryans, it was perfect among the races to which the name Rakshasas was applied; and that what was their system gave its designation to the exceptional, although permitted, marriage by capture among the Kshatriyas. This is the more probable, since, so far as we can ascertain, there is nothing in the name – Rakshasa – itself, descriptive of the mode of marriage.

From another point of view, it may be observed that the Rakshasas hold nearly the same place in Hindu tradition that giants, ogres, and trolls occupy in Scandinavian and Celtic legends. They are supernatural beings – robbers and plunderers of human habitations – men-devourers and women-stealers. The giants and ogres of the north share the characteristics of Ravana. The cruel monsters are always carrying off kings' daughters. As Rama's exploits culminate in the recovery of Sita, so the northern giant-slayer is crowned with the greatest glory when he has rescued the captive princesses and restored them in safety to the king's – their father's – palace. [1860/ 1970:123–4]

One could say that Balinese formulations of their own marriage system and Western formulations of exotic marriage systems are cognate. Both descend (although through dialectics of cross-breeding rather than unilineally) from distant understandings of the *Ramayana*: Bali's on the one hand, McLennan's on the other. If nothing else legitimated a comparative study like the present one, the common reference point of Balinese and anthropological typologies would.

McLennan's suspicions about Rakshasas and giants, expressed in an evolutionary framework, echoes a Sanskrit–German connection mentioned by romantic philologist F. von Schlegel two generations earlier: "The lower German is generally of importance in regard to the etymology, the old form being often exactly retained. *Roksho* and *rakshoso* may be the ancient *recke* [giant]" (Schlegel 1860:430–1). Finally, McLennan's concluding speculations illustrate the inevitable difficulties with historicist interpretations of the *Ramayana* and texts like it, even in our own day: "Are we to hold all such beings – giants, ogres, trolls, etc. – wherever they occur, as representing savage races, between whom and the peoples in whose legends they appear as supernatural beings, there was chronic hostility?" (1860/1970:124).

That the *Ramayana* itself cannot be so construed is underscored by its central place in traditions far from South Asian history. In fact, what the *Ramayana* "becomes" in export enables us to modify speculations about what the *Ramayana* "was" in situ. (It is possible that such texts are in a way "always exported," not susceptible of definitive editions, not centralized, not canonical). In Bali the *Ramayana* stands first among epic, mythic, and dramatic traditions (cf. Robson 1972:316). Yet the events of Balinese "history" afford no program that, so to speak, explains the *Ramayana*'s meaning as their allegory. Nevertheless, Balinese culture's *reception* of the *Ramayana* confirms the significance of Rama–Sita consorts and Rakshasa-capture – not as McLennan's evolutionary source-custom eventually yielding in turn matriliny and patriliny, but as components in a total Indo-Pacific marriage system.

In order to suggest how an Indic literary tradition penetrates the Balinese context, let me venture a provisional reading *between* India's *Ramayana* and Bali's culture.[9] The *Ramayana* opens with Dasartha's "political" infertility, his lack of male progeny. The solution promises conflict as four sons (avatars of Visnu) are born of three wives whose fertility was enhanced by different amounts of divine aphrodisiac; as I work it out: "Rama, son by first wife Kausalya (½ of beverage); Bharat, by third wife, Kaikeyi (⅛ of beverage); Lakshmana and Satrughna, twins, by middle wife, Sumitra (¼ + ⅛ of beverage; ³⁄₁₆ per son?)." Accordingly the two sons with highest factors of seniority, mother's seniority, and beverage, Rama and Lakshmana, perform with the sage the initial demon killing. Bharat, through the devices of his mother, assumes the throne; the impropriety of this event is underscored by the implicit but unstressed rival, Satrughna. Obviously *artha* is out of gear; only *kama* will restore the balance, but never permanently, never compromisingly.

Back to the story. Heirless Kosala is echoed in heirless Videha. King Janak's only potential alliance credit is the adopted Sita (her obscure origins enable the events of the narrative to reveal her ultimate nature: Rama's cosmologically perfect spouse). A political alliance between the houses is arranged, but excessively, as many Kosala men prepare to marry Videha women. The uxorilocal setting of the marriage festivities counters regular Balinese marriage; in fact the entire episode suggests a *sentana* "borrowed-son-in-law" pattern in Balinese practice. But the multiple marriages complicate this sentanalike arrangement even more (in fact Balinese rules preclude one-way exchange relations repeated between lines or houses – cf. Boon 1977: chap. 6). From the outset everything is fraught with imbalance and excess: four sons and four daughters are expended on the same alliance, a *nyentana*-like ceremony (a real option, polygyny, is never entertained). The precise ranks of the sons cannot perfectly mesh with respective ranks of the daughters, who include no explicit twins, although Urmila is Sita's sister. But Urmila marries Lakshmana. Thus, we have sisters (Sita and Urmila) divided between half-brothers (Rama and Lakshmana), and whole brothers (the twins) divided between nonsisters (Urmila and Srutakriti). The ambiguous Bharat marries Janak's brother's daughter, underscoring his secondariness. The *Ramayana* thus poses excessive marriage alliance (type II) that will have to be counterbalanced by excessive passionate capture (type III) that in turn reveals the arch-spouses Rama and Sita as, more than just an alliance match, cosmological complements: like incestuous twins (type I) – as outlined above (pp. 182–83).

The values of alliance fracture at once. Rama is uneager to rule; in the idiom of romance, he requires experience. Then Rama and Sita appear as a prematurely complete couple in *tapas* rather than as producers of progeny or as centers of a kingdom. Intrigue is apparent. Kaikeyi's ambition for Bharat; the background of the boons promised her by the king that place Bharat on the throne and banish Rama to a hermit's life, uncomplaining. Subsequent scenes portray Rama and Sita in truncated, complacent love in their *ashram*, free of social or cosmological consequence. This is the false solution, the love-couple:

> Years will pass in happy union – happiest lot to woman given –
> Sita seeks not throne or empire, nor the brighter joys of heaven,
> Heaven conceals not brighter mansions in the sunny fields of pride,
> Where without her lord and husband faithful Sita would reside!
> Therefore let me seek the jungle where the jungle-rangers rove,
> Dearer than the royal palace, where I share my husband's love,
> And my heart in sweet communion shall my Rama's wishes share,
> And my wifely toil shall lighten Rama's load of woe and care!
> [R. Dutt trans. 1910]

The false, partial solution (like a cosmological metonymy) fails to convey the ideal, totalized *suspension*.

Upon Dasartha's death Bharat himself tries to restore Rama to his throne, but Rama remains in exile to fulfill his father's vow. Into this false solution – Rama, Sita, and Lakshmana tranquil and complete in their Panchavati retreat, with home and society mere memories – the Rakshasas intrude.

Surpanaka, sister of Ravana, king of the Rakshasas, is smitten by Rama. Rama's joke again contradicts birth order when he suggests that she (a king's sister) should consider not himself but his younger brother. Her wrath then provokes Lakshmana's dismembering of her nose and ears. The fundamentally incomplete harmony of the love retreat is obliterated by the great slaughter of Rakshasas at Panchavati.

We need not follow the *Ramayana*'s episodes step by step to their conclusion or supplements. Once the Rakshasas and in particular the monkey-warriors enter the scene, the full conjunction of extremes becomes patent. It is the capture of Sita, the monkey antics, and Sita's ordeal that dominate Balinese performances, especially masked dance-dramas (*wayang wong*). From the point we have reached, typical Balinese versions of *Ramayana* themes proceed selectively as follows:

To avenge [Surpanaka] Ravana sent the rakshasa Marica in the semblance of a deer,
to lure away the hunter Rama, thus leaving Sita unprotected. Sita fell into the trap;
she was so captivated by the delicate mottled coat and "variegated countenance"
of the deer that she implored Rama to go and catch it for her as a playmate. He leaves
her in the care of his brother and goes off into the forest. But Sita becomes anxious
at his long absence and imagines she hears his voice crying for help. Nothing will
satisfy her but Lakshmana must go after him, and while she remains alone Ravana
gets admission to the house in the disguise of a mendicant and carries her off to his

kingdom of Lanka (Ceylon). The bird Jatayu, which owed its life to Rama, is
mortally wounded in an attempt to win her back, but survives to deliver Sita's ring
to Rama, and tell him what has happened. Rama, despairing in the forest, meets
the monkey-king Sugriva, who promises the help of all his monkey host if Rama will
destroy his twin brother Subali, who has taken his wife and kingdom from him.
Subali is killed and the monkeys, led by Hanuman, build a bridge across the sea to
Lanka, and after a long and terrible war defeat and kill Ravana. Sita, on suspicion
of infidelity during her long captivity, undergoes the ordeal by fire. She emerges
victorious and accompanies Rama to his Kingdom of Ayodhya, but again the people
begin to murmur and again Rama listens, and banishes her to the Ganges, where in
the hermitage of the sage Valmiki (author of the *Ramayana*) she gives birth to two
sons. They are brought up by Valmiki and are only recognized by their father on the
occasion of a great horse sacrifice, when they visit his court and recite the epic
made in his honour. But just as he seems about to win back Sita, cleared of suspicion
by the solemn oath of Valmiki, she calls on the earth to take her and vanishes from
his sight. Rama eventually resumed his godlike being, and rejoined her in Svarga.
[De Zoete and Spies 1939:153]

If we zoom in on a segment of an actual performance, the emphasis on
Rakshasa thrusts and monkey antic reactions is conspicuous:

There are now two groups, Jatayu and his passive ladies, Ravana crouching in loud
despair between [his clown-servants] Delem and Sangut. At last he draws his kris,
and advancing in huge swirls of movement beats down the fluttering bird, round whom
all circle with loud cries. Jatayu, mortally wounded, drags his limp feathers without
aim over the ground like a wounded fighting-cock with trailing wing or severed leg.
Sita, still passive, is seized by Ravana and led off, of course through the air. Rama
and Lakshmana re-enter solemnly singing, and wind up the stage, while the bird flaps
madly round and round, beating the earth with its wings. They close round it as
it sinks into a lovely crouching posture, and in a high wounded voice tells its tale
to Rama, while Twalen interprets. This scene was again without [gamelan] music.
The death of the bird, swaying strangely before its final passionate fall, was very
moving. It rose and was led off. The music again grows wild. Rama dances, then
stands long motionless. A host of monkeys troop in in two files led by Sugriva and
Hanuman, the latter recognizable by his white tail. They address each other with
monkey cries, changing restlessly from knee to knee, moving about continually with
queer fastidious steps. The monkeys,...are in style quite carefully differentiated...
as well as by their distinctive masks. Sugriva now approaches with majestic but uneasy
gestures, never still, punctuating his gliding, darting steps with swift accents. He
is joined by Hanuman and the three so-called *alus* [refined] monkeys ...Subali,
identical with Sugriva in mask and voice, now whirls up the stage, the wings of
his dress held wide, a thin sash to toy with in his hand. They threaten each other
with the familiar gesture of two pointing fingers sharply withdrawn. They fight with
curious square poses and jagged cries, watched by the immobile Rama and commenting
Twalen. Sugriva is the first to fall, for Subali is invincible so long as he has only
a brother monkey to deal with. It is not until a flower or string is tied to him to
distinguish him from his twin, that Rama dares to shoot his arrow. [De Zoete and
Spies 1939:159]

The significance of Hanuman and Sugriwa/Subali as mediators in Balinese
symbology cannot be overestimated. They obviously conjoin different spheres:
animals categorized like gods/men (demonic Subali, like Ravana; princely

Sugriwa, like Rama; refined yet spritely Hanuman). Moreover, in Balinese wayang wong the uncompromising comic "multivocality" generally associated with clowns (*parekan*) – placing them, like Sancho Panza, in contrast with all levels of society and cosmos – extends to monkeys. As de Zoete and Spies remind us:

In *Wajang Wong* the role of Twalen and Merdah is much more restricted than in *Wajang Koelit*, where they mix themselves in the divine battles and are obstreperously comic. Everything is allowed to them as to old-fashioned and trusty servants, but their chief purpose in *Wajang Wong* is to advise their master, and to translate into Balinese the unintelligible Kawi of the main characters...They trot clumsily after their master in a dance style peculiar to themselves, progressing with awkward, inept movements, their arms bent and jerking like pump handles to and fro, their hands folded in a styleless, inconclusive manner, in striking contrast with the highly stylized movements of the hero. [1939:156]

I would contrast *wayang kulit* and *wayang wong* in roughly this way: *Wayang kulit's* primacy of joking clowns – who must, like the *dalang* (puppeteer) himself display all levels and modes of voice or speech (antic is secondary in puppets) – is transformed into *wayang wong's* coprimacy of clowns and monkeys, the latter displaying all levels and modes of antic and gesture. It would seem that *wayang kulit's* singular, intensive source of codes, the *dalang*, is epitomized in the generalized mediating of clowns, bridging all languages, voices, motions, gestures (the latter, however, restricted by the genre). *Wayang wong's* more diffuse source of codes – multiple performers with varied skills – is epitomized in the differentiated mediation of clowns (translators) and monkeys (acrobats), the one bridging language codes, the other bridging gesture codes that gain new prominence in dance. Regardless, like the clowns themselves but in a different register, Hanuman and his companions, implicated in all the forces at odds in *wayang* episodes, perform a dramatic conjunction of extremes: both refined and animal, both controlled and capturing, *both/and*.

The dynamics and dialectics we detected above in microcosm–macrocosm body symbols reappear in the realm of monkeys and *parekans*. This fact is suggested by iconographic conventions:

[*Parekan*] are among the most popular characters in the *wayang kulit* where their functions somewhat resemble those of jesters, or wise fools, in the pastoral idiom of Western art. Whereas Twalen and Merdah serve causes of righteousness, their counterparts, Delam and Sangut, function as the *parekan* of evil and demonic personages...Although all four possess certain traits of the *kras* or *kasar* [rough] type, only Delam and Sangut have round, bulging eyes [versus the narrow-refined eyes of Twalen and Merdah]. [Gralapp 1967:257]

Thus, the arch-*kasar* itself subdivides into rough/refined (cf. Peacock 1968). Such contrasts are relational and shifting. More subtly, as one moves across Balinese "genres" of ritual, art, and social structure, a particular set of symbolic "functions" subdivides for redistribution. Again, the clowns of *wayang kulit* mediate all idioms and styles across disparate realms: Heaven/Earth/ Underworld in both refined/rough aspects of all three. In *wayang wong* clowns specialize in speech – mediating (translating) *Kawi*, different levels of Balinese, and occasionally nowadays Indonesian; while physical mediation – exaggerated refined manners (parody), exaggerated clumsiness (pratfalls) is assumed partly by monkeys. Yet in both varieties of *wayang*, mediation occurs through the mutual exaggeration of extremes and the juxtaposition of all codes.[10]

It is not only dancing monkeys and bawdy clowns that enable Bali's *Ramayana* to underscore the adventuresome, demonic, and dislocating side of marriage. Indeed, Sita herself, at the victorious moment of proving her purity, alludes to the *kama*–capture complement of marriage symbols. Sita's ordeal is a major subject of traditional Balinese painting, a third genre or vehicle for the appearance of the forces of the *Ramayana*, this time as immobile figures. One typical version of the episode transposed into court painting stresses spiritual elevation (see, e.g., Gralapp, 1967: Fig. 14). Conventional divine aureoles predominate. Sita herself, preserved in the flames, inclines toward the right, relatively sacred side. Twalen and Merdah are both on the right, at a respectful distance from Sita's female attendant. Hanuman is elevated; no monkey intrudes raucously into Sita's sphere of repose. Even Wilmana, demonic bird-vehicle of Rakshasa king Ravana is restrained beneath an aureole. All is symmetry and hierarchy, ordered to the verge of sublimity. The entire scene, likened in Balinese conventions to a cremation (Sita leaps from a cremation tower or *bade*) – is in this case more precisely a *mukur*: "The imagery above the cremation tower recalls the Balinese custom of placing effigies of a bird and a lamp near the *mukur* tower for the guidance of the soul on its journey to heaven" (Gralapp 1967:266). Now, a *mukur* is a cremation of a cremation: reburning the body forty-two days later, without the body. The iconography could hardly be more explicit.

Set in the ritual register of *mukur*, Sita's ordeal appears sublime. This particular Balinese version could almost be set to a patently sentimentalized translation of the *Ramayana* suggesting that pure-Sita, restored blameless to Rama, is a *solution*:

> Slow the red flames rolled asunder, God of Fire incarnate came,
> Holding in his radiant bosom fair Videha's sinless dame,
> Not a curl upon her tresses, not a blossom on her brow,
> Not a fiber of her mantle did with tarnished luster glow!
> Witness of our sins and virtues, God of Fire incarnate spake,
> Bade the sorrow-stricken Rama back his sinless wife to take.
> Rama's forehead was unclouded and a radiance lit his eye,
> And his bosom heaved in gladness as he spoke in accents high:
> "Never from the time I saw her in her maiden days of youth,
> Have I doubted Sita's virtue, Sita's fixed and changeless truth.
> I have known her ever sinless – let the world her virtue know,
> For the God of Fire is witness to her true and changeless vow!"
> [R. Dutt 1910]

But this sort of reading of the *Ramayana* as depicted in Balinese painting would fail to explain why pictures of Sita's ordeal *vary*. If my suggestions about Balinese symbo-logics are accurate, we would expect the register of divine sublimation (in death-ritual terms, *mukur*) to be complemented by a register that suggests demonic agitation. Such is indeed the case. Another version of the episode (see, for example, Gralapp 1967: fig. 13) at first glance looks similar but in detail is a polar extreme. No *mukur* ritual items enhance the scene. The ritual register is rather cremation itself (*ngaben*), body and all. Sita inclines toward the demonic left. The flames around her have not been decoratively conventionalized into an aureole motif; Wilmana, too, is unconstrained by the visual code of divine influence. Hanuman remains next to Sugriwa; symmetry is unsettled, the bottom of the hierarchy accentuated. Twalen himself is situated on the demonic left. Most conspicuously: "At bottom center, with the assistance of Merdah, Twalen, in a typical note of erotic comedy, parodies the central event by testing the chastity of Sita's servant, Pengeruan. A further comic touch is furnished by the monkeys who impudently, if rather apprehensive [?], climb on the lotus throne and the ramp of the *bade*" (Gralapp 1967:266). The painting is actually even bawdier than Gralapp suggests. Twalen's hand extends under Pengeruan's skirt, a standard gesture in Bali–Hindu iconography. Clinging to Sita's fiery sphere is a large monkey with a netherly orifice (because of the blending of front, profile, and rear views in Balinese painting, it is hard to tell which one) exposed just above Pengeruan's head.

Gralapp's informative reading of assorted Balinese paintings mentions that the other refined version "has the effect of minimizing the human drama of the event while giving greater emphasis to its hieratic and doctrinal significance" (ibid.). But he suggests no thoroughgoing contrasts such as *ngaben/ mukur*. Moreover, it is crucial to note that the "human drama" neglected in a *mukur* variant is more precisely the demonic, lusty, sensual realm of capture and kama. Thus in Balinese cremation as well, symbology is relational and shifting; and every variant alludes to the total scheme. Although *ngaben* following exhumation is at one level the purer rite, contrasted to prior burial, it appears relatively demonic beside elevated *mukur* (just as, in reverse, the burial of an upper-title corpse is less demon threatened than the burial of an inferior).

In sum, looking between and moving across Bali's dramatic genres and institutions, we learn a basic lesson of their symbology: Balinese variations on the *Ramayana* never forget that pure Sita enflamed and sullied Sita abducted are two Sitas in the same. In fact they are three: by spanning areas of convergent meanings in Balinese ideals and action, we can now read Sita herself as a triad of extremes – the essence of capture (captured by Ravana and captured back, thanks to Hanuman); the essence of political alliance (Kosala *cum* Videha); and the essence of incest (divine consort of Rama), like an immolated sister spouse with a vagina in her foot.

Toward interpretive tantrisms

Typologically and comparatively, Balinese symbology contrasts with aspects of religious development that Hocart deemed "the Good," which recalls Weber's notions of world-rejection involved in reformism:

> By 500 B.C. a great change had come over religious thought: worldly welfare was considered an unworthy aim; spiritual elevation became the goal of the religious leaders. The objective of the preachers is still welfare, but welfare is differently conceived; it is to a large extent identified with goodness. It is better to be good than to be healthy and wealthy, and so a ritual which leads to goodness takes the place of a ritual that only gives material prosperity.
>
> India has not been unique in undergoing this transformation. A tendency to cast the sober hue of morals over all seems a recurring phenomenon in the life of civilizations. As they get older, they exalt the spirit higher and higher above the flesh, till at last the flesh becomes a thing to be ashamed of, bodily wants are tolerated as an unfortunate necessity, not enjoyed. Ritual has either to conform to the fashion or perish. At first, ritual falls into discredit, because the moralists, being intellectuals and individualists, are hostile to a materialistic and intensely social ritual. In the end however the ritual saves itself by adopting the new moral tone.
>
> The causes of these ethical movements are not known. They have generally been accepted without question as stages in the evolution from low to high. As a matter of fact they seem to herald the fall of civilizations. The more decadent a people, the higher the moral tone.
>
> . . . we have to accept [these ethical movements] as *facts* which go under the name of Buddhism, Christianity, Islam, philosophical Hinduism, Confucianism, and the rest. The rituals we may label ethical rituals. [Hocart 1970:72]

With a unique combination of ethnological and philological insight, Hocart suggested that the *rituals* of "life" (renewing a diversified social organism), rather than *ceremonies* of moral betterment, predominated in contemporary Fiji, as they must have done during South Asia's Vedic period. I have argued that such a ritual basis – similar to both Pacific social forms (cf. Sahlins 1976a:42–6) and certain Indic traditions – underlies Balinese resistance to ethical aspects of Hinduism, Buddhism and, of course, Islam. This resistance qualifies Balinese variations on renunciation, monasticism, literalist and legalistic rationalism, and karma doctrine as well.

Balinese culture contains many traces of "ethical rituals" (and even a dash of devotionalism), but the "new moral tone" has never pervaded the whole. Although Indic renunciation may imply a total social antithesis (cf. Dumont 1970b; Tambiah 1970), the Balinese renouncer tends rather to reinforce social bonds of kinsmen who intensify their ancestor rituals in light of his example. Even in the Brahmana sector, ascetic ideals are embedded in kinship and the related state mode of organization, with the accent on fertility and descendants. Similarly, tantric tapas, the "heat of asceticism," appears in Balinese texts and lifestages based on the South Asian paradox of fertility/release:

Throughout [South Asian] mythology, whether or not *tapas* is accepted as a valid means of creation, it is practiced for another goal: immortality, freedom from rebirth. In the Vedas, *tapas* is able to accomplish the chief desideratum, fertility; in the Upanishads, *tapas* is the means to a new goal, Release. Both are forms of immortality, both promising continuation of the soul without the body – Release giving complete freedom of the soul (or absorption into the Godhead), progeny giving a continuation of the soul's life in the bodies of one's children. [O'Flaherty 1973:76]

In this particular domain Balinese culture as a whole is less coextremist than textual Tantrism: Given the progeny/release dichotomy, Bali privileges progeny; fertility encompasses release. I suspect that any bifurcation of tapas-Release (Upanishads) and tapas-fertility (Vedas) into distinct alternatives has been precluded in Bali by its Indonesia-style ancestor cult and ideology (Boon 1977: chap. 4).

Yet that Balinese culture fails to accentuate equally the fertility/release polarities of mythology and Tantrism hardly implies reformism. Bali's modification slants not toward ethics (the social equivalent of tapas-release minus the social equivalent of tapas-fertility) but toward progeny, what Hocart called "life."

Indeed, wherever the progeny/asceticism contrast appears in Balinese traditions, emphasis finally falls to immortality through "the bodies of one's children." For example, in Indic traditions: "According to the *Ramayana* and *Padma Purana*, however, (the sage) remains with [the courtesan and forsakes] the forest, while the *Mahabharata* suggests a compromise of considerable significance in the context of the Indian ascetic paradox: Rsyasrnga returns to the forest, but with his wife" (O'Flaherty 1973:49). Again, Balinese culture echoes the *Ramayana*, perhaps contrasting with Java's emphasis on the *Mahabharata* (cf. Geertz 1960:263). Like the *Ramayana* itself, Balinese culture (a "text" in its own right, when read comparatively), although admitting the co*ritualism* of *pedanda* and *istri pedanda*, rejects the compromised coasceticism of the hermitage couple. Throughout Bali's dramatic and social genres, ultimate implications point to the full cosmological and social order: ancestral and descendant.

In the more specifically Southeast Asian context, Bali and other Indonesian cultures conspicuously deemphasize monasticism, that is, institutions organized around chastity or celibacy, mediation, group and residence, and literacy-writing-reciting-chanting. (In Bali some of these functions fall to casual reading clubs or *sekaha bebasan*). Of course, historically in the traditional Hindu-Buddhist states of Indonesia, priestly functions were associated with the courts; scribes complemented the legal, textual, calendrical, and temple dimensions of state rituals in rajas' spheres of influence. In Bali no monastic institution or path finally styled itself as a total alternative to ancestor groups, temple networks, and political organization. Those ethical components elsewhere consolidated into monasticism remained diffused and suspended in

Bali's ideas, action, institutions, and texts. Or, to recall Weber's terms from Chapter 3, in Bali monasticism never became the "single dominating confession."

If we compare religious symbol systems at the broadest level of ideal-types, Hocart's sense of "the Good" (versus "life-maintenance") illuminates dilemmas inherent in monasticism as a *social value*. Nonmonastic traditional systems, including, I would argue, both tribes and Tantrisms, are *generalized*. (Again, Tantrism can contain monastic and ethical elements, but they do not symbolize the whole.) In a generalized order, each smaller division – two exogamous clans, say, or some other type of alliance partners – replicates the full degree of differentation recognized; small-scale wholes engage in rituals of the total whole. Compared to such systems monasticism appears revolutionary, or at least antithetical: Celibacy, which must remain ambivalent or even deviant in tribal (or tantric?) systems, becomes institutionalized in monasticism. "Asociality" is legitimated as an alternative to "society." From the vantage of society and its perpetuation, the monastery epitomizes incompleteness: not self-regenerating, often not self-sustaining. Yet although the monastery can survive only through recruitment, it presumes to represent the entire cosmos, society included. Hence from the vantage of "life" there is a fundamental discrepancy: The cosmic whole is lodged in a social part (*ceremonies* of monks), not in the social whole (*rituals* of clans or ancestor groups).

If one assumes with believers that religious merit is vital to society's perpetuation as well as to ultimate release, then monasticism achieves what Durkheim called "organic solidarity" with an incremental level of differentiation: reciprocity between two specialist sectors or categories, one producing merit and release, the other producing successors and subsistence. Neither lay nor monk alone can reproduce the socioreligious totality. Opposed to the extreme monastic alternative, the lay sector appears relatively homogeneous; the monk/lay distinction overshadows any other ones. The nearest tribal equivalent to this lay/monk distinction is male/female: In other words, the only ideal tribal division that is not self-reproducing is one sex or, analogously, one exogamous clan. In tribal systems (and I think indirectly in tantric ones as well), *the whole is implied in society's sexuality*, in *coitus itself*. (Tantric forms suggest a sort of nostalgia for this symbolic basis of solidarity in radically divided social orders like caste systems.) In contrast, monastic systems totalized around celibacy rather than sexuality replace coitus and ritual with *lettres* and ceremony as their primary symbolic media. In the "primitive classifaction" of generalized tribal kinship, ideally every marriage and ritual exchange conjoins representatives of the extremes of social and cosmic divisions. In contrast, monasticism totalizes cosmic order through the organizing power of specialized writing, chanting, and liturgical canons: all these alternatives to fertility, all these ingredients of "historical society" and of the idea of "History" itself.

I broach such immense issues – at once Weberian, Hocartian, Durkheimian, and structuralist – both to accentuate Bali and to allow Bali to illuminate

Western social theories considered in Chapter 3. Balinese symbology, which I have tried to show is broadly more tantric than reformist, reveals specialized institutions of writing, reading (*sekaha bebasan*), and text-based performances; this differentiation parallels monastic systems. But like tribal cultures, any symbolic totality in Bali obtains from a fertility of variant extremes. Thus a problem in interpretive method arises. Standard approaches to literate cultures proceed as if aspects of monasticism necessarily underlie textual values and as if history moves such cultures progressively either away from the perfections imagined in texts (golden ages of prior kingdoms) or toward such perfections (revolutionary utopias, religious release). Western analysis of literate cultures often aims for singular, literal translations, and canonical interpretation. Rationalized analysis assumes, indeed often 'imposes, centralized, uniform literate standards. One might say that philological and historical approaches to literate cultures are themselves "monastic." I have suggested that applying such reformist assumptions to a generalized, "unethicalized" symbology like Bali's can obscure a recurrent tripartism, an emphasis on complementary sexuality, and a pervasive dynamic variation stretching well beyond the courtly and priestly sectors.

Yet that Balinese culture and symbology is less reformist than many historical societies should imply neither stagnation nor archaic "traditionalism" (a concept sustained in part by analyzing exotic civilizations from documentary evidence such as courtly chronicles). Traditionally Bali contains elaborate regulations: legal spheres (*adat*), rules for hamlet and irrigation control (*awig-awig*), and so on. Yet even neighboring locales reveal elaborate variations in their rules (cf. Korn 1932). Their complex dynamics have not moved irrevocably toward the sort of centralized, uniform code we associate with bureaucratic rationalization.

The traditional Balinese state itself perhaps never tended toward a centralized status quo (cf. C. Geertz 1973: chap. 12; 1980a). Yet the Sanskrit-oriented scholarship on Balinese royal courts long emphasized the idealization of Majapahit Java, the alliance of Siwaic Brahmana and raja-enthroned (recalling the Mitra/Varuna duality in Indic sovereignty — cf. Dumézil 1966–71), the state temples, royal chronicles and cremation, and the legal, priestly, and literary texts of the courts. Less attention was paid to the plentiful institutions, rituals, and lettres that counterbalanced any centralization by dislocating, shifting, and renewing the center from the periphery. Bali's refined, Brahmana-backed courts have been regularly qualified in social action by rival ancestor groups, trance practices, local temple lore, the demonic register of rituals, and, of course, the conspicuous clowns of dramatic performances. A centrist status quo – whether royalist, colonialist, or now nationalist – has remained in Bali a Dulcinea-like ideal, continually and essentially fractured by the Panza-like play inherent in ideas and actions (Boon 1977: Part I).

Balinese symbology confirms the point. It operates less through symbolic partials implying a solution than through symbolic multiples implying a suspension – not monks, but clowns and monkeys. As a pure, ideal-type of mediation and totalization, monks convert variant codes into a conformist canon that promises ultimate, radical, rarified release. In contrast, clowns exaggerate variant codes, never converting and consolidating them but juxtaposing them incongruously. Comparative anthropology invites us to take clowns seriously and monks playfully, to help them complement each other. Ultimately, perhaps, so does Tantrism, as an ideal-type, itself. (Ultimately, perhaps, so does semiotics, as an ideal-type, itself.) Most conspicuously of all semiotic endeavors, comparative anthropology – in its writing and practice – savors of tantric extremes. Of course, no actual culture or discipline is a pure type; even Theravada cultures are not thoroughly monastic; even Balinese Tantrism is not thoroughly "ludic." There is a bit of the monk in the latter and a bit of the clown in the former.[11]

The heady brew of social and textual forms in Balinese culture – marriage and politics, religion and ritual, myth and narrative, dance and drama – reflects no monolithic substantive theme, no deep religiosity, no exploitative power. Rather, the forms act as complex commentaries on each other (cf. Geertz 1973: chap. 15). Moreover, they act as figurations of something relatively lacking in Balinese culture: ethical ideals such as monasticism, karma, and the like. At the fullest comparative level, we must interpret Balinese meanings in terms of *both their multifarious presences and this pervasive absence.*[12]

Tantric cultures (to coin a type), revolve around a generalized *ritual* symbology; this fact recalls principles of tribal cultures themselves. In Balinese culture even ultimate Release is thought to be embodied in the ashes of the cremated corpse (cf. Soebadio 1971:52; Boon 1977:219), ashes that result from rituals performed by the deceased's descendants who will in their turn, particularly if fertile, gain Release. In Bali even final liberation is dramatic, episodic, recurrent, and embedded in "life." This fact is nowhere more evident than in symbols of incest, alliance, and capture, all conjoined in – to chant the mantra one last time – a systematic suspension of complementary extremes.

Reflexivity

Let us imagine that in Toledo a paper is discovered containing a text in Arabic which the paleographers declare to be in the handwriting of the cide Hamete Benengeli from whom Cervantes derived the *Quixote*. In this text we read that the hero . . . discovers, after one of his many combats, that he has killed a man. At that point the fragment ends; the problem is to guess or conjecture how Don Quixote would react. [Three standard conjectures follow] . . . There is another conjecture, which is alien to the Spanish orb and even to the orb of the Western world and requires a more ancient, more complex and more weary atmosphere. Don Quixote – who is no longer Don Quixote but a king of the cycles of Hindustan – senses, standing before the dead body of his enemy, that killing and engendering are divine or magical acts which notably transcend the human condition. He knows that the dead man is illusory, the same as the bloody sword weighing in his hand and himself and all his past life and the vast gods and the universe.

J. L. Borges, *Labyrinths*

Balinese culture's weaving of dance, drama, and narrative arts into general motives and action calls to mind the autofiguration of *Don Quixote* with the clowning Sancho in the history of Western discourse:

In the second part of the novel, Don Quixote meets characters who have read the first part of his story and recognize him, the real man, as the hero of the book. Cervantes's text *turns back upon itself, thrusts itself back into its own density, and becomes the object of its own narrative*. The first part of the hero's adventures plays in the second part the role originally assumed by the chivalric romances. Don Quixote must remain faithful to the book that he has now become in reality; he must protect it from errors, from counterfeits, from apocryphal sequels; he must fill in the details that have been left out; he must preserve its truth.
    . . . having first read so many books that he became a sign, a sign wandering through a world that did not recognize him, he has now, despite himself and without his knowledge, become a book that contains his truth. [Foucault 1973:48; emphasis added]

"Thrusts itself back into its own density" – like Balinese symbology, which never thoroughly embraced monasticism, the source of discourse that is literalist, singular, historicist, reformed. Not so Bali: It is dramatic, multiple, turned back upon itself.

Cultures and books are both discursive; how appropriate, then, that what ethnographers do is write. Moreover, a culture's boundaries are equally "blurred" (cf. Geertz 1980b):

The frontiers of a book are never clear-cut: beyond the title, the first lines, and the last full stop, beyond its internal configuration and its autonomous form, it is caught up in a system of references to other books, other texts, other sentences: it is a node within a network . . . [The book's] unity is variable and relative. As soon as one questions that unity, it loses its self-evidence; it indicates itself, constructs itself, only on the basis of a complex field of discourse. [Foucault 1972:23]

Both books and cultures allude explicitly or implicitly to what they are not – each culture being not other cultures and each book being not other books; and each ethnographic book being not the culture it would re-present, the culture whose truth it would contain. As surely as any book, any culture (even literalist–historicist ones, although repressedly) is reflexive. Balinese culture, for example, "becomes the object of its own narrative," like Don Quixote ("who is no longer Don Quixote but a king of the cycles of Hindustan"), and other comparatively unethicalized, reflexive, discursive books of books and books of cultures–like this one.

What would be the analog of Bali's (not-India's) Lady Uma in our own culture? Perhaps it would be the very book – or some epitome of it, or some enterprise of which it is a part – that you are reading. Here discourse replaces intercourse to bridge the world of difference:

Who gives the Bride, chants the Hindu?...

Man Woman, Woman Man
Tristan Iseut, Iseut Tristan.[13]

7. Structuralism/Romanticism, reciprocally

If, therefore, we preserve the language of Romanticist hermeneutics when it speaks of overcoming the distance, of making "one's own," of appropriating what was distant, other, foreign, it will be at the price of an important corrective. That which we make our own – *Aneignung* in German – that which we appropriate, is not a foreign experience, but the power of disclosing a world which constitutes the reference of the text.

Ricoeur, "The Model of the Text"

Sometimes one can scarcely resist the idea that two minds might actually belong together like separate halves, and that only in union could they be what they might be.

F. Schlegel, *Aphorisms*

This chapter explores a major source of anthropological structuralism: the transformation of an ideal of social solidarity (documented in exotic tribes and commended to the fragmenting West, cf. Chapter 3) into a mode of discourse. I then searchingly suggest a parallel aspect of the history of romanticism, when Western philosopher-translators longingly invoked select social and discursive properties of Indic Brahmins.

Indic Brahmins are different from the Balinese Brahmanas discussed above. Indeed a more apt comparison would link Balinese Brahmanas with German romantics: Both have sought to inform their sense of themselves and their exclusive role in society and literature by referring to Sanskrit texts and to Indic ideals of literary priesthood. In a way the Herders, Schlegels, and Novalises of Germany occupy a position vis-à-vis India analogous to that of the *Ida Bagus*es and the *pedanda*s of Bali.

Here, however, we are concerned not with equating aspirations of Bali's Brahmanas and ideals of *blaue Blumen*, two equally strange distortions of India. Rather, we trace a meaningful comparison between romanticism – this self-conscious, programmatic ideology that advocated an encounter of exotics – and a pursuit against which it stands in strongest contrast: structuralism. Yet, what is Lévi-Strauss if not a Goethe (of the *Farbenlehre*) come lately, when interpretive metaphors of organic growth and mysterious antinomies have been replaced (substituted) by metaphors of communicative exchange and relational opposition?[1]

207

A poetics of exogamy

At the heart of structuralism throbs an ideal of not philosophical (mind/body) dualism or theological (good/evil) dualism but tribal dualism. Durkheim's principle of organic solidarity, Mauss's theory of exchange, Lévi-Strauss's structures of marriage and totemism all revolve around aspects of "communication" – social, ritual, stylistic – that became conspicuous in works on unlettered, nonstratified aboriginals. Fully elaborated, or rather, condensed, the ideal poses two sides of a contrast reciprocally and holistically.

Dualism can characterize two categorical halves of a total society, just like two halves of an opposition. In full-flowering structuralism this social principle perceived in other cultures is transformed into a principle of structuralist discourse itself. That is, ultimately the order of structuralist discourse is modeled on, inspired by, the order of tribal society. This model-inspiration grew out of a recognition that societal dualism is analogous to the dualism of the sign in Saussurian linguistics and, derivatively, to the systems of distinctive features (extended to semantics) in Jakobson's poetics.

Chapter 3 reviewed principles of tribal clans, each requiring another to be complete and to perpetuate both. A social structure of exogamous clans requires marriage exchange: Conventions whereby one clan trusts another will provide it with spouses (positive marriage rules) because other conventions (incest taboos) prohibit a lone clan's self-provisioning. Through complementary descent rules the exchange produces legitimate descendants and a perpetuated, differentiated total society.

These conventions have often been labeled dualism, evidenced in rules of intermarriage or some other regularized exchange, such as reciprocal totemic obligations (a particular clan associated with a particular species) or craft specialization, each part of a system requiring all for social, environmental, ritual, and mythic totality. Again, in the crisp formula of a member of Durkheim's circle: "Dualism, which is essential to the thought of primitives, dominates their social organization. The two moieties or phratries which constitute the tribe are reciprocally opposed as sacred and profane" (Hertz, 1973:8). This sort of dualism is reciprocal rather than exclusivistic: Each side is both sacred and profane with respect to the contrary characteristic of the other. Durkheim's celebrated sacred/profane distinction becomes in structuralism not substantive but relational and complementary. "Binary opposition" looms, and reciprocity pervades, either directly or indirectly (through an intermediary) in light of the entire system.

Outside Durkheim's circle, a dualist basis of moieties was compellingly evoked by Hocart; to enlarge an earlier quotation:

We have here, practically complete, the pattern of behavior between two moieties: mutual aid combined with playful hostility, intermarriage, interburial. I have elsewhere attempted to derive the whole etiquette of moieties from one fundamental principle – that, for some reason or other, there must be two parties to the ritual. We may call these "god and worshipper," "victim and sacrificer," "principal and ministrant," "king and priest," or by whatever terms we choose to fit the particular case; they are all mere variant applications of the principle. A further rule is that the two parties must belong to different lines. If one line is principal, the other must be ministrant.

The Fijians call such a reciprocal relation "mutual ministry" (more literally "facing one another," or "worshipping one another"), and I propose to adopt this term. It means that if the deceased belongs to one line, the other buries him (Winnabagoes), or mourns for him (Trobriands), or otherwise plays the vis-à-vis. *If the bridegroom comes from one side, the bride comes from the other.* [Hocart 1952:186]

We may, I think, extend Hocart's insight from social entities of discourse: Two clans (from the two moieties), two chapters, two descent lines, two poem lines, two rhymes, two books, two genders, two myths, two mythologies, two isms – are related dualistically if they can be shown reciprocally to "play the vis-à-vis."

In social systems so inclined, divided society appears almost sonnetlike, each clan a stanza. Or better (because simultaneous and not necessarily "territorialized"), society is motetlike, each clan a voice. As in motets of old, voices may sing different texts and even different languages (church Latin with vernacular French). Yet the motet (the society) remains a structured whole, its diversity notwithstanding. A totalized order of exogamy, like polyphony, keeps the "voices" both distinct and interrelated. Their structure must not be reduced to a compromised harmonics.[2]

In French structuralist formulations a social ideal – clan exogamy – was found to resonate through tribal cosmologies, institutions, and practices. We recall from Part II that endogamy/exogamy assumes a semiotic complexity comparable to Saussure's signifier/signified, provided societies are approached as total systems. Populations with divisions interrelated through positive rules of exogamy (not just negative rules, as in our customs not to marry within a nuclear family) became central to the concerns of French, Dutch, and American ethnology in particular and to British anthropology as well. Cross-cousin marriage rules take on enormous importance, because they automatically articulate an alliance system of either directly or indirectly spouse-exchanging exogamous units. Dravidian-type kinship terminologies found in South Asia, Australia, and elsewhere seem to work similarly (cf. L. Dumont 1966).[3] (In this chapter these complexities recede; "clan" is used loosely to designate social units defined with reference to exogamy, not necessarily identified with McLennan's capture-marriage; caste, in particular Brahmans, is a social unit defined with reference to endogamy: all for the sake of a comparison and contrast of isms, which is continuous with the comparison and contrast of cultures.) Finally, structuralist thinkers who turned their attention to such rules have, following Durkheim, hoped to rectify Western maldevelopment by, if not restoring, at least keeping us partly in touch with an always-lost reciprocity. Through the efforts of comparative sociological science and by the grace of socio-logic awareness, the pathology of rabid individualism (anomie) would be cured and organic solidarity reconstituted, such that any set of social divisions – occupations, estates, classes, and so forth – would be conscious of its complementary role with all others.

Durkheim and Mauss together placed tribal-dualist principles at the heart of "primitive classification":

> Society was not simply a model which classificatory thought followed; it was its own divisions which served as divisions for the system of classification. The first logical categories were social categories; the first classes of things were classes of men, into which these things were integrated. It was because men were grouped, and thought of themselves in the form of groups, that in their ideas they grouped other things, and in the beginning the two modes of grouping were merged to the point of being indistinct. Moieties were the first genera; clans, the first species. Things were thought to be integral parts of society, and it was their place in society which determined their place in nature. We may even wonder whether the schematic manner in which genera are ordinarily conceived may not have depended in part on the same influences. It is a fact of current observation that the things which they comprise are generally imagined as situated in a sort of ideational milieu, with a more or less clearly delimited spatial circumscription.
>   ...the unity of knowledge is nothing else than the very unity of the collectivity, extended to the universe. [1903/1963:82–4]

British structural functionalists, assuming from such remarks that group determines thought, obscured Durkheim's and Mauss's sense of collectivity as basically differentiated, with any determinism revolving around social categories rather than homogeneous group.

On the other hand French structuralism embraced the ambiguities of causality in Durkheim's and Mauss's celebrated formulation that "the classification of things reproduces the classification of men." It developed implications of Durkheim's ultimate view, traced in Chapter 3, of the generalized quality of social order: "At bottom, the concept of totality, that of society, and that of divinity are very probably only different aspects of the same notion" (1912/1965:490). Moreover, structuralists discarded the archaic illusion from "primitive classification" to yield a sense of structure, an order (interrelations of contrasts) equally removed from all evidence, ideal and actual, superstructural and infrastructural. M. Mauss and Lévi-Strauss shifted emphasis from social isolates (even Durkheim's ideal/actual classifications of differentiated yet solidary men plus things) to those mediators – the gift, the spouse, the sign, the myth – whose systems constitute the conditions of possibility of any and all relationships whatsoever: economic, social, linguistic, semantic. Thrust by events or epistemes beyond the lingering positivist optimism of Durkheim, Lévi-Strauss wedded Mauss's insights about reciprocity to Saussure's concept of language as systems of signifier/signifieds and to an abbreviated form of Peirce's view of symbols as replaceables (Lévi-Strauss 1973: chap. 1). The resulting structuralist concept of society and discourse suggests that any system of exchange reveals orders of conventions that allow units (at one level alike, at another level different) to replace each other. This is true within a system: Spouses and siblings replace each other, words and sensations replace each other (issue of transformation). It is true across systems: One type of spouse replacement is itself replaceable by another type of spouse replacement in the different varieties of elementary kinship structures; or one set of word replacements, that is, one language, is itself replaceable by another set (issue of translation).

In *Le totemisme aujourd' hui* Lévi-Strauss traced tribal modes of transforming natural surroundings, social relations, ritual, and myth into reciprocal codes that convert different levels of continuity into interrelated discontinuities:

> Totemism as a system is introduced as *what remains* of a diminished totality, a fact which may be a way of expressing that the terms of the system are significant only if they are *separated* from each other, since they alone remain to equip a semantic field which was previously better supplied and into which a discontinuity has been introduced. Finally the two [totemic] myths suggest that direct contact..., i.e., a relation of contiguity, is contrary to the spirit of the institution: the totem becomes such only on condition that it first be set apart. [1963a:26]

Moreover, like such totemic operations, the book *Totemism* dismantles the conditions of possibility of hypostatizing its own topic. Similarly, *The Savage Mind* imploded the notion of any discrete preliterate mode of meaning by collapsing historical understanding itself into oppositional structures.

Again, in tribal-totemic institutions and codes, a closed set of contrasts must, to endure, to be repeated, imply complementarity. Were, for example, Americans so organized, a Republican Catholic might necessarily wed a Democrat Baptist, producing offspring who are Republican Baptist or Democrat Catholic, depending on which parent was which and on the related descent rule. Moreover, distinct forms, contents, and sectors of experience are associated with one-not-the-other possible combination. Society itself operates antiphonally both at a given moment and in duration.

In discourse proper, analogues of this tribal-totemic tendency abound. Rhymes divided into "genders," both genders required to fashion a complete stanza, are quintessentially dualistic. Rhyme, alliteration, in fact any convention limiting the paradigmatic set of candidate terms that can occupy a syntagmatic position implement such order, ultimately identifiable with the whole texture of metonymy/metaphor. In prose as well, stylistic, rhetorical, and grammatical conventions heighten opportunities for a text's components to stand vis-à-vis each other. The convention of entitlement establishes such a relationship between title/work, each a replaceable of the other. Of course, the distinction poetry/prose is itself such a difference.

My point is that literary discourse (and even more so music, whether in score or in performance) echoes – or should I say completes through displacing? – tribal orders of out-marriage, totemism, and semantic classification. A discourse conscientiously produced to amplify these dimensions assumes many guises. Elsewhere I have argued that it may resemble a symbolist, synesthetic poem in place (on the page), or perhaps a Rousseauesque reminiscence or a Proustian paragraph in time (reading). Definitely this conscientious discourse resembles *Tristes tropiques*. Many structuralist and poststructuralist critics have attempted to interpret *Tristes tropiques* as a discourse of autobiography (e.g., Mehlman 1974). I resist this tactic because it makes much of that work and all of Lévi-Strauss's remaining corpus appear but so much obsessive digression; "*auto*biography" is precisely what, through tribal codes, his discourse "ironizes."[4]

In Lévi-Strauss's *Tristes tropiques* syllables, words (*Brésil/grésiller*), phrases, paragraphs, images inscribed, episodes recollected, chapters, parts, organize themselves, so to speak, reciprocally – like the out-marrying clans and moieties of tribes and the out-servicing ritual-occupations of castes that in structuralist formulations stand opposed to tribes. The discourse of this prose becomes "exogamous," speaking figuratively now, to every point of view, every stylistic mode, every epistemological certainty it would establish. From the opening "*fin des voyages*" to the final extinction of any isolated (phenomenological, existential) self – the constitutive *oubli* – *Tristes tropiques* engenders codes through transformations, finally even assembling metamorphoses of substances in a transformation of codes: "in the contemplation of a mineral more beautiful than all our creations; in the scent that can be smelt at the heart of a lily and is more imbued with learning than all our books."[5] Sky and sea codes *se transforment*; social structure and music codes *se transforment*. To travel is to activate *pensée sauvage*: "Travel is usually thought of as a displacement in space. This is an inadequate conception. A journey occurs simultaneously in space, in time and in the social hierarchy" (p. 81). Writing-travel-reminiscence is that much more again. Each inscription becomes the source of metaphor/ metonymy to articulate a contrary inscription. Traveling inverts:

The first contact with Rio was different. For the first time in my life, I was on the other side of the Equator in the tropics, in the New World. By what major sign, I wondered, was I about to recognize this three-fold mutation? What voice would provide me with evidence of it, what note as yet unheard would be the first to strike my ear? My initial observation was a trivial one: I felt I was in a drawing-room. [p. 80]

Irony replaces irony in another "major sign": "From being poor I had become rich, first because my material circumstances had changed, and secondly because the prices of local produce were incredibly low. A pineapple cost twenty sous" (p.81). Recollecting-writing-traveling inverts inversions, orders them, mythlike converts diachrony to synchrony, collapses introspection and retrospection into description, and yields structure against all odds:

Rio is the opposite of Chittagong, in the Bay of Bengal; there, each small, cone-shaped mound, rising above the marshy plain and with its orange-colored clay glistening

through the green grass, is occupied by a solitary bungalow, a rich man's fortress
to protect him against the oppressive heat and squalor of the swamps. Rio is just
the opposite: the globular domes, formed of granite in solid blocks like cast-iron, throw
back the heat with. . . [p. 84]

These constructions replicate the originality of metonymy/metaphor. Everything emerges as a contrastive replaceable for its complement, but dynamically. Rio, at one level the inverse of Chittagong (with reference to internal
topography) is at another level the inverse of New York (with reference to
what each looks out on):

The Sugar Loaf Mountain, the Corcovado and the much-praised natural features appear
to the traveller entering the bay like stumps sticking up here and there in a toothless
mouth. Since these eminences are almost always swathed in a thick tropical mist,
they seem totally unable to fill the horizon, for which in any case they would be
inadequate. If you want a satisfactory view you must look at the bay from the landward
side and look down upon it from the heights. On the seaward side, the optical illusion
is the opposite of the one which obtains in New York; here, it is nature which has
the appearance of an unfinished building-site. [p. 75]

New York and Rio, like Rio and Chittagong (and by implication New York
and Chittagong via Rio) are mutually exogamous, requiring one another to be
both distinct and completable. Out of these doldrums of strained, prefabri-
cated analogies-through-contrast, Lévi-Strauss's discourse sails into a recognition of the self-same limits in tribal constructs, his ultimate contrast–
complement. "We are not alone" (p.470).

Tristes tropiques – narrative prelude to *Mythologiques*' discursive "twilight
of man" – retained a forgetting-*raconteur* as ostensible center, yet a center
ironically displaced with each successive episode, rendered literally unreliable
in the play-within-the-story, "The Apotheosis of Augustus," an allegory
begging to be construed as representational of the very account we are
reading (chap.37). Sentimentally centered in a narrative voice, *Tristes tropiques*
is the result of forgetting ("Forgetfulness has done its task. . . Fifteen years
have lapsed"): the "opposite of a voyage," all departures having "blended
together in my memory" (pp. 54–5). The process ushers continuity into
discontinuities, arranged discontinuities. Remembering (like myth) is forgetting; who could fail to be reminded of Proust, here recalled in Walter
Benjamin:

For the important thing for the remembering author is not what he experienced, but
the weaving of his memory, the Penelope work of recollection. Or should one call
it, rather, a Penelope work of forgetting? Is not the involuntary recollection, Proust's
mémoire involuntaire much closer to forgetting than what is usually called memory?
And is not this work of spontaneous recollection in which remembrance is the woof
and forgetting the warp, a counterpart to Penelope's work rather than its likeness?
For here the day unravels what the night was [*sic*] woven. When we awake each morning, we hold in our hands, usually weakly and loosely, but a few fringes of the
tapestry of lived life, as loomed for us by forgetting. [1969:204]

Tristes tropiques, this discourse of forgetting, the sunset of Lévi-Strauss's voyages, recognizes itself in nature's own involuntary memory, her ritual automythologizing of dusking fragments:

Daybreak is a prelude, the close of day an overture which occurs at the end instead of the beginning, as in the old operas...Sunset is quite a different matter; it is a complete performance with a beginning, a middle and an end...Dawn is only the beginning of the day; twilight is a repetition of it...The operations of consciousness can also be read in these fluffy constellations. When the sky begins to brighten with the glow of sunset (just as, in certain theatres, the beginning of the performance is indicated, not by the triple knocking customary in France, but by the sudden switching on of the footlights), the peasant pauses...[Who could fail to be reminded of...?] Remembering is one of man's great pleasures, but not in so far as memory operates literally, since few individuals would agree to relive the fatigues and sufferings that they nevertheless delight in recalling. *Memory is life itself, but of a different quality*. And so, it is when the sun declines towards the polished surface of calm water, like alms bestowed by some heavenly miser, or when its disc outlines mountain summits like a hard, jagged leaf, that man...[pp. 56–7; emphasis added]

Lévi-Strauss here implicates his own metaphoric extravagances along with the solar extravagances, as he will soon through his discourse implicate tribal mythic extravagances, all of which both pale and gain significance, "since the insignificance of external events in no way justified any extravagant atmospheric display" (p. 57). Or can we distinguish these sunset–memory metaphorical extravagances from tribal mythic extravagances? This is the ambiguity deepened into *Mythologiques*; to trace it requires setting portions not just of *Tristes tropiques* but of Lévi-Strauss's entire corpus into complementarity.

What is *Tristes tropiques* like? Forgetting-remembering. What is forgetting-remembering like? A sunset. What is a sunset like? A theatrical performance, whose rays "as they gradually declined (like a violin bow which is placed at different angles to touch different strings), made each network in turn explode into a spectrum of colors that one would have said was the arbitrary and exclusive property of each" (p. 60). What is a sunset color spectrum like? An incandescent octopus: "At times, the light would be withdrawn, as if a fist had been clenched and the cloudy mitten would allow no more than one or two stiff and gleaming fingers to appear. Or an incandescent octopus would move out from the vaporous grottoes and then there would be a fresh withdrawal" (p.59). Such riotously wide-angled metaphors are, of course, the very figure of language itself as a replaceable for all these replaceables. In fact the incandescent octopus of a sunset – ironically offered as a fragment from Lévi-Strauss's shipboard notes, not having materialized through fifteen years of forgetting – represents a victorious, or tentative, transformation of event into discourse:

With the beginner's lack of sophistication, I watched enthralled from the empty deck as, every day, for the space of a few minutes, in all quarters of a horizon vaster than any I had ever seen before, the rising and the setting of the sun presented the beginning, development and conclusion of supernatural cataclysms. *If I could find a language* in which to perpetuate those appearances, at once so unstable and so resistant to description, if it were granted to me to be able to communicate to others the phases and sequences of a unique event which would never recur in the same terms, then, so it seemed to me – I should have discovered the deepest secrets of my profession: however strange and peculiar the experiences to which anthropological research might expose me, there would be none whose meaning and importance I could not eventually make clear to everybody. [p. 55; emphasis added]

Lévi-Strauss discovers the parallel between analytic sunsets, nature's self-codes, and myths, culture's self-codes. Seeking a language to communicate those appearances, he offers an incandescent octopus. Is this transformation, this transposition, a communication? Finally, whose language is it?

That last question points us outside *Tristes tropiques* into *Totemism*, where we learn what an incandescent octopus is like:

The form of a system of relations is thus extended, in a coherent fashion, to a situation which at first sight might appear quite foreign to it. And, as among the Ojibwa, a second system of relations with the supernatural world, entailing food prohibitions, is combined with a formal structure while at the same time remaining clearly distinct from it, though the totemic hypothesis would incline one to confuse them. The divinized species which are the objects of the prohibitions constitute a separate system from that of clan functions which are themselves related to plant foodstuffs: e.g., *the octopus, which is assimilated* to a mountain, the streams of which are like its tentacles, and for the same reason, *to the sun and its rays*; and eels, both fresh-water and marine, which are objects of a food tabu so strong that even to see them may cause vomiting. [1963a:28–9; emphasis added]

Was Lévi-Strauss already writing *Totemism* (and *Mythologiques*) in the ostensible recollection of *Tristes tropiques* (in 1955)? This is a suspicion perfectly appropriate to structuralism, to dualism, and to transformation as a mode of ordering myth doubled into a mode of ordering discourse through myths; because

La pensée mythique est par essence transformatrice. Chaque mythe, à peine né, se modifie en changeant de narrateur, que ce soit à l'intérieur du groupe tribal ou en se propageant de peuple à peuple; certains éléments tombent, d'autres les remplacement, des séquences s'intervertissent, la structure distordue passe par une série d'états dont les altérations successives préservent néanmoins le caractère de groupe. [Lévi-Strauss 1971:603–4]

Mythic thought is by essence transformational. Each myth, barely born, is modified through changing its narrator, whether this occurs within a tribal group or in being propagated from population to population; certain elements succumb, others replace them, sequences are inverted, the twisted structure passes through a series of conditions whose successive alterations nevertheless preserve the character of a set. [Lévi-Strauss 1971: 603–4; my translation]

As "sunset" was perhaps "languaged" as incandescent octopus only through the translated mediation of Ojibwan codes, so structuralist terms themselves, indeed the very concept of transformation, take on significance only oppositionally. The famous *finale* of *Mythologiques*, professed twilight (sunset?) of Lévi-Strauss's oeuvre, converts all the opponents of structuralism and its own analytic rejoinders into fragments arranged in a display more extravagant than events would justify, with its teasing possibilities as to the extra-*Mythologiques* explanation for the display, none any more credible than would be an external explanation of myth:

> *A moi-même en tout cas, qui ai entrepris ces* Mythologiques *pleinement conscient que je cherchais ainsi à compenser, sous une autre forme et dans un domaine qui me fût accessible, mon impuissance congénitale à composer une oeuvre musicale, il apparaît certain que j'ai tenté d'édifier avec des sens un ouvrage comparable à ceux que crée la musique avec des sons: négatif d'une symphonie dont, un jour, quelque comsositteur pourra être légitimement tenté de tirer l'image positive; d'autres diront si les contributions déjà demandées à mon ouvrage par la musique s'inspirent ou non d'un tel dessein.*

To me (myself) in any case, who undertook these *Mythologics* totally aware that I thus sought to compensate – under another form and in a domain that was accessible to me – for my congenital impotency to compose a work of music, it appears certain that I tried to construct with meanings [*sens*] a production comparable to those that music creates with sounds [*sons*]: negative of a symphony, for which one day some composer will legitimately be tempted to print the positive image; others will say if the contributions already demanded of my production by music are or are not inspired by such a plan. [1971:580; my mythic transposition]

The bottom of all this finale is left to others, as it began with others – Ojibwans? The scathing polemics against existentialism, geneticism, and sundry scholarly rivals end finally by setting themselves into doubt, as Lévi-Strauss returns his discourse of *Mythologiques* into the *je*-eclipsing mode of Jean-Jacques initiated in *Tristes tropiques*, as if to place several thousand pages of uncompromising, path-breaking analysis of tribal codes into quotation marks:

> *Les réflexions qui précèdent ne constituent pas un thèse. Elles prétendent moins encore ébaucher une philosophie, et je souhaite qu'on les prenne pour ce qu'elles sont:* une libre rêverie, *non exempte de confusion et d'erreurs, à quoi le sujet s'abandonne durant le court moment où, délivré de sa tâche, il ne sait encore dans laquelle il lui adviendra une nouvelle fois de se dissoudre. Jetant un ultime regard rétrospectif sur le labeur de huit années bientôt promis à me devenir aussi étranger que s'il eût été l'oeuvre d'un autre.*

The preceding reflections do not constitute a thesis. Still less do they claim to sketch a philosophy, and I hope that they will be taken for what they are: a free reverie, not devoid of confusion and errors, to which the subject abandons himself during the brief moment when, delivered from his task, he does not yet know into what it will come about for him to be dissolved anew. Casting an ultimate retrospective glance on the work of eight years soon guaranteed to become for me as foreign as if it had been the work of an other.

In the subsequent, crucial antepenultimate paragraph we discover that we have never left the sunset, like an incandescent octopus:

Moi-meme, selon que je considère mon travail du dedans où je l'ai vécu, ou du dehors où il est maintenant et s'éloigne pour se perdre dans mon passé, je comprends mieux qu'ayant moi aussi composé ma tétralogie, elle doive s'achever sur un crépuscule des dieux comme l'autre; ou, plus précisément, que termiñe un siècle plus tard et dans des temps plus cruel, elle anticipe le crépuscule des hommes, après celui des dieux qui devait permettre l'avènement d'une humanité heureuse et libérée. Parvenu au soir de ma carrière, la dernière image que me laissent les mythes et, à travers eux, ce mythe suprême que raconte l'histoire de l'humanité, l'histoire aussi de l'univers au sein de laquelle l'autre se déroule, rejoint donc l'intuition qui, à mes débuts et comme je l'ai raconté dans Tristes tropiques, *me faisait rechercher dans les phases d'un coucher de soleil, guetté depuis la mise en place d'un décor céleste qui se complique progressivement jusqu'à se défaire et s'abolir dans l'anéantissement nocturne, le modèle des faits que j'allais étudier plus tard et des problèmes qu'il me faudrait résoudre sur la mythologie: vaste et complexe édifice, lui aussi irisé de mille teintes, qui se déploie sous le regard de l'analyste, s'épanouit lentement et se referme pour s'abîmer au loin comm s'il n'avait jamais existé.* [1971:619–21]

Myself, according to whether I consider my work from within where I lived it or from without where it now exists and moves away to become lost in my past, I better understand that, I too having composed my tetralogy, it must conclude with a twilight of the gods like the other one; or more precisely, that, completed a century later and in crueler times, it anticipates the twilight of men, after that of the gods which ought to allow the advent of a humanity happy and freed. Arrived at the evening of my career, the last image myths leave me – and through them the supreme myth related by the history of humanity, the history also of the universe in whose midst the other unfolds – thus rejoins the intuition which, at my beginnings [*débuts*] and as I related it in *Tristes tropiques*, made me seek in the phases of a setting sun, awaited since the installation of a celestial scenery which complicates itself progressively to the point of becoming undone and abolished into the annihilation of night, the model of facts that I was later going to study and of problems that I would have to resolve on mythology: vast and complex construction, it too iridescent with a thousand hues, which deploys itself under the gaze of the analyst, slowly fades and closes up, engulfing itself in the distance as if it had never existed. [1971:619–21; my transplant]

Thus in this structuralist discourse, all sections, movements, metaphors, books become with respect to each other mutually "exogamous." Structuralism appears the inverse of textual hermeticism (autoeroticism?). Like tribal codes, each part of structuralism constitutes itself only in counterdistinction to another: an embrace without unity, transformation without substantive metamorphosis. How nonromantic! Yet there was *another* in romanticism, too: desired, translated, but never conjoined.

An endogamy of poets

Willst du den Himmel, die Erde mit einem Namen begreifen,
Nenn ich, Sakontala, dich, und so ist Alles gesagt.
Goethe "epigrammed" by Herder

Like Hamann, Herder calls for cleansing (*läutern*) and rejuvenating (*verjüngen*). An individual genius will show his worth by the boldness of his idiom, breaking his way through heavy ceremoniousness down into the bowels of the language, down through rocky clefts to find gold. Even if what he finds is but a shapeless lump, there may be opportunity for chemistry [alchemy?]. Would there were many such miners and smelters in Germany! Did not the great Leibniz tell us that German was the language of miners and hunters?

Eric A. Blackall, *The Emergence of German as a Literary Language, 1700–1775*

Romantic cross-cultural ideals dawned during the heady period of early translations between Sanskrit and European literatures, in particular English and German.[6] The "first-generation" philosopher-translators championed C. Wilkins' *Bhagavad Gita* and the dramatic language of *Sakuntula*, translated via Latin into English by W. Jones and from the English into German by Forster, to profess the desirability of both the contents and institutions of Indic poetic–priestly traditions. Soon after, translation would fall away from philosophy, in spite of F. Schlegel's advice before his own disenchantment with India:

Indian study and research in general should be pursued with the grander views and opinions of those able men of the fifteenth and sixteenth centuries, who first revived the study of Greek and Eastern literature; for it must not be imagined that a bare knowledge of the language is sufficient to entitle its possessor to the reputation of a learned man; and, indeed, there were few among the classical scholars of that period who did not unite with their knowledge of language an earnest study of philosophy, and the whole abundance of historical science. [Schlegel 1860:522]

For the brief heyday of such grander views, before translation was routinized into philology with its lexical standards, definitive editions, and aim of literal accuracy, Herder, Novalis, Schlegel, and other scholars confronted Indic traditions, directly or indirectly, and managed to compare themselves implicitly or (as in the case of the brothers Schlegel) explicitly to Brahmans. What an ideal to penetrate the Western sector of Indo-European ideology: an in-marrying priest-poetship, whose progeny would cultivate their legacy of esoteric texts, occasionally instructing inferiors, but essentially self-perpetuating.[7] Brahmans: hermetic, priestly poets, both ascetic and erotic, both polygynous and endogamous. Echoing values more Rosicrucian, Masonic, or even kabalistic, Brahmans represented in a sense the antithesis of all Western orthodoxies, whether Catholic (celibate), Protestant (reformed), or free-thinking (rational). Could romantics rival Brahmans?

I raise the question to augment its suggestiveness. The complex history of Brahman stereotypes in Western letters had set the stage for this ultimate romantic attraction. Ancient Greek frameworks for Hindus included vegetarianism, widow immolation, and what we would now call caste-endogamy. Reputed links of Pythagoras and Plato to Indic sages reinforced associations between Brahmans and hermetic wisdom: astrological, mathematical, eventually poetic. Qualities of both license (polygyny, concubinage) and asceticism (recluses, teetotalers, scholars) attached paradoxically to the idea of Brahmans.

Over the centuries, reports confirmed their exclusivism and secrecy. In the later eighteenth century, Alexander Dow and Voltaire, among others, remarked that non-Brahman sects, Sudras, and foreigners alike were forbidden access to Sanskrit texts. Christian Dohm forged obscure notions of Brahmans' ancient sublimity into the image more familiar to us from later pathological, provincial, and self-aggrandizing versions: "that India was the true fatherland, the cradle of the human race" (Willson 1964:26).

Such variations of W. Jones's Aryan thesis had been foreshadowed in earlier Dutch works, for example, Baldeus's crediting the Brahman doctrine of metempsychosis to early Germanic tribes. Moreover, it was another Dutchman, Rogerius, whose *De Open-Deure* (1651) included "the first direct adaptation of a Sanskrit work into a Western tongue"; he provided information on the Vedas, Brahmanical rites and special privileges under law, and other aspects of the context of "Sanscortamish, a language esteemed by the Brahmans as is Latin in Europe by the scholars, a language which contains all the secrets of the heathen" (Willson 1964:8ff.).

Thus by the mid-seventeenth century, Rogerius sought to describe Brahmanical traditions. By the late eighteenth century, Romantics meant to emulate Brahmans, to become – through a complex of poetry, philosophy, and translation – Brahmanical. The discourse dimension of their idealization is clear:

> Herder never spoke more rapturously of anything native to India than he speaks of *Sakontala*. The Indic studies of Herder found their peak in his devotion to this play, his *indische Blume*. In this drama he finds the ideal he has sought: innocence and unity with nature, the marvelous treated as ordinary, tangible incidence, a supreme harmony of the arts. He exclaims: "*Sakontala* heisst mein Drama: ein Indisches Schauspiel, von Kalidas gedichtet, von W. *Jones* herbeigeschafft, und ins Englishe, aus dieser Sprache von G. *Forster* ins Deutsche so gut übersetzt, dass es sich fast besser als das Englische Original lieset." [Willson 1964:70]

It is Forster's German – or some contrast in "readability" between Forster's German and Jones's English – that actually embodies the Indic discourse Herder so desired. The implication that a translation of a translation might *sich fast besser lieset* is a telling sign of romantic hopes. Moreover, the suggestion of some subterranean system of affinities that allowed a translation of a translation to move nearer the Original works to Herder's own advantage. F. Schlegel himself, the ultimate romantic Sanskritist-philosopher, attributes to Herder extratranslation powers:

> Lessing is too much a philosopher, and too little an artist in his criticism. He wants that energy of fancy by which Herder was enabled to transport himself into the spirit and poetry of every age and people. It is this very perception and feeling of the poetical, in the character of natural legends, which forms the most distinguishing feature in the genius of Herder. . . His mind seems to have been cast in so universal a mould, that he might have attained to equal eminence either as a poet, or as a philosopher. [Schlegel 1846:405]

This romantic view of Herder persists even today in works themselves interpreting Romanticism. Willson, for example, salutes Herder's *Gedanken einiger Bramanen* for improving the very translations from Sanskrit he relied on:

> The genius of Herder's spirit, which revealed itself in the empathy with which he was able to project his sensitive awareness and grasp the essence of an idea – an alien idea, clothed clumsily in the phrases of a sequence of three translations – can be shown in the four instances where Von Bohlen, translating directly from the Sanskrit, found Herder's renderings admirable enough to be retained.
> ...these examples may suffice to illustrate Herder's happy aptitude for striking through the entanglement of Rogerius' too formal grammar and verbiage and plumbing the ethos of the Sanskrit thought by a kind of extrasensory empathy. [p. 68-9]

This telltale possibility, which remains always open to Romantics – namely that a translation translated may return toward the Original – lies ruined in the uncompromising irony of Benjamin, even as he restores legitimacy to this "mode":

> For any translation of a work originating in a specific stage of linguistic history represents, in regard to a specific aspect of its content, translation into all other languages. Thus translation, ironically, transplants the original into a more definitive linguistic realm since it can no longer be displaced by a secondary rendering. The original can only be raised there anew and at other points of time...
> ...a translation touches the original lightly and only at the infinitely small point of the sense, thereupon pursuing its own course according to the laws of fidelity in the freedom of linguistic flux. Without explicitly naming or substantiating it, Rudolf Pannwitz has characterized the true significance of this freedom...Pannwitz writes: "Our translations, even the best ones, proceed from the wrong premise. They want to turn Hindi, Greek, English into German instead of turning German into Hindi, Greek, English. Our translators have a far greater reverence for the usage of their own language than for the spirit of the foreign works...
> The higher the level of a work, the more does it remain translatable even if its meaning is touched upon only fleetingly. This, of course, applies to originals only. Translations, on the other hand, prove to be untranslatable not because of any inherent difficulty, but because of the looseness with which meaning attaches to them. Confirmation of this as well as of every other important aspect is supplied by Hölderlin's translations. [Benjamin 1969:78–81]

For Benjamin every transplanting – whether a translation or a reading from an inevitably different stage of linguistic history – raises the original into more specific accessibility. Translation, then, becomes the very figure of interpretation, a process hoping to turn itself into a foreign spirit but, as in scriptural exegesis, necessarily reducing the original to narrowed ruins. Thus Benjamin simultaneously elevates both the original and those more definitive transplants that would be faithful to it but whose very specificity renders them, as translation, untranslatable. Every translation must proceed from the original: Where would this leave Herder? Where, indeed, would it leave Romanticism, Structuralism?

The combined play and profundity of Benjamin is most apparent when he stipulates:

Therefore it is not the highest praise of translation, particularly in the age of its origin, to say that it reads as if it had originally been written in that language. Rather, the significance of fidelity as ensured by literalness is that the work reflects the great longing for linguistic complementation. . .

For to some degree all great texts contain their potential translation between the lines; this is true to the highest degree of sacred writings. The interlinear version of the Scriptures is the prototype of or ideal of all translation. [1969:79, 82]

Benjamin manages to distinguish in translation truth from literalness and to isolate intimately the translator with the original, each the other's complement, free of the institutional weight of a cumulative philological or hermeneutic enterprise. This unspeakably delicate position – an anti-ism – either may be equally removed from both romanticism and structuralism or may augur the late structuralism of *Mythologiques*, which necessarily makes any distinction between original/translation ironically reciprocal.

Regardless, in the case of Herder, his translator-longing arose, if only indirectly from the language of Kalidasa's *Sakuntala*, directly from its contents and imagery: its portrait of the Brahman Kanna – ascetic yet sensuous, guardian of harmony among nature, humanity, and divinity. But Herder's admiration of Brahmans went beyond the dramatic–yogic variation of Kanna's grove and beyond metempsychosis as well. He emphasized their rank and authority as apical caste, their juridical functions, and their importance in religious–poetic intensity and continuity:

[For Herder] it is in the Brahman that the lofty conception of God has maintained its purity, whereas long centuries have contaminated the idea among the common people. The Brahman, the keeper of religion and law, the depository of wisdom of medicine, astronomy, mathematics, and other sciences, taught the youth and thus propagated his wisdom through succeeding generations.
Concerning the place of the Brahman as a molder of philosophy, Herder says (evidently after Dohm) that the path to a humanistic philosophy is more efficacious through moderation of sensual enjoyments than through a thousand artificial abstractions. The very essence of Hindu culture centered in the Brahman. [Willson 1964:59]

What then of the social dimension in this idealization of Brahmans? We know that Herder's Romantic successors strived for Brahman-like *lettres*. The more ambiguous problem in Romantic discourse, and in the Romantic movement, concerns the extent to which the social setting and institutional framework of Brahmans was an object of longing as well. This question points toward the pivotal formulation of our comparison: In its fullest elaboration, structuralism converts an exotic social ideal (clan exogamy, complemented in tribal "discourse" by totemic myth) into a mode of Western discourse. Did, in reverse, Romanticism in its fullest elaboration dream of converting an exotic discursive ideal (sacred, high-caste hermetic literature, complemented in Indic society by in-marrying castes) into a mode of Western society? Did Romantics desire an endogamy of poets?

The question, or its implications, can be felt behind the works of Novalis. Willson has reviewed Novalis's efforts to synthesize Christian and Indian religion, in particular that "mystery in personification" of the *blaue Blume*:

> The Romantic mythical image of India found its most poetic expression in *Heinrich von Ofterdingen* (1800), in which it finally is transfigured and absorbed into the new mythology, the mythology of poesy, through the suprarational, magical qualities of the *blaue Blume*. This supreme Romantic symbol has been imperfectly comprehended because of the slighting by scholars of Novalis' allusions to India, the result of the poet's acquaintance with Indic lore in his time...
>   ...the primary concept of the *blaue Blume* as a symbol is in its use as the object suggesting the unfolding of poetic growth, the development of poetic vision, the germination of poetic accomplishment. A collateral and increasingly important symbolistic function in the course of the novel is its use as the mediator in the reconciliation of divergent religions, a motif of perfect, transcendental love, and a symbol of the merging into harmonious synthesis of the disparate qualities of man and nature. [pp. 155, 157]

Willson carefully considers Indic influence on the flower symbolism pervasive in Romantic works to prepare us for the central episode in Novalis's tale of Heinrich's heightening in a grotto into blueness:

> *Dunkelblaue Felsen mit bunten Adern erhoben sich in einiger Entfernung...der Himmel war schwarzblau und völlig rein. Was ihn aber mit voller Macht anzog, war eine hohe lichtblaue Blume, die zunächst an de Quelle stand, und ihn mit ihren breiten, gläzenden Blättern berührte...Er sah nichts als die blaue Blume...die Blütenblätter zeigten einen blauen ausgebreiteten Kragen, in welchem ein zartes Gesicht schwebte.*

Dark blue boulders with variegated veins arose at some distance...the heavens were blue black and entirely pure. What appeared to him with even more power was a great light blue blossom that lay next to the spring and touched him with its broad, splendid leaves...He saw nought but the blue blossom...the petals revealed a blue outspread collar, a tender countenance suspended therein. [P. 160; my translation]

But where is the social dimension in this ultimate literary image, ostensibly uniting Germany and India, actually hermetically sealing German literature? We see the social ideal in, for example, a tale within the tale of Heinrich, about a princess of a *morgenländischen Königsfamilie* obliged to marry a poet:

> *Seine Dichter hatten ihm unaufhörlich von seiner Verwandtschaft mit den ehemaligen übermenschlichen Beherrschern der Welt vorgesungen, und in dem Zauberspiegel ihrer Kunst war ihm der Abstand seiner Herkunft von dem Ursprunge der andern Menschen, die Herlichkeit seines Stammes noch heller erschienen, so dass es ihn dünkte, nur durch die edlere Klasse der Dichter mit dem übrigen Menschengeschlechte zusammenzuhängen.*

His poets had sung to him incessantly of his relationship with the former superhuman rulers of the world, and in the magic mirror of their art the condition of his descent from other men, the glory of his ancestry was made clearer to him, so that it seemed to him only through the noble class of the poet to be connected with the rest of mankind. [p. 161; my translation]

In the conventions of Indo-European ideology at its furthest reaches, such a marriage has two possible implications. If the poet is low-born (a bard?) the marriage would appear as *swayamvara*, a union of a superior woman with an inferior (normally forbidden): her champion, her worthy, evidenced through some achievement other than birth. If the poet is higher born than the princess, he is necessarily a Brahman, and conventions of hypergamy allow the woman to marry her caste-superior. (Hypergamy involves regulations and values requiring the women of a social category to wed only their equals or superiors; hypogamy means the contrary. Hypergamy and its related codes of purity/pollution are compatible with caste systems; hypogamy is a complex of values and practices often associated with chieftainship, the chief tying lesser lines to his own by marriages with his daughters.)[8]

Regardless, the crucial fact is that marriage is ideally regulated with reference to "poethood." Ultimately in Indic variants of Indo-European traditions, this registers as endogamy (with hypergamy allowed). Tracing the ideal of marriage within a population of poetic-*semblables* would carry us from Novalis's relations with his fiancée Sophie von Kuhn (whom he called "Sakontala") to Wagner and Cosima's domestic variations on Schopenhauer's mythic image of Buddhism. I do not mean to imply that the Brahmanical social ideal alone sustained Romantics' yearnings for an endogamous poethood. Certainly medieval guild traditions – remembering Nuremberg and its singers – and various Rosicrucian and Freemasonic brotherhoods and sisterhoods conveyed a comparable desire. But that Brahmans were not just magical–hermetic (like miners) or material-philosophers (like alchemists) but *literary*–philosophical–poetic–hermetic–pedagogic–sensuous-ascetics-*cum*-progeny suggests that their texts and social usages most fully embodied Romantic ambitions, overt or covert.

The perhaps prematurely post-Romantic discourse that completely elaborates and/or parodies these ambitions emerges with E. T. A. Hoffmann. Whether in a register of Indic fantasy, Kabbalism, mysterious guilds, or Masonic orders, his tales of discovery of a poetic *Beruf* include an endogamous consort. The celebrated "Der goldne Topf " both describes and achieves hermetic metamorphoses of literary substances, like a German transmogrification of Indic philosophical transmigration. The tale revolves around the imaginary or real identity of Anselmus's intended: Serpentina or Veronica? Alchemical–poetical consort or daughter of Conrector Paulmann?[9]

Even in tales less obviously fantastical, less loaded with the "Oriental bombast" and "Romantic idiocy" of Anselmus and Archivarius decried by Paulmann and Heerbrand, the ideal of hermeticism and endogamy is never far away. It is explicit in "Tobias Martin":

"A wonderful story," said Paumgartner. "Still I don't see how this prophetic song of your old grandmother has any connection with your obstinate determination to give Rosa to nobody but a master cooper."

"What can be clearer," said Master Martin, "than that the old lady, specially enlightened by the Lord during the last moments of her life, declared in prophecy how matters are to go with Rosa, if she is to be happy and fortunate? The wooer who is to bring wealth, luck and happiness into her dwelling with a beautiful house; who can that be but a clever cooper, who shall finish his masterpiece, the beautiful house of his building, in my workshop? In what other house do streams of sweet savour flow up and down but in a winecask? And when the wine is working it rustles, and hums, and splashes; and that is the singing of the angels as they float on the tiny ripples. Ay, ay! no other bridegroom did the old grandmother mean but the master cooper. And that it shall be!"

"Good Master Martin," said Paumgartner, "you interpret the old lady's words after your own matter."

Finally, hermetic endogamy pervades "The Mines of Falun" even in snippets, here translated and transplanted, but still like ideal Brahmans-transposed:

"It gives me real satisfaction to listen to you, youngster," said the old miner. . . ."Heaven could have given you no more precious gifts; but you were never in all your born days in the least cut out for a sailor. How could the wild, unsettled sailor's life suit a meditative, melancholy Neriker like you?. . .Take my advice, Elis Froebom. Go to Falun, and be a miner. . ."

. . .more and more vivid grew his words, more and more glowing his face. He went, in his description, through the different shafts as if they had been the alleys of some enchanted garden. The jewels came to life, the fossils began to move; the wondrous pyrosmalite and the almandine flashed in the light of the miner's candles, the rock crystals glittered and darted their rays.

. . ."Elis Froebom," said the old man at last, "I have laid before you all the glories of a calling for which Nature really destined you."

Driven hither and thither by all these fancies, [Elis] looked down into the water, and then he thought he saw the silver ripples hardening into the sparkling glimmer in which the grand ships melted away, while the dark clouds, which were beginning to gather and obscure the blue sky, seemed to sink down and thicken into a vault of rock. He was in his dream again, gazing into the immobile face of the majestic woman, and the devouring pain of passionate longing took possession of him as before.

. . .when he looked at these fine, handsome fellows, with their kindly, frank faces, he forgot all about the earthworms he had seen coming up the shaft. The healthy gladsomeness which broke out afresh in the whole circle, as if new-fanned by a spring breeze, when Pehrson Dahlsjoe came out, was of a different sort from the senseless noise and uproar of the sailors' Hoensning. The manner in which these miners enjoyed themselves went straight to the serious Elis's heart. . .

When his song was ended, Pehrson Dahlsjoe opened his door, and all the miners went into his house one after another. . .The miners all stood up, and a low murmur of pleasure ran through their ranks. "Ulla Dahlsjoe!" they said. "What a blessing Heaven has bestowed on our hearty alderman in [his daughter]!"

. . .then the [old miner] cried. . .:"Down here you're a sightless mole, and of no use up above either – trying to get hold of the pure Regulus; which you never will – hey! You want to marry Pehrson Dahlsjoe's daughter; that's what you've taken to mine work for, not from any love of it. Mind what you're after, doubleface. . ."

". . .is it your highest aim to be engaged to Ulla? Wretched fool! Have you not looked upon the face of the queen?"

"...I only want to tell you, my beloved Ulla," [Elis] said, in a faint trembling voice,"...everything has been revealed to me in the night which is just over. Down in the depths below, hidden in chlorite and mica, lies the cherry-coloured sparkling almandine, on which the tablet of our lives is graven. I have to give it to you as a wedding present...we shall see and understand the peculiar manner in which our hearts and souls have grown together into the wonderful branch which shoots from the queen's heart, at the central point of the globe...I will be back in a little while."

"Here's the old St. John's Day grandmother," the miners said. They had given her this name because they had noticed that every year she came up to the main shaft on Saint John's Day and looked down into its depths...
    The moment she saw the body she threw away her crutches, lifted her arms to Heaven, and cried, in the most heart-rending way:
    "Oh! Elis Froebom! Oh, my sweet, sweet, bridegroom!"
    ...the miners closed around. They would have raised poor Ulla, but she had breathed out her life upon her bridegroom's body. The spectators noticed now that it was beginning to crumble into dust. The appearance of petrifaction had been deceptive.
    In the church of Copparberg, where they were to have been married fifty years earlier, the miners laid in the earth the ashes of Elis Froebom, and with them the body of her who had been thus "Faithful unto death."

Between heaven and earth, sky-sea and shaft: endogamous miners (Ulla of the society of miners become the majestic subterranean Queen, consort in hermetic–poetic knowledge). Between the desire of endogamy and its storied realization, through death and narrative, stretches Hoffmann's disourse.

Epithalamium written

Yet if that ultimate synthesis toward which dialectical thought moves turns out to be unattainable it must not be thought that either of the terms of that synthesis, either of the conceptual opposites which are its subject and object, are any more satisfactory in their own right. The object considered in itself, the world taken as directly accessible content, results in the illusions of simple empirical positivism, or in an academic thinking which mistakes its own conceptual categories for solid parts and pieces of the real world itself. In the same way, the exclusive refuge in the subject results in what is for Adorno the subjective idealism of Heideggerian existentialism, a kind of ahistorical historicity, a mystique of anxiety, death, and individual destiny without any genuine content. Thus a negative dialectic has no choice but to affirm the notion and value of an ultimate synthesis, while negating its possibility and reality in every concrete case that comes before it.

Fredric Jameson, *Marxism and Form*

"The world of the Hindu," writes Herder, "is a stream of facile metamorphoses." The world of the preliterate, writes Lévi-Strauss, is a system of possible transformations. Romanticism and structuralism elaborated their own metamorphoses and transformations partly in response to exotic examples. The one: exclusivist Brahmans, endogamy, hermetic–substantive expression, literature. The other: clan-divided tribes, exogamy, reciprocal-codes-exchanged, preliterateness. Yet some of each example must characterize both, or else the one would never be communicated, the other never palpable, never felt.

However much Romantics wished to transmogrify German into Sanskrit, or rather literary German into something Sanskrit-like, and to transform its institutionalization into something Brahmanical, insofar as the process required translation, it remained at base transformationist. (The idealized other of Sanskrit kept Romanticism, for a while, from collapsing into its own hermeticism.) However reciprocally external (like exogamous clans) structuralism and tribal systems remain, structuralist discourse presumes to embody a metamorphosis of preliterate life.

We have been flirting, unashamed, with a revealing anthropologicocentrism: in their motives of and for translation and interpretation, isms emerge less from History unfolding than from the dialectics of cultures crossing, constituting themselves with reference to idealized others. This process is common to Romanticism and structuralism, among other isms, because Herder and Durkheim, and Schlegel and Lévi-Strauss, like all Romantics and structuralists, early and late (and like all ethno*graphers*), write. Tribes, castes, preliterate and literary myth, in fact any exotic ideal materializes across cultures only through discourse, in Foucault's sense:

Discourse in this sense is not an ideal, timeless form that also possesses a history; the problem is not therefore to ask oneself how and why it was able to emerge and become embodied at this point in time; it is, from beginning to end, historical – a fragment of history, a unity and discontinuity in history itself, posing the problem of its own limits, its divisions, its transformations, the specific modes of its temporality rather than its sudden irruption in the midst of the complicities of time.[10]

Moreover, it is with discourse as it is with society: Discourse units – signs, sounds, words, languages – circulate. Social units – spouses, roles, institutions, divisions – circulate, in space and time. Structuralism's basic argument is that one such circulation can, at some specifiable remove, replace another. Sundry indigenous traditions confirm the argument, including some that Romantics themselves found desirable; Lévi-Strauss:

Marriage is thus a dramatic encounter between nature and culture, between alliance and kinship. "Who has given the bride?" chants the Hindu hymn of marriage: "To whom then is she given? It is love that has given her; it is to love that she has been given. Love has given; love has received. Love has filled the ocean. With love I accept her. Love! let her be yours." Thus, marriage is an arbitration between two loves, parental and conjugal. Nevertheless, they are both forms of love, and the instant the marriage takes place, considered in isolation, the two meet and merge; "love has filled the ocean." Their meeting is doubtless merely a prelude to their substitution for one another, the performance of a sort of *chassé-croisé*. But to intercross they must at least momentarily be joined, and it is this which in all social thought makes marriage a sacred mystery. At this moment, *all marriage verges on incest*. More than that, it is incest, at least social incest, if it is true that incest, in the broadest sense of the word, consists in obtaining by oneself, and for oneself, instead of by another, and for another. [1969a:488; emphasis added]

Rules of exogamy set such risks of social hermeticism in abeyance. But in society, the noncirculation of spouses (incest) – like, in discourse, the noncirculation of signs (silence) – remains *sous-entendu*. There is a murmur of hermeticism behind every circulation, every exchange.

In the dense, Delphic pages concluding *The Elementary ~~Forms~~ Structures of ~~Religious Life~~ Kinship*, Lévi-Strauss brings the necessities of communicating–circulating back round to the mysteries of noncirculating, of "staying home":

> In this way, language and exogamy represent two solutions to one and the same fundamental situation. Language has achieved a high degree of perfection, while exogamy has remained approximate and precarious. This disparity, however, is not without its counterpart. The very nature of the linguistic symbol prevented it from remaining for long in the stage which was ended by Babel, when words were still the essential property of each particular group: values as much as signs, jealously preserved, reflectively uttered, and exchanged for other words the meaning of which, once revealed, would bind the stranger. . .
>
> Passing from speech to alliance, i.e., to the other field of communication, the situation is reversed. The emergence of symbolic thought must have required that women [I would say spouses], like words, should be things [signs, gifts] that were exchanged. In this new case, indeed, this was the only means of overcoming the contradiction by which the same woman was seen under two incompatible aspects: on the one hand, as the object of personal desire, thus exciting sexual and proprietorial instincts; and, on the other, as the subject of the desire of others, and seen as such, i.e., as the means of binding others through alliance with them. . .In contrast to words, which have wholly become signs, woman [I would say spouse] has remained at once a sign and a value. This explains why the relations between the sexes have preserved that affective richness, ardour and mystery which doubtless originally permeated the entire universe of human communications. [p. 496]

Exogamy pushed past the limits of constituting a system is marriage by choice (in Indic traditions *swayamvara*), independent of categorical restrictions: too exogamous, oblivious to the relative endogamy in a system of exchange. The reciprocal clan-exogamy admired in structuralism *is* limited. Exogamy out of control would yield (has yielded?) rabid individualism, like the anomie Durkheim feared. Would it be going too far to suggest that the discourse-equivalent of such excessive exogamy is Barthes' very *Fragments d'un discours amoureux*: metonymic, alphabetic, everyday, profane, verbose, *par hazard*. For if, as we saw above, every marriage implies incest (social and discursive), so every potential love letter implies onanism (social and discursive). Barthes' poststructuralist discourse-fragments (like a structuralism out of control) of lovers' discourse-fragments propose "a portrait – but not a psychological portrait; instead, a structural one which offers the reader a discursive site: the site of someone speaking within himself, amorously, confronting the other (the loved object), who does not speak." Barthes suggests that "an always present *I* is constituted only by confrontation with an always absent *you*. To speak this absence is from the start to propose that the subject's place and the other's place cannot permute."[11] The *Fragments* mark the end of reciprocity and romance; they read like an exogamy, uncompleted by the endogamy (at the logical extreme, incest) placed in abeyance but only provisionally: for the moment, at a level. Remembering that both Barthes and the *Mahabharata* are, at comically different removes, variations on possibilities in Dumézil's "Indo-European ideology," I read the *Fragments* as Indic swayamvara run discursively rampant.

Endogamy pushed past the limits of constituting a system is incest: too endogamous, oblivious to the relative exogamy in a system of exchange. Instead of Barthes, we have here Wagner: metaphoric, leitmotivic, special occasion, sacred, musical, star-crossed. Needless to say, this romantic theme, glimpsed above in Novalis and Hoffmann, culminates in *Tristan und Isolde* (and Richard and Cosima), *Parsifal*, and "that other *tetralogie*" – all saluted by Lévi-Strauss at the twilight of *Mythologiques*. The murmur of incest (hermetics) that oppositionally constitutes any system of exchange – social or discursive – represents the Romantic coefficient that persists in structuralism.

Structuralism "itself" (oxymoron) is as incomplete as the exogamous clans (social metonymies) it idealizes. Yet Romanticism, too, remained incomplete insofar as it idealized a closed Brahmanical essence it could never become. It would seem that the promise of structuralism can be fulfilled only if it places itself in opposition to something *other* – and marries it. As I once proposed an alliance with French literary symbolism, I here propose German philosophical–poetic Romanticism, leaving in dark ambiguity whether this would not be a wedding of siblings. The *blaue Blume* and an incandescent octopus. To mean anything as discourse, structuralism, alone contentless, must be exogamous and – like Bali's Lady Uma – polygamous.

8. Conclusion: Dead moons or eclipsed?

Ah! How the old sagas run through me!

Herman Melville, *Mardi*

The significance of anthropology often fails to penetrate sister disciplines whose devotees assume that kinship and marriage pertain merely to society's domestic sector or that ritual and myth are extracurricular imaginative flings. To the contrary: The experience of tribal and traditional populations reveals that kinship and marriage are a metainstitution and myth and ritual a metaclassification: an institution of institutions and a classification of classifications. Studying situations where kinship is economics is politics is religion helps dissolve any comfortable sense of the disjunction of such components in presumably rationalized social systems (as analyzed by rationalized investigators). In a generalized system, rank, authority, rights and obligations, property, specialization, production, and redistribution pertain to a common set of symbolic values. Generalized systems are languagelike symbolic orders that contain, at least implicitly, their own antitheses and thus their own conditions of possibility of change. Examples include histories moving to the rhythm of one or another cross-cousin marriage exchange; ideologies revolving around ideally closed sets of social and religious categories; or societies in which kinship is the encompassing order. Anthropology sometimes startlingly detects generalized systems where they are least expected; as when David Schneider locates in American culture values that operate our political, religious, and perhaps even economic sectors in accordance with symbols of kinship and coitus (1980).

Many debates that continually animate anthropology pertain to such generalized symbols (cf. Boon 1973). One recent example is the Marxist/structuralist dispute in France, resolved by Sahlins in the following terms: "What structuralism seems to offer, even beyond a conception of the continuity in history that Marx recognized for certain precapitalist societies, is an explicit statement of the culture in the praxis, the symbolic order in the material activity" (1976a:3). Weber's work likewise begged the difference between the ideal and material in the interpretation of generalized symbolic orders. Cultural

229

interpretation and historical hermeneutics as well reveal dialectical dimensions of generalized symbols. Many such investigations disclose an order of orders, neither ideal nor material: not an historical–synthetic construct but an operation of culture and/or structure based on a total system at odds with itself, hence motivated for its actors and locatable in a field of contrasts with other such systems.

Anthropology, like Weber, weds the pursuit of the generalized to an insistence on the fracturing of human experience into languages, cultures, and histories. It fosters a radical sense of the mutual peculiarity of all cultures and times, and of anthropology's peculiarity as well. Scholars like Hocart, Frazer, and others we have discussed convey the "strangeness" of comparing cultures routinely: an activity certainly as strange as shamanism. Polycultures in anthropology seem almost to recall polydeities in religion. Anthropology stands to, say, sociology (or psychoanalysis?) as polytheism to monotheism; it offers a regular orgy of "defamiliarization."

Chapter 7 implied that scholars like Walter Benjamin are polytheists, so to speak, of History. They at least acknowledge a fractured plenitude, over and against any traditional Judaeo–Christian ideology of a monolithic, substantive flow of time (culminating in Hegel and Marx). They resign themselves to fragments of mutual "alienation," *Verfremdung, ostranenie*: languages always lapsed from Adamite unity; snapshots of presences that never quite were. The model of history – even of *our* history – becomes something very much like cultures: integrated, well yes, but only through discontinuities (never substantively).

This very modern view has emerged in the works of very different writers. One of its earmarks is a set of graphic devices as exhilarating to some as they are irritating to others. Semiotic writing is particularly symptomatic. A kind of hyphenitis creeps in (it is rampant in poststructuralism). Why? Because hyphens remotivate, in the Saussurian sense, lapsed significances. Hyphens are to polysyllables what semiotic anthropology is to polycultures: marks dislodging normalized, standardized, homogenized, habituated meanings. A hyphen elevates an oblivion (break-fast) into a discrimination, in fact a bridgeable difference. Works like the present one tend as well to employ a logical–graphic device (/) that many associate with structuralism's obsessive oppositions. Yet at the broadest level (Saussure/Peirce, Romanticism/structuralism, Durkheim/ Weber) it serves as a shorthand for strategies for comparative–contrastive interpretation of extremes, stretching from Benedict's Zuni/Kwakiutl/Dobu to Dumont's India/us or *Homo hierarchicus/aequalis*. (Were one to succumb to Mallarméan–Derridaesque scriptive terms, one might say that the glyph of semiotics is the – whose trace is the /).

Yet however inscribed, the critical point is that cultures are more than just empirically comparable: They are intrinsically comparative. Cultures have their own / built in. Like languages, cultures are fundamentally beside themselves:

inside out as well as outside in. Analytically, cultures are constituted contrastively, from an "operational point of view:"

What is called a "culture" is a fragment of humanity which. . .presents significant discontinuities in relation to the rest of humanity. If our aim is to ascertain significant discontinuities between, let us say, North America and Europe, then we are dealing with two different cultures; but should we become concerned with significant discontinuities between New York and Chicago, we would be allowed to speak of these two groups as different cultural "units."

. . .anthropologists usually reserve the term "culture" to designate a *group* of discontinuities which is significant on several of these levels [familiar, occupational, religious, political, etc.] at the same time. That it can never be valid for all levels does not prevent the concept of "culture" from being as fundamental for the anthropologist as that of "isolate" for the demographer. [Lévi-Strauss 1963b:288]

Chapter 4 suggested that this very condition of contrast (see Saussure, Lévi-Strauss) is at some level implicated in the symbolic integration of the lives of social actors in each culture *as a culture* (Peirce, Geertz). An anthropology at once semiotic and dialectical follows Durkheim in continually arguing this simultaneous integrity/differentness of cultures. It thus becomes contrary to the nature of any culture, to whatever degree interpreted, to end in a definitive study.

Bali, for example, like all cultures, is autodislocated: "In an ordinary, quite un-Hegelian way, the elements of a culture's own negation are, with greater or lesser force, included within it" (Geertz 1973:406). Romanticism, like all isms, is autodislocated – inclined toward contrastive others. Structuralism, I would suggest, operationalizes this fact, making itself reflexive. In Saussurian and post-Saussurian terms, every culture is, by absence, all cultures; each occupies a position the others are not: "*la véritable contribution des cultures ne consiste pas dans la liste de leurs inventions particulières, mais dans* l'ecart différentiel *qu'elles offurent entre elles*" (Lévi-Strauss 1973:417). One name for this irreducibly contrastive *condition humaine* is "translation."

Accordingly, in this study I have, sometimes openly, sometimes surreptitiously, compared isms and eras (really, epistemes) to cultures. The Enlightenment, for example, is certainly more exotic to me than Bali (and as integrated). Nor is this simply because I, like nearly everybody else, have been to Bali; after all we are still surrounded by the Enlightenment or by its residual disenchantments. Whether cultures, isms, or eras, each reaches toward the other discursively, dialectically, ironically. What do eras, isms, and cultures (even nonliterate ones) do? They, in a manner of speaking, "write," too. By some means of inscription – graphic glyphs just one among them – each culture both differs and defers itself from whatever its sense of substantive presence might have been.

But more systematically, any society at some level (families at least; sometimes clans, even moieties) has its members marry categorical *others* in order by descent to reproduce the differences both constituted and bridged by incest taboos in the realm of sexuality and exogamy rules in the realm of marriage. Moreover, any culture requires its actors to counterdistinguish themselves, irreducibly segmented, from others: other worlds (divine, extraterrestrial), other eras (past idylls, future utopias), other languages, other cultures. In structuralist terms any discourse at some level alludes to the absences it intrinsically sets in abeyance: whether being (versus conceptualizing), speaking (versus writing–reading), sexuality (versus textuality), music (versus lettres), and so forth. Every discourse, like every culture, inclines toward what it is not: toward an implicit negativity.

The distinction between mechanistic and semiotic approaches revolves around the presence or absence of this sense of negativity. As is semiotically proper, "symbols and signs" are invoked by authors who in fact occupy different sides of the distinction. For example, H. D. Duncan and Kenneth Burke have similar analytic vocabularies and are often cited together; yet Duncan's important works (1961, 1968) on "symbols in society" are basically functionalist, while Kenneth Burke's symbolic action and dramatism represent a milestone in semiotic interpretation (cf. Peacock 1975). Short of a dialectic semiotics, the inevitable compromise between mechanism and symbolism is a stratigraphic model, with the bottom layer looking fundamental. By stacking culture above society above psychology above biology, the bottom appears solid and the top gauzy, with the middles less of both. A stratigraphic model readily converts into a cybernetic model that connects all the levels fairly with feedback loops. Unfortunately, many social scientists read Talcott Parsons this way, along with the theories of Durkheim and Weber that he consolidated. However, semiotic anthropologists such as D. Schneider and C. Geertz have refined and elaborated Parson's views cross-culturally by emphasizing two points: (1) Culture is the most general, least determined level which symbolically condenses the conflicts and harmonies of the other levels; and (2) the significant way to move laterally in human affairs is from culture to culture to...(cf. Singer 1977, 1968).

Some semioticians insist that even this is not enough, and they would call the present study relatively mechanistic, because it discusses societies, institutions, and the like. An important review by D. J. Umiker-Sebeok poses this semiotic "bone of contention" over the "place of the traditional society–culture split":

But Schneider, unlike Sahlins (1976a) or Sperber (1975), is unwilling to give up the distinction between culture and society. In response to criticism that his theory does not pay enough attention to action, he merely places his own concept of culture within T. Parsons' general theory of social action, the parallel systems of culture and society being mediated by what he calls norms, or moral propositions operating as templates for social action. The study of culture is concerned...with the study of social action as a meaningful system of action, and it is, therefore, by definition, concerned with the question of "meaning in action" (1976:198-99). Peacock (1975) also expresses dissatisfaction with traditional approaches to the relationship between society and culture. Like Schneider, he borrows from Parsons and, like Hymes (1968) and Geertz (1973), from K. Burke. It would appear that in British and North American anthropology Sahlins is alone in pursuing Lévi-Strauss' ideas concerning communication to their logical conclusion...Others, while recognizing the arbitrary distinction between practical and symbolic, refuse to make a total commitment to a theory which does away with it, so that analyses tend to focus on an isolated set of symbols, such as a corpus of myths or rituals, the "symbolic," with an explicit attempt to point out the "practical" or "functional" nature of the set in relation to "society" and/or ways in which society is reflected in symbolic practices. [1977:128–9]

I gnaw away at this issue by preserving a society/culture distinction, but not with the hope of correlating anything either way, much less positivistically lodging one in the other; rather the distinction is preserved as a "polar" way of identifying either. Total commitment to a semiotic approach requires not doing away with the distinction between practical and symbolic but recognizing it as a symbolic distinction. Semiotics poses "society" against and in terms of "culture" as mutually symbolic; likewise, "culture" and "language." (We might here recall as well Adorno's "negative dialectics," designed "to keep the idea of system itself alive while intransigently dispelling the pretensions of any of the contingent and already realized systems to validity and even to existence" – (Jameson 1971:55). *Cultures, our own included, admit each other into the realm of the contingent.*

The abstracted levels and systems of culture and action, like the infrastructures/superstructures of society and myth, do not enable us to reduce the general to a privileged determinant. Semiotically, levels and substructures are adduced not for reductionist but for paraphrastic purposes. They are the source of information that says something of what it is not. Human kinship, for example, reduced to genealogy or to biology is not "kinship" at all. Rather, kinship *is* precisely (and variously across cultures) what biology (standard across cultures) *isn't*. Or consider music(s) – a cultural domain in which, acoustical science notwithstanding, the distinction between "term" and gloss is ultimately inoperable; in which either everything is paraphrase or nothing is paraphrase. Music – a persistent concern of extramusicological scholars as different as Suzanne Langer and Lévi-Strauss – conceivably provides a sense of pure cultural paraphrasis. Regardless, it exists as relational variants alone. Music is perhaps the very model of negativity in Kenneth Burke's sense:

If we employ the expression "symbolic action" to designate the use of symbol systems generally (in tribal vernaculars, mathematics, philosophic or scientific nomenclatures, dancing, music, painting, architectural styles, etc.), we can safely say that insofar as any symbol system refers to any aspect of the nonsymbolic realm (the realm of sheer motion and position) there is a *qualitative* difference between the symbol and the symbolized. For the symbol is necessarily referring to the symbolized in terms of something that the symbolized is not (in the sense that the *thing* tree is not a *word*). [1966:480–1]

Music confirms the fact: Semiotics embraces negativity; dialectics requires as much.[1]

But were any negativity itself deemed absolute, it would cease to be semiotic. Thus I have argued a plurality of negatives, particularly when placing the contrast between structuralism and pragmatism-dramatism in "suspension," without diluting or dissolving it (Chapter 4). (Simply to avoid the contrast would be unanthropological; such contrasts are, after all, cultural). Geertz has called the method of cultural interpretation hermeneutic (1979:240). (In keeping with a hermeneutic rhythm, we circled through plenitudinous texts in Chapters 2, 5–7). But in anthropology hermeneutic intepretation involves more than History (whether defined religiously or philosophically) pulling itself away from its own would-be presence and interpreters striving to obliterate the distance between the self and the lost. Anthropology offers an enriched field of multiple languages and plural cultures. Again, a hermeneutics appropriate to plural cultures and histories brushes alongside negative dialectics whose nemesis is standardized (Enlightened) uniformity and whose circles or spirals of interpretation (versus explanation) are nothing if not bumpy. Any anthropological hermeneutics becomes – like anthropology's social theory – a hermeneutics with a difference (cf. Szondi 1978).

Back on the structuralist side of things, Edward Said has provided one of the more interesting critiques: "Structuralism replaces the darkening glass of traditional religion and literature...with a ready antiphony of equal sights and sounds" (1975:337). Does it replace, or does it supplement? It would, I think, be more accurate to say that structuralism (at least in the writings of Lévi-Strauss with which Said is concerned) admits the darkening glass with all the other prisms; it then privileges none of them, preferring complex ambiguity to reduced transparency. Moreover, Said seems in error in another provocative observation (here as elsewhere he pays little regard to the kinds of tribal institutions that, right or wrong, lay at the heart of structuralism's inspiration): "For the structuralists the whole world is contained within a gigantic set of quotation marks. *Everything* therefore, is a text – or using the same argument, *nothing* is a text" (1975:338). This formulation is too monolithic, still Hegel-tinged. In structuralist anthropology as in structural linguistics, absence "itself" is multiple.[2] It would be more accurate – less absolutist and synthetic – to suggest that for structuralists "nothingnesses are texts." This point has in fact become a rubric of "cultural semiotics:" "Each type of culture has a corresponding type of 'chaos' which is by no means primary, uniform, and always equal to itself, but which represents just as active a creation by man as does the sphere of cultural organization. Each historically given type of culture has its own type of nonculture peculiar to it alone" (Uspenskij et al. 1973:2; cf. Geertz 1973:109 n.33). Each historically given, culturally embedded type of cross-cultural approach likewise conceals a corresponding type of "chaos": for example, hortatory negativity versus mute *indifférence*, the noncultures of cultural interpretation and structuralism, respectively.

I would not wish to synthesize these negatives. For any synthesis, even a dramatistic one, can appear a compromise; and compromise, inevitably diluted, is not our goal. Rather, a semiotic view of cultures (which must include a view of itself, which must be reflexive) should subscribe to an exhaustion of extremes, à la Hindu mythology:

> There are, in fact, scattered Sanskrit epigrams closely akin to the Greek *meden agan* that [E. M.] Forster thought he saw in the Maharajah: "Excess must be avoided in all things." But this is not the prevalent Hindu attitude, nor is it the attitude underlying the mythological texts, which by their very nature tend to exaggerate all polarities, including potentially dangerous excesses.
>
> Hinduism [that is, its mythology] has no "golden mean"; it seeks the exhaustion of two golden extremes. It was perhaps as a reaction against this extremism that Buddha called his teaching "the Middle Path," explicitly rejecting both the voluptuous life which he had known as a prince and the violent asceticism which he had mastered at the start of his spiritual quest. Although the Buddhists also stated the problem explicitly in positive terms, recognizing the merit of both goals, the final choice was a negative one: there are two pleasures, the pleasure of the householder and the pleasure of asceticism, but the latter is pre-eminent. For the Buddha taught nirvana – literally, the extinguishing of the flame – while Siva embodied the flame and danced within it. Hinduism has no use for Middle Paths; this is a religion of fire and ice. [O'Flaherty 1973:82]

The fire/ice–like golden extremes of anthropology are, I suggest, the tribal and the scribal. Throughout this study we have employed "tribal" in the ethnological and not the holy scriptural sense. Aboriginal tribes idealize divisions such as clans, each of which, recalling Hertz's formulation for dual moieties, is "reciprocally opposed as sacred and profane" (1973:8) As we saw in Chapter 7, one tribal moiety is not sacred and the other profane; rather, each is both, vis-à-vis the other. Dualism's dialectical basis ensures balance, differentiation, and holism: anything *they* are to us, *we* are to them. (Must writing and the powers producing it disrupt such desirable qualities?)

In a sense nothing could be further from this aboriginal "tribal" than biblical traditions like the following:

> It is consistent that [the Old Testament] should lay stress upon the unique importance of Jerusalem as the cult centre of the Jewish faith in which the tribe of Judah stands for the secular arm and that of Levi for the spiritual, and it is quite appropriate that the tone of Nehemiah and Ezra should be one of bigoted sectarianism which demands above all else that Jews shall separate themselves off sharply from all foreigners and that there shall be no intermarriage between Jew and Gentile. For Nehemiah and Ezra such intermarriage is the sin of sins. [Leach 1969:44]

This variety of "tribal" tradition underlies Judeo-Christian history and the ideals of reformed and homogeneous communities behind Protestantism, nationalism, utopian visions of a New Jerusalem, and other varieties of Weber's "rationalization." To bring the biblical tribal into conformity with Australian,

South and Southeast Asian, and Amerindian tribal ideals (and in Chapter 5 we found the Tudor scholar Grafton unwittingly attempting just that!), one of two total transformations would be necessary. If the biblical tribe is conceptualized as all-Israel, then Levi must marry Judah, so that the spiritual and the secular exist not exclusively but oppositionally and complementarily. Or if the biblical tribe is all humankind, then Jew and Gentile, or later Christian and Heathen, must exchange spouses or otherwise reciprocate, circulate, communicate, discourse. To phrase the distinction more abstractly: (1) Aboriginal tribal cosmology (defining the limits of humankind quite narrowly) organizes its system of differences as mutual necessities; (2) biblical tribal cosmology (desiring to propagate a universalistic ethic) organizes its system of differences as mutual exclusions, at least until the Apocalypse.

Some scholars suspect that the "scribal" dimension of history and the centralizing tendencies facilitated by writing doom the first kind of cosmology to the fate of the second, eventuating in a spiceless "monoculture" of our doleful globe (Lévi-Strauss 1955, 1973). Thus small-scale reciprocal clans are eventually converted into exclusivistic sects, or stratified castes, or exploitative classes. Whether or not this view is adequate, anthropology's boldest hope has been a *victimless interpretation*, a deprivileged inscription extended to all cultures, not just ones chosen by God, or emergent through History, or emboldened by military might or economic advantage; above all not just ones centralized, homogenized, rationalized.

In the extreme, anthropological writing transposes, at times even rivals, the rituals, forms, and institutions and messages of those who do not write: nonliterates. Or anthropology converts to writing aspects of literate cultures ignored or denied by their own institutional writing. Typically and paradoxically, anthropology writes the unwritten, (the oral, the ritual, the total); or it rewrites the written (history, literature, ceremony) in light of values accentuated by the otherwise unwritten (myth, action, ritual). The discourse of cultures produces texts of the tribal/scribal, like two moieties dancing coolly and culturally in each other's flame.

Recognizing that all such differences must be begged, this book has explored, discursively, reconciliations of the tribal and scribal, without cooling the fire or melting the ice: from the antecedents to Frazer's prose of rites to the implications in Geertz's rites of prose. Our discourse remains caught between the fire of fieldwork (speaking, being, procreating, describing, kama) and the ice of ethnology (writing, ordering, asceticism, comparing, tapas). Like Tantrisms. How can I write cultures into each other's texts-between-texts?

"On vera alors," writes Mauss, *"qu'il y a eu et qu'il y a encore bien des lunes mortes, ou pâles, ou obscures, au firmament de la raison"* (1950:309) ("We will see that there have been and are plenty of dead moons, or pale, or obscure, in the firmament of reason.") For his part Kenneth Burke traces

Augustine's surmounting of his own Manichaean dilemma in an age, it retrospectively appears, still awed: "In contrast with the Manichaean doctrine of two rival powers, Good and Evil (the powers of Light and Darkness), equally substantial and confronting each other in universal combat, Augustine would contend after his conversion that good alone is real, an *ef*ficient cause, while evil is but a *def*icient cause, that is, an *eclipse* of goodness" (1970:87). Theodicy aside, the *figure* of the eclipse – darkness in the absence of light – poses an antinomy containing its own transcendence, or a polar distinction in light of a positive resolution. (But the gloom could just as well be victorious: lightness in the absence of dark.) The point is that light/dark is no mere opposition; either side might be encompassing: hierarchy in reciprocity. In either case the history of writing cultures becomes a shifting collage of contraries threatening (promising) to become unglued: *blaue Blumen* versus incandescent octopoi; Patagonian giants versus Enlightenment measure; Balinese ideal incest, McLennan's theories, our own taboos; Freud's renunciation of a religious "oceanic" versus Weber's confession of religious "unmusicality"; swashbuckling Crow *bourgeois*; semiotic slashes and dashes; odorous Moluccas; Jacobean Kings. . . and other surrealist facts and phrases. Ours is a discourse of aphorisms and e(c)llipses. . .

What, then, is the rejoinder of cross-cultural interpretation – goaded by fieldwork, resulting in writing – to the specter of uniformitarianism? Their/our answer lies not in a language but in translation; not in a culture or an era but dialectically in between. Insofar as all passing forms of enchantment – "sweet and solemn they chime" – leave traces in ethnological discourse, the paradox of their fate, and that of the discourse itself, intensifies:

Oubli or reenchantment?
Dead moons or eclipsed?

Appendixes

Dans son effort pour comprendre le monde, l'homme dispose donc toujours d'un surplus de signification.

Lévi-Strauss, *Sociologie et anthropologie*

The aptly named "structuralist controversy" (Macksey and Donato 1972) emerged in the postwar period as something of a structuralectics. Although anthropological functionalism was centered in the standard monograph, structuralism, semiotics, poststructuralism, and cultural interpretation as well – apart from a few extended corpora by a few central figures – have developed via articles, essays, and critiques, occasionally kindly, more often testy. The following pieces, a kind of postlude, touch on debates that have proliferated across disciplines, whose methods and isms seem at times to rival the diversity of cultures themselves.

Portions of Appendix A appeared as "What Little Girls Were Good For," *Psychology Today*, November 1978; a few paragraphs appeared in a review of C. Babcock, *Lévi-Strauss: Structuralism and Sociological Theory* (1976), in *Royal Anthropological Institute News*, May-June 1976; the opening paragraphs are revised from Boon (1973). A version of Appendix B appeared as "Anthropology's *Devata*" in *Semiotica* 21 (1977). Appendix C appeared in slightly different form in *Royal Anthropological Institute News*, August 1977.

Appendix A. Structuralectics

Reading Lévi-Strauss is, as he intends, a *Tristes tropiques*–like voyage into unexpected recollections of lingering structuralist processes. Perhaps the best place for an English reader to begin is *Structural Anthropology*, volume 2 (1973), a compilation of old and new essays and reviews that demonstrates Lévi-Strauss's consistency of approach, his sense of cultural relativity and "tolerance," and his hopes for structural–diffusionist studies on the scale of Wasson's overwhelming work on Vedic *Soma* (1968). Having seen how close Lévi-Strauss remains to Boas and Lowie, one can better profit from the many outstanding translations painstakingly produced by Rodney Needham, John and Doreen Weightman, and others. After swimming through the complete translation of *Tristes tropiques*, one might back-paddle to the original *Structural Anthropology*, using the "Social Structure" article as a diving board into *The Elementary Structures of Kinship*. Before totally submerging oneself in that sea of contention, one should come up for air into *Totemism* and then dip carefully into *The Savage Mind* (being wary of the poor translation of this particular book and the in-house Parisian discourse of the concluding chapter). Finally, after sampling Lévi-Strauss's aesthetic conversations with G. Charbonnier, one can plunge into the volumes of *Mythologiques* to swirl through the composer's final analogy of the nature of cultural variation and the limits we enjoy in comprehending it: *la musique*.

Lévi-Strauss's approach to "myth" employs complex texts (1) found in *multiple* versions across different groups and languages, (2) as evidenced *indirectly* by the translations of oral performances gathered by fieldworkers, (3) developed by and for members of the whole *society* (as is possible in small preliterate groups with their "communal censorship" of expressive forms), (4) at a more or less *unconscious* level of selection and interrelation of distinctive features from fragments of the groups' experience – which selection is influenced by, but in no simple and direct relationship with, the ethnographic context. In brief, *Mythologiques* studies a particular human capacity – the analogical capacity (first sketched as *la pensée sauvage*, which is defined as "analogical thought"). *Mythologiques* studies that capacity by concentrating on human phenomena that seem most confined to it, namely preliterate texts of the sort defined above.

Lévi-Strauss analyzes at a distance the mythic motifs that have been exchanged among groups with different social organizations and languages or maintained by two once-identical groups as their social organizations and languages diverge (or, if we follow his implications to the limit, perhaps social organization and languages have been exchanged across myths). He maps the patterns of principles behind differences the myths assume, as when one variant presents a set of elements in an inverse relation to the same set of elements in another variant. He calls what he maps "structure." As some portion of a myth is borrowed, transformations occur; or if a group splits, its once coterminous mythic corpus is differentiated in dialectic with the now-different ethnographic conditions and historical events. The most general principle behind the studies is that "matter is the instrument, not the object of signification. In order that it yield to this role, it is first necessary to impoverish it: retaining from it only a small number of elements suitable for expressing contrasts and for forming pairs of oppositions" (1964:346–7; my translation). His vast empirical demonstrations disclose codes of interrelationships across different orders of experience – as when myths depict the dawn of cooking and dining customs as norms or when concepts of cyclical time are symbolized by female biological cycles and solar and seasonal phenomena. Different societies can be culturally contrasted according to the different orders selected. Lévi-Strauss thus considers New World Indian myth as a continually selecting and reselecting totality but never a synthesized whole:

> From the start, then, I ask the historian to look upon Indian America as a kind of Middle Ages which lacked a Rome: a confused mass that emerged from a long-established doubtless very loosely textured syncretism, which for many centuries had contained at one and the same time centers of advanced civilization and savage peoples, centralizing tendencies and disruptive forces. . . [The set of myths], such as the one studied here, owes its character to the fact that in a sense it became crystallized in an already established semantic environment, whose elements had been used in all kinds of combinations – not so much, I suppose, in a spirit of imitation but rather to allow small but numerous communities to express their different originalities by manipulating the resources of a dialectical system of contrasts and correlations within the framework of a common conception of the world. [1969b:8]

Only by moving across groups and languages, as the myths themselves have, can we discern the principles of order that set societies apart from each other while leaving them interrelatable. As Lévi-Strauss concludes:

> Rarely seized upon at their origin and in a state of vitality, these relationships of opposition between myths emerge vigorously from a comparative analysis. If thus the philological study of myths does not constitute an indispensable preliminary approach, the reason for this lies in what one might call myths' diacritical nature. Each of the myths' transformations results from a dialectical opposition to another transformation, and their essence resides in the irreducible fact of translation *by* and

for opposition. Considered from an empirical point of view, every myth is at once pristine [*primitif*] in relation to itself, and derived in relation to other myths; it is situated not *in* a language and *in* a culture or sub-culture, but at the point of articulation of cultures with other languages and other cultures. Myth is thus never in its language [*de sa langue*], it is a perspective on *another language*...[1971:577; my translation]

Lévi-Strauss strikes a similar note in a sequel to *Mythologiques, La voie des masques* (1975a), a study of Northwest Amerindian masks and ritual and social contexts in light of his earlier mythic studies. Critics who complain that *Mythologiques* never correlates "myth" (which Lévi-Strauss construes as broadly as Boas did) with anything external will need to take fresh soundings of the myth volumes after pursuing this continuation into visual materials. The distribution of varying styles and motifs in the masks exchanged among Northwest Coast tribes again evidences the sort of oppositional codes and systematic inversions that, Lévi-Strauss insists, compose a semantic universe that identifies and differentiates New World preliterates.

Thus continuing his controversial and grandiose excursion into myth, Lévi-Strauss arrived at the culmination of his career – his mythic tetralogy complete, himself admitted to the Académie Française after wedging ethnology further into the highest resistant organization of French academia. Yet from this Olympian vantage Lévi-Strauss redescribed his life's work ultimately as a rejection of anthropological functionalism:

One of the most pernicious notions bequeathed us by functionalism – one which still holds many ethnologists under its sway – is the notion of isolated tribes [peuplades], closed in on themselves, each living on its own account a particular experience of mythic, ritual, or aesthetic order. One thereby fails to understand that before the colonial era and the destructive effects from afar exercised (even in the most remote regions) by the Western world with its pathogenic germs and exported goods, these more numerous populations were also more interlocking [*coude à coude*]. With a few exceptions nothing that transpired in one went unnoticed by its neighbors, and the modalities by which each explained itself and represented its universe were elaborated in a dialogue, uninterrupted and vehement. [1975a, Vol. 2:118–19; my translation]

Lévi-Strauss's rejection of functionalism is particularly vivid in *The Origin of Table Manners* (1978), the third and pivotal book in his four-volume study of traditional South and North American mythology. Indian populations never developed a permanent centralized state and lacked a standardized writing system; thus their myths emerge from various circumstances of language, environment, and social organization. Yet Lévi-Strauss seeks to understand myths and their contexts according to a total system of implicit meanings and not with an eye to any particular tribe, place, or time. He both detects the rules that transform one tribal myth to another and suggests translations of myths into our own logical, ethical, philosophical, and scientific paradigms.

Because myths are basically "in between," they are ideal subjects for the so-called structuralism Lévi-Strauss has championed in cultural anthropology. Myths establish connections between the different ways tribes acquire, prepare, and consume foodstuffs (hence "table manners") and how they organize diverse aspects of their languages, rituals, social structures, ecologies, music, and beliefs. The details of myths sound to us unseemly; for example, Plains Indian styles of trophy ornamentation: scalps, porcupine quillwork (the typical female craft), or human pubic hair (p. 404). Indeed many myths recall those Arapaho tales that "from a certain distance... appear rather like a cross between a picturesque and exotic Book of Genesis and a decorous version of *The Story of O*" (1978:227). But for Lévi-Strauss myths employ such contents to relate codes to codes: astronomical cycles, menstrual cycles, and seasonal cycles; social cycles and so forth. Myths signify signification. Their fractured metaphors and unexpected relationships – whether pubic hair trophies or swallowed chickadee songs – form part of mytho-logics in the same way that phonetic sounds are part of languages or "scaled" tones compose music.

Lévi-Strauss demonstrates that the ethical concerns of North American Indians focused on "good little girls." Different tribes obliged their daughters to dine, converse, groom, court, and, yes, menstruate, in strikingly different fashions, because each tribe felt its social harmony and balance depended on the distinctive etiquette of its daughters. This basic assumption of Indian societies (often made up of intermarrying clans) explains the elaboration, diversity, and seeming arbitrariness of customary restrictions of women:

> When a young Indian woman from the Chaco or the surrounding areas first began to menstruate, she was laced up in a hammock and remained suspended...throughout the west and north-west of North America, a girl menstruating for the first time was not allowed to touch the ground with her feet, nor to look at the sun...The Algonquin of the Great Lakes area merely required her to keep her eyes lowered. Any contact between her hands and her body or domestic utensils would have been fatal. Among several Athapaskan tribes, she wore mittens, used a scratcher for her head and back, and sometimes even for her eyelids, drank through a tube and picked up her food with a sharpened bone (unless some other girl was given the task of putting the pieces into her mouth one by one)...Menstruating girls could drink neither hot nor cold beverages, only tepid ones. Their solid food also had to be lukewarm; it could not be raw (in the case of the Eskimo who often ate their food raw), nor undercooked in the case of the Shuswap, nor fresh in the case of other tribes; nor boiled, in the case of the Cheyenne. The Klikitat, for their part, forbade the eating of rancid food. [1978:500–1]

How a particular tribe's daughters eat is part and parcel of how she is obliged to menstruate. By such differences tribal Americans ordered and distinguished their cultures. The meticulous culinary rules that set off different tribes were analyzed from other angles in *The Raw and the Cooked*, but the themes continue throughout *Mythologiques*. As always, Lévi-Strauss contrasts those rich tribal codes to our own rites of passage and dietary customs that have been homogenized, standardized, and seem universally imperative:

> We have changed our table manners then, and adopted others, the norm of which at least has been generalized throughout the Western world, where different ways of

chewing no longer denote national or local traditions; they are merely either good or bad. In other words, and contrary to what we have observed in exotic societies, eating habits for Westerners no longer constitute a *free code*: we opt for some habits and prohibit others, and we conform to the first in order to transmit a *compulsory message*. [1978:499]

The "free code" of tribal cooking customs and table manners complements the code of menstrual seclusion, providing that girls behave themselves. In fact, menstruating daughters are highly regulated and as crucial to a tribe's well-being as its warrior sons; for example: "The menstruating girl can drink neither hot nor cold liquids for the same reason that she is not allowed to eat fresh or tainted food. She is subject to a violent internal commotion, which would become even more violent if her organism ingested solids or liquids that were, in one sense or another, strongly marked."

Table Manners provides unprecedented perspectives on tribal gerontology, sex-role dichotomy, and ideals of socialization, all woven into meaningful relationships by myths. Just to suggest Lévi-Strauss's complex summary:

The myths use the theme of ageing...to introduce a fundamental category, that of periodicity, which modulates human existence by assigning it a certain duration, and by establishing, within this duration, the major physiological rhythms which have their seat in the female organism. We have also learned from other myths that the education of girls is mainly achieved by the mental and biological interiorization of periodicity.
    We now see that the absence of mediatory utensils such as combs, head-scratchers, mittens, and forks between the subject and her body causes the hair to turn white, the skin to wrinkle, etc. [1978:506]

In the concerted universe of tribal myths, old age, mortality, war rules, menstrual cycles, and domestic technology are culturally as interconnected as the natural fact of night following day – and following night.

Several words of caution. Controversy over *Mythologiques* has burgeoned since the series began appearing in French in 1964. For example, some critics have accused Lévi-Strauss of reducing the symbolic significance of women to their biological condition. But this charge ignores the fact that Lévi-Strauss investigates menstruation only as one cycle among the many cultural cycles outlined by the myths. Moreover, the myths themselves hardly suggest that women are "natural" and men "cultural"; rather, they pose women and men as transformations. Lévi-Strauss pursues a theme begun in *Tristes tropiques* (chap. 23) in *Table Manners*.

"According to the myths discussed in this volume, it was boys in South America and girls in North America who, at the onset of puberty, were the first repositories of these rules of good behavior." If females are "natural" from the vantage of North America, males are natural in South America. Lévi-Strauss underscores the variance recognized by the myths themselves, where women and men appear (for the purposes of meaningful codes) transformations of each other. This variance also allows Lévi-Strauss playfully to place North America together with European moral philosophy. The musical epigraphs of *The Raw and the Cooked* are replaced in *Table Manners* with ethical epigraphs – in turn replaced in *L'homme nu* (1971) with metaepigraphs – epigraphs on the nature and purpose of epigraphs. North American Indian etiquette is paralleled by excerpts from Erasmus, Montaigne, Chateaubriand, and particularly Rousseau, whose *Emile* likewise situated the well-being of civil society in the manners of regulated, that is to say educated, daughters.

Finally, besides male/female, senility/youth, and sex/death, *Table Manners* also considers less grandiose issues, like chickadees. To take one of the many comic mythic images Lévi-Strauss investigates, members of the Ojibwa tribe believed that "there will be a storm if the chickadee swallows the last syllable of its song: "*Gi-ga-be*; *gi-ga-be; gi-ga-me.*" Obviously, the swallowed syllable involves the m/b distinction of the phonological spectrum. But to understand how the chickadee's oral apparatus symbolizes units of time as well as language, we must turn to the more elaborate views of the Shoshones. Did you know that chickadees have barbed tongues? Traditional Shoshones could hardly forget it:

> The chickadee is usually non-migrant. But its tongue is barbed with filaments, of which – according to the Shoshone – there are six; one falls off each month and grows again six months later, so that it is possible to tell, by capturing a chickadee, which month in winter or in summer it is. This is why it is wrong to kill chickadees. . . The belief is sufficiently widespread to be also found among the Mandan and the Hidatsa, who reckon the months of the year from the Chickadee's tongue. [1978:236]

That chickadee tongues can symbolize different months explains their relevance to thunderstorms. Similarly, the entire volume explores relations among temporal, natural, and cultural cycles: seasonal change, menstruation, solar and lunar phenomena, the ritual organization of hunting and warfare, and ultimately the Amerindian logic that relates scalped men to menstruating women; for that story you must read the book!

Lévi-Strauss thus modulates the shriller issues of our "human condition" with the softer obsessions of Ojibwas. This fact helps explain his rejection of existentialism, expressed forcibly in *Tristes Tropiques, The Savage Mind*, and *L'homme nu*. He thinks that a self-centered existentialism arose from an arrogant humanism that assumed tribal orders were isolated and closed, when in fact the West itself was becoming a "reservation," trapped in the conformity of standardized *compulsory message*.

In contrast to such humanism, *Mythologiques* explores tribal myth without a synthetic vision of some conformist brotherhood or sisterhood of universal Man and/or Woman. Lévi-Strauss's science of mythology – challenging, controversial, contentious, and pervaded with ethnological *hauteur* – contains nevertheless a humbling ethical moral. Again, as demonstrated in the *Origin of Table Manners*, women's place in North American mythology is assumed by men in South American mythology. Neither Man nor Woman can more justly claim to be, as the humanist saying goes, "the measure of all things" than the Shoshones' lowly winter bird, the black-capped tit with the barbed tongue that subdivides time itself.

Appendix B. Trickstering

All languages are littered with such petrified bodies. The English -*ster* of *spinster* and *Webster* is an old agentive suffix, but, as far as the feeling of the present English-speaking generation is concerned, it cannot be said to really [sic] exist at all; *spinster* and *Webster* [*Webster's*!] have been completely disconnected from the etymological group of *spin* and of *weave* (*web*).

E. Sapir, Language

Edmund Leach has collected some structuralist chips from his workshop and organized them into *Culture and Communication*, a step-by-step manual for anthropological analyses of ritual and myth. The style is casual lecturese, full of warnings and disclaimers, which exercises the reader in a frame of mind without ever thoroughly defending the concept of "culture as communication." Many topics are dropped as soon as they are introduced – kinship and marriage, color codes, music, etc. – and much recent work in these areas is ignored. Leach prefers to emphasize the meanings of "customs other than verbal customs" until he comes to his own treatment of the Bible as an "ethnographic monograph" (not an ethnographic document) offered in lieu of those "potted ethnographies" he feels clutter other introductory texts. Whenever an explication of a custom or image is truncated, the student is implored simply to look about – whether at Judaeo-Christian rituals and texts or at slang usages and lexical taboos like the play between bunny/cunny and others earlier documented in the author's admirable "Animal Categories and Verbal Abuse" (1964a) – to see what Leach has been driving at.

The book should prove useful in the classroom, because it develops a few themes from several different directions, such as the following equivalences:
Symbol/Sign = Metaphor/Metonymy
             = Paradigmatic association/Syntagmatic chain
             = Harmony/Melody
This series alone could keep ardent semioticians arguing for months; and it is to Leach's credit that he never hesitates to disentangle an issue in order to initiate students in diverse structuralist and semiotic concerns, including distinctions of signs, symbols, signals, icons, indexes, and other matters bequeathed by Saussure and Peirce. Yet the drawback to such simplification

248

becomes increasingly evident as Leach gradually dilutes his major thrust to a truism of modern symbolic or cultural analyses: "A sign or symbol only acquires meaning when it is discriminated from some other contrary sign or symbol" (p. 49). Even Marxists, social structuralists, phenomenologists, and existentialists, who reserve some sort of essentialist base for communication codes – whether the material means of production, the group's organization, the personal and social "self," or the philosophical abyss – would at some level agree with this general tenet of linguistics and set-theory. Leach's own distinctive view of symbol systems – which stresses the emotive aspects of categorical infringements – appears in occasional sentences and quips but does not inform the book as a whole. This pedagogical exercise thus lacks much of the analytic incisiveness that has become its author's trademark; but it still provides an occasion for us to assess certain semiotic underpinnings of Leach's always-provocative outlook on symbolic forms.

Ever since *Rethinking Anthropology* (1961) Edmund Leach has tantalized comparativist scholars with analytic metaphors from mathematics, computer science, and experimental studies in perception: cross-cultural analysis as topology; mythic thinking as binary computer language (Leach has insisted on this idea even more than its earlier proponent, Lévi-Strauss); taboo as the repression of those inherent ambiguities that lie behind categorical distinctions. In this study as well the confirmed ex-engineer seems most comfortable when discussing the "mapping" of time and space (chap. 11). Similarly, in recent stateside lectures Leach has compared the "structures" in mythology to those invisible grids which one must unconsciously know to read a map at all, but which could only interfere with understanding the map if they entered the reader's explicit awareness. This is an apt metaphor: One cannot find anything on Columbus's charts without knowing the appropriate projection; but no map should be constructed as a picture *of* its projection system. Rather it is a picture of "the world" organized according to this logical scheme. So far this example is a neat visual analogue to Lévi-Strauss's celebrated, revisionist mechanical metaphor which likened structuralist abstractions in their relation to "empirical reality" not (as he attributes to Radcliffe-Brown) to the jigsaw puzzle itself but to mathematical formulae behind the shape and rotation of the cams which cut the puzzle-pieces (Lévi-Strauss 1963b). But Leach goes on in his work on ambiguity and taboo to insist that the blockage – again, one might almost call it the repression – of any awareness of the organizing apparatus is also crucial. We must necessarily repress the "structure" if we are to make use of what it organizes, whether map or myth. The necessity *not* to be thinking directly of the structuring apparatus explains the affect-laden response when classificatory boundaries are trangressed (and thus, so to speak, raised into consciousness) either exceptionally or during ritual events – the horror of incest, the disgust or comedy of inversion, the nervousness behind curse-words and sexual slang. Leach thus joins Mary Douglas, Victor Turner, and other margins-oriented scholars who find the blurred borders of distinguished entities to be supercharged with significance:

A boundary separates two zones of social space-time which are *normal, time-bound, clear-cut, central, secular*, but the spatial and temporal markers which actually serve as boundaries are themselves *abnormal, timeless, ambiguous, at the edge, sacred.* [p. 35]

By equating centers with the secular and borders with sacred-dangerous or taboo, they manage to set Durkheim's sacred/profane (= center/periphery) on its head, but in a way that is consistent with the master's sense of religious and intellectual categorizing.

As in his earlier studies of Genesis and Solomon (1969), Leach brazenly addresses scripture. This project directly rejects Lévi-Strauss's longtime, although lately somewhat modified, insistence that oral, non-literate, collectively rehearsed materials (those submitted to what Jakobson has called "communal censorship") are the only proper province for a thoroughly structuralist approach. Leach indeed reaches beyond small, face-to-face non-literate societies that classify themselves in counter-distinction to what they think of other groups and of their surroundings – the limited realm of Lévi-Strauss's *Mythologiques* – into texts that structuralists have in the past written off as either "literarized," distorted by political interest, or, worst of all, historicized. But Leach is, I think, on firm ground here, because he addresses precisely those aspects of Biblical organization, language, and imagery which structuralism has shown to be vital in message-sending. Leach asks neither how the Bible was composed nor what exact relations tie its assembled episodes to the complex contexts that produced them or to equally complex issues and commentaries (e.g., Maryolatry and Virgin-Birth) they have helped generate. Rather he asks the other kind of structuralist question: what possibly holds "the Bible" (and also later Biblical exegesis) together as a corpus of variants besides its binding? There are, after all, *four* gospels, not one, all telling what is considered to be the same revealed truth. The accounts are repetitive but not identical, and sometimes superficially inconsistent; and many episodes, especially as later developed in patristic and scholastic commentaries, hinge on logical contradictions, actually oxymorons:

Christianity affords some very striking examples: the concept of the Virgin-Mother of God is one; the proposition that God the Son was "begotten" of God the Father, even though God the Father, God the Son, and God the Holy Ghost have been one and the same and identical from the beginning, is another. Admittedly even devout Christians have great difficulty in "understanding" such mysteries, but it certainly cannot be argued that just because religious propositions are non-logical (in the ordinary sense) they must be meaningless. [p. 70]

Leach insists that redundancy and ambiguity are central to mythic message-making. What appear as obstacles for literalists become opportunities for structuralists who, following *Mythologiques*, pose the central question: What cross-referenced covert codes enable one to argue with increasing thorough-ness that some assortment of materials (some set of variants) is a corpus? Various properties of Biblical discourse appear sensical if they are approached from the vantage of mythic (in Lévi-Strauss's sense of communication by variants) as opposed to historicist means of organizing – and yes, even reveal-ing – things. One might say that the essence, such as it is, of myth is something that can only be said two or more ways. While not quite ineffable, the point of myth is the order among its contrasts, and its true significance lies between mere words, languages, or referential concepts. For Lévi-Strauss, and perhaps even more for Leach, myth is oxymoron that never quits.

Unlike literalist historians, Leach would not have the Bible or its subse-quent commentaries apologize for their structuralist nature. The Bible and the discourse of Biblical theology repeatedly surmount contradictions through transformations: Old Testament sacrifice appears retrospectively as a "figure" of New Testament crucifixion (and the Eucharist foreshadowing it); Old Tes-tament "prophets of tribes" become New Testament "father-sons of families," and the complementary imagery of prostitutes and virgins provides metaphors for expanding Judaeo-Christian paradoxes of faith.

Because we happen to know a great deal about the history of Christianity we can see that the cross-references and symbolic transformations in this particular case have been exceedingly involved. The Christian Mass, as a whole, is a transformation of the Jewish Passover, and the crucified Christ "is" the sacrificial paschal lamb, "the lamb of God." The bread and wine is on this account associated with the meat of the sacrifice not only by metaphor but also by metonymy (cf. Leviticus 23). [pp. 92–93]

We might note that Leach's Biblical analyses are really no more avant garde than those of typological approaches. His project perhaps complements the outlook of Biblical experts such as James Barr, who argues that the Old Testament story "spirals back and forward across history, sometimes coming closer to it, sometimes going farther away from it," and later deems the story itself "a massive literary form, made up from many sources but having its own integrity and consistency in the midst of multitudinous differences" (1976:8, 9). Good news indeed for structuralists!

Of course it is not Leach's purpose to compete with Biblical scholars on their own ground; rather he challenges us to include once again Biblical traditions within general theories of sacrifice, myth, and ritual as developed by ethnologists. Thus, the Parvati and Siva tales from Hinduism reveal the by-now familiar sort of ambiguities:

Siva is the most ascetic of all yogis and his divine power derives from asceticism; yet, as the consort of Parvati, the most beautiful woman in the universe, who was expressly created to seduce the unseducible Siva, he is the most passionate of all lovers.

Stories of this kind are not invented simply as exercises in the art of paradox, they contain practical implication. The devout Brahmin has a moral duty to produce male offspring, but he also has a moral duty to move progressively in the direction of sexual asceticism. The myth provides a charter for both modes of activity. The notions of divine purity, achieved through asceticism, and of divine power, achieved through ecstacy, are interdependent concepts, the one implies the other. [p. 74]

The "double-bound" Brahmin roles and the Christian oxymorons are examples of what Leach has elsewhere called the *devata* pattern in religious systems:

The purpose of all religious activity is to obtain benefit from this ultimate sacred source but, as a rule, direct approach to the *deva* is felt to be too dangerous. In defense against this danger, religions have created a great variety of secondary gods, goddesses, godlings, saints, prophets, mediums, who are thought to exercise supernatural power by derivation from the original source and who can, on that account, act as intermediaries between man and God. These secondary deities I label *devata*. [1962]

What is inadmissible as fence-sitting in political thought is productive as boundary-straddling in mythic thought. Tricksters, saints, dying gods, elephant eunuchs, bodhishatva, monks, repentant profligates, virgin-like prostitutes – such *devata*-types display all sorts of emotive and experiential excesses in order to bridge the necessary gaps of religious cosmology.

No more fitting image could be found to characterize Leach's own creative role in comparative anthropology. The Cambridge provost's trickster-like provocation has grown proverbial, not only in his discussions of bunny/cunny, but in the driest analytic issues of kinship analysis. Thus in a technical discussion of kin terms and descent, Leach can assert:

The link between matrilineal descent and this particular kin-term usage (father's sister = father's sister's daughter) is a matter of logic. The correlation can be directly inferred from the operations necessary to produce a satisfactory definition of the expression "matrilineal descent group." What is surprising is not the empirical association of facts but the lack of it. [1968a:340]

This off-hand dismissal of G. P. Murdock's statistical catalogues of cross-cultural correlations (between things like descent principles and terminological usages) has a doubtless intentional ring of Gibbonian irony: compare ". . . instead of inquiring why the Roman Empire was destroyed, we should rather be surprised that it had subsisted so long." It is this intellectual agility, particularly conspicuous in post–WW II British anthropology, that helped Leach's *Political Systems of Highland Burma* (1964b) and *Rethinking Anthropology* (1961) enliven so many areas of anthropological theory. Leach still writes mischievously – whether ending an awkward summary of Lévi-Strauss's musical analogy of mythic arrangement and analysis with a purposefully clumsy pastiche of a French reflexive ("We engage in rituals in order to transmit collective messages to ourselves," p. 45), or abruptly glossing "dyadic" as "two-faced" (p. 11).

Some of the provocative irony in Leach's later works stems from his fundamental, yet unclarified, ambivalence about structuralist methods themselves, and in particular about Lévi-Strauss. Sometimes Leach commends an analysis which Lévi-Strauss bases on relationships by inversion between two codes (Leach 1967); sometimes any hint of inverting codes is scathed by Leach as just one more instance of Lévi-Straussian chicanery (Leach 1970:117). The tone of such disputes degenerated with the aggravation of the feud between Leach and Lévi-Strauss over who edged out whom in penetrating the systematic implications of Kachin matrilateral cross-cousin marriage. If Leach finds inversion of codes admissible in some instances (such as when Lévi-Strauss confirms the Tsimshian explicit opposition of sky/earth by a transferred and implicit opposition of sky/water in his analysis of the Asdiwal *geste*) but not in others (such as when Lévi-Strauss argues that the New World code of honey as sperm is confirmed by evidence of the perfect inversion of honey as menstrual blood), shouldn't he specify the conditions he feels distinguish the two cases (cf. Leach 1970 versus Leach 1967)?

Beyond these technical disputes, the feud between Leach and Lévi-Strauss is probably more profound than either has ever clearly admitted. Leach remains, as all his talk of "charters" suggests and as he has increasingly confessed, semi-functionalist even as he pursues structuralist ends:

Both viewpoints accept the central dogma of functionalism that cultural details must always be viewed in context, that everything is meshed with everything else. In this regard the two approaches, the empiricist (functionalist) and the rationalist (structuralist) are complementary rather than contradictory; one is a transformation of the other. [p. 5]

It is precisely this transformation that Leach himself means to embody. In his own works, Lévi-Strauss has increasingly distanced himself from functionalism, especially insofar as it tends to reify and isolate closed groups in space and time (Lévi-Strauss 1975a, II:118–19). The larger issue reflected here is that Lévi-Strauss has moved more and more toward one kind of semiotic viewpoint, while Leach has not.

Lévi-Strauss has discarded various functionalisms and formalisms earlier tried on for size. Well into *Mythologiques* we hear no more of periodic charts of mythic "mental enclosures" or of some hoped-for calculus of mythic materials, presumably because differentials in a calculus must be distinguished by relations to a *constant* of the sort Lévi-Strauss has ultimately rejected. Leach retains metaphors both of a calculus and of "deep structures," whether positivistic ones or heuristic ones – metaphors which have vanished from Lévi-Strauss's concerns. The few early allusions by Lévi-Strauss to parallels between structures of the brain and structures of myths were transferred in *La Pensée sauvage* to the more ambiguous concept of *esprit*. And by *Mythologiques* Lévi-Strauss seems satisfied to describe his trajectory as a dialectical movement from text, to text, to text. . .(remembering that contexts themselves are by selection and disjunction converted into mythic texts) – each new variant affording a fuller translation of New World mythology, but no final analysis being closer to anything mental or innate or anything else; "only the voyage is real" (cf. Boon 1972: chap. VI):

...both the natural and the human sciences concur to dismiss an outmoded philosophical dualism. Ideal and real, abstract and concrete, "emic" and "etic" can no longer be opposed to each other. What is immediately "given" to us is neither the one nor the other, but something which lies betwixt and between, that is, already encoded by the sense organs as well as by the brain, *a text* which, like any text, must be first decoded to translate it into the language of other texts...Never can man be said to be immediately confronted with nature in the way that vulgar material- ism and empirical sensualism conceive it. For nature appears more and more made up of structural properties undoubtedly richer although not different in kind from the structural codes in which the nervous system translates them, and from the structural properties elaborated by the understanding in order to go back, as much as it can do so, to the original structures of reality. It is not being mentalist or idealist to acknowledge that the mind is only able to understand the world around us because the mind itself is part and product of this same world. Therefore the mind, when trying to understand it, only applies operations which do not differ in kind from those going on in the natural world itself. [Lévi-Strauss 1972:241][1]

In contrast, Leach's latest lectures still invoke "deep structures" as well as isolated human brains; and he suggests that a mythic or ritual pattern gives direct insight into these objective things whenever he cannot relate it to something specifically located in time and space, that is to something functionalist.

Yet however far apart Leach and Lévi-Strauss now stand, they still share a reluctance to address the critical issue of developing a genuine typology of mythology in the way, for example, a genre theory develops typologies of literature. (There is just a brief hint of this in *Mythologiques III*, when Lévi- Strauss poses "serial myths" as a specialized development of general myth.) In fact, if one explains *devata* figures merely as evidence that human minds or brains work this way, as Leach is still prone to do, one ignores the whole issue of variability. Or if, *d'après* Lévi-Strauss, one rolls fulsomely from myth to myth to myth in an ever surging crescendo of cross-cultural insights into the so-called conditions of possibility afforded by sets of mythic distinctions and relations, one can never articulate anything typological about Semitic myth versus pan-Indo-European myth (cf. Dumézil 1966–71), versus Oceanic myth (cf. Boon 1977: chap. 9), versus New World myth, etc. Somewhere between Leach's localism-as-evidence-of-brain-skills and Lévi-Strauss's sometimes rarified cosmic-universalism, there is a lot of mediating work to be done.

This is not, however, to gainsay Leach's own vigorous contributions to the anthropology of myth and ritual. By managing to keep one foot in empiricism, functionalism, and positivism, and another foot in rationalism, structuralism and dialectics (not to mention all the other feet – such are the advantages of a mythic Brother Trickster!), Leach has brought to anthropological studies that very ambiguity/ambivalence that he has championed in cultural studies of symbolic systems. Occasionally in *Culture and Communication* and repeatedly in earlier articles and books, Sir Edmund Leach manages, by bridging a basic epistemological chasm of comparative research, to rival those very *devata* that he has, perhaps more than anyone else, helped to illuminate.

Appendix C. Dia-tribes

Toward the end of Stanley Diamond's important collection of essays, *In Search of the Primitive*, appears the dour warning: "For structuralism, epitomized in Lévi-Strauss, is the intellectual ideology, and the immanent logic, of a new, technocratic totalitarianism" (1975:297). Readers who have, perhaps unwittingly, been exposed to such pernicious influence should not recoil too hastily, because they might inadvertently step back into yet another case from Diamond's very long list of such totalitarian and/or technocratic tendencies in the history of the West's views of other cultures. Indeed, the list stretches at least from Plato's *Republic* to "Parsonian and related systematics" (p. 213). While Diamond's concerns were expressed judiciously in the 1950s, by the late 1960s developments in the U.S. – Vietnam, counterculture – had convinced him that the complex historical process called civilization or state formation (which entails literacy, stratification, and property ownership, along with their related alienations) is itself epitomized by its cruelest results:

Fascism is grounded in state capitalism, bureaucratic autonomy and class collaboration; its goal is the "integration" of all into the hierarchical system, by reducing persons to integers.
What I am getting at is that the link – let us call it the Mylai link – between the bureaucratic personality and affective dissociation, the link that leads to murder at a great psychic distance no matter what the proximity of the victim, is not fortuitous, but necessary for the ultimate success of the system, even though it means the destruction of the counter culture's potential. [pp. 354, 355]

Now, taking, as Diamond does, the Nazi *Schutzstaffel*, Mylai, and Biafra to stereotype this dimension of human history recalls taking infant marriage, widow burning, and beef-prohibition-despite-the-starving-masses to stereotype archaic Hinduism – or taking nudity, polygamy, and infanticide to brand "the primitive." This last example of sensationalistic selectivity is one of the fallacies Diamond insistently rejects in the earlier chapters of *In Search of the Primitive*. Why he is increasingly unable to appreciate the pitfalls of such stereotyping for "civilization" – defined by Diamond purely

255

in opposition to the primitive – is an intriguing aspect of this degenerative book.

Several of Diamond's constructive chapters reinvigorate anthropology's role in general social theory. His central theme is "an inductive model of primitive society informed by the problem of civilization" (p. 206); put most grandly:

> The search for the primitive is, then, as old as civilization. It is the search for the utopia of the past, projected into the future, with civilization being the middle term. It is birth, death, and transcendent rebirth, the passion called Christian, the trial of Job, the oedipal transition, the triadic metaphor of human growth, felt also in the vaster pulse of history. And this search for the primitive is inseparable from the vision of civilization. [p. 208]

This book is an integrated set of reflections on the sense of civilization that has characterized diverse state systems and on the place of the primitive in Western letters – in particular as it is militated against by Plato, repressed in the Book of Job, properly situated as an axiom for conceptualizing civility by Rousseau, and prophetically returned to in action by Marx.

For example, Diamond rightly credits Rousseau, "the parent of our retrospective tendency," with first forging the two components, an interior-personal and exterior-civic, of what must be the same anthropological quest:

> Rousseau, alienated by the rising bourgeoisie, the new urbanism, the pervading commercialism and acquisitiveness, the droning bureaucracies and the estrangement of men from the natural and human rhythms, devoted most of his energies to the retrospective search for the means of uniting technical education and a more fully human socialization...But it is important to recall that this was a matter of emphasis. Despite the epigrammatic Voltaire, Rousseau never counseled a return to any historically specific "state of nature," such a return he dismissed as impossible; although he did wonder that men should have abandoned that relatively creative life which we would probably designate as early neolithic, a problem that is far from solved. [p. 220]

Here we have Rousseau just where anthropology needs him (and where several other scholars, including Lévi-Strauss, have placed him): insisting that one must necessarily posit the primitive in order to investigate either civilized states and polities or civilized selves.

The core of Diamond's study is, in good anthropological tradition, an ideal-type primitive society where, within the web of kinship, one finds: affective nurturance; a sense of self, confirmed by manifold personal relationships throughout the life cycle; institutionalized public deviancy and dramatic rituals; a heightened sense of reality and emphasis on physiological functions; full participation in culture; values on artisanship; and most important, socioeconomic risks equally distributed throughout society. In short, primitive personalism, nominalism, individuation, and existentialism (versus alienation) appear to form the very inverse of the modern dilemma that Diamond deems a pathology marked by "our dedication to abstractions, in our collectivism, pseudo-individualism, and lack of institutional means for the expression and transcendence of human ambivalence" (p. 173).

His discussions of primitive personalism are the freshest, since Diamond employs Paul Radin's studies to extricate total tribal persons from the homogeneous tribal "groups" often suggested by Radin's contemporaries. Yet increasingly along the way, Diamond takes his own ideal-type literally and historically and, forgetting the lesson of Rousseau, simply laments our somehow having lost it all. Thus, during an excellent discussion of ritual and the role of the trickster (again, Radin) in primitive life, we read:

The primitive ritual also differs from ritualized group occasions in civilized society; the latter strive toward repression of ambivalence rather than recognition and cultural use. One can hardly imagine a "burlesque of the sacred" taking place at, let us say, a patriotic ceremony; in this sense all state structures tend toward the totalitarian. But, among primitives, sacred events are frequently and publicly caricatured, even as they occur. In primitive rituals, what we would call the fundamental paradoxes of human life – love and hate, the comic and the tragic, dedication and denial, and their derivatives – are specified, given free, sometimes uninhibited, even murderous "play" in quite the sense that Huizinga uses that word. [pp. 153–4]

Elsewhere Diamond alludes to drama and theater as token, isolated instances of any civilized "play," thereby explaining away as mere vestige and remnant Shakespearean fools, religious carnivals, theaters of the absurd, and a host of artistic forms in otherwise civilized contexts. The possibility that such "dramatistic" events are just as vital (to civilization) as is goose-stepping is never entertained by Diamond, who tends increasingly to convey that antidramatic, untricksterlike, literal-minded seriousness vis-à-vis ritual form that is most often associated politically with both the extreme left and the extreme right. Many observers of rituals in stratified societies, such as A. M. Hocart, Robert Bellah, Victor Turner, Kenneth Burke, Louis Dumont, Clifford Geertz, and Edmund Leach have found more caricature and "play" – from rituals of inversion in feudal orders and autocratic city-states to the weekends, vacations, and games of postmodern nations – than Diamond can allow.

Later in a critique of the U.S. "mental health movement" which specifies the civilizational pathology as paranoic schizophrenia, Diamond again grants genuine ritual to primitives alone: "Rituals and ceremonies permit the expression of ambivalent emotions and the acting out of complex fantasies in a socially prescribed fashion. It is customary for individuals or groups of people to "go crazy" for self-limiting periods of time without being extirpated from the culture" (p. 254). Diamond stereotypes civilization's answer to this primitive capacity by citing mental hospitals and asylums rather than by drawing the parallel of "sports freaks" (although the United States reveals more football addicts than inmates) or cocktail sets (which he would presumably dismiss as comprising extirpated and alienated individuals while admitting drug-induced vision quests of tribesmen as socially prescribed). All this reasoning may or may not be accurate; the trouble is that Diamond simply takes it for granted because of his increasing rigidification of the primitive/civilization contrast and his refusal to admit any of the ideal-type of the former as an integral (rather than a vestigial) part of the latter. If Diamond is right about Radin and rituals and tricksters, to fully criticize even civilization would take more than just a Marxist; it would take a *playful* Marxist, a notably rare breed. Rather than invoking "primitive play" to question civilization itself, Diamond should perhaps use it to question the very frameworks, borrowed from Sartre, Marx, and others, that he employs to assess the worth or authenticity of civilized experience.

Turning now to the political state, we find an interesting treatment of Plato's *Republic*, this landmark of an antithesis to the primitive – antifamily, prospecialization. Diamond's reading is compelling, although his secondary theme of the Dahomean protostate as an ethnographic–historical parallel to Plato is less convincing, as are all the sketchy empirical examples. Moreover, possibly Diamond's field experiences in Nigeria distorted his view of the general process of state formation as inevitably imperialistic. What, then, of the historic centerpiece, the material, of Diamond's book: the origin of the state, the rule of law, and the dawn of landed property and wealth?

His implicit panorama of the rise of the state-civilization-fascism is wondrously simplified:

In fact, acculturation has always been a matter of conquest. Either civilization directly shatters a primitive culture that happens to stand in its historical right of way; or a primitive social economy, in the grip of a civilized market, becomes so attenuated and weakened that it can no longer contain the traditional culture. In both cases, refugees from the foundering groups may adopt the standards of the more potent society in order to survive as individuals. But these are conscripts of civilization, not volunteers. [P. 204]

His standard and norm for this view is the Anaguta who, Diamond conjectures, made a "single conscious decision not to try to adapt to the new world growing up around them" and were "bent upon preserving their historical existence, not denying it, by withdrawing from civilized contact" (pp. 66–7). Diamond views world history as continual defeats of this image of the Anaguta; every social change advances the ineluctable degeneration of the world's population into an alienated proletariat. From the outset Diamond's generalizations are as sweeping as they are unverifiable: "No rationalization for the existence of the early state can alter the fact that the majority of the people were always taxed in goods and labor far more [?] than they received from the state in the form of protection and services" (p. 8). This is merely doctrine clouded by historical mystique. No one disputes that countless unscrupulous and inhumane episodes riddle the histories of state formation, of colonialism, and of the process of standardization in the areas of law, language and literacy, taxation, and conscription. But to collapse every supralocal development into some emotive vector of political "cannibalizing" – "Law has cannibalized the institutions which it presumably reinforces" (p. 257); "The Nazi Party and its supporters cannibalized the institutions of German society" (p. 258) – is to ignore the specificity of historical processes that it is ethnography's major claim to respectability to have helped reveal.

Consider, for example, this reviewer's Anaguta – Indonesia and Southeast Asia – in light of the view of law as "symptomatic of the emergence of the state" (p. 259). Diamond advances this theme by adopting the position that custom, the "modality of primitive society," is among other things "spontaneous, traditional, corporate and relatively unchanging." Law or "the instrument of civilization," we are to assume, is the inverse. Diamond then illustrates law with standardized legal codes – the Roman, the Napoleonic, and (he supposes) the Islamic – that are said to tear apart the fabric of kinship and to wrest criminal accountability from the immediate corporate kin groups. There are enormous problems with this devolutionary, very nineteenth-century view. First, to call custom "corporate" overlooks societies that display differences (but not necessarily inequality) by studiously distinguishing customs across clans by means of totemic classifications, positive marriage rules, and so forth. More to the point, the implication that legal systems such as Islam are monolithic codes that ride roughshod over local usages ignores the lessons that fieldworkers (even civil servants within the British, Dutch, and French colonial regimes) have preached to experts in the Great Tradition throughout the century. Any literate canon – whether a legal one or a religious one (and most are both) – is culturally unfinished. Consider, for example, S. Tambiah's (1970) demonstration that orthodox Theravada Buddhism and its literate, liturgical, and legal programs are in essence incomplete until filled out in diverse particulars by local social organization, as in matrilineally inclined Northeast Thailand (cf. Kirsch 1977). In these areas careful ethnography suggests that "conquest" is not the primary characteristic, either literally or figuratively, of state formations. Many so-called despots, whether earlier rajas or later sultans, never owned the virgin or irrigated lands; ownership remained largely in local hands. Moreover, both Hindu laws and later Islamic codes were meticulously altered – were in effect completed – with reference to variable customary practices. Such legal systems tend to reserve special duties (and not just despised ones) for upland rustic populations and for groups in the plains conceived as less refined but as equally essential to the proper state. In a similar way, in and around South Asia (cf. Barth 1965) a caste-based ritual division of labor can serve to insulate segments of the population from the detribalization that Diamond decries, as when nomadic herders are viewed as an endogamous and polluted occupation group. As a result the herders themselves remain in part independent, self-sufficient, and proud tribesmen who disparage the settled populations with whom they trade as much as they themselves are disparaged. Finally, it is even possible that in places like Bali, Hindu-Buddhist statecraft advanced partly because local units of customary tradition promoted from their ranks overlords to affiliate with so-called upper-caste houses that helped expand controlled water distribution without expropriating irrigated lands (Geertz 1980a). These examples are meant to suggest not that state formation proceeded fairly and prettily but only that Diamond's "single complex imperative" obscures any general processes that might be involved.

Diamond raises many important points, especially the concept of civil crimes (rape, homicide, most paradoxically suicide) and other personifications of the civil order. Moreover, one can certainly sympathize with his dismay over the "progressive reduction of society to a series of technical and legal signals, the consequent diminution of culture, that is, of reciprocal, symbolic meanings" (p. 280). Earlier he had invoked Weber: "The evolution of the state toward what Max Weber called maximally politicized society, the unprecedented concentration of bureaucratic and technological power, which economically and culturally dominates the rest of the world, creates a climate in which all problems cast a political shadow" (p. 275). But in that whole aspect of history that Diamond analytically slurs as civilization–state–imperialism–fascism, he never envisions the elements Weber called legitimation; or motivation, which ties acts and deeds, even those of supposed despots, to social meanings; or charisma, whereby a leader complements the cultural integrity of his followers. Indeed, anthropologists are, as Diamond suggests, concerned with reciprocal, symbolic meanings. However, there can be – to invoke an interpretive tradition running from Durkheim to Louis Dumont – reciprocity in hierarchy. Diamond, by doctrine, simply eliminates this possibility from the outset. He acknowledges that upper classes require an "image of themselves"; but he never suspects that the advantaged may in their self-images necessarily relate to the images held by those beneath them. So simplified, how could Diamond's approach handle classic ethnographic complexities, such as inferior matrilineal Nayars (a dominant Sudra caste), who traditionally esteemed their unions with patrilineal Nambudiri Brahmins as legitimate hypergamous marriages, while the Brahmins (often cadet sons) viewed the unions as mere concubinage, enabling the children's descent to be reckoned matrilineally? In this case (and it is more complex than here suggested) who, if one insists that social stratification entails simple coercion-after-conquest, coerces whom?

Diamond avoids such matters, because after one offhand allusion to the "single-mindedness of Soviet technicians" he feels justified in generalizing: "The point is that the imperialist imagination can neither permit nor conceive alternatives in subordinate areas and will use all means to abort them if they should develop. Thus, imperialism fulfills its own prophecy; and the metropolitan power seeks to impose its concrete form of society as a theory of growth" (p. 28). However well-intentioned Diamond's mission, these reified abstractions verge on fighting fire with fire, a dangerous policy in combating imperialism. There are reactionary, perhaps even totalitarian overtones to a concept like "the imperial imagination." Contrary to Diamond's own imagination, what often happens in history and ethnography is altogether less melodramatic – neither noble courts and cities against iconoclastic barbarians nor noble savages against inevitably exploitative states – than he portrays it.

The shortcomings of Diamond's brand of critique become blatant in his penultimate chapter, which seeks to discredit Lévi-Strauss, his structuralist method, and along the way any other rationalist or even systematic endeavor. During these unfortunate pages, which scar this often thought-provoking book, Diamond reduces Lévi-Strauss to an incarnation of Sartre's notion of the inauthentic Jew. Diamond apparently hopes to purge Western intellectual life of such influence by rallying someone (he never specifies whom) to retribalize something (he never specifies what). Anyway, for Sartre: "Jewish authenticity consists in choosing oneself as Jew, and abandoning '*the myth of the universal man.*' Thus the Jew knows himself and wills himself into history as a historical and damned creature. '*He understands that society is bad*'; for the naive monism of the inauthentic Jew he substitutes a social pluralism" (p. 329). Even if the application of this framework to Lévi-Strauss in particular were not outlandish, one might rightly remain skeptical that "pluralism" in the ordinary sense of the term would inevitably result from such a process of self-authentication. If, as Diamond insists, Lévi-Strauss needed (because he is inauthentic) to repress his personal–ethnic–racial essence, why did the Belgian-born ethnologist cast his remarkable intellectual autobiography in the feeling-tone produced by his exile with other French Jewish intellectuals during World War II? Diamond disregards this dimension of *Tristes tropiques* so that he can better accuse Lévi-Strauss of all the worst crimes: objectivity, in fact scientism; elitism, and bourgeois elitism at that, since Lévi-Strauss illustrates a musicological point with Debussy; fetishizing cognition – and on and on.

Diamond, who elsewhere admires tricksters, lacks self-reflection; he ignores Lévi-Strauss's irony and misunderstands his efforts to refine Durkheim and Mauss by situating the "social" and its classifications at an epistemological level analogous to that occupied by "language" in structuralist linguistics. At one point Diamond proclaims Lévi-Strauss the "ultimate academic critic, rationalizing and policing, rather than creating, the world" (p. 302). Turning the page, we then find a footnote in which Diamond officiously censors Lévi-Strauss's aim to "assimilate conceptions to perceptions" (a tendency Diamond applauds *chez* primitives) as an "inadmissible undertaking" (p. 304). Having thus unintentionally demonstrated his own solution to who polices the policeman, Diamond proceeds to condemn Lévi-Strauss, as might a one-man legal system with no alienating apparatus of due process to encumber it.

Unsurprisingly it is the prosecutor, judge, and jury himself who gets off scot free. For throughout the case he makes against Lévi-Strauss, Diamond never explains or repents his own part in disseminating to the reading masses the views of this "descendant of Plato, Descartes, and Spinoza" and even worse of this "system builder" (p. 320). If Diamond is right in his diatribe of 1974, whatever possessed him to incude Lévi-Strauss's reanalysis of Winnebago myths in a collection of essays to honor Paul Radin (*Culture in History*, 1960)? To be true to his own tenet of authenticity (a word as dangerous as "truth"), Diamond might today be expected to burn the very books he once edited.

Finally Diamond informs us:

The position of Lévi-Strauss becomes decisive; he demonstrates how the Western intelligentsia can make imposing careers out of their alienation. And we can understand why a distinguished anthropologist, a member of the most alienated of all professions, should now occupy a central position in the intellectual life of the West.

Authentic anthropologists will not make careers out of their alienation, but will understand it as a specific instance of a pathological condition, demanding political commitment and action; that is, they will reject the reified identity: "anthropologist." [pp. 305, 330]

But what if, in Diamond's own terms, an "authentic anthropologist" *could* become a central figure in Western intellectual life? For the sake of argument, let us assume that Diamond himself is such an authentic figure. (As *In Search of the Primitive* and his enviable professional role as chairman of Anthropology at the New School for Social Research prove, whether or not central, Diamond is hardly marginal.) Does not then the fact that he and the other "poets" have yet to be expelled from the Republic suggest that the imperialist imagination is less thoroughgoing than he supposes? Might there be a bit of the trickster in many state systems and, I would add, a bit of the imperialist in any primitive system? Perhaps champions of the personal, the ritual–dramatic, and the creatively ambivalent are not automatically excluded even under conditions of extreme bureaucratization – as Weber himself half-hoped in his effort to guarantee institutionalized value-freedom. Of course, unlike Diamond I would include Lévi-Strauss, promoter of totalizing mythical orders, and many other systematic anthropologists in the ranks of such Rousseau-like champions who enrich our pigeonholed lives.

In short, if Diamond's book is ultimately right about capitalist states and all the other polities and academies he considers imperialist, the book should not even be here to say so. Thus as a die-hard academic anthropologist (and therefore, I think, also as a bit of a trickster), I propose logically that since Diamond's book is obviously here saying so, it is wrong. Furthermore, for this reason, because a trickster is never totally doctrinaire, I recommend we check it out of the library (GN320 D53) and read it, rendering it more wrong still.

Notes

1. Introduction: The exaggeration of cultures

1 For concise descriptions of these three influential centers of anthropological research, see Lévi-Strauss (1946) and Needham (1963); Stocking (1974); and P. E. de Josselin de Jong (1977); (see Chapters 3, 6). For a representative overview of the anthropology of religion, see Lessa and Vogt (1979).

2 A programmatic call to examine "the activity through which anthropologists determine and represent what they know in the writing of ethnographies" appears in Marcus (1980:507). It is still news that Frye, K. Burke, etc., pertain to what anthropologists (like historians) do; it remains headline news that ethnography is a rhetorical genre; and Lévi-Strauss and Bateson still appear somehow marginal as far as description goes – and this state of affairs suggests anthropology's ingrained faith in "representational" writing. Although Marcus seems too readily to oppose knowledge and writing, he makes telling comments on the reflexivity of recent efforts by Rabinow (1977) and Jean-Paul Dumont (1978) as a "thing in itself" whose relationship to standard ethnographic writing remains unexplored.

   Experimental ethnographies often try to burst the shackles of old-fashioned, establishment description, often by merely stressing rather than disguising a first-person pronoun. It would seem more pertinent to find a way to reveal the intense conventionality of standard ethnography (cf. Boon 1977: Part I), to engage in a reflexivity that ushers rival formats into critical self-consciousness.

3 For a consideration of Boas' reputation for being "dubious of analogies, opposed to deduction, suspicious of hypotheses and of theory," see Stocking (1974:15). See also Stocking (1976, 1979).

4 Actually, even the early Mead employed a deductive strategy, even in Samoa. In *Blackberry Winter*, she reveals: "I took into the field all the questions about deviance [Benedict] had raised, and I tried to *discipline my perceptions* by imagining what would have been the fate of the very definite personalities I knew – Franz Boas, Ruth Benedict, Leonie Adams, Edward Sapir – if they had been born Samoans" (1959:202; emphasis added). If only all fieldworkers were this candid, and not thirty years later!

5 Here, and again in Chapter 2, on Durkheim, I employ for polemical ends several offhand, published remarks of the late E. E. Evans-Pritchard. I do so not to reduce his views to such remarks but to accentuate a major irony in academic routinization: When scholars, even ones as complex as Evans-Pritchard, set about devising tenets, they standardize the activities of successors much more narrowly than their own endeavors. (The same Evans-Pritchard who here slaps nonfieldworkers' wrists elsewhere champions Levy-Bruhl, 1965: chap. 4.) Ultimately, of course,

Evans-Pritchard rejects functionalist abstraction and consolidates history and ethnography as few have managed to. On Evans-Pritchard's corpus, see Beidelman (1979).

6   There is currently extensive restudying, reanalyzing, and rereading of Malinowski, both of what he investigated and of what he wrote. For some recent thoughts on kula exchange, see Damon (1980) and Weiner (1976); see also Young (1979). Malinowski's diary (1967) is put to creative use in Herbert (1980). My aim here is not to review works on Malinowski's ethnography and texts but to state vividly the Malinowski/Frazer distinction between monograph and romance in order to shake it loose. Recent studies that make relations between writing and ethnohistory problematic include Errington (1979) and Siegel (1979). Interesting uses of natives' and ethnographers' time lapses characterize M. Rosaldo (1980) and R. Rosaldo (1980) as well.

7   Ethnographic discourse is "tropic" in the same way that, according to H. White (1974, 1978), historical texts are. Even conventional-looking ethnographies – for example, Mead's work on the Arapesh, Mundugumor, and Tchambuli of New Guinea (1963) – do strange things with first-person pronouns. An example may help illustrate ethnography's "tropic" qualities. G. Genette's influential study of narrative structures (1979) singles out in Proust's prose a device he calls the "pseudoiterative," posing events dense with accumulations of excruciating particulars, as if they were *typical*; something like: "It was one of those days when starlings and crickets sing sweetly and Aunt L. would have her recently returned runaway cook make extra efforts to please the palates of a visiting dignitary, just recovered from a bout of. . ." Ethnographic monographs' inherent concern with the bizarre, the everyday, and the palpable universal makes their discourse a field day for the pseudoiterative. Some anthropologists seek to debunk pseudoiteratives in standard ethnography without pausing to consider why they are there; as when M. Douglas remarks: "In my opinion it is less accurate to say that most Africans are nature-worshipers than to say most London journalists are Greek Orthodox" (1975:75). One might have to construe ethnological generalizations, and the ethnographic pseudoiterative, as contrastive propositions rather than as reportage.

8   Immense bibliographies could be developed to justify blurring conventional dividing lines between fiction and ethnography. My own would stress two formats: Menippean satire (see Chapter 7, note 4), including works like (!) Multatuli's *Max Havelaar* and Thomas More's *Utopia*; and thoroughly cross-cultural comedies of manners, like Forster's *Passage to India*. The anthropologist in me would then risk proclaiming literature "itself" as intrinsically both cross-cultural and multilingual and only in disguise a uniform spacetime-language. Starting points for sorting out relevant sources, including the relation of folklore and comparative mythology (both as practices and as ideals) to such issues, include E. Bruner (n.d.) on ethnography as narrative and articles by Dennis Tedlock (1977, 1979) on the distortions writing and translation bring to oral genres; see also a sensitive essay by Clifford (1980). Among many collections that help beg a literature/ethnography distinction are Basso and Selby (1976), Babcock (1978), and Dolgen et al. (1977). It is worth perusing journals ranging from *Semiotica* and *New Literary History* to *Alcheringa* and *Parabola* and many others that advertise themselves in the pages of those that I have named. For other sources, see Boon (1972).

9   On *Morganthropus exchangenesis* and his/her kin, see the revealing study of the marketing of "human nature" as a commodity by Channel and Macklin (1974). On ludic man, see Huizinga's classic (1949) and works on trickster or the grotesque, such as Radin (1972) and Bakhtin (1968). See also the representative

collections on carnivalization, ritual irony, etc., by Babcock (1978). I have learned much about institutional and typological components of clowning from papers by and conversations with J. Eidson.

2. Shades of the history of ethnology

1   For an alternative view see Rowe (1965); for other representative ideas on anthropology's history, see Darnell (1974). I broached related issues in Boon (1973:2–7).
2   It is irresistible here as elsewhere (see Chapter 7) to invoke F. Schlegel: "To some of my hearers it may appear as idle and superfluous to write against the philosophy of the eighteenth century, as it would be to fight with the shadow of a departed enemy. In truth, however, the cases are not at all parallel ones, although I can easily suppose they may seem so to such as form their judgments entirely from the external appearances of things. The evil is by no means annihilated, although it has become less visible. In England the disease of the age never broke out openly, and for that very reason has never been radically cured" (1847:377).
3   Similar standards characterize Malefijt (1974).
4   Other recent, helpful works on pre-Enlightenment and pre-Baconian interpretive traditions include Eliade (1978) and all the books of Frances Yates, for example (1972). See also Levin (1969) and the earlier chapters of Manuel and Manuel (1979).
5   Voltaire, cited in Lovejoy (1964:290). Lovejoy contends that Bolinbroke's assumption of a universal and unvarying code was "the root from which grew most of the principles of neo-classical criticism." For a fuller sense of such principles, see Gay (1966). With specific reference to "overcoming" language diversity, see Knowlson's excellent volume (1975).
6   Foucault's oppositional formulations, while rich for anthropologists' blood, raise vital issues in the history and practice of the discipline. Many enduring concerns – "primitive classifications," exogamous tribal clans, traditional hierarchies – recall a preclassical episteme as Foucault discloses it. Indeed, the history of anthropological debates over magic, religion, and ritual often read as a rescue-mission of native hermeneutic ideals and actions from their misanalysis by observers lodged in a classical episteme, the latter reaching even to Malinowski's functionalist successors.
7   Horkheimer traces Enlightenment impulses much further still: "In fact, the notion of the Enlightenment underwent a basic change in the forties. Instead of being the cultural correlate of the ascending bourgeoisie, it was expanded to include the entire spectrum of Western thought. 'Enlightenment here is identical with bourgeois thought, nay, thought in general, since there is no other thought properly speaking than in cities,' Horkheimer wrote Lowenthal in 1942. In *Eclipse of Reason* he went so far as to say that 'this mentality of man as the master [which was the essence of the Enlightenment view] can be traced back to the first chapters of Genesis' " (Jay 1973:258).
8   See also Elliott (1973). For sources from Columbus see Landström (1966). The Indian/cannibal distinction and related concepts are reviewed in Sanders (1978), which is marred by a too-monolithic notion of racism. For additional sources see Hahn (1978); relevant articles in Chiappelli (1976); and Honour (1975).
9   These allusions to Indo-European traditions and ideology rely on the sweeping comparative studies by Georges Dumézil (1966–71); see below, Chapters 6–7.
10 For a recent scholarly treatment of the inaccuracy of this translation, see Sturtevant (n.d.). Many similar episodes in cross-cultural encounters of a later period are discussed in Adams (1962).

11 I cite Darwin here from a collection of excerpts from *The Voyage of the Beagle* (1845) published for children in 1873. Elsewhere Darwin qualified such remarks. For example, in his letter on the "moral state of Tahiti," reflecting on the fate of two Fuegians transported to London, he wrote (in 1836): "Surely if three years sufficed to change the natures of such cannibal wretches as Fuegians and transform them into well behaved, civilized friends, there is some cause for thinking that a savage is not irreclaimable, until advanced in life, however repugnant to our ideas have been his early habits" (Darwin 1977). Here, however, we are concerned with those opinions written by Darwin that became routinized in social Darwinism. (I am indebted to D. J. Greenwood for suggestions about Darwin's contradictory opinions.) On the evolutionary views in the history of anthropology, see Stocking (1968). Oldroyd (1980) provides some guidance in the recent related issues welling up out of sociobiology. For some cultural anthropological responses, see Sahlins (1976b).

12 Just one example: "The natives [of Australia] were punctilious, so far as they still could be, about the observance of their laws of incest and marriage. When they saw that 'every native law regarding tabus was apparently set at naught by white people' – e.g., a man might share a hut hugger-mugger with his mother, mother-in-law, and nubile sisters – they charged the whites with 'group marriage and promiscuity' " (Bates 1938:75). That few such native opinions have been recorded should in no way suggest that few such native opinions have existed.

13 The history of ideas of Bali is instructive. In 1597–98 this complex, literate civilization was inscribed by the first Dutch visitors who employed similitudes of widow burning, in analogy with customs in Portuguese Goa, and orderly irrigation, in analogy with Holland's new canal systems (Boon 1977: Part I). Both images contained a degree of ethnographic accuracy; yet they were coined in pre-Enlightenment terms; and my point is that neither positive (Eden, irrigationist) nor pejorative (Nebuchadnezzar, widow burning) similitudes of exotics wholly separated the human species into measurably separate types. Rather, they applied sectarian polarities universally. (See chapter 5).

14 I agree with Scholte and others that anthropologies themselves are culturally mediated and that anthropological thought (I would say texts) requires contextual analysis, which itself must be dialectical and reflexive (Scholte 1973:431–7). It is when everything starts sounding emancipatory that I sense Enlightenment prejudices (they go under many guises) creeping uncritically back in.

15 The works I am alluding to, beginning with *Axel's Castle*, are listed in the bibliography; the subtitle of *To the Finland Station* could serve as well for the whole of Wilson's corpus: "A Study in the Writing and Acting of History." For a writer's version of his own motives for such diverse, yet concerted, enterprises of translating and writing, see Wilson (1977).

3. Social theories with a difference

1 Throughout this chapter I emphasize not the abstract tenets of social theorists but the complex texts – especially at points of intricate transition, whether thematic, methodological, or stylistic. Tenets routinize; texts envelop. Some literary readings of recurrent metaphors in Darwin, Marx, Freud, and Frazer appear in Hyman (1966). Elaborate phenomenological, structuralist, and poststructuralist readings of Freud and Marx are now commonplace; see, for example, Felman (1977). My own strategy in reading texts in social and cultural theory is to focus on any nexus where complex institutions are inscribed in a prose that shifts abruptly into inten-

sified stylistic intricacy. This tactic is most apparent in my discussions of Dumont and Lowie later in this book.

2   As the references in this section reveal, I have drawn on many recent secondary sources. I stress the comparativist ideals and projects associated with *L'année sociologique*, as they anticipated developments in structuralism. For general background, see Lukes (1973); Tiryakian (1978) (contrast this work with Coser 1960); and Wolff (1960), especially the essays by Peyre and Honigsheim. Bohannan (1960) remains helpful on *conscience collective* and culture. For additional sources, see the references in the text.

3   Two convenient reviews of the anthropology of aboriginal Australia to the present are Maddock (1972) and Yengoyan (1979), with its extremely helpful bibliography. For some remarks on Durkheim's last comments on Australia (made in response to a letter from Radcliffe-Brown criticizing his analysis of matrimonial organization), see Peristiany (in Wolff 1960).

4   Traugott (1978:12–13) makes interesting observations about Durkheim's "controverting the usual associations" by calling "mechanical" a form of society conventionally deemed more "natural" and calling "organic" a more intricate sort of organization.

5   A central issue is whether Durkheim saw society as fundamentally consensual; see, for example, the charges in Coser (1960); LaCapra (1972) also stresses consensus as the end point of Durkheim, leaving aside what I join Murphy in calling his dialectical side. The latter is most apparent in the connection between Durkheim's tribal studies and his notions of the state and other historical institutions. Lukes makes fine distinctions in Durkheim's views; he emphasizes his prewar optimism for internationalism and calls him a "moralistic conservative and a radical social reformer (1973:546). Equally important is Lukes's discussion of Durkheim's hopes for occupational organizations that would ensure communication and diversity by elevating private functions to the dignity of public ones (1973:537ff.).

6   See Chapter 1, note 5. In his most general statement on primitive religion, Evans-Pritchard isolated "two different sorts of religious experience": the static variety of closed, "primitive" societies and the dynamic mystical variety of open, universalistic societies (1965:115). My interrelating of Durkheim and Weber is meant to challenge this kind of conviction. For another effort to dissolve any closed/open or religious/secular pigeonholes, see Douglas (1970, 1975); however, she, like Radcliffe-Brown, seriously truncates Durkheim.

7   Durkheim's commentary in 1914 on his own discussion in the *Elementary Forms* underscores the complexities of his views; any crowd psychology is less the determinant than the vehicle of a sense of unison (contrast "union"): "Collective representations originate only when they are embodied in material objects, things, or beings of every sort – figures, movements, sounds, words, and so on – that symbolize and delineate them in some outward appearance. For it is only by expressing their feelings, by translating them into signs, by symbolizing them externally, that the individual consciousnesses, which are, by nature, closed to each other, *can feel that they are communicating and are in unison*" (1960a:335–6; emphasis added). Difficulties in assessing Durkheim's view of religion are apparent even from his own opening and closing footnotes to the preliminary questions in *The Elementary Forms* (1912/1965:37, 63), where he modifies earlier definitions of religion, which were in ways closer to what would eventually be designated by Lévi-Strauss "the intellect" (versus the social). Later still Durkheim shifts back toward an earlier position that would reemerge in Lévi-Strauss, when he crisply contrasts his own efforts to detect in primitive forms "the principle of

contradiction in an exaggerated fashion" to Levy-Bruhl's notion of prelogical "participation" (Durkheim 1978:145–9).

8   A similar relational formulation occurs in Durkheim's 1914 essay on *Homo duplex* (1914/1955) – full of reifications of sacred/profane distinctions that presumably form "the constitutional duality of human nature." Nevertheless, he finally operationalizes distinctions such as sacred/profane, soul/body, ideal/material, society/individual heretofore posed substantively: "Absolute egoism, like absolute altruism, is an ideal limit which can never be attained in reality. Both are states that we can approach indefinitely without ever realizing them completely" (1960a:329). Dialectics thus emerges. Earlier in the essay Durkheim treats concepts and morals as social, indeed languagelike. To these he contrasts individual sensations of color, hunger, etc. (1960a:327). Lévi-Strauss managed to collapse this very distinction, by treating sensations of color, sound, etc., as culturally ordered, languagelike selections. This view he has in common with ethnoscientists; but ultimately the latter tend toward formalism, whereas he tends toward dialectics of multiple variations.

9   For sources debating the implications of Dumont's views on caste, see Chapter 6, note 3. A reaction presumably in the name of both Marx and Untouchables is Mencher (1974; and subsequent issues of *Current Anthropology*). Dumont responds to many critics in his preface to the revised, complete *Homo Hierarchicus* (1980). A recent field study of Untouchables is Moffatt (1979).

10   Formulas of Dumézil's views are provided in Chapter 6, note 4, and Chapter 7, note 7. My sources on Weber and the portions of his corpus I emphasize should be clear from the text. Recent essays by Roth and Schluchte help correct inaccurate stereotypes of Weber; they stress his ambivalence toward rationality and his rejection of the fashionable attitude of *Kulturpessimismus* (1979:192). Jameson (1974) attempts to detect a narrative structure in Weber without examining very closely the actual fabric of his arguments or (most important, I think) his transitions. Although the epigraph by Geertz at the head of this section is dated, it remains true that Weber's comparativist breadth has not had the impact in anthropology one might expect. A recent indication of this fact is Sahlins' *Culture and Practical Reason* (1976a:95, 107) – so generous to Durkheim – which mentions Weber only twice, once to accuse him of solipsistic reductions (!), then in an unexplained juxtaposition with Malinowski, both opposed to Durkheim. These remarks are all the more peculiar when we stop to consider that Weber's social and cultural theory is so compatible with the views of another scholar whom Sahlins rightly applauds, Hocart. We might note the mutual emphasis on asceticism (cf. Hocart 1952: chap. 15), or Hocart's interest in Hebrew history with motives identical to Weber's: "Iconoclasm and centralization went hand in hand in Palestine. Local idols meant power dispersed; a central cult in Jerusalem meant power concentrated at headquarters. We now know that the centralizers pursued their aim with no more regard for truth than any political faction of the present day. They are said to have emended and expurgated the ancient records so that it should appear their faith was the original one, and polytheism a degeneration. The Hebrew rationalists ignored everything in the ancient records that did not fit in with their conception of the rational man. Fortunately for us they accidentally left in hints of image worship in ancient Palestine; for instance, the brazen serpent" (Hocart 1970:246). If, as Bendix insists, the distinction between society and polity is the fundamental theme of Weber's work as a whole (1962:478), the same is true of Hocart's *Kings and Councillors* (1970). Both Hocart and Weber legitimate anthropology's concern with cultures (tribes) and institutions (e.g., with "families") in

which a society/polity distinction is radically problematic: generalized systems. For more on Hocart and Weber, see Chapter 6.

11 In a footnote Parsons elaborates: "The most comprehensive treatment of this movement so far available is, to my knowledge, H. Stuart Hughes, *Consciousness and Society* (1961). My own *Structure of Social Action* (1937/1949) dealt with the more directly sociological aspects, especially, besides Weber, Durkheim and Pareto, and some of the relations to the tradition of economic individualism. Now it seems to me particularly that Freud, and the American pragmatists and social psychologists, such as G. H. Mead and John Dewey, have played a very important part" (1971:48, n.1). In anthropology both Weberian and pragmatist dimensions have been developed by C. Geertz (see Chapter 4). I should note Parsons's view of French social thought as well – including Rousseau, St. Simon, Comte, and Durkheim – as "intermediate between the German and the British and subsequently, though not in Weber's lifetime, . . . an essential intellectual bridge between them" (1971:31). This article by Parsons was presented at Heidelberg during the centennial of Weber's birth, with representatives of the very trilemma Parsons was assessing, including Raymond, Horkheimer, Habermas, and others (see Stammer 1971). I emphasize the article in part because Parsons himself did, stressing changes in his views over the years (Parsons 1975). See also the responses by Parsons to critical assessments of these theories in M. Black (1962b).

12 I consider the critical issues to be not whether the comparative social theories of Durkheim and Weber are convergent, as Parsons often argued, or divergent as Pope et al. (1975) insist; but whether their differences can be set into some kind of active complementarity. Short of making Durkheim's and Weber's respective comparativist enterprises an organic solidarity, we can still see them as variant ideal-types. This is not at all to synthesize them; it is, rather, to do to Weber-versus-Durkheim what Weber does to varieties of economic ethics and religious systems. Pope et al. (1975) oppose Durkheim's emphasis on society's imposed norms to Weber's emphasis on subjectivities. They tend to underestimate Weber's suggestions that subjectivities are not private but mediated by institutions (whether traditional ones or more rationalized ones). It is the institutional level in Weber that approximates the "society" level in Durkheim. I would also dispute Pope et al. in the claim of incompatibility between Durkheim and Weber's views of market behavior; Weber's treatment of *jajmani* alone conforms to Durkheim's (and later Mauss's) interest in noncontractual exchange relations embedded in society's divisions. They also overlook Durkheim's attention to variations of clans in a primitive society, which level would tie in with Weber's sense of "the systematic differences in religious ideas and interests among different status groups within a society" (Pope et al. 1975:424, 423). (I thank Doug Vermillion for several references in these debates.)

13 My remarks on music are obviously speculative. But it would be thoroughly uncharacteristic of Weber not to connect this project both methodologically and theoretically with his more patent analyses of institutions and values. His materials on rationalization in Western music are all the more intriguing because they were written in 1911 (although not published until 1921), near the time (circa 1913) of two provocative pieces on religious "social psychology" and "world-rejection," cited extensively above. The fluid format of these essays contrasts with *Economy and Society*, which in Weber's terms represents something of a rationalized routinization of his ideas, categories, and, I would add, texts.

14 I make no effort to review even part of the immense literature on Marx or even on Marxian anthropology. Rather, I bring Marx and Mauss into contrast at a point suggested by Mauss's notion of the gift as a total social fact. I am by and large

sympathetic with the elaborate work on related matters by Sahlins (1972, 1976a). For an interesting review and critique of anthropological economics with an eye on distribution, see Gudeman (1978), which ranges over Marxist, structuralist, and center/periphery models.

15   A typical summary of Mauss in terms of types of exchange, which inaccurately makes reciprocity just one variety among others such as redistribution and markets, appears in Codere (1968). Recent anthropological work on ritual and economic exchange is too copious to cite here.

16   Lévi-Strauss fleetingly applies the notion of mechanical solidarity to both restricted and generalized varieties of elementary structures; but he hastens to confess he has "used the terms 'mechanical' and 'organic' more loosely than Durkheim intended and than is generally accepted" (1969a:xxxiv, n.2). Moreover, his criterion of identical function of each segment vis-à-vis the other segments obtains only if one abstracts the social system. At the level of interrelated social units tied to interrelated ideals (both systems of contrasts, as in totemism), an organic solidarity of systematic differences comes into play. It is worth noting the moment in *Tristes tropiques* when Lévi-Strauss turns back to Amerindian social and mythic systems after confronting South Asian castes: "It is tragic for mankind that this great experiment failed; I mean that, in the course of history, the various castes did not succeed in reaching a state in which they could remain equal because they were different – equal in a sense that there would have been no common measure between them – and that a harmful measure of homogeneity was introduced which made comparison possible, and consequently led to the creation of a hierarchy" (1977:153–4).

17   These pages on Lowie and a few contempories merely indicate some intricacies in his writing and a thoroughness of historical vision seldom appreciated. I feel that the works of Boas and his students (along with many other ethnographers) should be viewed as texts and not just as information. Moreover, the motivations of their pursuits cannot be reduced to the bare tenets of their professional pronouncements. For an enriched sense of Boas's motives, see Stocking (1979). A particularly fertile textual terrain includes the works of the late Margaret Mead and of those whom she influenced: Fortune, Bateson, Benedict, Belo, and others in Bali, etc. One component of this story is the eventual rise of a Margaret Mead cult and canon. I am among those who feel that Mead's works demand serious, on-going critique and not homage-embalming.

4. Assorted semiotics and dialectics

1   A recent review article on anthropological structuralism is Kronenfeld and Decker (1979), with 138 references. It couches polemical points in a flat style and does little to relate structuralism to other methods with which – by structuralism's own tenets – it must be meaningfully compared and contrasted. The article includes many sources in linguistics, literary theory, and critical theory; yet it ends by expressing disappointment at not finding a standardized, centralized, patently structuralist output in America or Britain (or even France!). Careful reading of the materials reviewed, particularly Lévi-Strauss, would have corrected such expectations from the outset.

2   One gains a sense of both the impossible range and the endless precisions of semiotics and semiology by perusing *Semiotica* (under the editorial direction of Thomas A. Sebeok) from 1969 to the present; it stresses every kind of signifying activity from bees to burlesque. For an overview of semiotics, see also Eco (1976). It must be cautioned, however, that a synthesis (or an architectonics) of

all semiotics is itself a kind of symbol. Structuralism and poststructuralism place in the forefront paradoxes like: Does a synthesis include itself? I find it better to think of semiotics as a reductionist-resistant activity rather than as an accumulation of final results or even fixed methods. One of the great merits of semiotics is that it is not new; see the extremely constructive discussion of some antecedents in Ladner (1979).

3   An interesting use of "proto" concepts in the cultural and ideological realm is Dumézil (1966–71), although his sense of the locus of proto-Indo-European ideology seems to me to change over the years. For a sensitive treatment of the play between protoconstructs and mythic texts in the course of history, see P. Friedrich (1978).

4   This point invites consideration of many issues in sociolinguistics, theories of performance and competence, and characteristic displacements of communicative forms in creoles, pidgins, and related linguistic phenomena more prevalant than once assumed. For reviews of some of these problems, see, for example, Halliday (1978). An interesting application of creole linguistics to multiethnic societies is made in Drummond (1980).

5   Culler is, of course, alluding to poststructuralism, which considers the speech/writing difference in some form or other to be inherent in language. Language is decentered and nonpresent. Properly understood, the writing dimension of language is a matter not merely of script (versus speaking) but of the basic removedness of language from any spoken-presence. Language is in a way prealienated. For guides to poststructuralism vis-à-vis structuralism, semiotics, and many varieties of interpretation, see especially Harari (1979) and Culler (1976, 1981). A recent critique of Derrida's earlier basic view is Hans (1979).

6   Donato (1975), an often perceptive reader, misconstrues Lévi-Strauss by tracing a theme of "distanciation" from *Mythologiques* (where Lévi-Strauss converts himself to object in order to approach tribals as object-to-object) back to his kinship studies. Donato assumes cousins are of interest to Lévi-Strauss because they represent a compromise between siblings (near) and strangers (distant). In fact, what cross-cousins represent is the dialectics of any near/distant distinction. It is true that in ideal elementary structures of kinship, cross-cousins are the closest collaterals one may marry (Lévi-Strauss 1969a:98). But a cousin *category*, distinguished into parallel cousins (sibling equivalents) versus cross-cousins (spouse equivalents) irreducibly coinstitutionalizes near/distant at the heart of communication. The cousin category is no compromise between siblings and spouses; rather, it ensures that their respective features remain integrated in perpetual, systematic contradiction.

7   In the interview that furnished the epigraph for this section, Lévi-Strauss adds, "The full splendor of the French language is also illustrated in the Rousseau-Chateaubriand dyad" (1979:22). He develops points about Rousseau/Chateaubriand somewhat further in (1980:17), helping to clarify the role Chateaubriand plays in the epigraphs of *The Origin of Table Manners* (1978). Who could resist comparing Malinowski's entry in his field diary, dated May 21, 1918: "I am reading Chateaubriand. Entirely without stuff and stuffing" (Malinowski 1967:277)?

8   Durkheim notes that pragmatism "affirms that the mind remains free in the face of what is true." He goes on to explore pluralist notions of mind and reason. He finally concludes that "the pragmatist theory of truth is a logical utilitarianism" but does not stipulate the consequences if utility is itself plural. Durkheim wrestles with the works of James, Peirce, Dewey (and Nietzsche!), earnestly seeking "a formula that will preserve the essentials of rationalism, and at the same time, answer the valid criticism that pragmatism makes of it." Many of his provocative

digressions have helped stitch together the present study. For example: "We must also note certain common traits between pragmatism and romanticism, notably the feeling of the complexity, richness, and diversity of life as it is given to us. Romanticism was in part a revolt against the simplistic element in the rationalism and social philosophy at the end of the eighteenth century. This feeling for the complexity of things human, for the insufficiency of eighteenth-century philosophy, is also found at the basis of sociology" (1914/1955 [1960a]:387, 390, 436). The section on Geertz/Lévi-Strauss is offered as a kind of homage to Durkheim's course on pragmatism and sociology toward the end of his life. The similar/different opponents have altered: Pragmatism has become pragmatism-dramatism and *sociologie* has become structuralism. Nor is this development contrary to Durkheim's outlook, less oblivious to change than detractors make him appear: "The role of the social being within our single [individual?] selves will grow ever more important as history moves ahead" (Durkheim 1960a:339). For more on Durkheim and history, see Bellah (1959) and Traugott (1978).

9   It is worth quoting Lévi-Strauss's proclamation in its entirety: "*Cela va de soi et les linguistes nous l'ont appris. Tout système – linguistique ou autre – est* en déséquilibre constant avec lui-même, *c'est le moteur de son dynamisme interne. Mais, pour moi, ce n'est pas là exactement l'historie, en tout cas pas toute l'histoire. C'est la dimension que, dans notre jargon, nous appelons diachronique, de l'évolution des structures, et que personne ne conteste. Mais, en plus de cela, il y a autre chose, que nous ne pourrons jamais réduire. L'histoire est là devant nous, comme quelque chose d'absolu devant quoi il faut s'incliner*" (1975b:183; emphasis added). The intimate–contrastive bonds between time and cultures form a major theme of *Structural Anthropology*, which does not separate history from ethnology but makes them moieties, each the opposite-complement of the other and neither possible independently (1963b: chap. 1). This history of cultures is also the source of both sadness and resignation in *Tristes tropiques* and *Mythologiques*. Nor is this "constant disequilibrium" far from Sapir's sense of "drift" (1921/1949:99–100, chap. 7).

10 A prime theme in Geertz's work is that cultural symbols are public, not mentalistic. This continues the criticism by F. S. C. Schiller, James, and Dewey against traditional rationalism, which separates thought from existence, as though "thought is in the mind; existence is outside it" (Durkheim 1914/1955 [1960a]:405–7). As Durkheim observed, "To connect thought with existence, to connect thought with life – this is the fundamental idea of pragmatism." Along with the idea that truth is human, personal, mutable, concrete, plural; a "living thing that changes ceaselessly" (1960a:407, 409).

11 For further comments in this vein, see Boon (1982); cf. Boon and Schneider (1974). An important rereading of Freud's *Totem and Taboo* appears in Paul (1976).

12 Just before the passage quoted, Burke observes: "Since Hegelian metaphysics is so close to theology, much the same sort of structure can be discerned in the Hegelian dialectic. [Cf. Parsons 1979 on Marx.] Given the genius of the negative, the term 'thesis' of itself implies 'antithesis' – and both together imply 'synthesis,' the element of communication between them. At one point, one might object: 'But the Hegelian "antithesis" is *antagonistic* to "thesis," whereas the Son as the Word, is rather in a like-father-like-son relationship.' And such could indeed be the case, since so much nineteenth-century thinking was under the sign of antithesis. . . But we should point out that the idea of *opposition* can yield to the idea of *counterpart*" (Burke 1970:30). This view brings us close to the moiety-ties that we shall join *sociologie* and structuralism in idealizing (in Chapter 7). In fact moieties manage to institutionalize opposition *as* counterpart!

13 See especially Needham (1963) on Durkheim and Mauss (and Needham 1970 on harmonies between Hocart's views and theirs) and Josselin de Jong's introduction (1977) to the history of Leiden ethnology. I have tried to rectify misplaced archaisms about Bali, stemming from the work of W. H. R. Rassers on Java, in Boon (1977: chap. 9; n.d.).

5. Jacobean ethnology: An East–West intercourse

1 Hodgen mentions only Purchas's *Pilgrimage*; on publication of all his works, see E. G. R. Taylor (1934:60ff.), E. G. R. Taylor (1930:536–9); and William Foster (1946:47–61). All references to Purchas in this chapter employ Samuel Purchas, *Hakluytus Posthumus; or, Purchas His Pilgrimes* in twenty volumes (Glasgow: James MacLehose, 1907).

2 Taylor underscores the fact that slurs on Purchas have become *topoi* of standard bibliographical and biographical accounts. Purchas and "Jacobean" tend to be identified pejoratively; for example: "The sudden exuberance and national pride of the earlier period gave place to the gloom and introspection of the late Jacobean and Caroline age, in which the confident optimism of Bacon and Hakewill seemed out of place: in which the fussy and self-important Samuel Purchas constituted himself heir to the dedicated patriot Richard Hakluyt" (Christopher Hill 1965:11).

3 Sande Cohen has recently formulated a structuralist attitude toward history, based on the works of Michel Foucault, as follows: "The aim of Structural theory is to view texts as arguments and arrangements of sense which articulate and carve out communication from an historical continuum and thereby perform a signifying function of generating signs that 'stand for' " (1978:197).

4 On symbols of Astraea, see Frances Yates (1975a). I shall refer frequently to Yates, Roy Strong, and other scholars who have been investigating Tudor and Stuart symbology, whether Anglican, "Rosicrucian," or their rivals in counter-reformation Catholic programs for legitimating rulers, realms, alliances, and intellectual and practical endeavors.

5 Space does not permit consideration of Hakluyt versus Purchas; their ties to De Bry and others; the interests and writings of James I himself; crucial issues of Bancroft's and Laud's factions in the Church of England; and related matters refractive of ethnology. Many of Purchas' arguments conform to ideals of patriarchalism; on their anthropological, ideological, and moral dimensions that predate Filmer, see Schochet (1975–98).

6 On ideals and actualities of "print culture" and the transformation between scribal and typographic traditions, see Eisenstein (1979). Her study is particularly valuable for understanding Purchas because it reveals complexities in the impact of printed books as a cultural form on literati (not just the masses) long after the mere technological development. Purchas's tomes read like a last gasp of print-shop-style cosmopolitan ideals, before either pamphleteers or editorial offices gained standardized control. Eisenstein's discussions of Puritan values of reading versus the way print settled into other sectarian habits seem to me crucial for pondering how books like those of Anglican Purchas were meant to be experienced. Here, however, we verge on *Rezeptionssoziologie*.

7 Herman Melville, for example, who happens to have cited Purchas (and everything else), develops a perhaps apocalyptical literary language, reading at times like a pastiche of many Jacobeans (I name not Shakespeare). Like them, Melville wrote at a time of vivid factions when sectarian views faced encroaching standardization, and Puritanesque texts (e.g., Hawthorne) were rivals for universal imagery and meaning. Consider Melville's *Mardi*, in which names and phrases

often perfectly wed Near Eastern and Malayo-Polynesian-type sounds and syllables – from his book reading in the first case and from his travel reading in the
second (Cf. Finkelstein, 1961). Melville's cherished nautical narratives themselves represent a kind of sailor-*Sprache* evoked in *Mardi*: "Now in old Jarl's
lingo there was never an idiom. Your aboriginal tar is too much of a cosmopolitan
for that. Long companionship with seamen of all tribes: Manilla-men, Anglo-
Saxons, Cholos, Lascars, and Danes, wear away in good time all mother-tongue
stammerings. You sink your clan; down goes your nation; you speak a world's
language jovially jabbering in the Lingua-Franca of the forecastle" (Melville
1849/1970:13). So Melville (and, it seems to me, Purchas) wrote. The technical
vocabularies in comparative anthropological jargon – totem, tatoo, taboo, hapu,
mana, and so on, complemented by anima, connubium exogamy – are, I suspect,
not unrelated to such motives of interpretation.

8 I cite an excerpt of Hariot's famous account included in Frank Kermode et al.,
The Oxford Anthology of English Literature, vol. 1 (1973:547). In a footnote the
editors remark: "[Hariot's] misinterpretation of the Indians' totemic attachment to
the book itself is ironically generous; it represents what a Christian humanist who
believed in natural reason would want to be true" (p. 547). This statement itself
is, ironically, a misinterpretation. Recent anthropological work suggests that
"totemic attachments" construed as a substantive confusion between groups and
species (or book!) is an idea that itself represents what literateurs who believe in
essentialist symbols would want to be true. (Cf. Lévi-Strauss, *Le totemisme
aujourd' hui* [Paris: Presses Universitaires de France, 1962]). Such misinterpretations – which, like "misreadings," occur for interesting reasons – are the fabric of
the history of ethnology. (I thank Stephen Greenblatt for help with Hariot's
dates.)

9 The Jacobean idea and term *Fama* are difficult to extricate from "Rosicrucian"
traditions; see Frances A. Yates (1972: appendix).

10 On Purchas and Bali and the history of distortions his text helped reinforce, see
Boon (1977: Part I, chap. 9). An indication of Dutch sensitivity to the value of
royallike symbols of nationhood lies in the iconographic theme of Belgia; see
McGrath (1975).

11 Some of these themes in New World imagery are reviewed in Sanders (1978).
Extremist views are presented in L. Glaser (1973). See also Bucher (1977). For
additional illustrations, see Michael Alexander (1976:11) with comments on the
DeBry–Hakluyt connection. I should note that circumcision was equally important in Purchas's review of Christian sects; to cite one of many examples: "In all
Ethiopia, they circumcise their children in their owne houses without any Ceremony, but for a certaine ancient Custome, cutting away the Prepuce from the
Males, the Nympha from the Females: being asked, whether they beleeve Circumcision necessary to salvation, he answered, they know that it is now ceased,
and that it is no longer necessary" (1625/1907, vol. 1, 405). For a brief review of
papal epithets – Antichrist, Whore of Babylon, Beast and Hydra – in Luther and
in succeeding traditions, see M. Dorothy George (1959:introduction).

12 For the Jacobean side of things, see Roy Strong (1973) and Harris, Orgel, and
Strong (1973), just two examples from a burgeoning literature. For some Indonesian analogues, see Clifford Geertz (1977a). On Javanese–Balinese symbols of
widow burning and court suicides, see Chapter 6.

13 I employ the studies of Hill and Raymond Williams because their concern with
infrastructures helps us vastly expand the province of themes in Purchas's views
of exotics. Also, their works suggest how rhetoric of "others" – whether in
ethnological, sectarian, or class variations – never dies, only shifts.

14 For a review of the more immediate issues concerning Indians in the James River region, see Gary B. Nash's lively summary of imagery throughout the eighteenth century revolving around episodes such as Roanoke Island and the Rolfe–Pocahontas union. He makes note of Alexander Whitaker's recommendation in 1614 that "the dual policy of ruthless militarism and political intermarriage was the best policy" (1972:83). The intricate story of Pocahontas is of course involved with ideals of royalty and marriage (I thank Kathryn March for suggestions on this point). However, the part of Nash's review most relevant to Purchas concerns developments contrary to such idealizations of Indians; in particular the major change in relations in Virginia after 1612: "The Virginia Company of London gave up its plans for reaping vast profits through Indian trade on the discovering of minerals and instead instituted a liberal land policy designed to build the population of the colony rapidly, and ultimately to make it an agricultural province of such productivity that land sales would enrich its investors. When the cultivation of tobacco was perfected, giving Virginia a money crop of great potential, and further promotional efforts were rewarded with a new influx of settlers after 1619, the availability of land became a critical question for the first time in the colony's existence" (Nash 1972:69); on Purchas and Captain John Smith, see Sanders (1978: chap. 23).

15 See Boon (1977:10–19, 68). These accounts, of course, contrast with Cavendish (via Portugals) on Javanese potentates.

16 On these French views and their illustration, see Alexander (1976: chap. 1).

17 For a cross-cultural typology of kingship rites and institutions, see Hocart (1970).

18 It is worth noting that some of the accounts Purchas edited report seeking exotic spouses for captains, at least. Of course, a fundamental ethnological issue in colonial history – Portuguese, Spanish, British, Dutch – concerns rules, codes, and taboos on intermarriage and, if they were allowed, on the status of descendants. On symbolism of endogamy/exogamy in the New World, see Bucher (1977).

19 For suggestions about some covert codes in Genesis as written, see E. Leach (1969). Here I mention Grafton's imaginative "accretion" only to suggest that in Elizabethan and Jacobean symbols, it was not only masques connecting foreign lands that, to be complete, would have required ideals of *connubium*.

6. Balinese incest recaptured: A discourse

1 Cf. Boon (1977: chap. 4, p. 224). The fieldwork on which portions of this article are based was sponsored by Lembaga Ilmu Pengetahuan Indonesia and funded by a NIMH Combination Research Fellowship (1972–3). An earlier trip (1971) was made possible by the Ford Foundation and a later one (1981) by the American Philosophic Society. "Localization" in Southeast Asia is a theme of recent work by Oliver Wolters, Professor of History and Asian Studies, Cornell University.

2 Aspects of religious rationalization in certain sectors of Bali are discussed in C. Geertz (1973: chap. 7) and in Boon (1977: Part II). In areas of religious change, subsistence control, leadership, and so forth, Bali embeds principles of legitimacy in cyclic, ritual formulations. It is thus disconcerting to see Bali used to resurrect the old notion of "linear time" with a stress on individuals *versus* detemporalized "ritual communication" in Bloch (1977). Oddly, Bloch uses C. Geertz (1973: chap. 14) to illustrate an example of cultural anthropology overlooking everyday practical affairs. He calls on us to move past concern with esoteric, ritual "idioms" and to proceed with serious study of hard facts, such as entrepreneurship, overlooking the fact that Geertz's first extensive publication on

Bali (1963) treated, precisely, postcolonial entrepreneurship. Geertz showed how cyclic, ritual formulations in courtly traditions are intimately involved in influencing others, organizing any activity, and transforming praxis. To call "ritual communication" in Bali an *idiom* is to miss much of the power and subtlety of a generalized ritual system.

3 Of particular note regarding samsara is the Bhima cult in Java. See, for example, the interesting analysis by Johns (1970) of *Bhimasuci* with its ascetic and tantric components. Johns emphasizes the "radical monism" of Bhima's enlightenment in which everything "is the product of the One Mind, the microcosmos is the macrocosmos, Nirvana is Samsara, there is no duality" (p. 146). In the following discussion I try to refute an oversimplified dualistic analysis of Balinese materials, not, however, to champion monism. I find the monism/dualism distinction (itself dualistic?) oversimplified. Johns allusively rejects the "shade of Durkheim" (and by implication, I suppose, Rassers); perhaps this is appropriate for materials from the Javanese *kraton*. Yet in Balinese symbology distinctions are not collapsed into any ultimate rarification; this maintenance of distinctions strikes me as more compatible with the "dualism" of Durkheim's *L'année sociologique* than with any monism. For a fuller sense of Durkheim's dualism (implying organic solidarity) with reference to Indic traditions, see L. Dumont (1970). An elaborate debate over India between "monists" and "dualists" has been waged recently in the *Journal of Asian Studies*; see Richards et al. (1976); Marriott (1976); Barnett, Fruzzetti, and Ostör (1977). Durkheim (1960a) rejected both idealistic and empirical monisms, the latter identified with utilitarian motives. Other karma symbols of the Javanese palace are reviewed in Gonda (1970); see also Gonda (1975).

4 Tripartite Indo-European ideology as developed by Dumézil links three "functions": sovereignty (cosmic and juridical order); prowess; life-maintenance. On transposing the flexible scheme to Bali, see Boon (1977:238–40). Incest has many symbolic complexities in Bali (Boon 1977: chaps. 6, 9). Sibling incest has positive connotations if associated with godly marriage. Claimed by or attributed to a ruling group, it apparently could be used to argue their divinity if all other signs confirmed it or their criminality if not. Of course, opposed parties would differ. These cultural aspects of incest values are crucial if one is to make sense of traditions such as the records and chronicles of rival ruling houses, recently reviewed, for example, in Hanna (1976: chap. 5ff.).

5 This part of my argument attempts to add specifics and systematics to another comment by J. Hooykaas, in fact a parenthetical one: "In the 'Tantu Panggelaran' Siwa mostly appears as Batara Guru, the Divine Teacher. The whole book is principally concerned with the teaching of the Saiwa religion in Java. It deals with the founding of *mandalas* on the slopes of Java's mountains, which were places for religious concentration as well as for teaching. Many stories have been woven through this main Saiwite thread. One motive which keeps returning time and again in these stories is that of gods in their anger turning into demons, and what is done to placate their wrath. (A student of Balinese religion finds much in present-day Bali which calls to mind the 'Tantu Panggelaran.' The Balinese too are constantly preoccupied with gods who can become or might have become demons; this belief consequently necessitates continual rites of exorcism)" (1960:269). A parallel I would emphasize in ritual and symbolic action is this: High-level marriage alleviates threats of the bride being stolen just as cremation alleviates threats of the corpse being stolen. Parallels, perhaps even identities, between aspects of death and aspects of marriage demand concerted study in Balinese symbolic action, popular as well as courtly.

6 For insights into body symbols that remain, however, somewhat "architectonic," see Douglas (1970). A compendium of standard microcosm/macrocosm views in Bali runs through Covarrubias (1937). For other sources, particularly Dutch ones, see Boon (1977). For comments on more recent studies, such as Hobart (1978), see Boon (n.d.).

7 For variants of the riddle (one with an answer) in different esoteric texts, see C. Hooykaas (1973:167, 247, 257). Again, J. Hooykaas's rendition and her relating of Lady Uma's themes to tales of the Half-One and other folk traditions points toward the locus proper for anthropological concerns with how symbolic schemes mediate actions and texts. Compare also themes discussed by Sweeney in his important study *The Ramayana and the Malay Shadow Play*, in particular its ritual aspects: "This drama is parallel to, and clearly a version of the Javanese exorcistic *lakon Murwakala/Purwakala*, of which versions also exist in Bali. Kelantan has, in common with several Javanese/Balinese versions, the following major features: (1) Kala's hunger, (2) his taste for blood, (3) his right to eat certain persons, (4) a riddle which prevents his eating his father, (5) his chasing a victim, (6) a wayang within a wayang, (7) the victim is saved by the wayang" (1972:282–3).

8 For criteria of "deep" versus "shallow" cultural forms, see C. Geertz (1973: chap. 15). Additional implications of Balinese kinship as a cultural system are discussed in H. and C. Geertz (1975) and Boon (1974, 1978).

9 In this suggestive reading I try to remain between many variants of the *Ramayana*, including Valmiki's translated texts, outright sentimentalizations (e.g., Dutt) and related lore. The process extends in Bali not just to variants within a code (the textual) but to variants of the codes themselves (texts, rites, dance, illustrations, social regulations, etc.) My interest in the *Ramayana* centers on what it can *become* in translation, transposition, and transformation – an important issue in pursuits as different as structuralist analysis and *Rezeptionssoziologie*.

10 Many complexities and paradoxes of hierarchical vocabularies and speech styles enter into such considerations. To develop these issues would require a focus on performance rather than, as here, on typology. I would also stress *transmission* of codes through the generations. It is worth rethinking recent work on Balinese rites and symbols along more dialectical lines; see Boon (n.d.). On Javanese wayang kulit and its epistemologies plus performance, see in particular Becker (1979). For some suggestions about Javanese wayang beber, see Anderson (1974). On wayang in Lombok, see Eklund (n.d.).

11 For examples of relevant comparative studies of different Buddhist cultures, see Kirsch (1977), Holmberg (1980). There are glimmers of a comparative approach to Tantrism as a backdrop for contrasting varieties of Hindu and Buddhist traditions in Dumont. He points out the tantric components in Brahmanic rites and temples; he then provocatively concludes that Tantrism is "a truly fundamental variant of Hinduism, in which renunciation is replaced by reversal. While constituting and codifying Hindu ritual, while mixing intimately with other currents and without ever forming a sect in the proper sense . . . , the movement has kept an esoteric side. Also, by its very nature it is in contact with folk religion and can give expression to some aspects of it which the restricted formula would exclude, such as the complementarity of sex, and blood sacrifices to the Goddess" (L. Dumont 1980:281–2). See also Zoetmulder (1965:335ff.).

12 By the same token those South and Southeast Asian cultures pervaded by the "sober hues" of karma can be expected to conceal a muted dialectic with extremist rituals of "life."

13   This gloss of the Tristan/Isolde theme is taken from Campbell (1976). On bride-giving Hindus, see the conclusion to Chapter 7. My own text here verges on global Menippean satire (see Chapter 7, note 4).

7. Structuralism/Romanticism, reciprocally

1   Goethe and Shakespeare are the last two authors Lévi-Strauss salutes (along with an allusion to Wagner) in the finale of *Mythologiques* (1971:620–1). He expresses an affinity with Goethe and a difference with Hamlet's absolute (existentialist?) dilemma between being/not-being. Friedenthal (1963: chap. 36) summarizes Goethe's *Farbenlehre* and his wish to rescue the affective polarities of blue/yellow and their offspring colors from Newton's hated spectrum. Lévi-Strauss seeks in different ways, via tribal myth, to rescue from overabstraction the light spectrum (especially the chromatic–seductive rainbow of Amerindian myth), the musical scale, and other systematic discontinuities organizing sensuous material. On some methodological parallels between Goethe and structuralism, see M. Schneider (1979), most interesting on *Elective Affinities* and hermetic themes.

2   Cf. Boon (1972: chaps. 2, 4, 5). For helpful paragraphs on Rousseau's hostility to harmony that foreshadow Lévi-Strauss's stance against recent music's "polyphony of polyphonies," see Ryklin (1978). Readings of Lévi-Strauss that accentuate musical organization and duration appear in Ballour and Clément, ed. (1979). I attempted to incorporate certain musical dimensions of Lévi-Strauss in Boon (1980).

3   The terms "endogamy" (marriage within the tribe) and "exogamy" (marriage outside the tribe) were devised by J. F. McLennan (1865/1970), but it was L. H. Morgan who first recognized the relational aspects of the concepts: that every society is at one level ideally endogamous, at other levels exogamous. On complexities in these concepts, see the introduction by P. Rivière in McLennan (1865/1970). A helpful review of kinship and marriage theory, emphasizing alliance versus descent, is Buchler and Selby (1968).

4   Cf. Boon (1972: chap. 5). Lévi-Strauss's pervasive irony, perhaps akin to Romantic irony, is also underestimated when a particular episode is isolated and elevated into a presumably transparent moment in the writer's "metaphysical" distortion; a case in point is Derrida (1976). To isolate either *Tristes tropiques* or one of its episodes is to miss the structuralist form of the corpus (the set) that they precisely *partially* constitute. The poststructuralist response to Lévi-Strauss has been littered with insights, such as Derrida's remark that Lévi-Strauss always preserves "as an instrument something whose truth value he criticizes" (1978:284; cf. Lévi-Strauss 1963a). Yet literary critics have focused on the seemingly autobiographical material (in the first person) rather than on the unsettled boundaries between narrative and ethnography. So perceptive a textual critic as Culler (1981) still takes *Tristes tropiques'* famous sections on Lévi-Strauss's intellectual formation as reportage rather than as an exercise in conventionalized constructions of a quest-tale that occupy a position analogous to the myths that the quester later collects. *Tristes tropiques* does not offer representation of some biography external to it (any "biography" behind *Tristes tropiques* may be compared to any "natural event" behind myth: They are not what the texts are about; rather, they are what the texts constitute; they are its material-for-structure). The work is more an exercise in the "omnitemporal" and the "very "threshold of achrony," like that which G. Genette (1979:70, 79) detects in Proust and Rousseau – two authors whom Lévi-Strauss continually imitates (cf. Boon 1972: chap. 5). *Tristes tropiques* adds an omnispatial dimension as well; but the whole still unfolds in a narrative

tenor that could be parodied in this way: "Ah, well I remember two and a half
decades ago at the age of three anticipating writing, when eight and twenty, a
brief reminiscence." Nor do these dimensions pertain just to "literary" *Tristes
tropiques*; as we see in Chapter 7, they continue implicitly, and ultimately reemerge explicitly, in *Mythologiques*. In both works the multiplicity of voices,
shifts of person and actual meanings of narrative pronouns, collage of writing
(presumably pasting together author's contemporary prose with notes left from
the past), abrupt shifts from lyric to expository modes, prosody nestled within
ostensible prose, radical relativity intrinsic to modern anthropology, obliteration
of both idealist and materialist absolutes, and a pastiche of all genres (all woven
into a "medley" – cf. Payne 1981:4) recall conventions of Menippean satire (see
also Frye 1957; Bakhtin 1968). Most characteristically, there is no authorial
center and only relative authorial authority: the author's vantage is another myth
among all the other myths. A recent brief article by Goodson (1979) recognizes
Tristes tropiques as text but denies it much of its own irony by citing only the
opening few chapters where the first person apparently reigns. The mode of
operation of the work's retrospect becomes apparent only in light of the tribal
institutions that cue it; and the retrospection is variant precisely in the way that the
institutions are. (To most literary readers, the ethnography doesn't seem to matter
much.) Although Goodson's study overlooks most of the secondary literature on
Tristes tropiques, it does turn the tables on Derrida's myopic reading of Lévi-
Strauss as archaic–nostalgist (Goodson 1979:701, n. 15).

5   Lévi-Strauss (1977:473–4). I use John and Doreen Weightman's full translation
of *Tristes tropiques*, with an occasional reminiscence of John Russell's earlier
partial translation. I studiously place Lévi-Strauss's more analytic points first in
his original French, and I place his more "literary" points in translation in the first
place, thus ensuring their "mythicness" or translatability (see Appendix A). I
reverse this process for Novalis.

6   Herder's rendering of Goethe is cited and discussed in Willson (1964). I have
relied heavily on this book's review of the Romantic passion for Sanskritic traditions in trying to examine some of its conclusions in light of structuralism's
contrasting exotic ideal. Other important sources are Schwab (1950) and many
works in the extensive bibliographies and excerpts in Feldman and Richardson
(1972). On links between images of Indic Indians and New World Indians, see
Hahn (1978), which helps tie together my chapters in Part III. Willson's study
devotes little attention to Romantic irony, a topic that would, I think, help demonstrate how two minds like Schlegel's and Lévi-Strauss's actually belong together.
See, for example, J. L. Haney (1978), which provides interesting comments on
Schlegel and summaries of views on irony of Paul DeMan versus Wayne Booth
(1974).

7   We have already encountered in Chapter 5 "Indo-European ideology," the driving
concept of the comparative studies of G. Dumézil (1966–71). Dumézil detects a
tripartite scheme of relations among cosmic laws, military prowess, and basic
prosperity. The complex of values – which relates religious ideals to institutional
practice – seems to underlie hierarchical systems from India to Europe. For a
summary of Dumézil's views, emphasizing their Durkheimian basis, and their
operationalized concept of "proto," see Littleton (1973).

8   For a review of endogamy and hypergamy with regard to India, see L. Dumont
(1980). The issue is pervasive in comparative anthropology and in all areas
affected by Indo-European principles. For example, Indic ideals have influenced
both native genres in Bali and Western scholarship devoted to them. In a way
both Bali-Hindu traditions and their perception by outsiders present a later flower-

ing of Willson's "mythic image," although philological work on Bali, largely Dutch, developed (with the exception of W. von Humboldt's work on Kawi) after the routinization (and the divorce from philosophy and poetry) that Schlegel feared had set in. On related matters, ethnographic and comparative, see Boon (1977; n.d.).

9 Exerpts from Hoffmann's tales are taken from the translations by E. F. Bleiler (1967): first "Tobias Martin, Master Cooper, and His Men" (pp. 236–86), then "The Mines of Falun" (pp. 285–307). I cite these tales because they are explicit on an endogamy–hermetic theme. Regarding Hoffmann's discourse itself, and our reading of it, "Der Goldne Topf" most thoroughly absorbs itself into the process I am describing. The social analogues of such discourse – a virtual riot of hypergamy and endogamy – are developed (parodied?) in the occult, kabbalistic, and Rosicrucian games of "Die Königsbraut," which first weaves hermetic spheres around the couple and then ends with a comic return to normalcy: "But it was not long before [Herr] Amandus opened his eyes again, jumped to his legs, clasped Fräulein Aennchen in his arms, and cried, with all the rapture of affection, 'Now, my best and dearest Anna, we are one another again!' " (p. 419). The would-be Queen of the Vegetable Kingdom returns to supervising her servants in their garden work. Finally, I employ Bleiler's translation of *"Die Bergwerke zu Falun"* because, unlike the recent version by L. J. Kent and E. C. Knight (1969), it ends, suitably, I think, with the motto itself.

10 Foucault (1972:117). It is worth contrasting the sort of exotic discourse I am accentuating with a recent work by E. Said, *Orientalism* (1978). Said explores discursive properties of Western "textualities" of the East. For our purposes, he overgeneralizes the "imperialist" thrust to stereotypes of "the Oriental." His views of power as the determinant of discourse cannot explain the attraction of German early romantics to India (nor do they illuminate the attraction of French intellec- tuals to tribal systems far from their colonies). Said neglects the fact that some colonial powers – the Dutch, for example – involved with both Hindu and Islamic societies, recognized as much difference between these traditions as between either or both of them and Holland. Nor does he notice that Eastern cultures produce stereotypes of each other: Hindu versus Muslim views of each other; Buddhist views of Brahmanical traditions and vice versa; etc. These stereotypes are as exaggerated and partial as Western stereotypes of the Orient; and all such stereotypes, whether positive or pejorative, are inevitably simplifications. Scholars of cross-cultural discourse through history would do well to recall Spinoza's insights about what Durkheim might have called the "negative reciprocity" of understanding others: "The hatred of Turks against Jews and Christians, of Jews against Christians and Turks, and of Christians against Jews and Turks is derived...from ignorance and hearsay; the latter is the lowest grade of knowl- edge" – *Tractatus Theologico-Politicus*, paraphrased in L. S. Feuer (1964:264). Nor is it certain that fieldwork and/or empathy can transcend such mutual distanc- ing (sometimes in a positive, romantic register), no matter who is crossing cul- tures – a point confirmed by Said's critique. Finally, that the "Oriental" of most concern to Said – Islam – is often (like Protestantism and Judaism) represented by Westerners in ideal-types of moralistic, homogenizing reformism (according to some scholars, an earlier source of capitalist ethics than Protestantism) may pave the way for inadequate stereotypes to criticize themselves, as in Lévi-Strauss's deeply playful comment in *Tristes tropiques* that "Islam is the West of the East." One would expect more opportunities for stereotypes to self-debunk in Said's discourse theory (based in part on Foucault). But this dimension seems to have been purged by Said's own avowed moral mission and motive (1978:25–8).

11 *Fragments d'un discours amoureux*, transplanted as *A Lover's Discourse: Frag-*
ments (Barthes 1978:3, 13). See also Lévi-Strauss's spirited letter to the late
Barthes, "Sur *S/Z*," which contrasts castration to alliance; included in Bellour and
Clément (1979:495–7).

8. Conclusion: Dead moons or eclipsed?

1 A recent stimulating review by Lidov (1980) joins musicological analysis to
comparative semantics in a way that strikes me as compatible with Lévi-Strauss's
reading of myth. Lidov assesses Noske's (1977) interpretation of *texted* music,
drawing interesting contrasts with Langer (1953) and Meyer (1956, 1973) (but
disappointingly omitting Rosen [1972]). He highlights the "hetereogeneous fair-
ground of opera": "Opera raises the prospect of a comparative approach. Like
speech, music is temporal and auditory. Like the graphic arts, it fills its allotted
space, i.e., time, with a continuous and plastic sensuous material. Like gesture,
dance, and acting, it has an unmistakable, if also ineffable, alliance with movement. Like mathematics, music has an abstract aspect. Music might seem to be
the link mediating differences between many other signifying media... Music has
a semantic field of its own, different from that of speech, though one that can be
indicated by speech" (Lidov 1980:371–2). For a parallel between opera and
cultural performances that stresses similar dimensions, see Boon (1973). The
major musical theme of Lévi-Strauss's *Mythologiques* – the increasing chromati-
cism (small intervals) of mythic distinctions – culminates in *The Origin of Table
Manners* (1978:191) yet modulates on through *L'homme nu* (1971), ultimately
returning to Wagner's Isolde.

2 Merleau-Ponty concludes his *Adventures of the Dialectic* with a rejection of both
Hegel and Sartre, as he evokes "what remains dialectic if one must give up
reading history and deciphering in it the becoming-true of society" (1973:204).
Merleau-Ponty located pervasive dialectics in mutual being-in-the-world and in
the fact that the difference between two subjects "opens onto that world, because
we are imitatable and participatable through each other in this relationship with it"
(1973:204). I find a harmony between Merleau-Ponty and Lévi-Strauss (who
dedicated *La pensée sauvage* to his memory), but only by means of a transformation. Merleau-Ponty exalts subject-to-subject relations: Each "I" acknowledges
the other as in its own right an "I" who reciprocates the acknowledgment. Lévi-
Strauss, on the other hand, is willing to see self converted to object in order to
establish an object-to-object reciprocity (cf. totemism). Yet both Merleau-Ponty
and Lévi-Strauss deny that subject/object (ultimately master/slave) relations are
the essence of society; hence their respective rejections of Sartre. For Lévi-Strauss
totemisms institutionalize reciprocal object–object relations from the viewpoint of
the totalizing classification system (langue). For Merleau-Ponty pronouns, art,
and so forth institutionalize reciprocal subject–subject relations (artists and pronouns "view" objects as subjects) from the viewpoint of intersubjectivity. (See
especially Merleau-Ponty 1964b.) On Merleau-Ponty's affinities and differences
with structuralism, see Edie (1971). Merleau-Ponty discussed Mauss and Lévi-
Strauss in *Signs* (1964a).

Appendix B. Trick*stering*

1 Lévi-Strauss elaborated related points in a vivid interview with R. Ballour after
the completion of *Mythologiques*. He clarified allusions in *The Savage Mind* to
Marx and infrastructures: "*Quant à la question du déterminisme, je ne pense pas*

que Marx lui-même ait jamais conçu un déterminisme rigoureux qui aille dans un seul sens: il est clair que quand je me réfère aux infrastructures il s'agit surtout pour moi de souligner qu'il n'y a rien, dans la pensée de l'homme, que ne soit pensée du monde, en entendant par monde le monde physique et le monde social pris ensemble. Bien sûr, les constructions mythologiques constituent des sortes de relais, si je puis dire, qui eux-mêmes interviennent ultérieurement dans le déterminisme de la pensée. . .Autrement dit, les infrastructures n'agissent jamais en tant que telles, c'est-à-dire comme une réalité qui serait donnée objectivement et extérieurement à l'homme. Elles n'agissent que pour autant qu'elles sont pensées, et du moment qu'elles sont pensées, elle sont déjà mises dans une certaine forme qui a quelque chose d'obligé. L'esprit ne se trouve pas en tête à tête avec un monde qui lui soit complètement extérieur: il l'appréhende sous forme de texte dont l'élaboration commence aux niveaux les plus élémentaires de la sensibilité" (1979:160-1; emphasis added).

Bibliography

Dates in parentheses refer to the original publication or to the approximate time of writing; the first date refers to the edition quoted in the present study.

Adams, Percy G. 1962. *Travelers and Travel Liars, 1660–1800*. Berkeley: University of California Press.

Alexander, Michael, ed. 1976. *Discovering the New World*. Based on the Works of Theodore de Bry. New York: Harper & Row.

Anderson, Benedict R. O'G. 1974. The Last Picture Show: Wayang Beber. *Proceedings of the Conference on Modern Indonesian Literature*. Madison: Center for Southeast Asian Studies, University of Wisconsin.

Aron, Raymond. 1976. Interpreting Pareto. *Encounter 47*(5): 43–53.

Ashley, Maurice. 1973. *England in the Seventeenth Century*. New York: Penguin Books.

Auerbach, Erich. 1957. *Mimesis: The Representation of Reality in Western Literature*. W. Trask, trans. New York: Doubleday (Anchor Books).

Babcock, Barbara A. 1980. Reflexivity: Definitions and Discriminations. Introduction to *Semiotica* 30(½): 1–14.

____ ed. 1978. *The Reversible World: Essays in Symbolic Inversion*. Ithaca, N.Y.: Cornell University Press.

Bakhtin, Mikhail. 1968. *Rabelais and His World*. H. Iswolsky, trans. Cambridge, Mass.: MIT Press.

Barnes, J. A. 1966. Durkheim's *Division of Labor in Society*. *Man 1*(1): 158–75.

Barnett, Steve, L. M. Fruzzetti, and A. Ostör. 1977. On a Comparative Sociology of India. *Journal of Asian Studies 36*(3): 599–601.

Barth, Fredrik. 1965. *Political Leadership among Swat Pathans*. London: Athlone.

Barthes, Roland. 1972. To Write: An Intransitive Verb? In R. Macksey and E. Donato, eds., *The Structuralist Controversy*. Baltimore: Johns Hopkins University Press.

____ 1977. *Image, Music, Text*. S. Heath, trans. New York: Hill & Wang.

____ 1978. *A Lover's Discourse: Fragments*. R. Howard, trans. New York: Hill & Wang.

Basso, Keith H., and Henry A. Selby, eds. 1976. *Meaning in Anthropology*. Albuquerque: University of New Mexico Press.

Bates, Daisey. 1938. *The Passing of the Aborigines: A Lifetime Spent among the Natives of Australia*. London: Murray.

Bateson, Gregory. 1958 (1936). *Naven: A Survey of the Problems Suggested by a Composite Picture of the Culture of a New Guinea Tribe Drawn from Three Points of View*. Stanford, Calif.: Stanford University Press.

283

1972. *Steps to an Ecology of Mind.* New York: Ballantine Books.

Bauckham, Richard, ed. (n.d.) *Tudor Apocalypse.* Oxford: Courtenay Library of Reformation Classics.

Baugh, A. C., ed. 1967. *A Literary History of England.* New York: Appleton-Century-Crofts.

Becker, A. L. 1979. Text-building, Epistemology, and Aesthetics in Javanese Shadow Theatre. In A. L. Becker and A. Yengoyan, eds., *The Imagination of Reality.* Norwood, N.J.: Ablex.

Becker, A. L., and A. Yengoyan, eds. 1979. *The Imagination of Reality: Studies in Southeast Asian Coherence Systems.* Norwood, N.J.: Ablex.

Becker, Carl L. 1932. *The Heavenly City of the Eighteenth-century Philosophers.* New Haven, Conn.: Yale University Press.

Beeching, Jack. 1972. Introduction to R. Hakluyt, *Voyage and Discoveries.* J. Beeching, ed. New York: Penguin Books.

Beidelman, T. O. 1979. Evans-Pritchard, E. E. *International Encyclopedia of the Social Sciences. Biographical Supplement.* New York: Free Press.

Bellah, Robert N. 1959. Durkheim and History. *American Sociological Review.* 24: 447–61.

Bellour, Raymond, and Catherine Clément, eds. 1979. *Claude Lévi-Strauss.* Paris: Gallimard.

Bendix, Reinhard. 1962. *Max Weber: An Intellectual Portrait.* New York: Doubleday (Anchor Books).

Benedict, Ruth. 1961 (1934). *Patterns of Culture.* Boston: Houghton Mifflin.

Benjamin, Walter. 1969. *Illuminations.* Harry Zohn, trans. New York: Schocken Books.

    1978. *Reflections: Essays, Aphorisms, Autobiographical Writings.* E. Jephcott, trans. New York: Harcourt Brace Jovanovich.

Berlin, Isaiah. 1976. *Vico and Herder.* New York: Viking Press.

Black, Max. 1962a. *Models and Metaphors.* Ithaca, N.Y.: Cornell University Press.
    1968 *The Labyrinth of Language.* New York: Praeger.
    ed. 1962b. *The Social Theories of Talcott Parsons: A Critical Examination.* Ithaca, N.Y.: Cornell University Press.

Blackall, Eric A. 1978. *The Emergence of German as a Literary Language, 1700–1775.* 2d ed. Ithaca, N.Y.: Cornell University Press.

Bloch, Maurice. 1977. The Past and Present in the Present. *Man 12*(2): 280–91.

Boas, Franz. 1916. Tsimshian Mythology. *Annual Reports of the Bureau of American Ethnology, 31.* Washington, D.C.
    1927. *Primitive Art.* New York: Dover.
    1963. *Introduction of the Handbook of American Indian Languages.* Washington, D.C.: Georgetown University Press.
    1965 (1911). *The Mind of Primitive Man.* New York: Free Press.

Bohannan, Paul. 1960. *Conscience collective* and Culture. In K. H. Wolff, ed., *Essays on Sociology and Philosophy by Emile Durkheim et al.* New York: Harper & Row.

Boon, James A. 1972. *From Symbolism to Structuralism: Lévi-Strauss in a Literary Tradition.* New York: Harper & Row.
    1973. Further Operations of Culture in Anthropology: a Synthesis of and for Debate. In L. Schneider and C. Bonjean, eds., *The Idea of Culture in the Social Sciences.* Cambridge: Cambridge University Press.
    1974. Anthropology and Nannies. *Man 9*(1): 137–40.
    1977. *The Anthropological Romance of Bali, 1597–1972: Dynamic Perspectives in Marriage and Caste, Politics and Religion.* Cambridge: Cambridge University Press.

1978. The Shift to Meaning. Review of K. H. Basso and H. A. Selby, eds., *Meaning in Anthropology. American Ethnologist* 5(2): 361–7.

1980. *A Sound Portrait of Claude Lévi-Strauss.* National Public Radio series; A Question of Place.

1982. Introduction to M. Izard and P. Smith, eds., *Between Belief and Transgression,* J. Leavitt, trans. Chicago: University of Chicago Press.

(n.d.) Balinese Machinery, Balinese Culture, Balinese Text. In E. Bruner and V. Turner, eds., *The Anthropology of Experience* (forthcoming).

Boon, James A., and David M. Schneider. 1974. Kinship vis-à-vis Myth: Contrasts in Lévi-Strauss' Approaches to Cross-cultural Comparison. *American Anthropologist* 76(4): 799–817.

Booth, Wayne C. 1974. *A Rhetoric of Irony.* Chicago: University of Chicago Press.

Borges, Jorge Luis. 1964. *Labyrinths.* New York: New Directions.

Bottomore, Tom, and Robert Nisbet, eds. 1978. *A History of Sociological Analysis.* New York: Basic Books.

Bouissac, Paul. 1979. Semiotics and Surrealism. *Semiotica* 25(½): 45–58.

Bruner, Edward, M. (n.d.). Ethnography as Narrative. In E. Bruner and V. Turner, eds. *The Anthropology of Experience* (forthcoming).

Bruner, Jerome. 1976. Psychology and the Image of Man. *Times Literary Supplement.* Dec. 17.

Bucher, Bernadette. 1977. *La sauvage aux seins pendants.* Paris: Herman.

Buchler, Ira A., and Henry A. Selby. 1968. *Kinship and Social Organization.* New York: Macmillan.

Buffon, Georges-Louis de. 1971. *De l'homme.* Paris: François Maspero.

Burke, Kenneth. 1966. *Language as Symbolic Action.* Berkeley: University of California Press.

1968. Interaction: Dramatism. *International Encyclopedia of the Social Sciences.* New York: Free Press.

1970. *The Rhetoric of Religion: Studies in Logology.* Berkeley: University of California Press.

Campbell, Joseph. 1976. *The Masks of God.* 4 vols. New York: Viking Press.

Cassirer, Ernst. 1951. *The Philosophy of the Enlightenment.* Princeton, N.J.: Princeton University Press.

1953. *The Philosophy of Symbolic Forms. Vol. 1: Language.* New Haven, Conn.: Yale University Press.

Channel, Ward, and June Macklin. 1974. *The Human Nature Industry.* New York: Doubleday (Anchor Books).

Chiappelli, Fredi, ed. 1976. *First Images of America.* Berkeley: University of California Press.

Clifford, James. 1980. Fieldwork, Reciprocity, and the Making of Ethnographic Texts: The Example of Maurice Leenhardt. *Man* 15(3): 518–32.

Codere, Helen. 1968. Exchange and Display. *International Encyclopedia of the Social Sciences.* New York: Free Press.

Cohen, Sande. 1978. Structuralism and the Writing of Intellectual History. *History and Theory* 17(2): 175–206.

Coser, Lewis A. 1960. Durkheim's Conservatism and Its Implications for His Sociological Theory. In K. H. Wolff, ed., *Essays on Sociology and Philosophy by Emile Durkheim et al.* New York: Harper & Row.

Covarrubias, Miguel. 1937. *Island of Bali.* New York: Knopf.

Crawley, Ernest. 1960 (1927). *The Mystic Rose: A Study of Primitive Marriage and of Primitive Thought in Its Bearing on Marriage.* New York: New American Library (Meridian Books).

Culler, Jonathan. 1976. *Structuralist Poetics*. Ithaca, N.Y.: Cornell University Press.
    1977. *Ferdinand de Saussure*. New York: Penguin Books.
    1981. *In Pursuit of Signs: Semiotics, Post-Structuralism, Literature*. Ithaca, N.Y.: Cornell University Press.
Damon, Frederick H. 1980. The Kula and Generalized Exchange. *Man 15*(2): 267–92.
Darnell, Regna, ed. 1974. *Readings in the History of Anthropology*. New York: Harper & Row.
Darwin, Charles. 1879. *What Mr. Darwin Saw in His Voyage Round the World in the Ship Beagle*. (Edited for children; reprinted as *What Darwin Saw.*) New York: Weathervane Books.
    1977. *The Collected Papers of Charles Darwin*. P. H. Barrett, ed. Chicago: University of Chicago Press.
    1859, 1871. *The Origin of Species and The Descent of Man*. New York: Random House (Modern Library).
DeMan, Paul. 1971. *Blindness and Insight: Essays in the Rhetoric of Contemporary Criticism*. New York: Oxford University Press.
Demetz, Peter. 1978. Introduction to W. Benjamin, *Reflections: Essays, Aphorisms, Autobiographical Writings*, E. Jephcott, trans. New York: Harcourt Brace Jovanovich.
Derrida, Jacques. 1976. *Of Grammatology*. C. Chakravorty Spivak, trans. Baltimore: John Hopkins University Press.
    1978. *Writing and Difference*. A. Bass, trans. Chicago: University of Chicago Press.
Detienne, Marcel. 1979. *Dionysos Slain*. M. and L. Muellner, trans. Baltimore: Johns Hopkins University Press.
De Zoete, Beryl, and Walter Spies. 1939. *Dance and Drama in Bali*. New York: Harper's Magazine Press.
Diamond, Stanley. 1975. *In Search of the Primitive: A Critique of Civilization*. New Brunswick, N.J.: Transaction Books.
    1980 (1960). *Culture in History: Essays in Honor of Paul Radin*. New York: Farrar, Straus & Giroux (Octagon Books).
Dolgen, Janet S., D. S. Kemnitzer, and D. M. Schneider, eds. 1977. *Symbolic Anthropology: A Reader in the Study of Symbols and Meanings*. New York: Columbia University Press.
Donato, Eugenio. 1975. Lévi-Strauss and the Protocols of Distance. *Diacritics 5*(3): 2–12.
Douglas, Mary. 1966. *Purity and Danger*. New York: Praeger.
    1970. *Natural Symbols*. New York: Random House (Vintage Books).
    1975. *Implicit Meanings: Essays in Anthropology*. London: Routledge & Kegan Paul.
Drummond, Lee. 1980. The Cultural Continuum: A Theory of Intersystems. *Man 15*(2): 352–74.
Duchet, Michèle. 1971. *Anthropologie et histoire au siècle des lumières*. Paris: François Maspero.
Dudley, Edward, and M. E. Novak, eds. 1972. *The Wild Man Within: An Image in Western Thought from the Renaissance to Romanticism*. Pittsburgh: University of Pittsburgh Press.
Dumézil, Georges. 1966–71. *Mythe et épopée*. Vol. I: L'idéologie des trois fonctions. Vol. II: *Types épiques indo-européens*. Vol. III: *Un héros, un sorcier, un rois*. Paris: Gallimard.
Dumont, Jean-Paul. 1978. *The Headman and I: Ambiguity and Ambivalence in the Fieldworking Experience*. Austin: University of Texas Press.
Dumont, Louis. 1957. *Une sous-caste de l'Inde du Sud*. The Hague: Mouton.

1966. Descent or Intermarriage? A Relational View of Australian Section Systems. *Southwestern Journal of Anthropology* 22(3): 231–50.

1970a. *Homo Hierarchicus*. M. Sainsbury, trans. Chicago: University of Chicago Press.

1970b. *Religion/Politics and History in India*. The Hague: Mouton.

1975. Understanding Non-modern Civilizations. *Daedalus* 104(2): 153–72.

1977. *From Mandeville to Marx*. Chicago: University of Chicago Press.

1980. *Homo Hierarchicus: The Caste System and Its Implications*. Rev. ed. Chicago: University of Chicago Press.

Duncan, Hugh Danziel. 1961. *Language and Literature in Society*. New York: Bedminster Press.

1968. *Symbols in Society*. New York: Oxford University Press.

Durkheim, Emile. 1955 (1914). *Pragmatisme et sociologie*. Paris: J. Vrin. (Translated in part in K. H. Wolff, ed., *Essays on Sociology and Philosophy by Emile Durkheim et al*. New York: Harper & Row.)

1960a. The Dualism of Human Nature. In K. H. Wolff, ed., *Essays on Sociology and Philosophy by Emile Durkheim et al*. New York: Harper & Row.

1960b. *Montesquieu and Rousseau: Forerunners of Sociology*. Ann Arbor: University of Michigan Press.

1964 (1893). *The Division of Labor in Society*. George Simpson, trans. New York: Free Press.

1965 (1912). *The Elementary Forms of the Religious Life*. J. W. Swain, trans. New York: Free Press.

1974. *Sociology and Philosophy*. D. F. Pocock, trans. New York: Free Press.

1978. *Emile Durkheim on Institutional Analysis*. Mark Traugott, trans. Chicago: University of Chicago Press.

Durkheim, Emile, and Marcel Mauss. 1963 (1903). *Primitive Classification*. Rodney Needham, trans. Chicago: University of Chicago Press.

Dutt, Romesh C., trans. 1910. *The Ramayana and the Mahabharata: Condensed into English Verse*. New York: Dutton.

Eco, Umberto. 1976. *A Theory of Semiotics*. Bloomington: Indiana University Press.

Edie, James M. 1971. Was Merleau-Ponty a Structuralist? *Semiotica* 4(4): 297–323.

Eggan, Fred. 1961. Introduction to R. H. Lowie, *Primitive Society*. New York: Harper & Row (Torchbooks).

1973 (1950). *Social Organization of the Western Pueblos*. Chicago: University of Chicago Press.

Eisenstein, Elizabeth. 1979. *The Printing Press as an Agent of Change: Communication and Cultural Transformations in Early-modern Europe*. 2 Vols. Cambridge: Cambridge University Press.

Eklund, Judith. (n.d.) A Preliminary Analysis of the Sasak Shadow Play (Wayang). *Journal of Asian Studies* (forthcoming).

Eliade, Mircea. 1978. *The Forge and the Crucible*. 2d ed. Chicago: University of Chicago Press.

Elliott, J. H. 1970. *The Old World and the New, 1492–1650*. Cambridge: Cambridge University Press.

1973. The Discovery of America and the Discovery of Man. *Proceedings of the British Academy, 58*.

Engels, Fredrick. 1972 (1884). The Origin of the Family *and* Private Property and the State. In R. C. Tucker, ed., *The Marx–Engels Reader*. New York: Norton.

Errington, Shelley. 1979. Some Comments on Style in the Meanings of the Past. *Journal of Asian Studies* 38(2): 231–44.

Evans-Pritchard, E. E. 1940. *The Nuer*. New York: Oxford University Press (Clarendon Press).

1956. *Nuer Religion*. New York: Oxford University Press.

1962. *Social Anthropology and Other Essays*. New York: Free Press.

1965. *Theories of Primitive Religion*. New York: Oxford University Press (Clarendon Press).

Feldman, Burton, and R. D. Richardson. 1972. *The Rise of Modern Mythology, 1680–1860*. Bloomington: Indiana University Press.

Felheim, Marvin. 1969. Introduction to M. Twain and C. D. Warner, *The Gilded Age: A Tale of Today*. New York: New American Library (Signet Classics).

Felman, Shoshana, ed. 1977. *Literature and Psychoanalysis, the Question of Reading: Otherwise*. Yale French Studies, 55/56.

Feuer, L. S. 1964. *Spinoza and the Rise of Liberalism*. Boston: Beacon Press.

Finkelstein, D. M. 1961. *Melville's Orienda*. New Haven, Conn.: Yale University Press.

Firth, Raymond, ed. 1957. *Man and Culture: An Evaluation of the Work of Bronislaw Malinowski*. London: Routledge & Kegan Paul.

Forster, E. M. 1924. *A Passage to India*. New York: Harcourt Brace.

Fortune, Reo F. 1963 (1932). *Sorcerers of Dobu*: New York: Dutton.

Foster, William. 1946. Samuel Purchas. In E. Lynam, ed., *Richard Hakluyt and his Successors*. London.

Foucault, Michel. 1972. *The Archaeology of Knowledge*. A. M. Sheridan, trans. New York: Harper & Row.

1973. *The Order of Things: An Archaeology of the Human Sciences*. New York: Random House (Vintage Books).

Fox, James J. 1977. *Harvest of the Palm: Ecological Change in Eastern Indonesia*. Cambridge, Mass.: Harvard University Press.

Franklin, H. Bruce. 1963. *The Wake of the Gods: Melville's Mythology*. Stanford, Calif.: Stanford University Press.

Frazer, James G. 1980. *The Golden Bough: A Study in Comparative Religion*. London: Macmillan Press.

1911–15. *The Golden Bough*. 12 Vols. New York: Macmillan.

1959. *The New Golden Bough*. Theodore H. Gaster, ed. New York: New American Library (Mentor Books).

1961 (1922). Preface to B. Malinowski, *Argonauts of the Western Pacific*. New York: Dutton.

Freud, Sigmund. 1961 (1930). *Civilization and Its Discontents*. J. Strachey, trans. New York: Norton.

Friedenthal, Richard. 1963. *Goethe: His Life and Times*. London: Weidenfeld and Nicolson.

Friederich, R. 1959. *The Civilization and Culture of Bali*. Calcutta: Susil Gupta.

Friedrich, Paul. 1978. *The Meaning of Aphrodite*. Chicago: University of Chicago Press.

1979. *Language, Context, and the Imagination*. Stanford, Calif.: Stanford University Press.

Frye, Northrop. 1957. *Anatomy of Criticism*. Princeton: Princeton University Press.

1973. *The Critical Path*. Bloomington: Indiana University Press.

1976. *The Secular Scripture*. Cambridge, Mass.: Harvard University Press.

Gay, Peter. 1966. *The Enlightenment; An Interpretation*. 2 vols. New York: Knopf.

Geertz, Clifford. 1960. *The Religion of Java*. New York: Free Press.

1963. *Peddlers and Princes*. Chicago: University of Chicago Press.

1968. *Islam Observed*. New Haven, Conn.: Yale University Press.

289   *Bibliography*

1972. The Wet and the Dry. *Human Ecology 1*(1): 23–39.

1973. *The Interpretation of Cultures*. New York: Basic Books.

1977a. Centers, Kings, and Charisma. In J. Ben David and T. N. Clark, eds., *Culture and Its Creators*. Chicago: University of Chicago Press.

1977b. Found in Translation: On the Social History of the Moral Imagination. *Georgia Review 31*(4): 788–810.

1979. From the Native's Point of View. In P. Rabinow and W. Sullivan, eds., *Interpretive Social Science: A Reader*. Berkeley: University of California Press.

1980a. *Negara: The Theater State in Nineteenth Century Bali*. Princeton: Princeton University Press.

1980b. Blurred Genres. *American Scholar 49*: 165–82.

ed. 1974. *Myth, Symbol and Culture*. New York: Norton.

Geertz, Hildred, and Clifford Geertz. 1975. *Kinship in Bali*. Chicago: University of Chicago Press.

Genette, Gerard. 1979. *Narrative Discourse* J. Lewin, trans. Ithaca, N.Y.: Cornell University Press.

Gennep, Arnold van. 1960 (1909). *The Rites of Passage*. M. B. Vizedom and G. L. Caffee, trans. Chicago: University of Chicago Press.

George, M. Dorothy. 1959. *English Political Caricature to 1972*. New York: Oxford University Press (Clarendon Press).

Giddens, Anthony. 1971. *Capitalism and Modern Social Theory: An Analysis of the Writings of Marx, Durkheim, and Max Weber*. Cambridge: Cambridge University Press.

Girard, René. 1973. Lévi-Strauss, Frye, Derrida, and Shakespearean Criticism. *Diacritics 3*(3): 34–8.

1977. *Violence and the Sacred*. P. Gregory, trans. Baltimore: Johns Hopkins University Press.

Glaser, Lynn. 1973. Indians or Jews? Introduction to a reprint of Manasseh ben Isreal, *The Hope of Israel*. Gilroy, Calif.

Gonda, J. 1970. Karman and Retributive Justice in Ancient Java. In H. B. Sarkar, ed., *R. C. Majumdar Felicitation Volume*. Calcutta: K. L. Mukhopadhyay.

1975. The Indian Religions in Pre-Islamic Indonesia and Their Survival in Bali. *Handbuch der Orientalistik*, Vol. III. Leiden.

Goodson, A. C. 1979. Oedipus Anthropologicus. *Modern Language Notes 94*(4): 688–701.

Goslinga, Cornelis Ch. 1971. *The Dutch in the Caribbean and on the Wild Coast, 1580–1680*. Assen: Van Gorcum.

Gouldner, Alvin W. 1973. Romanticism and Classicism: Deep Structures in Social Science. *Diogenes 82*: 88–107.

Gralapp, Leland W. 1967. Balinese Painting and the Wayang Tradition. *Artibus Asiae 29*(2/3): 239–66.

Gudeman, Stephen. 1978. Anthropological Economics: the Question of Distribution. *Annual Review of Anthropology 7*: 347–78.

Hahn, Thomas. 1978. Indians East and West: Primitivism and Savagery in English Discovery Narratives of the Sixteenth Century. *Journal of Medieval and Renaissance Studies 8*(1): 77–114.

Hakluyt, Richard. 1972. *Voyage and Discoveries*. Jack Beeching, ed. New York: Penguin Books.

Haller, William. 1972. *The Rise of Puritanism*. Philadelphia: University of Pennsylvania Press.

Halliday, Michael A. K. 1978. *Language as a Social Semiotic*. Baltimore: University Park Press.

Haney, Janice L. 1978. "Shadow-Hunting": Romantic Irony, *Sartor Resartus*, and Victorian Romanticism. *Studies in Romanticism 17*: 302–18.

Hanna, Willard A. 1976. *Bali Profile*. New York: American Universities Field Staff.

Hans, James S. 1979. Derrida and Freeplay. *Modern Language Notes 94*(4): 809–26.

Harari, Josué, ed. 1979. *Textual Strategies: Perspectives in Post-Structuralist Criticism*. Ithaca, N.Y.: Cornell University Press.

Harris, John, Stephen Orgel, and Roy Strong. 1973. *The King's Arcadia: Inigo Jones and the Stuart Court*. London.

Harris, Marvin. 1968. *The Rise of Anthropological Theory*. New York: Crowell.

Hawkes, Terence. 1977. *Structuralism and Semiotics*. Berkeley: University of California Press.

Hayes, E. Nelson, and Tanya Hayes, eds. 1970. *Claude Lévi-Strauss: The Anthropologist as Hero*. Cambridge, Mass.: MIT Press.

Herbert, T. Walter. 1980. *Marquesan Encounters: Melville and the Meaning of Civilization*. Cambridge, Mass.: Harvard University Press.

Hertz, Robert. 1973. The Pre-eminence of the Right Hand: A Study in Religious Polarity. In R. Needham, ed., *Right and Left: Essays on Dual Symbolic Classification*. Chicago: University of Chicago Press.

Hill, Christopher. 1965. *Intellectual Origins of the English Revolution*. New York: Oxford University Press.

   1966. *Century of Revolution, 1603–1714*. New York: Norton.

   1975. *The World Turned Upside Down*. London: Penguin Books.

Hinzler, H. I. R. 1975. *Wayang op Bali*. Nederlandse Vereniging voor het Poppenspel.

Hobart, Mark. 1978. The Path of the Soul: The Legitimacy of Nature in Balinese Conceptions of Space. In G. B. Milner, ed., *Natural Symbols in Southeast Asia*. London: School of Oriental and African Studies, University of London.

Hocart, A. M. 1952. *The Life-giving Myth*. London: Methuen & Co.

   1954. *Social Origins*. London: Watts.

   1970. *Kings and Councillors*. Chicago: University of Chicago Press.

Hockett, Charles F. 1964. Scheduling. In *Cross-Cultural Understanding*, F. S. C. Northrope and H. H. Livingston, eds. New York: Harper & Row.

Hodgen, Margaret T. 1971. *Early Anthropology in the Sixteenth and Seventeenth Centuries*. Philadelphia: University of Pennsylvania Press.

Hoffmann, E. T. A. 1967. *Tales*. E. F. Bleiler, trans. New York: Dover.

   1969. *Selected Writings of E. T. A. Hoffman*. 2 vols. L. J. Kent and E. C. Knight, eds. Chicago: University of Chicago Press.

Holmberg, David H. 1980. Lama, Shaman, and Lambu in Tamang Religious Practice. Ph.D. dissertation, Cornell University.

Honour, Hugh. 1975. *The New Golden Land*. New York: Pantheon Books.

Hooykaas. C. 1973. *Kama and Kala: Materials for the Study of Shadow Theatre in Bali*. Amsterdam: Verhandelingen der Koninklijke Nederlandse Academie van Wetenschappen, afd. Letterkunde. 79.

Hooykaas, Jacoba. 1960. The Myth of the Young Cowherd and the Little Girl. *Bijdragen tot de Land-, Taal- en Volkenkunde 117*(2).

   1957. De Godsdienstige Ondergrond van het Praemuslimse Huwelijk op Java en Bali. *Indonesië 10*(2): 109–36.

Horkheimer, Max, and Theodor W. Adorno. 1972. *Dialectic of Enlightenment*. John Cumming, trans. New York: Seabury Press.

Huddleston, L. E. 1967. *Origins of the American Indians: European Concepts, 1492–1729*. Austin: University of Texas Press.

Hughes, H. Stuart. 1961. *Consciousness and Society*. New York: Random House.

Huizinga, Jehan. 1949. *Homo Ludens*. London: Routledge & Kegan Paul

Hyman, Stanley Edgar. 1966. *The Tangled Bank: Darwin, Marx, Frazer, and Freud as Imaginative Writers*. New York: Grosset & Dunlap.

Hymes, Dell. 1970. Linguistic Method in Ethnography: Its Development in the United States. In P. L. Garvin, ed., *Method and Theory in Linguistics*. The Hague: Mouton.

1971. The "Wife" Who "Goes Out" Like a Man: Reinterpretation of a Clcakamas Chinook Myth. In *Essays in Semiotics*. Julia Kristeva, ed. The Hague: Mouton.

ed. 1964. *Language in Culture and Society*. New York: Harper & Row.

1973. *Reinventing Anthropology*. New York: Random House. Izard, Michel, and Pierre Smith, eds. 1979. *La fonction symbolique*. Paris: Gallimard.

1982. *Between Belief and Transgression*. J. Leavitt, trans. Chicago: University of Chicago Press.

Jakobson, Roman. 1960. Concluding Statement: Linguistics and Poetics. In Thomas A. Sebeok, ed., *Style and Language*. Cambridge, Mass.: MIT Press.

1966. Franz Boas' Approach to Language. In Thomas A. Sebeok, ed., *Portraits of Linguists*. Vol. II. Bloomington: Indiana University Press.

Jakobson, Roman, and Morris Halle. 1956. Fundamentals of Language. Janua Linguarum I. The Hague: Mouton.

James, William. 1960 (1907–9). What Pragmatism Means; Pragmatism's Conception of Truth; The Pragmatist Account of Truth and Its Misunderstanders. In M. Konvitz and G. Kennedy, eds., *The American Pragmatists*. New York: New American Library.

1977. *A Pluralistic Universe*. F. Burkhardt, ed. Cambridge, Mass.: Harvard University Press.

Jameson, Fredric. 1971. *Marxism and Form*. Princeton: Princeton University Press.

1972. *The Prison-house of Language*. Princeton: Princeton University Press.

1974. The Vanishing Metaphor: Narrative Structure in Max Weber. *New German Critique 1*(1): 52–89.

Jarvie, I. C. 1969. *The Revolution in Anthropology*. Chicago: Henry Regnery.

Jay, Martin. 1973. *The Dialectical Imagination: A History of the Frankfurt School and the Institute of Social Research, 1923–1950*. Boston: Little, Brown.

Jennings, Francis. 1975. *The Invasion of America: Indians, Colonialism, and the Cant of Conquest*. Chapel Hill: University of North Carolina Press.

Johns, A. 1970. The Enlightenment of Bhima. In H. B. Sarkar, ed., *R. C. Majumdar, Felicitation Volume*. Calcutta: K. L. Mukhopadhyay.

Josselin de Jong, P. E. de, ed. 1977. *Structural Anthropology in the Netherlands*. The Hague: Nijhoff.

Kenner, Hugh. 1962. *The Stoic Comedians: Flaubert, Joyce, and Beckett*. Berkeley: University of California Press.

Kermode, Frank, and John Hollander, eds., 1973. *The Oxford Anthology of English Literature*. Vol. I. New York: Oxford University Press.

Kirsch, A. Thomas. 1977. Complexity in the Thai Religious System: *Journal of Asian Studies 36*(2): 241–66.

Knowlson, James. 1975. *Universal Language Schemes in England and France, 1600–1800*. Toronto: University of Toronto Press.

Konvitz, Milton R., and G. Kennedy. 1960. *The American Pragmatists: Selected Writings*. New York: New American Library (Meridian Books).

Korn, V. E. 1932. *Het Adatrecht van Bali*. 2d ed. The Hague: G. Naeff.

Kroeber, A. L. 1963. *Anthropology: Cultural Patterns and Processes*. New York: Harbinger Books.

1966. *An Anthropologist Looks at History*. Foreward by Milton Singer. Berkeley: University of California Press.

Kroeber, A. L., and T. T. Waterman, eds. 1931. *Sourcebook in Anthropology.* Rev. ed. New York: Harcourt Brace.

Kronenfeld, P., and W. Decker. 1979. Review article on structuralism. *Annual Review of Anthropology 8.*

LaCapra, Dominick. 1972. *Emile Durkheim: Sociologist and Philosopher.* Ithaca, N.Y.: Cornell University Press.

Ladner, Gerhart B. 1979. Medieval and Modern Understanding of Symbolism: A Comparison. *Speculum 54(2).*

Landström, Björn. 1966. *Columbus.* New York: Macmillan.

Langer, Suzanne K. 1953. *Feeling and Form.* New York: Scribner.

Leach, Edmund. 1961. *Rethinking Anthropology.* London: Athlone.

1962. Pulleyar and the Lord Buddha. *Psychoanalysis and the Psychoanalytic Review 49*: 80–102.

1964a. Anthropological Aspects of Language: Animal Categories and Verbal Abuse. In E. H. Lenneberg, ed., *New Directions in the Study of Language.* Boston: MIT Press.

1964b. *Political Systems of Highland Burma.* Boston: Beacon Press.

1968a. The Comparative Method in Anthropology. *International Encyclopedia of the Social Sciences.* New York: Free Press.

1968b. Ritual. *International Encyclopedia of the Social Sciences.* New York: Free Press.

1969. *Genesis as Myth and Other Essays.* London: Jonathan Cape.

1970. *Claude Lévi-Strauss.* New York: Viking Press.

1976. *Culture and Communication.* Cambridge University Press.

ed. 1967. *The Structural Study of Myth and Totemism.* London: Tavistock.

Lessa, William, and Evon Z. Vogt, eds. 1979. *Reader in Comparative Religion: An Anthropological Approach.* 4th ed. New York: Harper & Row.

Levin, Harry. 1969. *The Myth of the Golden Age in the Renaissance.* New York: Oxford University Press.

Lévi-Strauss, Claude. 1946. French Sociology. In G. Gurvitch and W. E. Moore, eds., *Sociology in the Twentieth Century.* New York: Philosophical Library.

1950. Introduction. Marcel Mauss. *Sociologie et anthropologie.* Paris: Presses Universitaires de France.

1955. *Tristes tropiques.* Paris: Plon.

1961. *Tristes tropiques.* John Russell, trans. New York: Atheneum.

1963a. *Totemism.* Rodney Needham, trans. Boston: Beacon Press.

1963b. *Structural Anthropology.* C. Jacobson and B. Grundfest Schoepf, trans. New York: Doubleday (Anchor Books).

1964. *Le cru et le cuit; Mythologiques I.* Paris: Plon.

1966a. *The Savage Mind.* Chicago: University of Chicago Press.

1966b. *Du miel aux cendres; Mythologiques II.* Paris: Plon.

1966c. The Scope of Anthropology. *Current Anthropology 7(2)*: 112–23.

1967. The Story of Asdiwal. In E. Leach, ed., *The Structural Study of Myth and Totemism.* London: Tavistock.

1968. *L'origine des manières de table; Mythologiques III.* Paris: Plon.

1969a. *The Elementary Structures of Kinship.* J. H. Bell and J. R. von Sturmer, trans. Rodney Needham, ed. Boston: Beacon Press.

1969b. *The Raw and the Cooked.* John and Doreen Weightman, trans. New York: Harper & Row (Torchbooks).

1971. *L'homme nu; Mythologiques IV.* Paris: Plon.

1972. Structuralism and Ecology. *Barnard Alumnae* (Spring): 6–14.

1973. *L'anthropologie structurale 2.* Paris: Plon.

1975a. *La voie des masques.* 2 vols. Geneva: Skira.

1975b. Discussions et polémiques. *L'homme* 15(3–4): 183.

1977. *Tristes tropiques.* John and Doreen Weightman, trans. New York: Pocket Books.

1978. *The Origin of Table Manners.* John and Doreen Weightman, trans. New York: Harper & Row.

1979. Claude Lévi-Strauss Reconsiders. Interview with Jean-Marie Benoist. *Encounter.* July 1979.

1980. Ce que je suis. *Le nouvel observateur.* June 28 and July 5.

Lichtenberg, Georg Christoph. 1970. Commentaries. In *Hogarth on High Life: The "Marriage a la Mode" Series.* A. S. Wensinger, ed. Middletown, Conn.: Wesleyan University Press.

Lidov, David. 1980. Musical and Verbal Semiotics. *Semiotica 31*(¾): 369–91.

Lienhardt, Godfrey. 1961. *Divinity and Experience: The Religion of the Dinka.* New York: Oxford University Press.

Littleton, C. Scott. 1973. *The New Comparative Mythology: An Anthropological Assessment of the Theories of Georges Dumézil.* Berkeley: University of California Press.

Lovejoy, Arthur O. 1964. *The Great Chain of Being.* Cambridge, Mass.: Harvard University Press.

Lowie, Robert H. 1927. *Origin of the State.* New York: Harcourt Brace.

1937. *The History of Ethnological Theory.* New York: Holt.

1948. *Social Organization.* New York: Holt, Rinehart and Winston.

1961. (1920). *Primitive Society.* New York: Harper & Row (Torchbooks).

1972. *The German People: A Social Portrait to 1914.* New York: Farrar, Straus & Giroux (Octagon Books).

1975. *Toward Understanding Germany.* Chicago: University of Chicago Press.

Lukes, Stephen. 1968. Mauss, Marcel. *International Encyclopedia of the Social Sciences.* New York: Free Press.

1973. *Emile Durkheim: His Life and Work.* London: Penguin Books.

Lynam, Edward, ed. 1946. *Richard Hakluyt and his Successors.* London.

Lyons, John. 1968. *Introduction to Theoretical Linguistics.* Cambridge University Press.

1977. *Semantics.* 2 vols. Cambridge: Cambridge University Press.

Macksey, Richard, and E. Donato, eds. 1972. *The Structuralist Controversy.* Baltimore: Johns Hopkins University Press.

Maddock, Kenneth. 1972. *The Australian Aborigines: A Portrait of Their Society.* London: Penguin Books.

Malefijt, Annemarie de Waal. 1974. *Images of Man: A History of Anthropological Thought.* New York: Knopf.

Malinowski, Bronislaw. 1929. *The Sexual Life of Savages in North-western Melanesia.* New York: Harcourt Brace.

1935. *Coral Gardens and Their Magic.* Vol. II. New York: American Books.

1944. *A Scientific Theory of Culture and Other Essays.* Chapel Hill: University of North Carolina Press.

1961 (1922). *Argonauts of the Western Pacific.* New York: Dutton.

1963. Introduction to R. Fortune. *Sorcerers of Dobu.* New York: Dutton.

1967. *A Diary in the Strict Sense of the Term.* New York: Harcourt, Brace & World.

Manuel, Frank E., and Fritzie P. Manuel. 1974. Sketch for a Natural History of Paradise. In C. Geertz, ed., *Myth, Symbol and Culture.* New York: Norton.

1979. *Utopian Thought in the Western World.* Cambridge, Mass.: Harvard University Press.

Marcus, George E. 1980. Rhetoric and the Ethnographic Genre in Anthropological Research. *Current Anthropology 21*(4): 507–10.

Mariott, McKim. 1976. Interpreting Indian Society: A Monistic Alternative to Dumont's Dualism. *Journal of Asian Studies 36*(1): 189-95.

Martindale, Don, and Johannes Riedel. 1958. Introduction to M. Weber. *The Rational and Social Foundations of Music*. Carbondale: Southern Illinois University Press.

Martinet, André. 1966. *Elements of General Linguistics*. E. Palmer, trans. Chicago: University of Chicago Press.

Marx, Karl. 1967 (1867). *Capital: A Critique of Political Economy*, Vol. I. S. Moore and E. Aveling, trans. F. Engels, ed. New York: International Publishers.

Mauss, Marcel. 1950. *Sociologie et anthropologie*. Paris: Presses Universitaires de France.

1967 (1925). *The Gift: Forms and Functions of Exchange in Archaic Societies*. I. Cunnison, trans. New York: Norton.

Maybury-Lewis, David, ed. 1979. *Dialectical Societies: The Ge and Bororo of Central Brazil*. Cambridge, Mass.: Harvard University Press.

McGrath, Elizabeth. 1975. A Netherlandish History by Joachim Wtewael. *Journal of the Warburg and Courtauld Institute: 38*: 182–217.

McLennan, John F. 1970 (1865). *Primitive Marriage: An Inquiry into the Origin of the Form of Capture in Marriage Ceremonies*. Peter Rivière, ed. Chicago: University of Chicago Press.

Mead, Margaret. 1959. *An Anthropologist at Work: Writings of Ruth Benedict*. New York: Avon Books.

1963. *Sex and Temperament in Three Primitive Societies*. New York: Morrow.

1971. *Coming of Age in Samoa*. New York: Morrow.

1972. *Blackberry Winter: My Earlier Years*. New York: Morrow.

Mehlman, Jeffrey. 1974. *A Structural Study of Autobiography: Proust, Leiris, Sartre, Lévi-Strauss*. Ithaca, N.Y.: Cornell University Press.

Melville, Herman. 1970 (1849). *Mardi and a Voyage Thither*. Evanston, Ill.: Northwestern University Press and the Newberry Library.

1972 (1851). *Moby Dick; or, the Whale*. Harold Beaver, ed. New York: Penguin Books.

Mencher, Joan P. 1974. The Caste System Upside Down, or the Not-so-mysterious East. *Current Anthropology 15*(4): 469–91.

Merleau-Ponty, Maurice. 1964a. *Signs*. R. C. McCleary, trans. Evanston, Ill.: Northwestern University Press.

1964b. *The Primacy of Perception*. J. M. Edie, ed. Evanston, Ill.: Northwestern University Press.

1973. *Adventures of the Dialectic*. J. Bien, trans. Evanston, Ill.: Northwestern University Press.

Meyer, Leonard. 1956. *Emotion and Meaning in Music*. Chicago: University of Chicago Press.

1973. *Explaining Music*. Chicago: University of Chicago Press.

Mitzman, Arthur, 1970. *The Iron Cage: An Historical Interpretation of Max Weber*. New York: Knopf.

Moffatt, Michael. 1979. *An Untouchable Community in South India*. Princeton, N.J.: Princeton University Press.

Montaigne. 1949. *Selected Essays*. Blanchard Bates, ed. New York: Random House (Modern Library).

Muhlmann, Wilhelm E. 1971. Max Weber and the Concept of Pariah-communities. In O. Stammer, ed., *Max Weber and Sociology Today*. Oxford: Blackwell Publisher.

Multatuli. 1967 (1860). *Max Havelaar, or the Coffee Auctions of the Dutch Trading Company*. Roy Edwards, trans. London: Heinemann.

Murphy, Robert F. 1972. *Robert H. Lowie*. New York: Columbia University Press.

1980. *The Dialectics of Social Life*. New York: Columbia University Press.

Nash, Gary B. 1972. The Image of the Indian in the Southern Colonial Mind. In E. Dudley and M. Novak, eds., *The Wild Man Within*. Pittsburgh: University of Pittsburgh Press.

Needham, Rodney. 1963. Introduction to E. Durkheim and M. Mauss, *Primitive Classification*. Chicago: University of Chicago Press.

1970. Introduction to A. M. Hocart, *Kings and Councillors*.

1974. *Remarks and Inventions: Skeptical Essays about Kinship*. London: Tavistock.

ed. 1973. *Right and Left: Essays on Dual Symbolic Classification*. Chicago: University of Chicago Press.

Nisbet, Robert. 1976. *Sociology as an Art Form*. New York: Oxford University Press.

Noske, Frits. 1977. *The Signifier and the Signified: Studies in the Operas of Mozart and Verdi*. The Hague: Nijhoff.

O'Flaherty, Wendy Doniger. 1973. *Asceticism and Eroticism in the Mythology of Siva*. New York: Oxford University Press.

1980. Karma and Rebirth in the Vedas and Puranas. In W. O'Flaherty, ed., *Karma and Rebirth in Classical Indian Traditions*. Berkeley: University of California Press.

Oldroyd, D. R. 1980. *Darwinian Impacts*. Atlantic Highlands, N.J.: Humanities Press.

Oswalt, Wendell Hillman. 1972. *Other People, Other Customs: World Ethnography and Its History*. New York: Holt, Rinehart and Winston.

Parsons, Talcott. 1949 (1937). *The Structure of Social Action*. New York: Free Press.

1971. Value-freedom and Objectivity. In O. Stammer, ed., *Max Weber and Sociology Today*. Oxford: Blackwell Publisher.

1974. The Life and Work of Emile Durkheim. In E. Durkheim, *Sociology and Philosophy*. New York: Free Press.

1975. On "De-Parsonizing Weber." *American Sociological Review* 40(5): 666–9.

1979. The Symbolic Environment of Modern Economies. *Social Research*, Autumn 1979: 436–53.

Paul, Robert A. 1976. Did the Primal Crime Take Place? *Ethos* 4(3): 311–52.

Payne, F. Anne. 1981. *Chaucer and Menippean Satire*. Madison: University of Wisconsin Press.

Peacock, James L. 1968. *Rites of Modernization*. Chicago: University of Chicago Press.

1975. *Consciousness and Change: Symbolic Anthropology in Evolutionary Perspective*. Oxford: Blackwell Publisher.

Peirce, Charles Sanders. 1955 (1893–1910). *Philosophical Writings of Peirce*. J. Buchler, ed. New York: Dover.

Penrose, Boise, 1962. *Tudor and Early Stuart Voyaging*. Washington, D.C.: Folger Books.

Peyre, Henri. 1960. Durkheim: The Man, His Time, and His Intellectual Background. In K. H. Wolff, ed., *Essays on Sociology and Philosophy by Emile Durkheim et al*. New York: Harper & Row.

Piaget, Jean. 1968. *Structuralism*. C. Maschler, trans. London: Routledge & Kegan Paul.

Pope, Whitney, J. Cohen, and Lawrence Hazelrigg. On the Divergence of Weber and Durkheim: A Critique of Parson's Convergence Thesis. *American Sociological Review* 40(4): 417–27.

Pudja, Gde. 1963. *Sosiologi Hindu Dharma*. Jakarta: Jajasan Pembangunan Pura Pita Maha.
Punyatmadja, I. B. Oka. 1970. *Pancha Cradha*. Den Pasar: Parisada Hindu Dharma.
Purchas, Samuel. 1907 (1625). *Hakluytus Posthumus; or Purchas His Pilgrimes*. 20 vols. Glascow: James MacLehose.
Rabinow, Paul. 1977. *Reflections on Fieldwork in Morocco*. Berkeley: University of California Press.
Rabinow, Paul, and William M. Sullivan. 1979. *Interpretive Social Science: A Reader*. Berkeley: University of California Press.
Radcliffe-Brown, A. R. 1952. *Structure and Function in Primitive Society*. New York: Free Press.
    1964 (1922). *Andaman Islanders*. New York: Free Press.
Radin, Paul. 1972. *The Trickster: A Study in American Indian Mythology*. New York: Schocken Books.
Richards, Audrey I. 1957. Culture in Malinowski's work. *In* R. Firth, ed. *Man and Culture: An Evaluation of the Work of Bronislaw Malinowski*. London: Routledge & Kegan Paul.
Richards, J. F., and R. W. Nicholas, eds. 1976. Symposium: The Contributions of Louis Dumont. *Journal of Asian Studies* 35(4): 579–646.
Ricoeur, Paul. 1963. Structure et herméneutique. *Esprit 322*: 596–627.
    1979. The Model of the Text: Meaningful Action Considered as a Text. In P. Rabinow and W. Sullivan, eds., *Interpretive Social Science: A Reader*. Berkeley: University of California Press.
Robson, S. O. 1972. The Kawi Classics in Bali. *Bijdragen tot de Land-, Taal- en Volkenkunde 128*(2–3): 307–29.
Rosaldo, Michelle Z. 1980. *Knowledge and Passion: Ilongot Conceptions of Self and Social Life*. Cambridge University Press.
Rosaldo, Renato. 1980. *Ilongot Headhunting, 1883–1974*. Stanford, Calif.: Stanford University Press.
Rosen, Charles. 1972. *The Classical Style: Haydn, Mozart, Beethoven*. New York: Norton.
Roth, Guenther. 1968. Introduction to M. Weber, *Economy and Society*. New York: Bedminster Press.
Roth, Guenther, and Wolfgang Schluchter. 1979. *Max Weber's Vision of History*. Berkeley: University of California Press.
Rowe, John Howland. 1965. The Renaissance Foundations of Anthropology. *American Anthropologist 67*(1): 1–14.
Ryklin, M. 1978. Rousseau, Rousseauism and the Fundamental Concepts of Structural Anthropology. *International Social Science Journal 30*(3).
Sagan, Carl. 1977. *The Dragons of Eden: Speculations on the Evolution of Human Intelligence*. New York: Ballantine Books.
Sahlins, Marshall. 1972. *Stone Age Economics*. Chicago: Aldine.
    1976a. *Culture and Practical Reason*. Chicago: University of Chicago Press.
    1976b. *The Use and Abuse of Biology: An Anthropological Critique of Sociobiology*. Ann Arbor: University of Michigan Press.
Said, Edward. 1975. *Beginnings*. Baltimore: Johns Hopkins University Press
    1978. *Orientalism*. New York: Pantheon Books.
Sanders, Ronald. 1978. *Lost Tribes and Promised Lands*. Boston: Little, Brown.
Sapir, Edward. 1949 (1921). *Language*: New York: Harcourt Brace.
Saussure, Ferdinand de. 1966 (1911). *Course in General Linguistics*. Wade Baskin, trans. New York: McGraw-Hill.

Schieffelin, Edward L. 1980. Reciprocity and the Construction of Reality. *Man 15*(3): 502–17.

Schlegel, Frederick von. 1846. *Lectures on the History of Literature Ancient and Modern*. J. G. Lockhart, trans. Edinburgh: Blackwood.

——— 1860. *The Aesthetic and Miscellaneous Works*. E. J. Millington, trans. London: Henry G. Bohn.

Schneider, David M. 1968. *American Kinship: A Cultural Account*. Englewood Cliffs: Prentice-Hall.

——— 1972. What is Kinship All About? In P. Reining, ed. *Kinship Studies in the Morgan Centennial Year*. Washington, D.C.: Anthropological Society of Washington.

——— 1976a. Notes toward a Theory of Culture. *In* K. Basso and H. Selby, eds., *Meaning in Anthropology*. Albuquerque: University of New Mexico Press.

——— 1976b. The Meaning of Incest. *Journal of the Polynesian Society 85*(2): 149–69.

——— 1980. *American Kinship: A Cultural Account*, 2d ed. Chicago: University of Chicago Press.

Schneider, Mark A. 1979. Goethe and the Structuralist Tradition. *Studies in Romanticism 18*(3): 453–78.

Schochet, Gordon J. 1975. *Patriarchalism in Political Thought*. Oxford: Blackwell Publisher.

Scholte, Bob. 1970. Epistemic Paradigms. In E. Hayes and T. Hayes, eds. *Claude Lévi-Strauss: The Anthropologist as Hero*. Cambridge Mass.: MIT Press.

——— 1973. Toward a Reflexive and Critical Anthropology. In D. Hymes, ed. *Reinventing Anthropology*. New York: Random House.

Schurtz, H. 1902. *Alterklassen und Männerbünde*. Berlin.

Schwab, R. 1950. *La renaissance orientale*. Paris: Payot.

Sebeok, Thomas A., ed. 1977. *Sight, Sound, and Sense*. Bloomington: Indiana University Press.

Siegel, James. 1979. *Shadow and Sound: The Historical Thought of a Sumatran People*. Chicago: University of Chicago Press.

Singer, Milton. 1968. The Concept of Culture. *International Encyclopedia of the Social Sciences*. New York: Free Press.

——— 1972. *When a Great Tradition Modernizes: An Anthropological Approach to Indian Civilization*. New York: Praeger.

——— 1977. Culture Theory's Tilt to Semiotics. *In* T. A. Sebeok, ed. *Sight Sound, and Sense*. Bloomington: Indiana University Press.

Smith, Bernard. 1960. *European Vision and the South Pacific, 1768–1850*. New York: Oxford University Press (Clarendon Press).

Soebadio, Haryati, ed. and trans. 1971. *Jnanasiddhanta*. Bibliotheca Indonesica. The Hague: Nijhoff.

Southern, Richard W. 1970. *Western Society and the Church in the Middle Ages*. London: Penguin Books.

Sperber, Dan. 1975. *Rethinking Symbolism*. Cambridge: Cambridge University Press.

Stammer, Otto, ed. 1971. *Max Weber and Sociology Today*. Kathleen Morris, trans. Oxford: Blackwell Publisher.

Steiner, George. 1975. *After Babel: Aspects of a Theory of Translation*. New York: Oxford University Press.

——— 1978. *On Difficulty*. New York: Oxford University Press.

Stocking, George W., Jr. 1968. *Race, Culture, and Evolution*. New York: Free Press.

——— 1974. *The Shaping of American Anthropology: A Franz Boas Reader*. New York: Basic Books.

1976. Ideas and Institutions in American Anthropology. In Selected Papers from the American Anthropological Association, 1921–1945. Washington D.C.

1979. Anthropology as Kulturkampf: Science and Politics in the Career of Franz Boas. In *The Uses of Anthropology*. Special Publications 11. Washington, D.C.: American Anthropological Association.

Street, Brian V. 1975. *The Savage in Literature: Representations of "Primitive" Society in English Fiction, 1858–1920*. London: Routledge & Kegan Paul.

Strong, Roy. 1973. *Splendor at Court: Renaissance Spectacle and the Theatre of Power*. Boston: Houghton Mifflin.

Sturtevant, William C. (n.d.) Patagonian Giants and Baroness Hyde de Neuville's Iroquois Drawings (forthcoming).

Sweeney, F. O. Amin. 1972. *The Ramayana and the Malay Shadow-Play*. Kuala Lumpur: Penerbit Universiti Kebangsaan Malaysia.

Szondi, Peter. 1978. Introduction to Literary Hermeneutics. *New Literary History* *10*(1): 17–30.

Tambiah, Stanley J. 1970. *Buddhism and the Spirit Cults of Northeast Thailand*. Cambridge University Press.

Taylor, E. G. R. 1930. Samuel Purchas. *Geographical Journal 75*: 536–39.

1934. *Late Tudor and Early Stuart Geography, 1583–1650*. London.

Tedlock, Dennis. 1977. Toward an Oral Poetics. *New Literary History 8*(3): 507–19.

1979. The Analogical Tradition and the Emergence of a Dialogical Anthropology. *Journal of Anthropological Research 35*(4): 387–400.

Thomas, Keith. 1971. *Religion and the Decline of Magic*. New York: Scribner.

Tiryakian, Edward. 1975. Neither Marx Nor Durkheim...Perhaps Weber. *American Journal of Sociology 81*(1): 1–33.

1978. Emile Durkheim. In T. Bottomore and R. Nisbet, eds., *A History of Sociological Analysis*. New York: Basic Books.

Traugott, Mark. 1978. Introduction to E. Durkheim, *Emile Durkheim on Institutional Analysis*. Chicago: University of Chicago Press.

Tucker, Robert C. 1972. *The Marx–Engels Reader*. New York: Norton.

Turnbull, Colin M. 1976. Review of Robert Ardrey, *The Hunting Hypothesis*. *New York Times Book Review*, May 23.

Turner, Victor. 1969. *The Ritual Process: Structure and Anti-structure*. Chicago: Aldine.

1974. *Dramas, Fields, and Metaphors: Symbolic Action in Human Society*. Ithaca, N.Y.: Cornell University Press.

1975. *Revelation and Divination in Ndembu Ritual*. Ithaca, N.Y.: Cornell University Press.

Twain, Mark, and C. D. Warner. 1969 (1873). *The Gilded Age: A Tale of Today*. New York: New American Library (Signet Classic).

Tylor, Edward B. 1958 (1871). *Primitive Culture*. Reprinted as *The Origins of Culture; Religion in Primitive Culture*, 2 vols. New York: Harper & Row.

Umiker-Sebeok, D. Jean. 1977. Semiotics of Culture: Great Britain and North America. *Annual Reviews of Anthropology 6*: 121–35.

Upadeça. 1968. *Upadeça: Tentang Ajaran-ajaran Agama Hindu*. Den Pasar: Parisada Hindu Dharma.

Uspenskij, B. A., et al. 1973. Theses on the Semiotic Study of Culture (as Applied to Slavic Texts). In J. van der Eng and M. Grygar, eds., *Structure of Texts and Semiotics of Culture*. The Hague: Mouton.

Vickery, John B. 1973. *The Literary Impact of the Golden Bough*. Princeton: Princeton University Press.

Voltaire. 1960. *Romans et contes*. Paris: Garnier.

Wagner, Roy. 1975. *The Invention of Culture*. Englewood Cliffs, N.J.: Prentice-Hall.

Wallis, Helen. 1964. The Patagonian Giants. In R. E. Gallagher, ed., *Byron's Journal of His Circumnavigation, 1764–1766*. Cambridge University Press.

Wasson, R. Gordon. 1968. *Soma: Divine Mushroom of Immortality*. (With a section by W. D. O'Flaherty.) New York: Harcourt Brace & World.

Weber, Max. 1958a. *From Max Weber*. H. H. Gerth and C. Wright Mills, trans. New York: Oxford University Press.

    1958b (1904–5). *The Protestant Ethic and the Spirit of Capitalism*. Talcott Parsons, trans. New York: Scribner.

    1967 (1916–17). *The Religion of India: The Sociology of Hinduism and Buddhism*. H. H. Gerth and D. Martindale, trans. New York: Free Press.

    1968 (1914–20). *Economy and Society: An Outline of Interpretive Sociology*. G. Roth and C. Wittich, eds. New York: Bedminster Press.

    1969 (1911, 1921). *The Rational And Social Foundations of Music*. D. Martindale, trans. Carbondale: Southern Illinois University Press.

Weiner, Annette B. 1976. *Women of Value, Men of Renown: New Perspectives in Trobriand Exchange*. Austin: University of Texas Press.

White, Haydon. 1974. *Metahistory: The Historical Imagination in Nineteenth-Century Europe*. Baltimore: Johns Hopkins University Press.

    1978. *Tropics of Discourse: Essays in Cultural Criticism*. Baltimore: Johns Hopkins Press.

White, Leslie. 1962. Symboling: A Kind of Behavior. *Journal of Psychology 59*: 311–17.

Whorf, Benjamin. 1964a. *Language, Thought, and Reality*. John B. Carroll, ed. Cambridge, Mass.: MIT Press.

    1964b. A Linguistic Consideration of Thinking in Primitive Communities. In D. Hymes, ed., *Language in Culture and Society*. New York: Harper & Row.

Williams, Raymond. 1973. *The Country and the City*. New York: Oxford University Press.

Willis, Roy, ed. 1975. *The Interpretation of Symbolism*. New York: Wiley.

Willson, A. Leslie. 1964. *A Mythical Image: The Ideal of India in German Romanticism*. Durham, N.C.: Duke University Press.

Wilson, Edmund. 1931. *Axel's Castle*. New York: Scribner.

    1956. *Red, Black, Blond, and Olive; Studies in Four Civilizations: Zuni, Haiti, Soviet Russia, Israel*. New York: Oxford University Press.

    1962. *Patriotic Gore: Studies in the Literature of the American Civil War*. New York: Oxford University Press.

    1969. *The Dead Sea Scrolls: 1947–69*. New York: Farrar, Straus & Giroux.

    1971. *Upstate: Records and Recollections of Northern New York*. New York: Farrar, Straus & Giroux (Noonday Press).

    1972. (1940). *To the Finland Station: A Study in the Writing and Acting of History*. New York: Noonday.

    1977. *Letters on Literature and Politics, 1912–1972*. Elena Wilson, ed. New York: Farrar, Straus & Giroux.

Wolff, Kurt H., ed. 1960. *Essays on Sociology and Philosophy by Emile Durkheim et al*. New York: Harper & Row.

Yates, Frances A. 1971. *Theater of the World*. Chicago: University of Chicago Press.

    1972. *The Rosicrucian Enlightenment*. London: Routledge & Kegan Paul.

    1975a. *Astraea: The Imperial Theme in the Sixteenth Century*. London: Routledge & Kegan Paul.

    1975b. *Shakespeare's Last Plays*. London: Routledge & Kegan Paul.

Yengoyan, Aram A. 1979. Economy, Society, and Myth in Aboriginal Australia. *Annual Review of Anthropology 8.*

Young, Michael W., ed. 1979. *The Ethnography of Malinowski; The Trobriand Islands, 1915–1918.* London: Routledge & Kegan Paul.

Zoetmulder, P. J. 1965. The Significance of the Study of Culture and Religion for Indonesian Historiography. In Soedjatmoko, ed., *An Introduction to Indonesian Historiography.* Ithaca, N.Y.: Cornell University Press.

Index